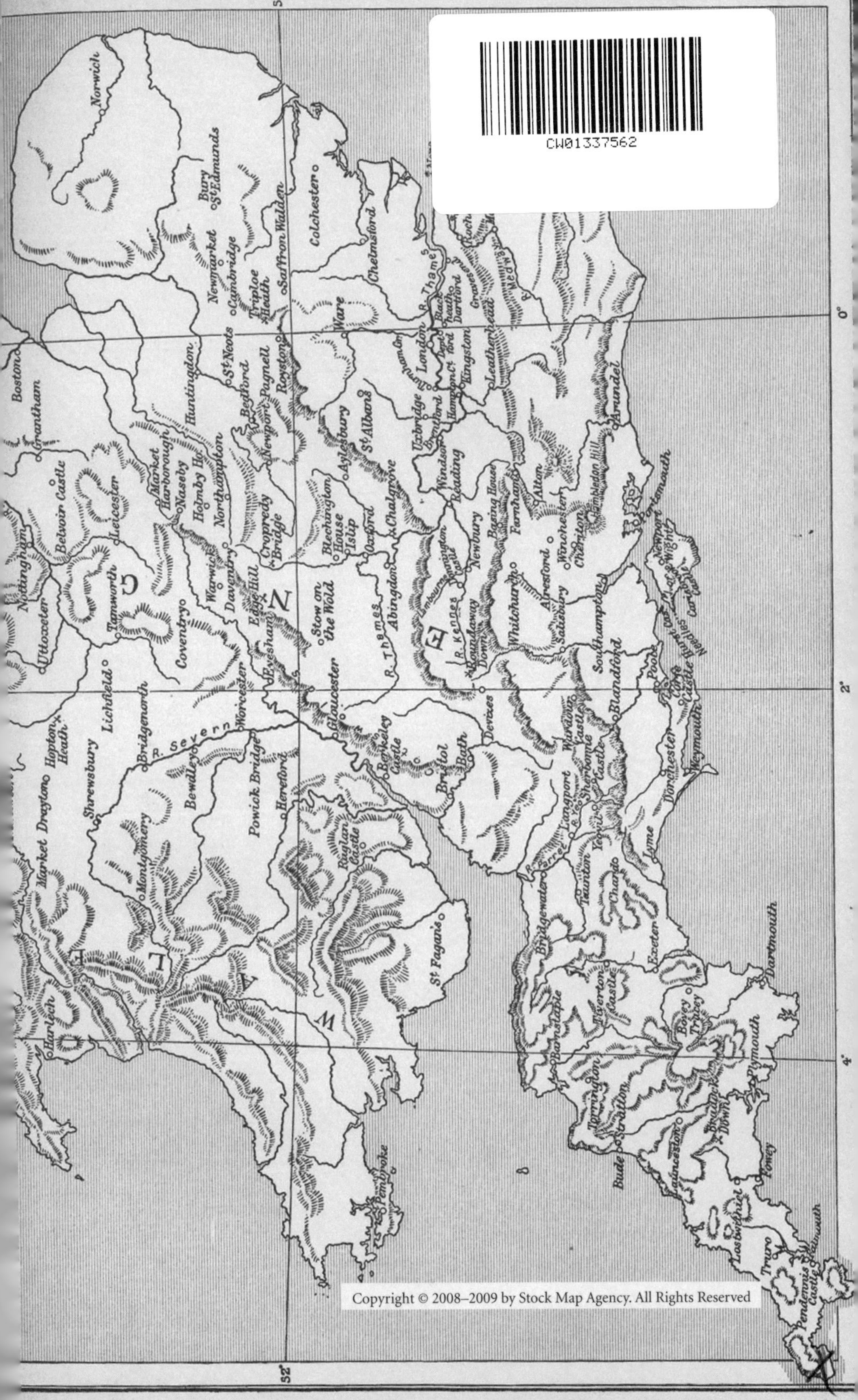

James Nayler: Revolutionary to Prophet

James Nayler:
Revolutionary
to Prophet

DAVID NEELON

LEADINGS PRESS, PUBLISHERS
2009

LEADINGS PRESS, PUBLISHERS
Becket, Massachusetts

Copyright © 2009 by David Neelon

Published by:
Leadings Press, Publishers
193 Long Bow Lane West
Becket, MA 01223-3226

All rights reserved. No part of this publication may be reproduced, stored in a retrieval system, or transmitted in any form, or by any means, electronic, mechanical, photocopying, recording, or otherwise, without the prior permission of Leadings Press, Publishers.

Neelon, David.
   James Nayler : revolutionary to prophet / David Neelon.
   p. cm.
   Includes bibliographical references and index.
   ISBN-13: 978-0-9817363-2-7
   ISBN-10: 0-9817363-2-7
      1. Naylor, James, 1617?-1660. 2. Quakers—England—Biography. 3. England—Church history—17th century. I. Title.
BX7795.N3N44 2009   289.6'092
                                                                                                 QBI09-600037

For Caroline Whitbeck

Preface

This book is the product of a decade's research, supported by the suggestions and contributions of a great many persons, most of whom are Friends in the religious sense of the word, i.e., Quakers, while others are not. I am thankful for the encouragement and assistance each one has provided. While I am sure that the story remains incomplete, I trust more will be revealed here than obscured. To the extent that this is so, many of those persons named below, and others I have regrettably overlooked, may look to their part in the work. For what is left out, misunderstood, or wrongly told, I alone am responsible.

Caroline Whitbeck, my dearest friend, Quaker wife, and teacher of religious and philosophical matters, made the suggestion that started this book. Then she lived with it patiently for years, reading and commenting on each of the many drafts, suggesting new directions, and putting the stymied author back on track when the next words could not be found.

Early in 1999 Liz Kamphausen taught a course at Pendle Hill Quaker Study Center near Philadelphia on Nayler's ministry and writings. It was here that I began to understand my subject and to test interpretations in long exchanges with Liz. We continued this process for several years. Doug Gwynn helped develop our dialogue about what Nayler thought he was doing in the Bristol reenactment. Fox biographer Larry Ingle encouraged me to go forward with my project, exchanged information on source materials, and suggested the importance of Anthony Nutter, minister of the Woodkirk congregation when James Nayler was a boy. Larry read the late drafts and provided extensive and useful commentary. Canadian Friend Jane Orion Smith dug through the original texts with me at Haverford and Swarthmore and contributed to the time line appearing in this volume. On a later visit to Pendle Hill, John Punshon encouraged me to write about Nayler's civil war involvement and the effect of war on his spiritual growth.

John and his wonderfully witty wife, Veronica, became tour guides and hosts to the Quaker historical sites in London, the Midlands, and the north of England, introducing Caroline and me to the social, political, and economic features of life in the 17th Century.

Of course, any research into Quaker history in England must include study at Friends House Library in London. For all its centrality to scholarship in the field, here is a calm and easy place to work. Librarians Joanna Clark, Tabitha Driver, and Josef Keith were most helpful in locating original materials.

The library at Woodbrooke Quaker Study Centre in Birmingham has another major collection, under the care of Ian Jackson, who was always quick to find not only requested obscure publications, but others possibly related to the subject.

Much of my findings about Nayler's home and his military service came from the West Yorkshire Archives Service, Wakefield. Also in Wakefield, Mr. John Goodchild, independent scholar and archivist, opened his remarkable document collection to me and guided me to a wealth of material pertaining to Nayler's church and community at Woodkirk, West Ardsley.

Yorkshire Quaker, Shirley Kearns of Ossett, located and drove me in the worst of rainy weather to important local landmarks in the story. Shirley referred me to local historians and collectors, including Mr. Jay Witham, authority on Howley Hall and the battles of Wakefield and Adwalton Moor. Mr. Peter Aldred, with his collection of maps and graphic materials, revealed the location of James Nayler's home, the Lee fairgrounds, the glebe lands and small industries of the Woodkirk monks, and Haigh Hall, where Nayler met with the first Independents in the area. Mr. Tom Leadly, historian of the fair, opened his own home, part of which dates to Nayler's time, and led me to other remaining structures that comprised his neighborhood. The present congregants of Woodkirk, including Mr. George Posthill, Warden, Mr. Matthew Haigh, and Mr. Eric Stephenson, welcomed me and contributed their parts of the history.

In Cumbria, the people of Appleby were similarly helpful, opening their Town Council chamber, which must have been the courtroom for Nayler's trial by the Assize Court. Mr. John Flanshaw of Orton corresponded with information on the town field involved in Nayler's visit to that town. Correspondents from both the Sealed Knot and the English Civil War Society provided information specific to the wars, which their reenactments commemorate. David Evans contributed materials on Christopher Copley.

Notwithstanding three enjoyable visits to England, most of the research and writing of this book was done in the United States. The microfilms containing Nayler's military record were accessed in the University of Akron library in Ohio. The Thomason Tracts, while seen in the original in the British Library in London, were studied at leisure in the fine public library of Cleveland, Ohio. The Smith Library at Case Western Reserve University, headed by Joanne Eustis, provided obscure historical works, including many rare volumes. The Quaker document collections at Haverford College and Swarthmore hold some of the greatest resources outside of England. Pat O'Donnell of Swarthmore and Betsy Brown of Haverford, along with their assistants, helped to locate documents and in some cases to read the old script.

I am especially grateful for the collegial assistance of contemporary scholars and authors. Historian Hugh Barbour emphasized that much of the story I needed to tell was in the letters of the itinerant Quaker evangelists, and told me where to find them. Leo Damrosch, always generous with his time, supported my progress through the research and patiently guided my efforts to negotiate the subtleties of academic publication. Michael Birkel, Earlham Bible scholar, offered insights to how early Friends read Scripture. Ben Pink Dandelion assisted in the publication of my article in Quaker Studies, in which parts of the civil war narrative in this book first appeared. Rosemary Moore, perhaps the most knowledgeable authority on Quaker writing and publication from the early period, contributed suggestions on points both obscure and obvious, then read and commented on the draft manuscript. Larry Kuenning helped me understand 17th Century Puritans. Licia Kuenning urged me again and again to get a better grounding in Scripture and early Friends' theology.

Licia's greatest contribution to our field of study, however, and to my work in particular, is her painstaking gathering and publication of the only complete collection of James Nayler's works.

Finally, I am grateful to my son, Caleb Neelon, for his special expertise in making things both written and pictured into books, and to my daughters, Sarah Neelon and Evelyn Whitbeck-Poorbaugh, for their consistently positive support while I carried on this writing.

Contents

Introduction		xiii
Timeline: James Nayler and his Contemporaries		xxi
CHAPTER 1	A Sense of Place: Woodkirk and West Ardsley	1
CHAPTER 2	Anthony Nutter and the Puritans	13
CHAPTER 3	Religious Dissent and Freedom of Conscience	27
CHAPTER 4	Charles I and Abuse of Personal Rule, the Prelude to Revolution	35
CHAPTER 5	The Outbreak of War	45
CHAPTER 6	Nayler as Officer in Councils of War, The End of Charles I	55
CHAPTER 7	From Epiphany to Arrest, the Itinerant Ministry Begins	67
CHAPTER 8	One of England's Prophets	81
CHAPTER 9	Traveling Ministry in the North	99
CHAPTER 10	No Protection Under the Law	107
CHAPTER 11	The Low State of Morality	115
CHAPTER 12	Quakers in London	125
CHAPTER 13	Enter the Adversary, Nayler Weakens	133
CHAPTER 14	The Ride Into Bristol, Blasphemy and Imprisonment	147
CHAPTER 15	Explaining the Events at Bristol	159
CHAPTER 16	Possession of the Living Faith, the Last Great Works	167
Notes		181
Bibliography		203

Introduction

In 1656 James Nayler marked his page in history with an outrageous reenactment at Bristol, England of Jesus's ride into Jerusalem. An adoring entourage of Quakers from the London area accompanied him in procession, singing hosanna, casting down their garments in the mud before him, proclaiming Nayler as a divine prophet. Some among them seemed to suggest that he was, or was soon to become, the returned Messiah. It was a time of enthusiastic expectation that the Day of the Lord was upon all England, when Christ would return triumphant and with terrible judgment for the unrepentant.

Nayler narratives often begin with his Epiphany and first Quaker ministry. Almost every reference to him that can be found in the general historical literature about 17th Century England focuses entirely on the peculiar demonstration at Bristol four years later and in a few cases, its aftermath. Nayler's contribution cannot be fully understood, however, if his life's story is treated as if it began when he was thirty six years old and culminated four years later.

Nayler was a product of the Puritan religious revolution, who as a rebellious soldier took part in the overthrow and execution of the King. He was a soldier long before there were any Quakers, and a religious dissident against the national church well before he ever met George Fox, the first Quaker evangelist. Nayler, with Fox and others, argued convincingly for the most unpopular goal of the revolution, that Oliver Cromwell might follow through on his representations that he would establish free religious expression and even, they hoped, a Godly state under law. In addition to his persuasive and charismatic spoken ministry, Nayler produced a body of literature, the last of which was written in prison and published around the time of his death. Here he laid out his final message, the description and exhortation to follow a mystical, solitary Christian passage into salvation. This written legacy, over the centuries, has been little understood and conveniently forgotten. It is the purpose of this book to make the memory of Nayler complete.

Early Quakers emphasized two principles of faith in particular. Together these formed a robust, intertwined thread of belief that strengthened and guided Nayler through his ten year course of prophetic ministry until his death in 1660 at the age of 43. The first principle was the understanding that within each person existed a spiritual life, separate and distinct, perceptible, sometimes audible, and even tangible in its way, partly comprehensible, insistent, ever present and wanting. That life, or as Nayler's colleague George Fox liked to call it, that seed, was Christ. More properly, it was Christ in some human and variable measure, different for each person, certainly incomplete, but no less divine for that. Its nature was, of course, confusing and ultimately unimaginable, as it could only be experienced or described by humans in human terms. This first principle was not unknown to many believers who were not Quakers, and so, it was at least disputable in gentle society. The second principle could be more problematical for Nayler and the Quakers, or Friends, their proper name.[1] That principle was that the revelation of God's truth, the unfolding of Christ's teaching, was not all written and bound in scripture as if completely delivered; it was ongoing.

From these principles came some practical experiences. Christ, who was present in varied and limited measure in each person, could be experienced. Because that experience consisted of a continuous, limitless flow, the leading, the direction, the understanding of what one should do to live up to the will of God, was available always. It could be accessible, and one could grow in the presence of Christ. The effort to do so was, at a human level, perfectible. If one took as one's direction the leading of Christ, one could follow that direction all the way to salvation. It would be the height of foolishness, in fact, to go any other way.

Still, to say that we could be led to follow Christ to salvation did not mean that we would do so. To say that we could apprehend the will of God from that divine presence within us, did not mean that even if we wished to do so, and we listened for that inner voice of guidance, we would hear correctly and from what we thought was the motion of the spirit within us, that we would act rightly. Error, even in our best intended actions, was in our nature.

The founding Quakers, George Fox, James Nayler, and about sixty others, believed most ardently that in this redeemed world Christ had come to teach His people, and Christ was within His people. The teaching was available from that inner spirit. It was possible, in fact, to speak and act from that spirit and to utter the words of God as they were given to individual Friends to speak. What would that utterance be? To give utterance to the word of God is prophecy, and so they were prophets. James Nayler declared in writing in 1652 that he was one of England's prophets, but not the only one. He never claimed that, nor did he ever claim to be the Messiah returned. He was one of the prophets, and if he were, they all were prophets, for the Friends spoke the word of God as it was given to them. Characteristically, they were confident of the truth of their utterance, and bold about speaking out.

The problem was this. In all earnestness, good intention, and belief, one could attempt to give utterance to the word of God and, unfortunately, be mistaken. When a Friend was so moved by the stirring within herself or himself that it seemed the inner voice must be Christ, how could that Friend be sure, and how could those

Introduction

who heard the word be sure? The problem was to discern, to pull it out of all the noise and error and say, yes, this is truth.

The ride into Bristol became Nayler's public disgrace and, once he had examined it, the turning point in his understanding of where his spiritual witness and ministry would lead. Convicted of an undefined crime called "horrid blasphemy" in a politically charged trial by Parliament, Nayler was publicly humiliated, tortured, and imprisoned for an indefinite term. As one of the foremost leaders of the fast-growing Friends religious movement, perhaps more influential at the time than George Fox, who is widely known as its founder, Nayler was used by the Puritan majority in England's government as an example to justify increased persecution and suppression of this troublesome sect. Fox turned Quakers away from Nayler, blaming him for compounding the jeopardy in which they stood. Nayler's death soon after the Restoration of Charles II to the monarchy in 1660, combined with Fox's opprobrium, meant that his ministry and writings were withheld from publication for over fifty years. Later generations remembered his demonstration at Bristol and its punishment, while they were forgetful of his prophetic ministry, his role in the itinerant evangelism, which helped to found Quakerism, and his part in the revolution that overthrew the monarchy and resulted in the beheading of King Charles I.

Because the sign, as it was called, enacted at Bristol was so noteworthy for its peculiarity, for the extreme political reaction it engendered, and for the graphic cruelty of its punishment, this event became known as Nayler's primary historic contribution, and a rather sad, failed effort at that. He should be understood as a far more influential figure than the Bristol matter and its aftermath seem to suggest.

His early religious life, deeply influenced by the Puritan movement, epitomized the widespread dissident reaction against the Church of England. Rejection of the state church formed the necessary foundation for the development of not only the Friends, but also many other sects. Some of the Friends' contemporaries have prospered, such as Baptists and Congregationalists; many others have disappeared, for example Fifth Monarchists, Muggletonians, and Familists. Religious dissidence from any quarter drew oppressive treatment from the monarch. Those oppressed in their religious practices protested, along with others affected by a variety of offensive royal imperatives in areas including the conduct of foreign wars, the taxation of trade, rejection of the peoples' rights to a Parliament, and more. Protestation from all classes of society extended against specific government ministers, the bishops, the King himself, and the entire tradition of monarchy by divine right, leading eventually to revolt, civil war, and regicide. Nayler expressed more eloquently than was common, a commitment to the revolution that merged in its ideal outcome the secular and the religious state. Nevertheless, similar to other contemporary believers who were to become pacifist in their most basic religious tenets and practices, he and about one hundred of those later identified as Friends came to that conviction through a futile effort to gain their ends by military means.

Political historians, looking beyond Nayler's explanation that he had a spiritual leading to conduct the Bristol reenactment, have focused on the effect of his action on the uncertain situation of law in England during the time when there was no King, and all government was trying to find its way after the great revolution. The role and power of Parliament stood in question in the incompletely defined tripartite organization of government under Oliver Cromwell's Protectorate. Undertaking to act in judiciary capacity, while at the same time considering the need for expanded legislation to deal with religious deviance from the national church's teaching, Parliament tested and demonstrated its capacities in a very public way, using Nayler's notoriety as forum. Protracted debate over the case revealed, among other things, that only a vague distinction existed in some Members' minds between a religious and a constitutional state. No great progress was made on the question of whether England was one or the other, and even the more limited question of defining blasphemy in public conduct was left no more clearly resolved. Parliament's standing was little improved by its efforts. When the Protector asked by what legal reasoning the whole proceeding was managed, perhaps in the hope of identifying some useful precedent for the legal administration of dissent in a republic, Parliament declined to answer. Military leadership avoided the debate, no doubt uneasy about its role in fostering dissent all through the civil war period, and about the possibility of being called in the near future to suppress its excesses. Quakers and other nonconforming sectarians remained offensive in public. To some they seemed to threaten possible subversion of the government, and what little control could be applied to their numbers continued so harsh and cruel that it only served to strengthen their unity.

James Nayler tested that remarkable unity, so critical to the longevity of the Friends as a body, in two important ways. The disaster culminating in his trial and punishment for the Bristol demonstration revealed a critical weakness in the internal process of Quaker ministry and the security of meetings. This fault required and received immediate and lasting attention to repair. It had to do with discernment and discipline. When persons' expression of faith and ministry ran out into self-serving error, untrue to internal spiritual guidance, what was to be done to discern that improper leading, to restrain it, and to correct it? How could Friends recognize when ministry that was supposed to be led by the Spirit was not in fact true? What right and responsibility had they to stop its utterance? If necessary, to what extent must they go to discipline the offenders? In the beginning of their prophetic ministry, the early Friends had not sufficiently attended to these questions, and the Nayler case proved the deficiency. Most especially, the case of his idolatrous supporters proved it. Many who were close to the London meeting believed that the leading to present Nayler as if he were the Saviour came first from his band of adherents, most of whom had also been involved in corrupting meeting practice in London and scandalizing George Fox and his leadership. Until after the enormous disgrace of the Nayler trial no sufficient discipline seemed to exist that could limit the errors of wild enthusiasts or of respected leaders of great stature, when they threatened the unity of Friends' meetings, and much less if they conducted public outrage dangerous to their fellows in the faith.

The second test of Nayler's prophecy grew out of the first, being his own recognition of his errors, his turning again to truly follow the inner leadings of Christ toward salvation, and his revelation in writings of what he discovered in this late stage of his passage. The first test, that of discernment and discipline within the meeting bodies was well met and dealt with by Fox and his contemporaries, but the same need for discernment continued to resurface and reassert itself throughout the generations, as new communities gathered and encountered this part of their processes of worship. The need for discernment remains as relevant in modern times as it was in the 17th Century and as relevant to many other denominations with prophetic traditions as it is to Friends. So too, Nayler's final ministry, but it is very hard to understand. It is mystical, as frightening as death, and, partly because the very writings in which it is found were suppressed, it is difficult to access. Nayler characterized his own journey as an effort to follow the life of Christ among men, which required a willingness to endure humiliation and crucifixion. Whether or not that called for death of the carnal body, and in his own case it did not, the death of self was most necessary, a complete sacrifice and giving over to Christ of everything one had held dear, and a plunge into the deepest parts, where Christ waited. This was the end of Nayler's spiritual journey, which he found after his own humiliation and crucifixion before the people of England and the Friends, during his years of confinement in prison. The end of his witness called for a lonely, solitary sacrifice, in which man met Christ. The community of Friends could carry one only as far as the awful edge of self-abnegation, where the only way forward was alone, and there was no looking back. Closely read, this part of his account stresses the adequacy of Quaker community support and unity to its limits and perhaps beyond, as much in our times as in his. Nayler did not live to offer any way for the community to pass that second test.

Most studies of Nayler end at about this point, where a charming, poetic epitaph, ostensibly Nayler's last utterance, puts the reader at ease, allowing closure of the book, with appropriate drama. A lingering distress persists, however, that the story perhaps has not been resolved after all. If the story began with the Bristol ride and ended with Nayler's last testimony, indeed it would be incomplete. It would be as if his life story were a play in three acts, and the audience had seen only the third.

Nayler was one of the prophets, as he claimed, but the same claim was made by others who were not Friends. England had all too many self-proclaimed prophets. The question remained the same as it was in ancient times, the times of Scripture, who among them had the truth?

Friends and English Puritans agreed on one thing. Truth, spiritual revelation, was to be found in the Bible. From that point onward their paths diverged. While the Bible, here called Scripture, was the Word of God (Fox insisted on "words"), to the Friends it was not the last word. As they experienced the moving of the spirit within them, they heard from within the words of God. So the Truth was not all contained in the book, perfect and complete, but rather it was continuously revealed, ongoing in God's own time. Furthermore, no priest or cleric, learned or not, was necessary to tell it to them, to read for them, to interpret the passages. Accepting Scripture as the truth revealed by God, Friends and other Christians believed in the prophecies that Christ would return to the world. Having the inward, personal experience of the Spirit, Friends further declared that Christ was present in their own time, that He had come to teach his people. They therefore preached a ministry of repentance, preparation for imminent judgment as also promised in Scripture, simplification of their lives, and centering down or listening to that Spirit, which was already a part of them, and they preached peace among God's creation. The redeemed and revealed kingdom was at once coming and here now, as close and promising as love, as sharply defined and fearsome as its alternative choice, the pit where Satan lived. England and its people had a choice in this moment, and they would have no other. To be sure, other Protestants, especially those still of a Puritan persuasion, agreed on the immediacy of the time for repentance, and called their people to the Church. The Friends argued that the people *were* the Church, not that it was some institution, separate, and in charge of the matter of salvation. The truth was at the same time much simpler than that, and much more demanding, for access to God and one's alignment toward salvation were all in the heart of each person, and the institution in the stone house at the center of town with its pretentious steeple was irrelevant and corrupt. Friends' outspoken adherence to this ministry was predictably offensive, unwelcome and threatening to the established church. Willingness to admit common ground was scarce, and compromise between the Quakers and established church was seldom sought by either side.

An apocalyptic expectation had some currency in popular thought in 17th Century England. Figures from the Book of Revelation turned up in political pamphlets and news journalism, as well as in religious tracts. Civil war heroes were compared to the four horsemen. The enemy, even the King, were called Antichrist, even as the King, in a Biblical epic of his own struggled to maintain the authority granted by God's own blessing of his crown. Battles more terrible than any ever seen before on English soil invited comparison with those of the days of judgment. Hunger and plague, too, were part of contemporary experience and were not confined to the imaginations of crones and ancients. Religious profession was enacted in the streets in apocalyptic metaphor, some of it by members of James Nayler's procession at Bristol. Very real threats to the government were presented by a small number of extremist radicals who took literally the prophecy of war against false leaders in the times of judgment and the establishment of a new kingdom on earth with the returned Christ at its head. Years of war and hardships had set chaos against hopes for order in a new and godly society. James Nayler came of age in the midst of this tumult, grew up in it, and conducted his ministerial mission at its peak. For this he had been well prepared.

The Puritan reaction to Elizabethan reforms to the Church of England, which began long before Nayler's birth, was an important influence in his early religious experience. That influence is traceable through the remarkable coincidence of the service of Anthony Nutter, a minister whose exceptionally long lifetime spanned the Presbyterian trials of the 1590's, service to and ejection from the very parish church where George Fox would later be brought up, and finally, many years of service to the church community into which James Nayler was born, and which Nayler eventually rejected after Nutter's death. Nutter, through his entire ministerial service right up until his death at Nayler's parish, was an active dissident against the episcopal model of the Church of England. Puritan in the original sense of the word, a conservative Christian minister who sought to base faith and practice entirely in Scripture, he was punished again and again by bishops' courts for his nonconformity to the liberalized state church. Nayler's part in the revolution to replace the monarchy of Charles I along with Archbishop Laud's reforms and the episcopacy in the Church of England, had its roots in Nutter's congregation. When Nutter was gone, harshly punished despite his advanced age by Laud's counterpart archbishop in the North of England, Nayler left the old congregation and took up with the dissident Independents. Among that diverse faction, hardly a cohesive group on a regional or national scale in its early years, were found other makers of the revolution in counties across the land, including Oliver Cromwell.

The Puritan dissidents' catalog of objections was remarkably consistent between the turn of the 16th into the revolutionary mid-17th century. A list of objections appearing in 1605 was republished in 1640, just before war broke out. Much of that list can be found repeated in Nayler's eventual rejection of the Independents in the early 1650's. Quaker dissent was built on a durable foundation of Puritan principle. What changed for Nayler, Fox, Fell, Dewsbury, and so many more Quakers was their experience of an inner illumination and access to the divine within their own hearts.

Christ was in them, in their measure, limited by the bounds of humanity. Just as had been so for the earliest Puritans, who had seen the Church of Rome behind even their own Church of England, the manual of faith was not the Book of Common Prayer, but the Bible. By Nayler's time popular access to Scripture was widespread. Various editions such as the contraband Geneva Bible had long been in circulation. The Authorized Version had been commissioned by King James I, and monopoly control of printing and pricing had been lost by his son Charles I. Those who could read, or be read to, could have a Bible, and many learned its contents completely. Scripture had become the common point of reference for religious argument, and not just among clergy, but among their congregants. Writers like Fox and Nayler could produce essays on ministry and discipline and find readership among people who had also read the source book and knew it well. Dialogue, criticism, and argument could be carried on by literate, if informally educated, common people, based on the Old and New Testaments. Anyone who had been convinced of Friends' ministry by what they found in Scripture and within their own hearts could, like Nayler, take the next step, and testify to their own experience of the divine. They found a ready audience with similar experience. Dissent had come far, and prophecy with it. The ancient Prophets had now their counterparts among the people, if prophecy were to give utterance to divine guidance personally received.

Timeline

James Nayler and His Contemporaries

1599	Oliver Cromwell born, Huntingdon.
	Thomas Fell born, Ulverston.
1603	Reign of James I begins in England.
	Millenary Petition presented, a protest by 1,000 Puritan clergy against Church of England practices and the Book of Common Prayer.
1604	Hampton Court Conference. Catholic restrictions are eased. Token improvements are made in Church of England governance in response to Puritan protests.
	King James I commissions a new translation of the Bible into English vernacular.
1605	Gunpowder Plot, an assassination attempt aimed at the King's family and members of Parliament. Catholics are charged, and persecution is reinstated.
	30 January: Anthony Nutter, Puritan dissident, is deprived of his church at Drayton-in-the-Clay by the bishop's court for refusing conformity to Book of Common Prayer.
	Ministers of Nutter's Lincoln Diocese deliver a tract containing objections to Book of Common Prayer.
	At some time between 1605 and 1616 Anthony Nutter becomes Chaplain to Howley Hall and minister of Woodkirk in West Ardsley, Yorkshire.
1611	Publication of Authorized or King James Bible.
1614	Margaret Askew (Fell) born at Dalton in Furness.
1616–1618?	James Nayler's birth, West Ardsley, Yorkshire. Family farm less than a mile from Woodkirk.
1619	Anthony Nutter, now at Woodkirk, is disciplined by the bishop of York for nonconformity with Book of Common Prayer.

1623	Anthony Nutter presented to his bishop again for sitting during communion. (Nayler is about 5 years old.)
	Martha Simmonds born at Meare, Somerset.
1624	George Fox born at Drayton-in-the-Clay, Leicestershire.
	James I calls Parliament to raise money for war in Palatinate to support Catholic monarchy there. Monopoly Act established, used to raise money, support royal favorites and impose unpopular costs on the populace. (One result is that Bibles are very expensive.) Power struggle between King and Parliament continues.
	Prince Charles, the future King, cements French alliance by marrying Princess Henrietta Maria, a Catholic.
1625	Charles I succeeds James I.
	Charles and Buckingham send an expedition to Holland to help Palatinate. Unfunded by Parliament, English soldiers suffer hunger and want of supplies.
1627	After several ill-fated military expeditions, Charles I levies a forced loan on gentry, under threat of imprisonment. Soldiers are billeted in private homes, martial law is enacted. In Yorkshire and elsewhere some local sheriffs and officials decline to raise the money, claiming hard times in their districts.
1629	Charles I asserts King's right to raise duties without Parliament.
	King takes active role in Church governance, supporting university trained theologians and clergy, episcopal authority, ceremonial form over Calvinist form of worship.
	Charles I's officers seize property of a Member of Commons for refusal to pay levies.
	Parliament is dissolved. King begins rule by personal prerogative lasting for 11 years.
1633	William Laud made Archbishop of Canterbury, enforces conformity to Book of Common Prayer, expands role of the bishops in church discipline.
	Charles I reissues *King's Book of Sports,* first published by his father in 1618, authorizing many games, sports, celebrations which are viewed by Puritans as pagan and blasphemous.
	Anthony Nutter is disciplined again for failing to read required prayers on designated occasions and refusing to wear the surplice. Nutter is excommunicated as a repeat offender, then fails to answer charges at York Chancery Court.

Timeline

Many ministers from West Riding of Yorkshire face similar charges and sanctions before Archbishop's courts. One enters plea on Nutter's behalf for old age as extenuating circumstance for failure to travel to York.

1634 Anthony Nutter dies in January, aged about 83. (Nayler is 16.)

The Independent congregation appears at Woodkirk, one of the first in this part of the country.

1637 Charles I raises troops in Yorkshire for a Scottish campaign. Ferdinando Fairfax is named colonel of a regiment of Yorkshire trained bands. His son, Thomas Fairfax raises troop of 160 dragoons, his first command. Now under the King's command, in five years they will be leading rebels against Charles I in civil war. Thomas Fairfax will command Nayler's cavalry troops.

1638 Scotland rebels against Charles's church innovations, denying episcopacy and the King's Prayerbook.

King's "Ship Money" tax imposition is supported by courts. Still, payment is often refused.

1639 James Nayler marries Anne, moves to Wakefield, adjacent to East Ardsley. James is 21.

1639–1640 Bishops' Wars (Prayerbook Rebellion) against Scotland, are conducted in two separate campaigns. Charles I defeated in both, humiliated, loses the north of England to occupation by Scotland until reparations are paid under the Treaty of Ripon.

1640 "Short Parliament" called, refuses to fund the war, is disbanded by the King.

"Long Parliament" called in November, will sit until 1660.

Thomas Fell, Margaret's first husband, is in "Long Parliament" Later an assize judge.

Army, largely made up of unwilling and unpaid conscripts, becomes unruly in many parts of England. In Wakefield, soldiers break into House of Correction and release the prisoners to riot in the streets.

Publishing monopoly for Bible collapses and price falls to point at which most people can afford to buy at 2s or less.

Lincoln Diocese tract of 1605 is republished, enumerating reasons for the abolition of the Book of Common Prayer.

1640, 1641, 1643 Nayler daughters born: Mary, Jane, and Sarah.

1641	Protestants object to reported massacre of Protestants in Ireland by Catholics. Rumors of as many as 50,000 killed are wildly exaggerated. Anti-Papist feelings aroused by John Pym in Parliament. King Charles I and his wife Henrietta accused of selling out England to Rome.
	Parliament has Charles's favorite, the Lord Deputy of Ireland, Thomas Wentworth, Earl of Strafford, executed for preparing to bring army from Ireland to oppose Parliament. King was forced by law to sign bill of attainder calling for execution of his friend.
	Archbishop Laud is imprisoned by Parliament for treason, to be held in the Tower until executed in 1645.
	Conflict between King and Parliament over retention of episcopacy, as well as over money to fight Catholic uprising in Ireland.
	Parliament passes a "Grand Remonstrance" against King's actions, calling for among other things, control of the militia.
1642	King personally invades Parliament to arrest Pym and four others, an outrage against the independence of Parliament. Resisted, he fails the attempted arrest, leaves London in self-defense.
	The civil war begins, King and royalist supporters against Parliament.
	Charles I denied entry to Hull in April by Parliament troops who capture King's weapons held there. Charles raises 2000 Yorkshire volunteers in May.
	Fairfaxes raise troops for Parliament in the clothing towns around West Ardsley: Wakefield, Leeds, Halifax and Bradford.
	Fighting starts in July at Manchester, August at Nottingham. Charles campaigns toward London, fails, sets up headquarters at Oxford.
	Ferdinando Fairfax chosen by Yorkshire Parliamentarians to command forces, his son Thomas to be general of horse.
	October: first action at Bradford, 300 Parliament troops fight off 700–800 Royalists. November and December battles at Pontefract, Wetherby, Sherburn, Leeds, Wakefield, Bradford return control of the clothing towns to royalists and divide Parliament forces from York and all supplies. Economic blockade must be broken or the clothing towns will starve in winter.
	December: attack on Bradford drives royalist forces out. Parliament then turns to attack royalists at Leeds in early January.

1643

James Nayler appears at Leeds in January, leading a bold charge of a small group of dragoons who break royalist stronghold and turn the tide of battle in Parliament's favor.

May 20: Nayler joins Captain Copley's cavalry at age 25, under Thomas Fairfax's command, as corporal. Troops gather at Howley Hall near Woodkirk and Wakefield,.

May 21: Whitsunday, Battle of Wakefield. Parliament forces take Wakefield from 3,000 royalists, later are forced to abandon it to the royalists.

June 30–July 1: Battle of Adwalton Moor near Bradford, a serious loss for Parliament. Nayler almost certainly present with Copley's troop.

July–September: Nayler is paid at Barnsley.

October 18: Nayler is paid in Gainsborough, Lincolnshire.

George Fox, age 19, is traveling in search of priests who can teach him.

1644

January 26: Battle of Nantwich, victory for Parliament, led by Fairfax. Copley's force, Nayler's unit, does well.

April 18: Nayler is paid at Compton, Yorkshire.

May 27: James Nayler promoted to Quartermaster of Copley's troop.

Scots enter England, allied with parliamentary army, in exchange for recognition and support of Presbyterianism, both in Scotland and England.

July 2: Battle of Marston Moor, a Parliament victory. The largest battle ever fought on English soil is a disaster for Charles I. Nayler present.

August 16: Quartermaster Nayler is paid at Whixley, near Knaresborough.

November 24: Nayler is paid at Halifax. There, Copley's troop is joined by Christopher Marshall as chaplain. Marshall will become Vicar of Woodkirk after war. Having a notable confrontation with George Fox, he arranges slanderous rumors about Nayler and other Friends. He was an Independent Puritan, who had been in Boston, Massachusetts before the war.

25th, Christmas: First Siege of Pontefract Castle begins. Thomas Fairfax, wounded, leaves Lambert to blockade Pontefract. Among officers who enter Pontefract Castle are Maj. Copley, Robert Lilburne (brother of John Lilburne, the Leveller), James Nayler.

1645 Archbishop of Canterbury, Laud, executed for treason.

In Parliament the religious argument heats up, dividing Independents (including Cromwell and Vane), who reject a national church and, generally, the monarchy; from Puritan Presbyterians, who hold for a national church (not episcopacy). Some support monarchy but not Charles I.

Book of Common Prayer is prohibited, replaced by a new Directory of Worship.

New Model Army established, a national army under Fairfax. Cromwell eventually commands cavalry. Independents and Levellers are prominent in its ranks.

Lambert is made Commissary General of Northern Army, not a part of New Model, headquartered in York. Task to secure royalist strongholds,

March: royalists recapture Pontefract Castle, driving out Parliament Army, which resumes siege. In April and May Nayler is paid at Pontefract.

July 19: Pontefract Castle is surrendered back to Parliament, ending second siege, which has lasted five months. Officers negotiating surrender include Copley, indicating that Nayler was present.

1646 May: Charles I surrenders to Scots.

May: Nayler is paid at York.

Episcopacy is abolished by Parliament.

Copley's cavalry is consolidated under Lambert's command. James Nayler becomes Quartermaster directly under Lambert.

1647 George Fox starts preaching, age 23.

January: Nayler at York, Lambert's headquarters, probably involved in efforts to settle army troops at end of this part of civil war. Troops and civilian vendors have not been paid.

Charles I handed over to English by Scots when they leave, is seized by parliamentary army, negotiates with Cromwell to end war, but without agreement.

October: Putney Debates. Army factions consider future forms of government without King, leading to Leveller 'Agreement of the People.'

November and December: King escapes, signs engagement with Scots. Royalist uprisings around country continue, second civil war breaks out. Scots ally with Charles under promise of establishment of presbyterian system.

	December: Nayler serving at Pontefract Castle.
1648	June: Pontefract Castle, reoccupied by Parliament, is turned over to royalists by turncoats within the castle. Third siege of Pontefract resumes.
	Nayler may have been at Pontefract during the summer, or with Lambert's troops dispatched to North to counter Scottish invasion. This would have put him in the area of Westmoreland, Appleby and environs, where his ministry later began and his imprisonment took place in 1652–1653.
	August: Battle of Preston, Scots defeated by Cromwell's forces. Scots accused of atrocities against civilians.
	December 12: Nayler attends meeting of Lambert's Council of Officers at Pontefract. Council decides to support, and Nayler votes for, Army's trial of King Charles I as a criminal, which event leads to the King's execution. Robert Lilburne, who sits on the same council with Nayler, also supports this vote, later goes to serve on committee which tries the King, and Lilburne is one of the signatories of the King's death warrant.
	December: "Pride's Purge." Parliament, at Fairfax's command, is purged of Presbyterians, leaving only the "Rump Parliament" consisting of a single party, the Independents, headed by Cromwell and his supporters, and heavily dominated by the army and the regicides.
	End of the Thirty Years War in Europe.
1649	January: Charles I executed for treason.
	House of Lords abolished.
	Group of Levellers in New Model Army mutiny, set out marching across country seeking support, until apprehended at Burford, Oxfordshire, by troops dispatched by Cromwell. Leaders executed.
	(James Nayler was charged in 1652 interrogation at Appleby and again in 1656, London, with being at Burford with Levellers, but declared he was in the North (Pontefract) not at Burford at the time. These charges were apparently a case of mistaken identity.)
	William Dewsbury, soon to be a leading Quaker figure, quits army "on a call" to lay down carnal weapons.
1649–1652	Ongoing efforts to suppress revolt in Ireland and in Scotland.
1650	August: Blasphemy Act passed, aimed at suppression of Ranters, Quakers, other troublesome sects. Fox is imprisoned at Derby under the Act, a six month sentence.

According to Fox "Justice Bennet of Derby . . . first called us Quakers because we bid them tremble at the word of God, and this was in the year 1650."

September 3: Nayler was in Cromwell's army, Lambert's regiment, at the Battle of Dunbar, Scotland, a decisive victory for Parliament.

Nayler was later reported to preach convincingly to a crowd of people at Dunbar, as a Quaker, but it's doubtful he was known as a Quaker at this time.

Nayler leaves Army sometime after Dunbar because of poor health, returns home.

1651

Battle of Inverkeithing, 20 July. Lambert's troops defeat Scots royalists, pursue them toward Worcester.

September 3: Battle of Worcester, defeat for royalists, Charles II flees England in disguise.

Fox is kept in prison at Derby beyond the expiration of his term for refusing impressment to Cromwell's force for battle of Worcester. He was first offered a captain's commission, refused, then was offered impressment money and refused again. Kept in prison a year and 3 weeks.

Released in October, Fox goes preaching in Yorkshire. At Lt. Roper's house in Stanley, near Wakefield, Fox meets Nayler, then age 33. Also present, William and Mary Dewsbury. All are convinced, according to Fox.

Publication of Thomas Hobbes's *Leviathan,* political philosophy taken as supportive of the Cromwellian Protectorate.

1652

Fox passes through Yorkshire again, holds second meeting at the Ropers' in May, where Nayler, the Dewsburys, Thomas Aldam, Richard Farnsworth and others are present. Fox visits the Woodchurch "steeplehouse" in West Ardsley, where Nayler had been a member of an Independent church. Fox challenges the pastor there, Christopher Marshall (1614–1673), who later excommunicated Nayler. Marshall accused Fox of what amounted to witchcraft.

Early Spring, barley planting season, Nayler's epiphany experience: hearing the voice of God while plowing his fields, Nayler fails to act on the call, falls gravely ill. After he recovers, he hears another call, to go into the west, and a promise, that God will always be with him. He joins in itinerant ministry with Fox and others.

James Nayler is 34, married about 12 years. Daughters are 9, 11, 12. Fox is 28, unmarried, Margaret Fell is 38, a mother, her husband, Judge Fell is 53.

Nayler goes with Farnsworth to Swarthmoor Hall, joining Fox and Margaret Fell. Judge Fell offers the use of his home to Quakers.

Fox and Nayler visit Walney Island, are met by an angry crowd, stoned, beaten and chased back to the mainland.

30 October: Nayler's earliest still extant letter, written from Kellet: *To Friends in Yorkshire,* relates the trial at Lancaster of Fox for blasphemy, at which Judge Fell was one of the presiding judges, and Fox was released.

Francis Howgill and Nayler, charged with blasphemy and vagrancy by a coalition of priests, are jailed at Appleby until the next meeting of the quarter sessions.

Nayler begins his pamphlet writing career while in jail, his first pieces co-authored with George Fox, *Several Petitions Answered* . . . and *Saul's Errand to Damascus* . . .

November: Nayler writes to Margaret Fell and George Fox from Appleby, describing his arrest, detention on unknown charges, false witnesses brought forward. Mentions sending some papers to be published.

1652–1656	Nayler produces nearly 50 publications.
1653	Cromwell replaces "Rump" parliament with hand-picked military council of state ("the Major Generals") and a new parliament, the "Barebone's Parliament." Parliament breaks down in December. Cromwell fills void by becoming "Lord Protector."

January: Nayler and Howgill tried by Assizes, begin an indefinite jail term at Appleby.

February: Nayler writes from Appleby *To Friends About Wakefield* and to Fox: . . . *Dear brother, I am here in peace and joy within, though in the midst of the fire* . . . Mentions Ann's visit, describes fasting, confinement in jailers' house, threats of low prison and irons.

March: *Saul's Errand to Damascus* published by Fox and Nayler.

April: publication of *A Discovery of the Wisdom which is from Beneath, and the Wisdom which is from Above* . . .

April: Nayler released from Appleby, holds meetings in Durham, Northumberland, and Westmoreland, Strickland, Appleby, Sedburgh.

June: Publication of *Several Petitions Answered.*

July: Nayler writes to Fox from Sedburgh, Mallerstang, Shap, all in Westmoreland.

August 1: George Fox jailed at Carlisle for 7 weeks, until late September.

August: Nayler writes to Fox from Newby, southeast of Penrith: *The work is great and many temptations, and a burthen there is upon me, and I am brought to silence within myself, and a willingness there is to be nothing.*

mid-August: meetings at Rampshaw Hall, home of Justice Pearson, the same Justice who had presided over Nayler's interrogation at Appleby Assizes in January 1652 and was thereby convinced to become a Friend.

September: Letter from Newby to Friends in Holderness. Fox is nearby at Great Strickland about same time, probably meets with Nayler, but soon has to hurry back to Swarthmoor Hall, as he learns that men are looking to arrest him under an outstanding warrant from Appleby.

November: Nayler publishes *A Lamentation (by one of England's Prophets) Over the Ruins of this Oppressed Nation.*

December: under the Instrument of Government, a form of Constitution, Cromwell becomes Lord Protector of England.

1654

Petition in Lancaster alleging Nayler and Fox are leading people to the fall and blasphemy under the recent Act. Nayler and Fox publish refutation, *Several Papers . . .*

The Stumbling Block Removed From Weak Minds says the Lord is manifest by strange works and acts where his people are inspired to go into the streets as a sign of his wrath to come.

March: Rampshaw Hall, West Auckland, Durham, home of Anthony Pearson was Nayler's base of operations for two weeks. The two traveled together from there up and down the coast until mid-April.

March: Nayler invites Fox to a general meeting on Easter. Fox's *Journal* references a large meeting at Pearson's house about that time. Then Fox goes toward Northumberland and Derwentwater, Nayler goes east toward the coast.

April: Letter to Fox from Durham: "... *who is sufficient for these things? ... we have had many great meetings & much convincement upon people's minds ... If some were sent into that county [Northumberland], I see much service in it.*"

April: Nayler writes public letter to Cromwell to abolish tithes and therefore paid clergy: *O ye Rulers of this nation, by whom we have been called to stand up against all oppression, and you have told us it was liberty of conscience you stood for, and for liberty of conscience did we join you valuing that before the King, Bishops, Estates, Lives or outward liberties . . .*

May: *All Vain Janglers* and *An Answer to the book Called The Perfect Pharisee Under Monkish Holiness.* This was shortly followed by an extended answer by Weld, Prideaux, Hammond, Cole, Durant, called: *A Further Discovery of that Generation of Men called Quakers.*

June: *A Discovery of the Man of Sin*, Nayler's response to Weld's latest in the Pamphlet Wars.

July: Friends London ministry begins, led by Edward Burrough and Francis Howgill who enlarge ministry begun by two Quaker women from the north who had begun Friends' work in the city.

Martha Simmonds is convinced "of the rightness of Quakerism."

July and August: Nayler visits meetings in Yorkshire, at Scalehouse, Brighouse, and Thornton, all clustered around Bradford, also Bradford and probably Wakefield. He intends to move on toward Pontefract.

Publications related to the Yorkshire ministries include: *To Friends About Scalehouse,* and *To the Town of Bradford.*

To Them of the Independent Society, addressed to the church at Woodkirk, where Nayler had been a member, enumerates the reasons why he is no longer a member of the Independent congregation. These bear comparison with the Reasons for Abolishment of The Book of Common Prayer, as published by Priests of the Diocese of Lincoln in 1605, when Anthony Nutter was ejected from Fenny Drayton, and republished in 1640 just before the civil wars.

Letters to George Fox from Yorkshire in August.

September: First Protectorate Parliament meets through January 1655, attempts to restrict religious toleration.

November: Nayler writes Fox from Nottingham where he met with Rhys Jones, who had contested with Fox some of basic tenets of Quakerism. Nayler finds Jones illogical, inconsequential.

December: Nayler at Chesterfield witnesses bull-baiting party and rowdy public behavior. Writes to John Billingsley, *To thee who calls thy self a minister of Jesus Christ and pretends to be called to this Town of Chesterfield,* from which follows exchange of letters and a public meeting. George Fox, with Nayler just before the meeting, described his feeling of concern about Nayler's condition.

1654–1655	Numerous Friends punished 1654–1655 under *An Act for the Punishment of Rogues, Vagabonds, and Sturdy Beggars*, an Elizabethan law, under which punishment consisted of whipping until the body was bloody and disposition either to the person's parish of origin, or to a house of correction, or if the person were considered "unreformable" to prison. Nayler wrote against this un-Christian practice in *A discovery of the first wisdom* . . . and elsewhere.
1655	Early in the year Friends purchase the Bull and Mouth Tavern, London, in which to have meetings. It can hold close to 1,000 people.

March: George Fox, arrested in Leicestershire, is taken to London to be interviewed by Cromwell to see if he is a threat to the Commonwealth. Fox delivers to him a version of what came to be known as the peace Testimony.

March: Richard Baxter, prominent nonconformist Puritan, completes his challenge to Quakerism, *The Quakers' Catechism*, a comprehensive work of many parts, addressed not only to its principles, but also to people of different persuasions attracted to convert to Quakerism. Nayler publishes a response.

March: Penruddock's uprising of royalist radicals attempting overthrow of the Protectorate is defeated.

April: all suspected of being Roman Catholics required to take an oath renouncing transubstantiation and the authority of the Pope. This was used against Quakers who could be jailed for refusal to take oaths.

May: Scottish rebellion defeated. Militia established, with eleven military districts, governed locally by the Council of State or "Major Generals" until 1657.

June: Nayler takes up London ministry. Now a leading figure among Quakers, a prolific writer and powerful preacher, he is viewed by some as "head Quaker."

July: Howgill and Burrough go to Ireland, leaving Nayler in London. Fox and Alexander Parker assist at several large meetings. At one, Judge Fell and Giles Calvert (religious publisher and brother of Martha Simmonds) are present.

September: John Camm and John Audland begin a highly productive ministry to Seekers, Baptists, and Independents at Bristol. No building is large enough, so they meet in public fields, where up to 500 people attend at first. This number soon grows to 3,000 and concerns authorities, but the Governor and Captain of the Castle are supportive.

November: Nayler's letter to Margaret Fell reports a gathering at Lady Darcy's attended by lords and ladies, army officers, and priests. Lady Darcy's son, Sir Henry Vane is present, a prominent member of the Commonwealth, recently fallen out with Cromwell.

A Salutation to the Seed of God and a Call out of Babylon, and Egypt . . .

Martha Simmonds, age 31, publishes pamphlet, *A Lamentation for the Lost Sheep of the House of Israel*, which in part may anticipate Nayler's Bristol event.

1655–1656 Many letters, later printed as *Epistles*, to such as *The Churches of Christ in the North, Friends in the City of York, The Called of God, Some That Were Backslidden*.

1656 Rebecca Travers hears Nayler debate Baptists, becomes his admirer and is subsequently converted. She is 46, a former 'zealous professor of the Baptists' and a 'woman of account'. She will be his loyal friend.

Love to the Lost and a Hand Held Forth to the Helpless . . .

January: Fox imprisoned at Launceston in Cornwall.

April: Nayler writes Burrough and Howgill of the need for assistance in the London ministry. Burrough arrives in April.

May: A letter to Friends at Lincoln: . . . *take heed that ye be not shaken in your Minds at the appearance of Satan's Wiles and Temptations, who must be revealed (at the Brightness of the Lamb's Appearance)*.

Spring: Richard Hubberthorne writes to Fell about Fox, Nayler, Simmonds.

June: Nayler's letter from London to Margaret Fell, later identified as the last letter written before he "runn out."

June: Nayler briefly visits Wakefield, Yorkshire at Fox's request.

June: A letter written from Wakefield To Friends in London patterned on Paul's second letter to the Thessalonians, an effort to heal divisions in congregation.

On return, a split is apparent in the movement. Enthusiastic supporters of Nayler, especially Martha Simmonds, disrupt preaching of other ministers, Burrough and Howgill. Nayler at first rebukes Simmonds, then retracts and apologizes. Tensions in ministry increase, as Nayler enters a time of personal questioning and anxiety.

July 25: Nayler taken to Bristol by Friends to preach (and to "pluck him away" from the grip of Martha Simmonds.) Simmonds follows him but is restrained from joining him. Friends recommend that he visit Fox at Launceston. Simmonds hurries to Fox at Launceston with her party.

August: Nayler and others head for Launceston, are intercepted, arrested as rogues and vagabonds, and jailed at Exeter. Nayler begins 2+ week fast, "waiting on the will of God."

Fox, jailed at Launceston, writes to Nayler, jailed at Exeter, outraged about Simmonds's disrespectful visit.

September 9: Fox released from Launceston.

September 20: Fox and Richard Hubberthorne arrive at Exeter. Several meetings between Nayler and Fox over several days. Fox asserts his leadership, elders Nayler about London and Martha Simmonds. Nayler offends Fox and Fox offends Nayler. Breach occurs between the two, though Fox continues to write several letters to Nayler. Fox then travels through the region, including visit to Friends at Bristol. Meanwhile, in London: "division, strife, and contention."

September: Second Protectorate Parliament meets in June 1657. Renewed attempts to restrict religious toleration.

October: Fox sends final letter to Nayler, outraged over his refusal to rebuke Simmonds, declares Nayler out of the Light.

October: Nayler's release from Exeter, secured by Simmonds in return for nursing Cromwell's sister.

October: Hubberthorne writes to Margaret Fell that all is in order now and that "JN and co. will miss of their expectations."

October 21: Nayler and several others reach Glastonbury and "the sign" takes shape. Nayler enters town on a horse, re-enacting Christ's entry into Jerusalem, similarly enters Wells and the next day, Chew Stoke, 5 mi. south of Bristol.

October 25: Nayler and entourage enter Bristol in re-enactment and are arrested at the White Hart Inn in Broadstreet. Nayler is 38, Martha Simmonds 32.

November 15: Examinations begin in London regarding Nayler's trial by Parliament for "horrid blasphemy."

December 6–17: Parliament debates and tries Nayler. Petitions from supporting friends, including letter from Fox are ignored. Nayler is found guilty of "horrid blasphemy" and sentenced. Further petitioning, including another letter from Fox regarding the sentence, are unsuccessful. A letter from Cromwell to Parliament questioning their legal reasoning in the case is unanswered.

December 27: At 11 a.m. JN is led by a cart through London and whipped by the hangman at each cross street (310 lashes), then pilloried for 2 hours. His tongue is then bored through with a hot rod. "B" for "Blasphemer" is branded on his forehead. He is returned to Newgate to await going to Bristol for the next stage of his punishment. His wounds are cared for by Rebecca Travers at Newgate.

During his stay at Westminster, Nayler, Simmonds, and Hannah Stranger co-author a pamphlet calling for repentance and announcing the second coming and the end times for the world, *O England: thy time is come* . . .

1657 January 17: Nayler is taken to Bristol, riding into town facing backwards on a horse. There he is whipped and pilloried again.

Committed to Bridewell Prison Nayler works for food and keep (hemp production – 25 lbs. For 9p) with no access to visitors, pen, paper, etc., solitary confinement for an indefinite term at Parliament's discretion.

January: Nayler's health very poor, Ann Nayler allowed to visit him at Bridewell, successfully petitions Parliament to ease his treatment. An elderly woman prisoner is appointed to nurse him, and his health improves.

Summer: Nayler receives visitors (e.g., John Audland, Richard Hubberthorne). From some time in 1657 onward Nayler is able write and get his work out to be published by Thomas Simmons, probably assisted by the nurse and his visitors.

A letter to Margaret Fell from Bridewell: *I beseech thee, cease not to share with me in my tears before God, until the end* . . .

Hidden things brought to light . . .

To Friends: *Dear Brethren, My heart is broken this Day for the Offense that I have occasioned to God's Truth and People* . . .

To A Friend: *Dear Friend, I would not grieve thee, or any way offend the People of the Lord* . . .

Laws are passed by Parliament to be used against Quakers.

Naylerites continue to disrupt meetings.

1658 While in Bridewell, Nayler is encouraged by William Dewsbury to write letters of reconciliation to Friends.

Two letters to Margaret Fell: *Thou hast been faithful, a mother not willing to cast off compassion* . . . and, *Truly for the hardness and unreconcileableness which is in some I am astonished and shaken* . . . *Thou mayest feel my heart in what I have written to thee, which I fear to do for others . . . yet to thee I am bold, having known thee near me in all things . . . whose spirit is simple and harmless towards fools and babes.*

A letter to Robert Rich: *Alas Dear Heart, I know there is that amongst them that must be purged . . . and better is it to suffer with them for a little time than to be tormentors of them . . .*

To all the people of the Lord . . . Nayler's apology, printed and distributed in 1659 by Thomas Simmonds.

Six letters To Friends are written at Bridewell, which are later published as Epistles X–XV:

. . . seek to support the wek . . .

So feel that which is lovely and meek to arise above self . . .

. . . often remember, ye were Enemies to God . . .

. . . the Remembrance of you arises in my Heart . . .

. . . Watch against all fleshly, selfish, hasty Motions . . .

. . . grow in Strength against that Spirit which hath many subtil Wiles to draw your Minds from the Bread of Life . . .

The Lamb's Warre Against the Man of Sinne . . .

A Message from the Spirit of Truth Unto the Holy Seed . . . with a preface by Rebecca Travers

Thomas Fell dies 8th month (June).

Cromwell sends his secretary to Nayler, who treats him curtly.

Cromwell dies soon after, in September. Oliver's son, Richard Cromwell, becomes Lord Protector.

Both Thomas Fell and Cromwell died at age 59.

September: A letter to Richard Bellingham and John Endicott: *Friends of New England, so-called Independents, you have taken the name to depend upon the Spirit of Christ Jesus alone for you Defence . . . But are found a people filled with Rage, Wrath, and Bitterness . . .*

1659

What the Possession of the Living Faith is, and the Fruits Thereof . . .

Spring: Nayler is ill again and under care.

Summer: A letter to Margaret Fell: *. . . my heart is to see thee when God wills . . .*

Autumn: Nayler and other Quakers are released from prison under a general amnesty.

Nayler attempts to visit Fox in prison at Reading, is refused.

Nayler visits Isaac Penington at Jordans (Chalfont), meets Burrough. Together they go far in the convincement of Thomas Ellwood, then about age 20. Ellwood, meeting Nayler one month after release from 3 years in solitary, finds him intellectually bright, articulate. Nayler goes to live with William and Rebecca Travers in London and resumes ministry with Burrough.

Richard Cromwell resigns in May. Parliament dismissed by army and recalled.

1660 Army commander Monck restores order, reestablishes parliament, Charles II invited to be king.

Restoration of Charles II as King. He enters London 29 May.

Margaret Fell's first trip to London.

Nayler publishes against corruption of Christian religion to support established churches.

February: Dewsbury arranges a meeting of reconciliation between Nayler and Fox. Fox requires Nayler to kneel before him. Nayler kneels.

June 3: A letter to Charles II: . . . *And now, O King, as we have been moved of the Lord, . . . seek the Fear of the Lord, and not Pleasure, do Justice and Judgment in this thy Day . . .*

June: A letter from London to George Fox at Reading gaol: . . . *And my heart is with thee to ye strength . . . against all that man intends against thee.*

July 5: *Milk for Babes and Meat for Strong Men* published with a preface by Mary Booth.

October: Tired and ill, Nayler leaves to visit home. Beaten and robbed not far from Huntington, the town where Cromwell grew up, he is taken to a Friend's house, where he dies. He is buried in an unmarked grave at Ripton Regis, Huntingdonshire on October 21, four years after enacting his notorious sign. He was 43.

There is a Spirit that I feel, that delights to do no evil . . .

1661 "Fifth Monarchist" radical Puritan revolt. The "Fifth Monarchy" is the Second Coming. World to be ruled by a "Rule of Saints." (Puritan elect.)

Quakers are mistakenly associated with this rebellion and many are jailed.

1662	"Quaker Act" requiring oaths, which Quakers refuse, leading to widespread imprisonment.
	Margaret Fell's second of her nine London visits from Swarthmoor Hall, over 200 miles distant, in efforts to secure better treatment of Friends by the government. She is 48. Her last trip will be at age 76.
1663	Margaret Fell, her daughters, and later George Fox, travel in ministry in the southwest and north of England.
1664	Fell, Fox arrested at Swarthmoor, jailed at Lancaster, released 1668.
1669	Margaret Fell & George Fox married at Bristol, leading to second Fell imprisonment, 1670–1671. Margaret is 55, George 45.
1671	George Fox with many Friends, but not Margaret Fell, sails for Barbados and the American colonies. He returns 1673.
1685	Charles II dies.
1691	George Fox dies, 67.
1702	Margaret Fell dies, 88.
1716	George Whitehead, a Friend of the early movement, the oldest survivor of the Valiant Sixty (and de facto leader of the generation after Fox) compiles, edits, and has published *A Collection of Sundry Books . . . by James Nayler . . .*

NOTE ON NAYLER'S WRITINGS:

In total, James Nayler wrote approximately 60 pamphlets. In the most prolific period of Quaker "pamphleteering," 1652–1656, of 250 published; 47 were by James Nayler, 41 by George Fox, and 25 by Richard Farnsworth. The first and, for two hundred eighty-seven years, only collection of Nayler's writing was Whitehead's, published in 1716 with an American reprint in 1829. Quaker Heritage Press published Volume 1 of a four volume Works of James Nayler in 2003. Three of the four volumes have now come to press, and the fourth is soon to follow. This collection is the first complete edition of Nayler's writing.

CHAPTER 1

A Sense of Place
Woodkirk and West Ardsley

At Ardislaw two miles from Wakefield . . . A husbandman.
—testimony of James Nayler

Today one may stand outside the southeast corner of the Woodkirk Church, look across the low swale of Heybeck, and see the footpath leading up toward the village of West Ardsley, stretched across the moor to the east and north. In the 17th century young James Nayler walked home from Woodkirk on such a path as this, across the glebe lands of the church and through common pasture fields of the village. He could have seen a wisp of smoke rising into the sky from a cluster of farm cottages just out of view in a neighborhood called Westerton. One of the cottages was his home. Among the neat red brick houses of the 20th Century suburban town, only a few buildings of Nayler's period remain. A house believed to have been a blacksmith shop stands down a lane almost next door to the Naylers. Some stone farmyard walls survive, alongside the ruin of a stone house built in the saltbox style common in Yorkshire in Nayler's time, and next to it a two-story house, renovated in recent times. Part of that house dates to 1450, two hundred years before James lived up the road. He must have walked past it on his way to Independent congregation meetings at Haigh Hall, a mile to the south of the Westerton crossroad. Haigh Hall still stands, the building expanded several times since the 1600's. The stone walls of its northwest back corner contain and reveal the outline of the original stone saltbox shape of the house, two stories in front, a long sloping roof extending back over the kitchen to a rear wall just higher than the height of a person, and in it a door opening into the farm yards. So much has changed that the visitor must look for the small details of each building, must follow the contour of the land to see where the old paths were, and must seek out the long-time residents who keep the pictures, maps, and the accounts of families, each a little part of the puzzle, incomplete. Assembled, such fragmentary images tell the story of this neighborhood, helping to form an impression of how it must have been when James Nayler was a young man.[1]

West Ardsley occupies high ground between the four principal "clothing towns" of 17th century West Riding of Yorkshire. Of those four, Wakefield is

Woodkirk, Nayler's church in West Ardsley, Yorkshire

nearest to West Ardsley and adjoins East Ardsley. East of the market square Wakefield borders the River Calder. Eight miles to the northwest of Wakefield and five miles northeast of the Ardsleys, is Leeds, overlooking the River Aire. West of Leeds, to the northwest of West Ardsley about eight miles distant is Bradford, and farther to the southwest is Halifax. These four rather ancient communities were in the process of transformation in the mid-1600's, from regional agricultural trading towns into pre-industrial centers. That is to say, the wool from Yorkshire sheep farms, brought here for trading, was beginning to be processed into cloth locally by skilled workers, rather than being transshipped onward as raw material to weavers and dyers far away. Population in the clothing towns was growing, as more and more people, displaced by enclosure and consolidation of farm land, and by the economic hardships of farming small holdings, moved into the towns to find employment and opportunity, not only in the industries associated with wool, but also in such urban occupations as merchant trade, shoe-making, and baking.

Some cottage industries, for example, weaving, expanded into pre-industrial, organized businesses around Wakefield and the Ardsleys, but Nayler's town was never destined to become an industrial city. Neither would large scale agriculture prosper here. Whether for crops or for grazing, its soils, terrain, and weather were not conducive to efficient farming. Nor was the town adjacent to the rivers that later became important transportation corridors both for the wool industry and for the coal and iron mined in the area. Mining in West Ardsley in Nayler's time was confined to small, open bell pits producing coal for local consumption. Several coal pits were located in the vicinity of Westerton and Haigh Hall. In the same area there may have been stone quarries.[2] This was high, rocky, windswept ground, where the landlords, primarily Lord John Savile and later his son, Thomas, did not find much advantage to consolidation of less efficient family farms into larger, managed holdings. Smaller farms continued, providing subsistence for their tenant families, who raised necessary livestock and grew staple grains such as oats, rye, and barley. Modest amounts of surplus grain and animal product went for sale in the clothing towns nearby. Wealthy families such as the Saviles, Copleys, Thornhills, and Shaws contributed to the local economy by investing in business ventures and commerce in the clothing towns. The Copleys and Saviles engaged in ironworks and coal mines elsewhere in the county. These prominent families supported as well the churches and schools used by their neighbors and tenants.

Since as early as 1843 James Nayler's home has been identified, tentatively and incorrectly, as a certain very large house, built in the style of a gentry family's house of the late 16th or early 17th Century. Two pictures from the collection at Friends House Library, London are labeled as Nayler's home, but in each case with a caution that their connection with Nayler depends on unproven local tradition. These pictures, one a hastily drawn sketch dated 1843,[3] the other an early twentieth century

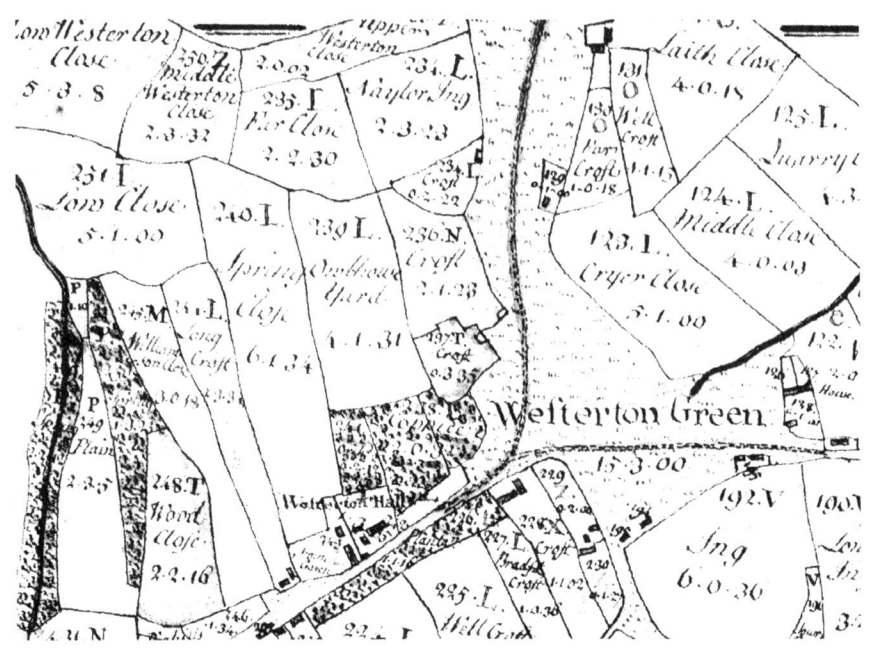

"Nayler Ing," (top center), at Westerton Green, West Ardsley, shown on a plot map by Sikes, 1735

postcard photograph[4] show the same house. Both are labeled, Ardsley Hall, known as the home of James Nayler. The postcard photograph is also labeled West Ardsley. The house shown still exists. Now known as Old Hall, it is located in East Ardsley, not West Ardsley, and it was not the family home of James Nayler.

Nayler's home, according to his own court testimony[5] and a good deal of additional evidence, was in the Woodkirk parish in West Ardsley, which was (and still is) a different parish with different parish records from East Ardsley. With that guidance and some locally provided evidence we can locate Nayler's home in the Westerton neighborhood of West Ardsley, down the road from another property called Old Hall, which appears to have been confused with the Old Hall in East Ardsley.

The Nayler family's economic circumstances were not such that they could have lived in a grand gentry house. James Nayler described his adult occupation as "husbandman" or farmer. Husbandman did not imply property ownership in 17th Century Yorkshire. The term yeoman, which has been used by others than himself to describe Nayler, sometimes implied landownership, and sometimes did not,[6] but it is much more likely that the family were tenants of Lord Savile, as will appear below. They could have had a respectable income, but were not likely to have been of the emerging affluent gentry class.

John Deacon, Nayler's earliest biographer, offered us a limited and biased description of Nayler's father, a "sowgelder" but also a man ". . . neither over-rich . . . nor over-poor" who "by his own industry . . . might have lived comfortably" and been able to provide a good education to his son. Deacon adds that James Nayler carried on his father's occupation of sowgelding until he enlisted in the army.[7]

Sowgelding (spaying sows so that they may be grown for meat production rather than breeding) was a legitimate agricultural specialty at the time, but unlikely to provide anything that might be described as a middling sort of income. Sowgelder could also be a term of insult, as such itinerant tradesmen were the subject of rough humor comparable to stories of traveling salesmen and farmers' daughters. Deacon was surely prone to insult. Yet his representation, based on hearsay, is all we have of James Nayler's father. We know nothing of his mother and have only hints about his siblings and children. Three daughters were recorded: Mary, Jane, and Sarah. A son, John, was the executor of Nayler's will in 1663. In his account, he referred to five children, presumably all living at the time. James's brother, William, was also listed, being owed money.[8]

The East Ardsley house, Old Hall, mistakenly identified as Nayler's, is an historic landmark, well documented by the Yorkshire Building Preservation Trust prior to its restoration in 1988, when it was subdivided into several private residences. The original part of the house was built in 1622 by a wealthy merchant from Leeds named Shaw. It was expanded about 1650, which accounts for a noticeable asymmetry in window arrangement between the two wings. The window configuration assists in visual identification of this building. Described in Scatcherd's History of Morley in 1830 and 1874 as the seat of the Copley family, it did not become a Cop-

A Sense of Place 5

ley property until the 18th Century when a Shaw daughter married into the Copley family. Scatcherd described it as the largest, grandest house in East Ardsley, calling it, The Manor.[9] The house is listed twice in Pevsner's definitive study of historic buildings. Listed under Ardsley, it is called Old Manor House, because a larger manor house was built in the Victorian era. Under the East Ardsley listing, it is called East Ardsley Hall.[10] A manor house would often carry the name of the village in which it was situated, hence the identification on the old pictures, Ardsley Hall, although its placement in West Ardsley was incorrect.

A collection of historic documents of West Ardsley includes a property ownership map of the village by Sikes, dated 1735, showing a single Naylor parcel,

*Pages of a land lease from Lord Savile, dated 1893,
showing Nayler farm at line 251*

located in the Westerton neighborhood, off what is now Haigh Moor Road. The parcel appears elsewhere in the collection on a page of a land lease from Lord Savile to a Mr. Audsley, dated 1893. Here, it is called "Naylor wife's ing." (James Nayler himself appeared to be indifferent to spelling the name with an e, or an o.) Ing is a Norse word in use in Yorkshire meaning field or meadow. The parcel is about 9 acres and is about a mile from Woodkirk church. On one sketch a windmill is shown nearby on the hilltop, about where a mill of more recent construction stands today. Shown in the immediate vicinity of the Nayler parcel are several field lots, which either were rented by local farmers, or were used in common. Fields abutting the Nayler parcel are identified, "Westerton." About 10 years after James Nayler's death a large home called Westerton Hall was built just around the corner from the Nayler property and is shown on the 1735 map. That owners' family outgrew the house, and they built another, even larger home across Westerton Road. The new house (not identified on the 1735 map) became known locally as New Hall, and the former Westerton Hall became Old Hall, called by the same name as the house in East Ardsley misidentified as the home of James Nayler. The Old Hall at Westerton, West Ardsley, was torn down early in the 19th century, but the one in East Ardsley survived and apparently became confused with the one associated with the Nayler family. James and his family did not live in either Old Hall, but they were probably close neighbors of the Old Hall on Westerton Road, West Ardsley.[11]

The argument presented above is not conclusive as to Nayler's particular property address in West Ardsley, even though the Old Hall in East Ardsley can be ruled out as his family home. The identity of the Nayler property in West Ardsley is not quite so clear. The map showing the Naylor property is dated 1735, and the same name appears 158 years later on the land lease. James Nayler died in 1660, 75 years before the date of the 1735 map. Nayler was a common name in the area, as we shall see in the civil war records that follow. It remains so today. Notwithstanding, no other Nayler properties are identified on the map, and "Naylor wife's ing" is unique wording, in that no other property on the town map is identified as belonging to anyone's wife. This may well be explained by James Nayler's notoriety as compared with other Naylers who may have lived in West Ardsley.

Nayler testified in the trial at Appleby that he and Ann moved to Wakefield after their marriage. How, then, did she end up with her name on the field back in West Ardsley? Nayler biographer Emilia Fogelklou stated that after James returned from the war he was unable to maintain their farm in Wakefield and had to move to a smaller farm. Its location was not identified. We know, from the Nayler will, that Ann, wife of James, inherited the family farm, but the estate account does not locate the farm or otherwise describe it. It appears that at some time the Naylers moved back to their family's property in West Ardsley. Who would be more likely to assist them in difficult times? It would be customary, if James were the eldest son, for him to inherit the farm on his father's death, whenever that occurred. When James died, the Nayler farm in West Årdsley most probably was left to Ann.

West Ardsley was also known as Woodkirk, which was the name of its parish and the name of the church in the parish. Nayler used both names in describing where he lived and in what congregation he was a member. While he did not leave much in writing to describe his relationship with the church or the parish, it is important to explore this place as his earliest spiritual home. In addition, the history of the church will help us to understand the community in which Nayler grew up, its strong placement in the region's social structure, and its contribution to the religious and political revolution of the middle third of the 17th Century. Woodkirk is also one of the few remaining physical structures in which James Nayler stood. It is a setting for parts of his story.

St. Mary's Church at Woodkirk is located on the present route A653, which roughly divides West Ardsley from the village of Morley. The road runs south to Dewsbury and Batley, and north to Leeds. Woodkirk is a Church of England congregation, as it was in Nayler's childhood. While the church building today is not just as it was in the 17th Century, in many ways it still reveals its antiquity. The church tower dates from the 13th Century.[12] A major fire damaged the building in 1831. The roof fell in, and some walls were so badly damaged that they had to be rebuilt. This work appears to have been done on the original foundations and plan. Significant portions of the building survived the fire as well. Woodkirk has been expanded a few times, and the modifications can be followed by observing the changes in stone work. Parts of the main body of the church also date from the original 13th Century construction, as for example the monks' door at the southeast end, where the building adjoins the ruined walls of what was the monks' house. This part, as well as the now unused front entrance at the west end probably remain as Nayler saw them. That the rebuilt church was not significantly different from its state before the fire is supported by Scatcherd's very detailed History of Morley, which contains a chapter on Woodkirk.[13] The first edition of this work was published in 1830, before the fire. The revised second edition, published in 1874, does not mention the fire or any reconstruction of Woodkirk.

A baptismal font in the church appears as old as the oldest parts of the building structure, but no record of its history has been found. Used today for the baptism of the congregation's infants, this artifact raises a question. If James Nayler were ceremonially baptized at all, was it done at this very font? We will return to this question.

A modern brass plaque seen in the Woodkirk church today commemorates all the known incumbent vicars, beginning with "The Black Canons, 1100–1539." Their individual names have not been recorded, though the names of almost all those vicars who followed up to the present day are presented.

Woodkirk, the Saxon name itself, reflects the antiquity of the place, suggesting a church in the forest, or a church built of wood. Some 17th Century documents identify it as Woodchurch. A church was listed in the Domesday Book of 1086, and in the 12th century an outlying cell of the Nostell Priory was established here. Nostell, located half way between Wakefield and Doncaster, now stands in its 18th Century rebuilt form, a grand mansion of Palladian design, but the original priory at that location dated to the Black Canons, or Augustinian order prior to formal foundation by King Henry I in 1122.[14] Nostell was established in a time of very active monastic life in England, and for a time was one of the most important priories in the North. Because it was a center from which outreach was extended to church communities as distant as Northumbria and Scotland, Nostell was valuable to the King and attracted considerable support from wealthy landowners in the North who sought his favor. Nostell was enriched by gifts of lands, and on some of these properties cells, or outlying branches of the priory, were established. One such cell was established at the parish of Woodkirk, given to Nostell Priory by William de Warrenne, who was Lord of the Manor of Wakefield and related by marriage to the royal family. Other cells of Nostell were located at Tockwith and Stokeskirk in Yorkshire, Hyrst at Axholme in Lincolnshire, Bredon in Leicestershire, and Bamburgh in Northumberland. Clearly Nostell's influence was widespread.[15] It was also one of rather few priories in which the monks of the out-lying cells actually took part in the ministry of the parish in which they were located. Hence the record of the Black Canons in the vicarage of Woodkirk.

King Henry I granted Nostell Priory a charter for a fair at Woodkirk, which became one of the sources of income for the Priory, as well as for the Woodkirk parish community. A fair such as this helped to establish the host town as a regional trading center. Part of the function of the royal charter was to protect that trading area, and so the Priory secured for the parish of Woodkirk a stable income source, which, as the charter was reconfirmed by Henry's successor, King Stephen, continued as a local institution. The fair established by the Black Canons of Nostell Priory in the 12th Century even now continues annually, reputed to be the oldest chartered fair in continuous operation in England.[16]

It is not clear just how much area was included in the original gift of Woodkirk parish to the priory, but it was certainly an extensive property, and one, which generated considerable income. That was the purpose of the benefactors making such gifts to the monasteries. Large income-producing landholdings could maintain financial support of the monastery and its work for generations to come. The Woodkirk parish holdings extended at least from the vicinity of Topcliffe Hall in Tingley to the north (now the northwest corner of the junction of the M62 with A653), where a water well used by the monks at the church was located, to the crossing of the Batley Road over Heybeck in the south, where the monks had a grain mill. The Woodkirk lands extended at least far enough to the west to include the site where Lord Savile's Howley Hall was later built, and as far east as the Westerton neighborhood of West Ardsley, where Nayler lived, and as we have seen, land leases from Saviles to the tenants continued into at least the nineteenth century.

The 1832 Topographical Dictionary of England shows West Ardsley parish as consisting of 2300 acres of fertile land, which approximates the area described above.[17] Nostell had substantial additional land holdings around Batley to the southwest of West Ardsley. The dissolution and sale of the monastery lands by Henry VIII brought the end of Nostell Priory close to the 1539 date shown on the Woodkirk plaque as the end of the Black Canons' vicarage at Woodkirk. After an interval of ownership by Dr. Lee, one of the King's commissioners in the property sale, Sir John Savile purchased land here some time before the 1590 construction of his elegant home at Howley Hall. With all the lands above described, Sir John Savile acquired the rights to what had come to be known as the Lee Fair. The fair, as well as a weekly market for farm products, was held on Woodkirk land in a field called Fairsteads.[18] By the mid-1500s Gypsies had become established in England. One of their business interests was the trading of horses, which regularly attracted them to the Lee Fair and helped to sustain a viable livestock market here. This trade is significant with respect to James Nayler's choice of cavalry service in the English Civil Wars.

The gift of Woodkirk parish to Nostell Priory and the establishment of the cell at Woodkirk had taken place in the 12th Century. Until the mid-16th Century the Black Canons managed this extensive property. For four hundred years, more or less, their influence here continued and fostered the growth of Woodkirk into an established community with the ancient stone church at its social, as well as its spiritual center. Indeed, as late as 1652, James Nayler still referred to his home, first, as Woodkirk, second, as Ardsley. The center of the community in the 17th Century was still the church, evolved and reformed into an institution far different from its constitution in the 12th Century. Separated from the Church at Rome by Henry VIII, Woodkirk survived and became West Ardsley's connection to the monarch's church, the Church of England. Through this connection flowed the powerful currents of Puritanism in Elizabethan times and afterward, then of independent religious thought and of revolution against oppression of free religious expression beginning when James Nayler was a young man.

Sir John Savile acquired the Woodkirk parish lands, in part, so that he could have built one of the grandest houses in the north of England. Howley Hall, finished in 1590, stood on high land overlooking the Valley of the Calder above Batley. Its beautiful site was improved with cherry orchards, gardens, and a bowling green. The two story mansion, measuring sixty yards square, was built around a courtyard with two grand entrances.[19] Howley Hall was about a mile directly west of Woodkirk Church, and less than two miles from the Westerton green in West Ardsley. Although Batley was the parish seat for the family, and the nearby church at Thornhill is where some family memorials are found, Woodkirk was nearer to Howley Hall. Savile supported Woodkirk as a chapel of convenience. He became influential in hiring the vicar, to whom Savile could offer, as part of the employment, the post of chaplain to his household at Howley Hall. Such local control of the village church, which had its counterparts all over England, came to enable Puritan dissidence and eventually independence to spring up in the face of the King's episcopacy.

The Savile family had been prominent in the region for over a hundred years, and their forebears, resident in the vicinity of Pontefract, 10 miles to the southeast of Wakefield, had even more ancient roots. The West Yorkshire Saviles, in the area of Wakefield and the Ardsleys, were divided into at least two family branches and two locales.[20] One had its properties to the north and east of Wakefield. Their family chapel was at Methley, and one of their seats was at Lupset Hall near Wakefield. George Savile, from this side of the family, was influential in the establishment of St. Elizabeth's Grammar School at Wakefield, which may have provided James Nayler's education. George Savile also granted the land for and supported the construction in 1595 of the Wakefield House of Correction, which figured in Nayler's entry into the civil war, and which later housed many Yorkshire Quakers, sentenced for crimes related to their religion. Lord William Savile, of the Methley branch of the family, was a prominent supporter of King Charles I and a Royalist leader in the early Yorkshire battles of the Civil Wars. James Nayler fought for the rebellious Parliament army against him.

Another Savile family branch was associated with the area around West Ardsley. John Savile, who supported the Woodkirk parish, was of this line. John became a member of Parliament, sheriff of Lincolnshire, held various other positions of power in the West Riding of Yorkshire, and sat in the privy council at London. He was made Baron Savile of Pontefract by Charles I at about the age of seventy, then continued for four years as controller of the royal household, until his death in 1630, at which time Nayler would have been 12 years old. Sir John's eldest surviving son, Thomas, was born about 1590, the time Howley Hall was built.

Thomas, 28 years older than Nayler, served Yorkshire in Parliament, part of his term overlapping with that of his father. Like Saviles before him he was favored with lucrative positions. Thomas was knighted and became warden and Lord of the Manor of Wakefield, surveyor of customs, and a member of the privy chamber, all positions, which had been held by his father before him. With each of these positions came opportunities to increase his wealth by benefiting from properties and fees. Upon his father's death, Thomas became the Second Baron of Pontefract, and being the eldest son, inherited much of his father's estate. He therefore became the landlord of the properties around Woodkirk where the Naylers lived and farmed. He must have been a well-known and central figure in the community life of West Ardsley in James Nayler's time.

Despite his wealth and connections with those in the highest positions of power, Thomas Savile earned a dark reputation with one outrageous exploit after another. He tried to seize property one of his sisters had inherited from their father. He was accused of forcing a tenant to sign away his interest by holding a dagger to his breast.

A Sense of Place

A few years later Thomas tampered with legal depositions in another matter, was tried by the Star Chamber and imprisoned in the Fleet jail, London, during part of 1638–1639. By the time of Thomas's release, King Charles I was embarking on the so-called Bishops' Wars against the Scots, without the willing financial support of Parliament. Because it was by no means certain that England would be able to mount the necessary force to prevail, Thomas made contact with the Scottish lords and apparently made an agreement with them that he and six other named noblemen would swing their allegiance and financial support to the Scottish invaders if they should succeed in crossing the border. The Scots were not entirely convinced by Savile's sole representation, however, and asked to see the other supporters' signatures on the agreement. Thomas Savile responded by forging the signatures of the six peers he had named to a written declaration of their support to the Scots. One would think that discovery of this crime would have been the end of Lord Thomas Savile, but no. He turned the treason to his advantage with the King.

Savile managed to convince the King that he had nothing but patriotic motives in his arrangements with the Scots. Indeed, his description of the affair was so persuasive that Thomas was named a commissioner for the King in the settlement negotiations leading to the Treaty of Ripon, which ended the Bishops' Wars. Not long after, when a series of dangerous political crises resulted in the death sentence for the King's favorite counselor, Thomas Wentworth, Lord Strafford, the Savile family's bitter adversary, Thomas Savile was promoted to posts formerly enjoyed by Strafford. (Strafford, as Thomas Wentworth, had taken over some of these offices in conflicts with Thomas Savile's father, Sir John Savile.) Thomas had so completely won the King's trust that he was made treasurer of the royal household in late 1641, just before the complete breakdown of relations between Charles I and Parliament, which led to civil war. The break with the King led Parliament to try to seize control of the mint at the Tower. Thomas Savile was assigned to look into the disastrous state of the King's finances, and to take the King's part with Parliament, where Savile still, somehow, enjoyed some support.[21]

Savile, meanwhile, raised a troop of 50 horse (cavalry soldiers) for the King, and he used his standing in Parliament to try to prevent delivery of a Yorkshire petition adversarial to the King.

King Charles, after confrontations with Parliament in London and military engagements with Parliament's army elsewhere, raised arms in Yorkshire in April of 1642 at Hull, where troops loyal to Parliament held a store of arms imported from Europe intended for the King's army. Savile, accustomed to backing both sides in the King's disputes, found himself in an open and untenable conflict. It was impossible for him to justify himself to his colleagues in Parliament, when he had been so clearly supportive of the King's interests. Parliament on June 6, 1642, declared Thomas Savile a public enemy and ousted him from office. Soon, Captain Hotham, who, on behalf of Parliament, had denied the King entrance to Hull, appeared at Howley Hall, seizing it and Savile's personal property "... to the valw of som £1300."[22]

Savile agreed to give Hotham £1,000 (a huge sum at the time) hoping that Hotham could secure for Savile and Howley Hall the protection of Parliament. The money apparently went to pay Hotham's troops, but no protection was provided. Soon the Royalist Lord Newcastle arrested Savile, taking him prisoner to await the pleasure of the King. Thus was Thomas Savile removed from six months of the Civil War. His house began to change hands between Newcastle's royalist forces and the Parliamentarian rebels of Lord Fairfax. The religious dimension of the intensifying conflict is suggested by Savile's correspondence. He described Hotham's men as needlessly destructive of his property, and no better than Newcastle's troops who were made up largely of Papists, whose services the King had been brought so low as to require for his own protection.[23] Savile was no lover of Papists.

Throughout the Civil Wars Thomas Savile continued to change sides. First he convinced the King of his allegiance. Then he declared for Parliament, then the King again, and Parliament again. He spent most of the war years in London, where he was made Earl of Sussex by the King, a title which did him little good when the King was executed. Thomas declared himself for Parliament and, as a former peer, was given its protection. During this time he attempted to treat again with the Scots royalists and was found out. He was twice committed to the Tower and twice released. At last he was fined £8000, which was reduced by negotiation to £4,000, to which the £1,000 he had paid Hotham was credited. He paid £2000, leaving a balance of £1000 that appears to have remained outstanding at his death.

Howley Hall may have been substantially ruined in the wars, but the Savile family continued to hold much of the manor lands around the Ardsleys and elsewhere. Though the Hothams, father and son, had both lost their heads for crimes of deceit and treason against Parliament not much more grave than Thomas Savile's, he died in relative peace and prosperity at Howley Hall about 1658, with his title, now Earl of Sussex, intact. His former prominence in the countryside had waned quietly as his former neighbor and probably his tenant, James Nayler, rose from unprivileged obscurity to a national prominence greater than his landlord ever knew, only to fall from the public view into a dungeon at Bridewell prison, London, leaving his wife and children to manage the farm.

CHAPTER 2

Anthony Nutter and the Puritans

. . . whatsoever is the convention of man is not to be allowed in the service of God.

—Anthony Nutter

Anthony Nutter was the minister incumbent at Woodkirk during James Nayler's childhood, arriving at the Yorkshire church not later than 1616. James Nayler's birth is variously dated between 1616 and 1618. Nutter died at about age 83 at the beginning of January 1634 (modern calendar), when James Nayler was about 16 years old. Although we find no mention of this part of Nayler's life in his discovered writings, we can be confident that the minister of his village church during most of his formative years would have influenced his religious thinking and spiritual experience. That the particular minister was Anthony Nutter, a prominent Puritan nonconformist throughout his career, suggests that Nayler would have been exposed during his early years to the principles of dissent against the established state church. As we highlight Nutter's points of opposition to the doctrine of the Church of England, we will find many of the points of controversy that appear later in James Nayler's own ministry. Nutter could have been the most important living figure in Nayler's religious experience before he met George Fox. Nutter's influence also could have touched Fox indirectly, as he was vicar of Fox's church in Fenny Drayton some years before Fox was born there.[1]

The Puritan revolution in England can be said to have begun with reaction against Roman Catholic influence in the church settlement of Queen Elizabeth. Passage of the Acts of Supremacy and of Uniformity in 1559 can be used as a reference point in this discussion. Puritanism certainly had earlier origins, but reaction against Elizabethan policies accelerated from this time and extended beyond the Civil Wars of the mid-seventeenth century, in which James Nayler took an active part. Anthony Nutter's career spanned fifty-five years from his ordination in 1578 during Elizabethan times, through the reign of James I, into the reign of his son, Charles I. Nutter died eight years before the English Civil Wars began.

Prominent features of the Puritan reaction against Elizabethan church reform included efforts to diminish the power of the bishops in church governance and to eliminate practices in the liturgy, which were brought over from Catholic tradition. The pyramidal authority structure of the English church had regional bishops answering to the archbishops of Canterbury and of York, who held authority under the monarch. This resembled the ecclesiastical authority structure of the Roman Catholic Church, and it was probably intended to do so. Early in her reign Elizabeth did not wish to confront the Catholics in England, as they were powerful and potentially subversive. Rather than to accommodate them, however, she may have hoped to absorb them into her Church, and so, may have chosen to keep it recognizable to them. Furthermore, a radical departure in liturgy and the liturgical calendar from what the common, illiterate people in the realm had always known would only serve to disturb the peace. Hence, the prayerbook of the Anglican church, established by Elizabeth in 1559, preserved many rituals carried over from Catholic practice and legitimized them in English law. The Puritans, however diverse their opinions turned out to be, agreed among themselves that the episcopal authority structure under the monarch politicized God's church, and even worse, that much of the ritual and artifacts of worship in the prayerbook were not only Catholic, but also lacked Scriptural authority. The Puritan objective was to restore the English church to its Biblical origins.

About ten years after his ordination Nutter was caught up publicly in this controversy. Two of the central figures in the drama were John Whitgift, Archbishop of Canterbury from 1583, and Thomas Cartwright, a prominent Puritan cleric and scholar. Whitgift was concerned to preserve the episcopal form of the Anglican church under the governance of the bishops and the discipline of the Book of Common Prayer. Thomas Cartwright regarded the Scottish Presbyterian church as a superior form, with its powers more widely dispersed among a preaching ministry, "His chief aim being the conversion of the Church of England into a Presbyterian body . . ."[2] Cartwright had lectured on Presbyterianism at Cambridge as early as 1570 and had been deprived of his position there by Whitgift. Concerned with church unity, however, he sought not to separate factions and divide the church, as some of the Brownists and Independents, forerunners of the Congregational movement, would do, but rather to reform the existing church along formal Presbyterian lines. In the belief that this could be done, Cartwright helped others of like mind to organize a series of Presbyterian styled conferences. Documentation of these meetings includes the series held at Dedham beginning in 1582 and held roughly annually thereafter until about 1588, as well as Warwickshire conferences held at Coventry.[3]

The Dedham Conferences, and others like them, were arranged like Presbyterian classis meetings, to be attended by senior clerics from the region, who would conduct discussions of theological and church governance matters, and would preach sermons, which were then critiqued by their peers. Sermons, not the ritual service called for by the Anglican prayerbook, were modeled as the central feature of Presbyterian worship. Apparently no great effort was made to obscure the intent of those present at the Conferences. The minutes of the 1583 meeting discussed, for example, "how far the pastor might go in reading the Book of Common Prayer"[4] Clearly, this was a provocative statement. Put another way it meant, "to what extent might a pastor decline to read those parts of the required liturgy with which he disagreed." Confrontation with Whitgift was forming up over not only the issue of use of the prayer book, but also over the basic authority for administering the church. The conferences of 1584 to 1586 dealt with the matter of suppression of clergy who had failed to subscribe to articles promulgated by the Archbishop in 1583. By subscription, the clergy were required to agree to three things:

1. Sovereignty and rule of the monarch over all things;
2. That the Book of Common Prayer and its ordering of bishops, priests, and deacons contained nothing contrary to the Word of God, that it was lawful, and that the clergyman would use it and no other in all conduct of public prayer and administration of the sacraments;
3. That the clergyman allows and believes that the Articles of Religion of 1562 are agreeable to the Word of God.[5]

The Archbishop meant to suspend from preaching any who would not accept this basic representation of the power of the Church. Puritans could not subscribe to a statement that anything other than Biblical scripture could stand in the place of the Word of God, or could in any contrived way expand on it. Whitgift thus forced the issue, not only of the authority of the prayerbook, but also of the authority of the bishops.[6]

Parliament became the next point of Puritan pressure, for the Church of England was, after all, the State Church. First, a Puritan prayer book was offered for acceptance by Parliament, and subsequently a full blown Book of Discipline was prepared as a Presbyterian alternative to the Book of Common Prayer. The discipline was adopted by the Presbyterian ministers' General Conference in 1586, but it was never passed into law by Parliament.[7]

At the Star Chamber in London in 1591, the Presbyterian movement was effectively put on trial. Whitgift's goal was elimination of the Puritans' "Church Within a Church," so called by John Field, who had written in about 1583 of an originally secret effort to introduce a Presbyterian core into the Church of England.[8] While discipline in church matters was customarily carried out in bishops' courts of the diocese involved, the government took the matter of Cartwright and his dissidents to a higher level as a national concern. Star Chamber, so-called because of the ceiling decoration in the chamber in Westminster where it met, originated from the King's Council, meeting in judiciary form to decide matters beyond the Common Law. Its powers had evolved, since the time of Wolsey in the court of Henry VIII, into very broad applications in the cause of maintaining public and often political order. Now a court both respected and widely feared, its purpose was enforcement of the laws, not settlement of differences. Appeal to its decisions, if any were in fact available, was only to the monarch, and was unlikely to succeed. With full powers of interrogation and deposition, as well as an almost complete range of sanctions, this was a court without much limitation on its actions. For example, although capital punishment was limited to verdicts obtained by jury trial, Star Chamber could use torture in its interrogations until about 1650.[9]

The 1588 Warwickshire Synod, by then a prominent and clearly Presbyterian conference, was subjected to investigation. Cartwright and other organizers were charged for holding this unauthorized Presbyterian classis, for preaching without proper license, and for speaking against the bishops. Others of those in attendance were questioned by interrogatory, including Anthony Nutter. According to his testimony, among the issues discussed at the Warwickshire meetings, were personal baptism (private ceremonies, sometimes arranged by the wealthy and noble), use of the sign of the cross, the reading of homilies from books, and the recognition of the power of bishops. In addition, the proposed Presbyterian Book of Discipline was presented in draft. Certain articles were discussed and agreed, and subscriptions to the new discipline were solicited from among those clergy present. Along with Thomas Cartwright, the discipline was subscribed by Anthony Nutter of Fenny Drayton.[10]

Cartwright, by this time a target long in Whitgift's sights, had already been tried by the High Commission for financial malfeasance and lesser charges. Whether these charges were justified or not is uncertain. We do not have a record of his own responses in that matter, because Cartwright refused to take the oath before that court, asserting that God did not require it of him. He did not use that defense before the court of Star Chamber. He admitted meeting in conference, but asserted the meetings were held in private, as students and ministers seeking further education in their faith. Others charged with him made similar admissions. The meetings were needed to answer the persistent threats of the Jesuits to the Church in England, and of schismatics like the Brownist separatists. The revised Book of Discipline was indeed discussed, and some did subscribe; but for such a document to move forward, he argued, unity was needed, and it was not ever reached.[11]

True, it was not, but Cartwright's defense was lost. He was effectively silenced by the Star Chamber, which saw to his removal from the processes of his Church. Cartwright was sent away and cut off from further influence. He was finished. It would be said of him in biography that his "... life-work was the pursuit of an apparently lost cause."[12]

Not so for Anthony Nutter. Though he had spent considerable time in jail as a result of his interest in advancing the Puritan ideals, Nutter's spirit was not broken, nor was his voice stilled. He went on to a long ministerial career marked by continuing dissent.

At least in some small part Cartwright's downfall before the Star Chamber was accountable to Nutter's answers to the court's interrogatories. Let us review how his testimonies were obtained.

In 1590 Nutter, among 18 participants in the conference or classis movement, was arrested and imprisoned in London, held for questioning about the classis activities. Here the testimony was developed that was used in the 1591 trial in Star Chamber of Cartwright and other prominent figures in the movement. Nutter and several others remained incarcerated for three years until 1593, when they were released without charges ever having been brought against them. As they were not influential Cartwright radicals, the court of Star Chamber had used them to get testimony against the leadership. Whether a bargain was struck or not for this, state's evidence has not been recorded, but that was certainly within the power of the Star Chamber.[13]

Nutter, who had come to Drayton-in-the-Clay (now known as Fenny Drayton) in 1582, returned to his preaching ministry at that church after his release from jail in 1593. Despite his recent ordeal, however, he did not conform to the dictates of the state church. In 1593 he defended a woman who refused to be "churched" after childbirth. In 1594 he was presented to the Bishop of Lincoln for various offenses, including failure to observe the Book of Common Prayer in all points (which he admitted), failure to wear the surplice, and for disciplining a parishioner himself in a case which should have gone to the Bishop's courts.

Note that charges against a parish minister were most often brought to the bishop's attention by some person or persons in the congregation who felt aggrieved by the action, or who were themselves church wardens, bound by church law to report, or present, any infractions, whether by another congregant or by the minister himself. It was not the case that the Bishop of Lincoln had to go into the countryside to root out dissidents against the church order. The bishop could and he did cause visitations to take place, but the process was facilitated by parishioners who reported the offenses. In addition, the Bishop could require responses from the ministers to his queries about their practices in a sort of discovery process. The point here is that at any time Nutter might face those in his flock who disagreed with his acts of nonconformity in the ministry enough to report him to the authorities. He might even be required, as an honest man, to incriminate himself.

In 1603 James I became King. He determined to hear the differences among various religious factions and perhaps even to satisfy their adherents with concessions consistent with his own will as King. In response to the moderate Puritan Millenary Petition, so-called because it was alleged to be approved by a thousand petitioners,[14] James I ordered the Hampton Court conferences, held in January 1604. Petitioners were invited to bring and air their differences. In return for their moderation, the King declared a long list of limited reforms. Chief among them was a commission for a new English Bible translation. In minor respects the rule of the King's bishops over the Church also was relaxed, but the following stipulation of unity was a blow to the Puritan movement, including Anthony Nutter.

In March 1604 the new King proclaimed the primacy of the Book of Common Prayer, reissued and up-dated from the 1559 Elizabethan version. His new

Archbishop of Canterbury, Richard Bancroft, who succeeded the deceased Whitgift, enacted the King's proclamation by calling for subscription to its Canon by all ministers of the Church. To put an end to nonconformity, ministers like Nutter soon faced charges. In October the Bishop of Lincoln Diocese summoned 93 ministers, including Nutter, for nonconformity to a variety of well-known charges, such as refusal to wear the surplice, improper performance of baptism, noncompliance with the orders of worship, and failure to use the proper prayers from the Book of Common Prayer. Nutter begged time to consider his responses and dragged out his considerations to an extent that must have suggested contempt for the discipline of the episcopal court proceedings. At last, some seven months after the King's decree, Nutter announced his decision, that indeed he had not conformed, and further that he was not at present conforming, and that in future he would not conform to the Book of Common Prayer, declaring that ". . . whatsoever is the convention of man is not to be allowed in the service of God."[15] The Bishop sentenced him to deprivation of his parish, to which Nutter appealed to a higher ecclesiastical court without success. 1605 found him without a church.

Ministers of Lincoln Diocese, of which Fenny Drayton was a part, delivered a document to King James I on the first of December, 1605, detailing their exceptions to The Book of Common Prayer, and their reasons for not subscribing to it. This statement can be seen as a declaration of civil disobedience and its justifica-

Church at Fenny Drayton, Leicestershire, where George Fox grew up. Earlier, Antony Nutter was vicar here, until dismissed by the Bishop of Lincoln in 1605

tion. It shares many points with the Millenary Petition given to King James in 1603, but is a quarrelsome document, both in tone and content, whereas the Petition to the new King, delivered while he was en route to his Coronation, was self-consciously moderate, even obsequious. The Millenary Petition, drafted in part by Thomas Cartwright, could have been supported as well by Anthony Nutter, but, regrettably, no one was recorded as signing the petition.[16] Out of concern over whether the new monarch would extend Elizabeth's antagonism toward Puritans, the petition claimed a thousand supporters, but was presented without their signatures. Similarly, it is likely that Nutter would have joined the Ministers of Lincoln Diocese on their petition to the King.

The Lincoln Diocese paper remained a durable statement of the Puritan case against Anglican practice and was reprinted for Parliament's consideration thirty-five years later.[17] It enumerated "above fifty" (if taken in detail, closer to one hundred) objections to The Book of Common Prayer, to the Tomes of Homilies to be read by curates, and to certain of the 39 Articles of Religion (promulgated in 1563 as the doctrine of the church, and written into law in 1571), including references to The Booke of Consecration of Bishops and Archbishops. In short, virtually the entire manual of Anglican Church practice came under attack, together with much of its Scriptural Canon. Taken in its entirety, the 13 page document was not only a tirade, but also a thoughtful critique of a corrupted institution.

The first exception, which may be seen as the central generalized objection to the current state of the Church, is that The Book of Common Prayer appoints an order for the reading of the Holy Scriptures so that, ". . . the greatest part of Canonical Scripture is never to be read to the Congregation." This was contrary to the practice of Jews before Christ, of the Primitive Church, and of "all the best Reformed Churches of this day," as well as to the teachings of the late Bishop Jewel, who was very well known by his Elizabethan contemporaries, and is recognized by modern historians as one of the earliest writers to distinguish the Anglican Church as a body of belief and practice separated from its Catholic ancestry.

This was the first of several references in which the Ministers of Lincoln called on support for their points by respected authorities. In addition to Jewel, the names of Fulke, Whitaker, Wilks, Calvin, Peter Martyr, Beza, Bucer, "our late Queen" (Elizabeth), Pilkinton, Humphrey, Andrews, Greenham, Hooper, Rogers, Reynolds, and several others were given as supporters of positions taken in the paper. Some of these remain well-known to historians of religion today; others may require some investigation to identify. Among them were some of the earliest proponents of the Reformation, as well as recent bishops and archbishops of the Church of England. All were coopted in this paper by the Ministers of Lincoln as supporters of their Puritan position, whether those named would have agreed or not. Their names were placed before the King along with the signatories of this offensive rejection of the Royal directive that all ministers (the King would have said "Priests") must subscribe to the prayerbook.

Indeed King James himself was reminded that he did "... sweare and subscribe... Wee detest all the false Doctrine of the Roman Antichrist, added to the Ministrations of the true Sacraments, wee detest all his vain Allegories, Rites, Signes, and Traditions brought into the Church without the Word of God."[18]

The argument to abolish the Book of Common Prayer, and the whole fabric of ritual practice in the Church which follows from it, focused on those very holdovers from the Roman Antichrist: which the King also detested, or so he said: allegories, rites, signs, and traditions. The argument against vestments, for example, described the bishop's prayer that wearing the surplice will protect the priest from "evil spirits." For that purpose it should also be worn by the lowest ranks of clergy and even by students. The vestment was dismissed by the Ministers as a "Popish Massing garment," an idolatrous and superstitious device. It was, after all, required of anyone conducting a Catholic Mass. Such things had no place in the Church of England.

Rituals and special observances were dismissed item by item. Use of the Sign of the Cross was rejected. The practice of standing for some prayers, kneeling for others, and for moving to certain parts of the church for recitations was dismissed. The "... gesture ... of kneeling in the very act of receiving the Bread and Wine in the Lord's Supper ..." was related to belief in the literal, physical presence of Christ in the Host, a point of basic difference in theology with the Catholics and a temptation by the Antichrist. The Liturgy in the prayerbook was described as too like the Catholic Mass. Furthermore, the length of the required Liturgy effectively foreclosed the opportunity of preaching, which by the Puritans was regarded as the greater part of worship. It was wrong, therefore, to call The Minister of the Gospel by the name, Priest. The Book of Common Prayer required particular observation of certain holidays above other days, even above the Lord's day in some respects, namely that only particular prayers, Scripture, and lessons be used on designated days, and some days were further established as Fasts. Examples considered incorrect in this regard included special observance of Christmas, Lent, Good Friday, Easter week, and Whitsun.

The whole practice of Baptism deserves special mention here, because on this subject not only did Puritans in general split from the Anglican Church, but also the sectarian Baptists divided away from others from about 1611, and the Baptists themselves further divided. The Ministers of Lincoln did not consider that Baptism was absolutely required by the Word of God. Nevertheless, they did not mention any objection to the practice of water Baptism, although some sectarians did object to this practice. Nor was the question of infant baptism itself specifically objectionable, but the way it was practised was offensive in many ways. First, use of the Sign of the Cross immediately defined the whole ceremony as Superstitious and Idolatrous. They argued so vehemently that this was fundamentally incorrect that we might speculate that, if only one thing could have been omitted from the Book of Common Prayer as a result of their objections, the Ministers would have preferred that it be the use of the Sign of the Cross in Baptism. The rest of the business of

Baptism was often incorrect, contradictory and even in some ways absurd. Private baptism was at best doubtful, but if it were needful, then the proper prayers should be used. Yet that was exempted from requirement. The interrogation of infants on the faith, with the answers and affirmations provided by the Godfather was absurd, as was conditional Baptism, i.e. "If thee be not Baptised already, I Baptise thee . . .."

Another broad area of discontent centered around administration of the Church, the careless and ingrown process of ordination, the establishment of Bishops and Deacons, and especially the allowance and encouragement of uneducated curates to read from the Tomes of Homily. These had no place in Worship. The Homilies were not in any way the Word of God and were full of confusion and falsehood.

Resistance to the rigid application of the prayer book was significant for both sides. Since refusal to conform meant the offending ministers denied the rule of the episcopacy, the bishops could hardly do otherwise than deprive men of their parishes and effectively bar them from their profession. Bad enough, but behind the bishops' sanction, stood the possibility of another, greater punishment. King James could have taken the position that when Nutter and others refused the prayerbook and resisted episcopal governance of the King's church, they did in effect refuse the King's authority to rule. Had the King taken offense at that level the offenders could have been subject to charges of conspiracy, perhaps even treason. Certainly the monarch did not wish to strip the Church of many of its ministers in such a confrontation. Neither side wanted to push the issue to its limits. King James saw fit to leave matters of dissent to the Bishops.

Anthony Nutter's case was not unique. Of some 746 ministers who were required to subscribe, about 90 refused countrywide and were deprived. Of these, nine were in Lincoln Diocese.[19] Punishment of clergy was handed out all over England, with varying effects. Some ministers humbled themselves and submitted to the discipline, effectively silencing their protests, while others like Nutter, perhaps inflexible in their beliefs, and sometimes well connected socially or secure financially, were able to continue ministry either as self-supporting itinerants without a parish appointment, or as with Nutter, in another parish supported by other benefactors.

The exact date of Nutter's arrival at Woodkirk is uncertain. He may have gone directly from Drayton-in-the-Clay, the same parish into which George Fox would be born nineteen years later, to Woodkirk in Yorkshire. The plaque in the Woodkirk church actually has his tenure there beginning in 1600, but this must be a modern-day approximation. He would not have begun his service at Woodkirk five years before he was ejected from Drayton-in-the-Clay. On the other hand, one scholar has not felt secure dating his tenure at Woodkirk before 1616, when Nutter was named among defendants in a Star Chamber law suit involving people and events around Mancetter, the village adjacent to Drayton-in-the-Clay, to which Nutter may have moved after his dismissal.[20] Marchant suggests that Nutter's tenure at

Woodkirk was well under way by 1619, the date of his first recorded conflict with the church courts in the Diocese of York. The testimony at that hearing suggests that Nutter had already been at Woodkirk for some time.[21]

We may ask how, after losing his parish ministry in one place as a result of publicly notorious and lengthy conflict with the bishops of the state church, could Nutter find employment in another church not so very far away? The answer may be found in the web of connection between rich and powerful families, which gave him recommendation and referral to another post. Nutter's parish at Drayton-in-the-Clay had long been a seat of Puritan nonconformity supported financially as well as politically by the powerful Purefey family. The Purefeys supported not only Nutter but also other ministers with Puritan reform convictions, both before and after his tenure.[22] When Nutter moved to Woodkirk, he went to the precincts of a similarly powerful family, the Saviles. Though not a member of any noble family or a university graduate, Nutter was educated in lower schools where he could have met young men of high station,[23] just as the young landed aristocrats became acquainted with each other. Such possible connections go unrecorded, if they ever existed, but this much is clear. Purefey was Lord of the manor, which contained Drayton-in-the-Clay. Sir John Savile was Lord of the Manor of Woodkirk, the Ardsleys, and much of the areas around Wakefield and Batley. Savile, acting like many of his counterparts elsewhere in the country, including the Purefeys, hired a Puritan nonconformist, Nutter, as his family chaplain at Howley Hall and had him installed at Woodkirk, which due to its proximity to the hall, was supported by the Savile family as a donative, similar to a chapel of convenience. The Archbishop of York may not have liked it, but the Savile family was far too powerful in that part of Yorkshire to offend by opposing their employment of a troublesome cleric in a donative village church. Nutter, because of his deprivation in 1605, could not be put forward to the bishop as a proposed vicar or rector. The chaplaincy was an acceptable compromise. What Nutter did with it still would be subject to the Archbishop of York's oversight, limitations, and sanctions.

Patronage was a widespread practise in England in a variety of social relationships, both secular and religious. As regards the Church, it involved especially the right of the patron to put forward a chosen candidate to fill a vacancy in the parish ministry. This secular control over the choice of local clergy did more than almost anything else to undermine the authority of the bishops, and so, was a great convenience to the Puritans. If patronage had not been so much a part of the livelihood of Puritan clergy, they must surely have opposed it, as the thousand Millenary Petitioners to the King had objected to the excesses then practiced by the bishops under their patronage rights in 1603.[24]

Nutter did not stay out of trouble at Woodkirk. At least three times he was charged for nonconformity in various matters. The first time, in 1619, was just after James Nayler's birth. In 1623, when Nayler was a little boy of about five years, Nutter was charged again with several offenses. The third set of charges came in

1633, only months before Nutter's death during a time when he was too infirm to travel the thirty miles to York.[25]

Nutter's offenses show very clearly that the same controversy with Anglican doctrine continued right up until his death as had occupied the man when he was with Cartwright at Star Chamber in Elizabeth's reign, as had been the cause of his loss of employment at Drayton-in-the-Clay fourteen years later, and as had been spelled out by the Ministers of Lincoln Diocese to King James in 1605.

In 1619 at Woodkirk, Nutter was presented to the archbishop's court for delivering Communion while he was seated and the recipients of the bread were standing, not kneeling as prescribed. Some of his congregants were also charged with refusing to kneel for Communion, and similar charges were brought elsewhere in Yorkshire as well. The issue around the Communion service ran directly to the question between Catholics and Protestants concerning transubstantiation, that is, whether Christ was actually, physically, and completely, present in the Communion host. Queen Elizabeth, on this and other matters between England's church and the church of Rome, had chosen to leave the question for the bishops and to let the ritual remain deliberately ambiguous, with the appearance at least of the Catholic practice. Nutter and many other Protestants would not let that question go, and refused to practice a Catholic ritual, which supported a basic tenet of belief they did not share. The question was, whether the word of the Catholic Church were the original arbiter of true faith, or Scripture was. One thing was certain to the dissenters. The authority was not The Book of Common Prayer.

Similarly offensive was the Baptism ritual. Not only did many Puritan nonconformists, Nutter included, refuse to use either the cross, or the sign of the cross, in Baptism. No such thing was found in Scripture. It was superstitious idolatry. In addition, it had become the custom in many parishes, especially larger ones in which congregants were diverse enough to make class an issue, to hold the baptism of babies of noble or gentry families in private. Puritan ministers refused this practice, asserting that Baptism was between God and his Church, which was to say, all the people. Another controversy centered on infant baptism, which became a focal point in the Baptist movement, as well as, in later years, one of James Nayler's issues with the Independents. We have no clear evidence of Nutter's position, but when charged with nonconformity with the ritual of Baptism at Woodkirk in 1619, he replied that he had never baptised there as far as he could remember. He may have meant that during the short time when he had been at Woodkirk, he had not baptised anyone.[26] On the other hand, he may have been inviting the dispute over whether any clergyman actually baptised the infant, or whether the ceremony attempted to take for man what was God's own, which definitely was offensive to Nutter.

It is here that the question is raised again of whether the ancient baptismal font in the Woodkirk church could have been where James Nayler was baptised. The answer remains quite uncertain, for even if we can assume that the font stood, then as now, in the church, we cannot assume that the minister would have used it for the Nayler baby or any other.[27]

Perhaps the most persistent offense charged against Puritan ministers was failure to wear the surplice, that white overgarment worn by Catholic priests and required as well by the Book of Common Prayer in the Church of England. A church near Woodkirk was found by the bishop's examiners not even to have a surplice in the church, and not to have owned one for many years. When Nutter was charged for the surplice offense at Woodkirk, the church wardens here, too, were unable to produce one for examination. They were charged to obtain one and certify to it, but the wardens failed to do so, and they were excommunicated.

The new Archbishop of Canterbury, William Laud, took charge of the Church of England with great vigor in August, 1633. He had been at King Charles I's side in matters of religion for several years already. In fact, part of the reason for the King's dissolution of Parliament in 1629 and his establishment of "personal rule" was the opposition from many in Parliament to the King's and Laud's Arminian church liberalism. Now the King and his Archbishops could get on with putting the church in order. Archbishop Neile of York, whose office was by ancient tradition co-equal with the Archbishop of Canterbury, was the effective administrator in the Diocese of York. Laud and Neile had been associated in the reform of the church since before the reign of Charles I began. In 1623 Matthew Wren had been chaplain to then Prince Charles, who was soon to become King. Laud was then bishop of St. David's, and Neile, bishop of Durham. These three were described as in the "van of the English Arminian movement," and destined to be among the leaders of the Church under Charles I.[28] Whereas Laud got the credit for church reform nationally, both during his own and in modern times, in Yorkshire his colleague Neile was the more active administrative party.

Laud's reforms for the national church were swift. First, he ordered that the Book of Common Prayer be restored to primacy in the conduct of worship. Then he attacked nonconformity to this rule, parish by parish. In the course of this enforcement frequent visitations by bishops and their staffs were undertaken to all churches, especially those in which nonconforming practices of worship were known to be carried on, as well as to those churches in which neglect of the physical facility had become a problem. Finally, Laud's program involved a marked increase in the capacity and activity of the bishops' courts.

Whereas in years prior to 1633 the High Commission of York tried twenty or so cases a year, the visitations and subsequent trials of 1633 were on a new and much more intense scale. Formerly, when visitations of the bishop's staff had resulted in trials, cases had been resolved in the local parish where the cases were discovered. Now, under Archbishop Neile, cases as serious as Nutter's, and many more like his, were transferred to the Chancery Court at York. The former court of High Commission had met perhaps once a month, with one judge hearing cases. Chancery court now sat with three Chancellors meeting weekly and trying many more cases, 41 cases of nonconformity in 1633.[29] That the firm episcopal actions in restoring church order were approved by the King is shown by a marginal note in Charles I's hand, made as he reviewed Bishop Neile's reports:

> "Neglect of punishing puritans breeds papists."[30]

Nutter's charges in 1633 included failure to read the required Litany from the prayerbook and failure to wear the surplice. Nutter could not or did not choose to attend the visitation hearings, which may have been held locally at Woodkirk, but more likely were held at the parish town, Batley, or the deanery town, Pontefract. He was excommunicated for his persistent nonconformity and his failure to appear before the court. That did not settle the matter, and soon his case was brought to the Chancery Court at York. Again Nutter failed to appear. Another local minister under charges, Thomas Gilbert, pleaded on his behalf for age and infirmity as extenuating circumstances, securing the dismissal of Nutter's current charges, but it is unclear whether the excommunication from the local visitation trial still held.

Perhaps not as harsh a penalty in 17th century practice as the word would imply today, nevertheless, excommunication of a minister meant loss of the minister's parish employment and his support by its tithes. Further, since leaving his position amounted to breach of his contract, he was required to pay the replacement minister out of his own funds. The penalty was clearly intended to bring the miscreant into line by means of financial deprivation. As such, in order to be effective, it was often temporary.

Financial hardship, however, was probably minimal in Anthony Nutter's case because of his support as Savile's chaplain and the fact that the Woodkirk church and its tithes were effectively Savile's to govern as well. There was no possibility that Woodkirk's minister of the past twenty-eight years would be left without financial support at the age of eighty-three or thereabouts. Indeed his estate at the time of his death in early 1634 included modest sums of money for several members of his extended family, as well as a small remainder interest to his elderly successor, "James Rigley, Clerke Minister of Woodkirke." In his will Nutter described himself simply, "Anthony Nutter of Woodkirk, Clerke and unworthy minister of Christ . . ." After fifty-five years of service and challenge to the Church of England, still he could not or would not claim any other title, however modest, for himself or his colleague, such as vicar or rector.[31]

By the time of Nutter's death the Church of England was in a turmoil. Though its main body of members continued their church-going ways and tried as best they could to avoid controversy, the leadership and their vocal opposition divided three ways, between Puritan Presbyterians like Nutter, Arminian Anglicans like Archbishops Laud and Neile, and those others who would form new Independent congregations, free of the heavy grip of bishops, their Prayer Book, and the national laws under which they held sway.

On the cusp of this division stood James Nayler, a young man at an impressionable age, apparently well enough educated in the issues of the controversies to find his way through them, and for now a member of a national church that had rejected his teacher and perhaps even figured in the old man's death. Not only Woodkirk, but the little churches round about were in turmoil. People were leaving their congregations to form new ones. However illegal, that was possible and not uncommon. The gathering place for one such Independent congregation was just down the road at Haigh Hall, as close to Nayler's home as Woodkirk was.

CHAPTER 3

Religious Dissent and Freedom of Conscience

I was a member of an Independent church at Woodkirk
—Testimony of James Nayler

The possibility of true revolution based on religious objections began to form early and in greatest earnest among the disaffected Independents. While it was economic suppression that ultimately forced the people of western Yorkshire to strike back against the King's allies, it was to a great extent the rallying cry of religious dissenters, the call for freedom of conscience, that sparked and sustained civil war based on ideals. The slogan called for more than free choice. Admission of choice in religion was never part of the King's law, nor had it been Catholic practice either. While the King represented absolute power on earth, under nothing but God's power, so too was conscience a gift of God, and the two in opposition had become irreconcilable. Thomas Fairfax, who with his father commanded the uprising in Yorkshire, wrote later that the resolve to war was based on religion, property, and commerce.[1] While property and commercial interests were negotiable categories, religion was not. The name of the dissenting congregations, Independent, described as well as any single word could the separation of its people from the King's dictated faith, his national Church.

James Nayler went among the Independents.

Independents also had begun the Puritan emigration to North America, driven by oppression of their intent to establish a truly godly society. Some of these were to return soon to the mother country to join in the civil war on home soil against the King's army.

A split in Woodkirk's community, dividing the Church of England congregation from a new Independent congregation, certainly could have resulted from the outrage felt by some congregants at the Church's renewed insistence on ritual practices that the people had long since rejected, as well as at the Archbishop's harsh sanctions against their old and familiar minister. By 1633 the situation at Woodkirk was anything but unique. Anthony Nutter was one of many easily identified irritants to the Archbishops. Neighboring parishes and their ministers also stood squarely in the way of the diocesan visitation program. Clergy and lay congregants around West Ardsley were charged with various sorts of nonconformity, including members on both sides of the divide between the old church and the Independents.[2]

By punishing Nutter and Presbyterian elders like him, on the one hand, and the much less stable band of Independent ministers, on the other, the Church of England attempted to take a progressive but moderate position between extremes. Apparently this was the King's intent as well as Laud's, the promotion of unity by way of diminishing the extremes of controversy.[3] By continuing steadfastly, however, to uphold the Book of Common Prayer and to support traditional clergy privileges and episcopal powers offensive to the people, the Church stirred up generations-old distrust of Catholicism, the Papacy, continental alliances, and now even of the monarch himself, for in much of Yorkshire the King was seen as a Papist. In a professed effort to restore order and prayerbook discipline and to cleanse the Church of sloppy practice and careless faithfulness, the bishops rejected stable and conservative ministers of worship like Nutter in favor of Laud's and the King's Arminian ritual practitioners. If all this offended young, enthusiastic, careful readers of the Scriptures like James Nayler, who had been brought up in Nutter's Puritan Presbyterian discipline, then small wonder that they might consider an Independent alternative more attractive.

James Nayler's presence in the Woodkirk congregation of Independents can be confirmed in four ways, but it cannot be dated. His membership in the Woodkirk Independents is affirmed in trial testimonies. It is elaborated in a suspect biographical claim. Church records refer to him by name, and finally Nayler's own correspondence with the Independents confirms that he was once among them. The circumstances of his coming, the nature of his work when he was with them, and the reason for his separation from their membership all remain uncertain.

In Nayler's trial at Appleby in 1652 he was questioned about where he was a church member, to which he answered, the Independent congregation at Woodkirk. Asked if he were not excommunicated from the Woodkirk congregation for his blasphemous opinions, Nayler answered. "I know not what they have done since I came forth, but before I was not, to my knowledge."[4] The Appleby trial, recorded in "*Saul's Errand to Damascus*," was taken down as if literally by a reporter, but nowhere in the document are we informed of who made the notes. A document in Friends House Library's collection, London,[5] suggests that it may have been Nayler himself who recorded the trial. His notes about what he meant in his answers to Scriptural questions are included with a record of the court testimony, which is believed to be in his hand. The same line of questioning was pursued in Nayler's trial before Parliament in 1656, and the same response was reported, as well as a variation. In the Parliament trial in London the questioning was conducted in a pretrial committee hearing, and a summary report of that proceeding was presented to Parliament as a whole. Another authority for this inquiry is the contemporaneous account, taken down as nearly verbatim as Member of Parliament Thomas Burton could make it, and presented in his diary.⁶ The consistency of this account with that of the Appleby trial is notable, but the official record of the London trial has it that Nayler was a member of an Independent church at Horbury, where Christopher Marshall was pastor and Nayler was cast out for adultery.⁷ Horbury is a village two miles south of Wakefield. Christopher Marshall briefly served both congregations at the same time. Nayler never mentioned being at Horbury, only Woodkirk.

The account of Nayler's membership and ejection from the Woodkirk Independent church found in John Deacon's biography of Nayler is unreliable.⁸ In this earliest account of Nayler's life Deacon asserted that Nayler was excommunicated from the congregation for adultery with a Mrs. Roper, whose husband was away at sea. (Mrs. Roper had hosted two meetings in which George Fox spoke. Fox reported in his *Journal* that Nayler, William and Mary Dewsbury, Thomas Aldam, and others had been convinced there.) Deacon went on to say that Nayler then moved to London where he took up with a Baptist congregation and was excommunicated from it also for adultery. The author of the Dictionary of National Biography article on Nayler, Alexander Gordon, stated that Deacon's whole story of repeated adultery and excommunications was a deliberate slander authorized by Christopher Marshall, who had become Independent vicar of Woodkirk about 1650, and was embarrassed there by George Fox right after the second meeting at the Ropers' house.⁹ It appears that Marshall was the source of the Deacon account as well as the line of questioning developed at Nayler's Appleby and London trials. This will be examined later in this volume, along with Nayler's steadfast denial of the adultery stories.

Nayler very likely was removed from a ministry position at the Woodkirk Independent congregation, which relocated to nearby Topcliffe. Scatcherd's History of Morley quoted from the registers of the Topcliffe Independent congregation,

> Church Members, 1655 . . . Besides Bro Elyard, Bro Legine, Bro Carver, *Jaimes Nailor*, Bro Bines, Bro Richardson, Sister Oxeley, Sister Hannah Cassley, Sister Easter Cassley. These departed from us, and some under Church Censures.¹⁰

Scatcherd described an arrangement without an incumbent clergy. Ministers, he said, were paid seven shillings when they officiated. Nayler (spelled Naylour in one account and Nailer in another) was one such occasional preacher. Expressing confidence that this was the "prophet," James Nayler, Scatcherd pointed out that he was obviously out of the fellowship of the congregation, not being styled, Brother, like the rest. That was because Nayler had become a Quaker, Scatcherd explained. Although this was the case in 1655, it is not clear when the congregation cast him out. The court in Appleby was under the impression that it had already happened in 1652.

Finally, while Nayler agreed that he was a part of the Independent congregation at Woodkirk and asserted he knew nothing of having been ejected from it, he did write a public letter to the Independents in about 1654 in which he said he was once a member, had not been among them for many years and detailed the reasons why.[11] Nayler did not acknowledge any discipline from the congregation, nor did he mention ministry, paid or freely given, while he was a member.

Could the growing interest in Independent forms of worship have been the direction in which Nutter was leading his congregation before his death? While tempting to conclude, this seems unlikely.

Nutter had long followed Presbyterian organizational structure. He had faced the Star Chamber before the turn of the century because of his presence at several of the classis-styled meetings in and around Coventry. He continued during the time he was at Woodkirk to attend the nearby Halifax preaching exercises, from which the only surviving notes of his sermons were taken, and these Halifax exercises were of Presbyterian structure.[12] Their emphasis was on preaching and peer criticism of sermons, a practice the Church of England deemphasized in favor of delivering less challenging and more familiar traditional ceremony. We must also remember Nutter's testimony at Star Chamber in 1590, that among the topics of discussion at his group in Coventry was a concern with the rise of Brownist separatists, who were a precursor group to the Independents. He was interested then, and apparently continued to be, in the maintenance of a strict Church structure in which preaching ministry was central. Nutter is much more likely to have opposed the Independent forms of organization than he is to have led his people toward them. If a separatist inclination developed in Nutter's congregation, we can be reasonably sure he did not lead it. About the time he died, early in 1634, however, Independent separatists did begin to form a congregation at Woodkirk, West Ardsley, one of the earliest Independent congregations in this part of Yorkshire.[13]

All around it others also formed within a short period. Independent churches emerged from the traditional Anglican congregations at nearby Morley, at Batley, of which parish both West Ardsley and Morley were a part, and at Leeds, the growing pre-industrial city to the north of Wakefield. In each case these nonconformist gatherings were potentially dangerous to their members, because conventicles, or unauthorized religious gatherings outside the Church, were prohibited, and those who held them, along with those who attended, were subject to presentment before the High Commissioners. Sanctions of imprisonment rarely if ever were used, but probationary limitations were common. Parishioners were ordered to conform in whatever way was appropriate to the infraction, and the courts followed up their orders with requirements of proofs of compliance and further intrusive charges for failure to submit to their orders. Church administrators from York certainly became unwelcome visitors to the parishes, and even church wardens attempting to conform to their responsibilities must have been seen as suspect by their neighbors. For these reasons the first gatherings of the Independent groups were informal meetings at private homes, not public events.

In the case of the Woodkirk Independents, the gatherings were first held at Haigh Hall, a farmhouse located south of the road from Wakefield to Batley and across from the foot of the lane that led up to the top of the moor at Westerton, where Naylor lived. If James had turned left leaving his house, instead of going west straight across the fields toward Woodkirk, he would have come, after a walk of about the same distance, a mile more or less, to this house where the first Independent meetings were held. Accounts suggest that one of the large front rooms was the meeting place of the congregation. They called this room in Haigh Hall, The Lord's Parlour. In a later account of his ejection from the church, it is reported that the elders met in this chamber to discuss Nayler's case.[14]

The Independents of this congregation later moved from Haigh Hall to Topcliffe Hall, a larger farmhouse in a more accessible location. Still only about a mile from Nayler's home, Topcliffe Hall was donated to the congregation by a prominent member of the old Woodkirk church, whose ancestor, Sir John Topcliffe, had been Chief Justice of the court at King's Bench under Henry VII and Henry VIII.[15] Topcliffe Hall, long gone now, stood in the neighborhood of West Ardsley called Tingley, in the vicinity of the present M62 junction with A653, the road, which passes Woodkirk, and A650, the road connecting Wakefield, West Ardsley, Morley, and Bradford. The Independents stayed many years at Topcliffe Hall until moving to a church building nearby in Morley after the Civil Wars.

Ministers from chapels and churches in this immediate area were caught up in the same program of visitations, presentments, and disciplines that ensnared Anthony Nutter. Nutter's successor at Woodkirk, James Ridgeley, was also summoned to Chancery Court in 1633 for nonconformity. Like Nutter, he did not appear due to age and ill health. Additional charges were brought against him, but within a short time Ridgeley died unpunished. Next to follow Nutter and Ridgeley as minister in the Woodkirk congregation was Samuel Newman, known as an Independent, who served only two years. Then came John Ridgeley, perhaps the son of James. This Ridgeley, who was also involved at Morley chapel, about a mile away from Woodkirk, was unlicensed to preach, as was Thomas Gilbert of Morley, who had spoken for Nutter when Nutter was too ill to travel to the court at York in 1633. Both Ridgeley and Gilbert were disciplined, although there was scant punishment for unlicensed preaching. Thomas Gilbert, when he was curate of Morley chapel, also was charged with failure to wear the surplice and for not observing the Book of Common Prayer, which he admitted. An Independent, he accumulated more offenses over the next five years and was excommunicated in 1638. That discipline apparently was lifted, as he served as rector and vicar in two more parishes before being convicted for nonconformity again. He emigrated to New England, where he served as pastor in Topsfield, Massachusetts until his death in 1673.[16]

Further infractions were charged in neighboring communities. Two men named Pearson were charged, one in Batley and Dewsbury, the other apparently in

East Ardsley, but this latter Pearson could not be found to answer his charge, having emigrated to Connecticut. John Reyner of Tingley was charged with holding conventicles, potentially one of the most serious charges of all, because it was viewed as outwardly subverting the organized Church. Indeed, due to the time and location, these conventicles may have been among the early Independent gatherings of disaffected Woodkirk members. It had been Reyner's custom, he admitted, to take notes of the morning sermon at Woodkirk and to read them at evening prayer meetings, so that the subject matter could be discussed.[17] People who might skip the proper service could still in the same day, after a fashion, hear the sermon, making a sham gesture of obedience to the law that they attend church. For Reyner to perform this service, however, was chargeable as preaching without a license, and those who skipped proper church services were still subject to presentment for failing to fulfill their obligations. Indeed it was the responsibility of church wardens to make this presentment, a form of legal accusation, to the diocesan authorities. In neighboring congregations some wardens were found lax in their office and were charged themselves for omitting to charge their neighbors.

The sanctions in this period were swift, frequent, and meticulous. The least offense could be noticed and the offender brought in to answer charges, a matter of time-consuming and sometimes expensive public embarrassment. It is no surprise then that it became attractive to some parishioners, long accustomed to a permissive discipline, to leave the national church and form their own, with local administration, and no bishops.

The name of the offshoot Independent sect changed over time to reflect its administrative form, Congregational. It was this name that stuck and eventually acquired respectability and some institutional establishment. During James Nayler's time, however, Independents had a less stable character, separatist, irregular, and above all, liberal and accommodating of innovation. Here was a refuge both for serious reformers and for the dissatisfied and recalcitrant, who enjoyed a chance to reject entirely the national church. Some Yorkshiremen, and those from other counties, went abroad to assert their Independence in New England, or in some cases in the Caribbean colonies. By 1634 concern over this emigration had risen to the point that formalities for clearance to ship abroad were promulgated, including the registry of names and the taking of oaths of allegiance. The extent, however, to which these were effective in deterring the departures is doubtful.[18] Independent emigrants included John Reyner of Tingley or Batley parish, who emigrated to New England in 1636 and served as minister in Dover, New Hampshire. Hatevil Nutter, a Puritan as strict and unyielding as his uncle, Anthony, went to America, also appeared in Dover about 1635, and there became an active member of the community and a scourge of Quakers.[19]

When Archbishop Abbott died in 1633, and William Laud replaced him, the Church of England needed reform of its own lax governance. For better or worse, that was what Laud undertook to do, and his efforts continued until his own impeachment in 1641. Laudian reforms made great progress in restoring the physical decline of the Church's real property, requiring that the reluctant parishioners, whether they liked it or not, spend real money and labor to repair buildings that were in danger of falling down in many cases.[20] The same system of visitation and reform was used to reinforce old forms of worship that might instead have been allowed to slide into disuse. In the 1630s the requirement of wearing the surplice was still just as current and objectionable as it was at the beginning of the century. People still were being punished regularly for ignoring it, though some churches had so thoroughly abandoned the practice that they had not owned such a vestment for years. Ministry was still a lackluster profession as practised by many, and its financial abuses burdened parishes more interested in the quality of the sermons than in ceremony. In 1603 the old practices of baptism had been brought to the new monarch's attention for change and laying down. The 1605 petition of the priests of Lincoln attacked baptismal excesses with even greater vigor, and by 1640, so little had changed in this and many other stipulations of the Book of Common Prayer that the same petition from Lincoln was deemed just as relevant as it had been thirty-five years before and was republished just before war broke out. The Church had changed very little, and in many ways its changes seemed retrograde toward its Catholic origins. Falling short of their intent to unify the Church community, Charles I and Laud had succeeded in opening the way for all sorts of dissent.

Even the promising Independent movement seemed failed to many who tried it, as James Nayler's epistle reflected. Writing well after the war to explain his rejection of membership in the Independent congregation, he noted again the deficiencies in ministry, continuation of the old forms of baptism, the corruption of Scripture. Furthermore, he named the effects of these free licenses with Christianity on personal behavior, as shown by the popularity of heathen sport and open slander in public life. Nayler concluded by stating that the Independents had committed the greatest error of all in limiting the Word of the Living God to that which was written on the page by others, when Nayler and "Hundreds in the Nation" could witness the hearing of the Word in their lives. He might not have been able to make that statement when he left Woodkirk for Haigh Hall, or even when he fought at Wakefield in rebellion against King Charles. Here, writing in 1654, Nayler focused on what he had come to understand as the purpose of the civil war just fought, that is, to take back into the hearts of people their practise of religion, or to put it in the words of his time, the exercise of Freedom of Conscience.

CHAPTER 4

Charles I and Abuse of Personal Rule, the Prelude to Revolution

... All things Going to Wreck, both in Church and State ...

—Joseph Lister

A neighbor from a town only eight miles from West Ardsley, Joseph Lister of Bradford (1627–1709) was about nine years younger than Nayler. His autobiography provides a vivid narrative of the growing chaos just before fighting began.[1] Of the period from about 1639 until the start of civil war in 1642, Lister wrote,

> ... all profaneness came swelling in upon us, swearing and sabbath-breaking, profane sports, and these even authorized by law; and the people of God not knowing what the end of these things would be, they being almost at their wit's end ...

Lister was twelve years old in 1639, so the judgments and observations in his autobiography reflect not only what he saw and understood for himself during those years, but also what he heard from the adults around him. Referring to the authority of law, Lister charged responsibility for the breakdown of order and morality to the King himself. Bad enough that after the 1627 publication of John Cosin's *Collection of Private Devotions* a whole list of saints' days with no basis whatever in Scripture had been glorified and added to the church calendar. Now the King published his own endorsement of celebrations with pagan origin. Charles I had republished the King's Book of Sports in 1633, reiterating his father's declaration of 1615 and endorsing many customary rituals, games, and celebrations that Puritans found objectionable. Archbishop Laud ordered the distribution of the Book of Sports to all the parishes, as the King's own order to his church. May Day games, Whitsunday and Christmas ales, midsummer Morris Dance festivals all gained what seemed to be equal approval with the Sabbath itself. The monarch appeared to enforce disorder on the people, a strange and incomprehensible policy indeed, thought Puritans like Lister, his family, and neighbors.[2]

The King and the bishops, of course, had a different agenda than to encourage immoral conduct. The purpose of the Book of Sports was to try to clarify the limits between allowable recreation and proper observance of the Sabbath. Where the King would allow traditional games, celebrations, and ceremonies after the conclusion of worship, the Puritans would reject as profane all drinking, gambling, and celebrations with pagan traditional origins, whether on the Christian Sabbath or on any day. Joseph Lister and James Nayler grew to adulthood with this controversy as part of their religious education and conviction, and it is clear whose side of the discussion was the Devil's in their judgment. It was the King's.

Lister attended The Free-School at Bradford, and was probably in attendance there as the early events of the wars unfolded. Nayler, about sixteen years old when Anthony Nutter died in 1633, had finished school, married, and had his first daughter by 1639. Where Nayler went to school is not recorded, but we can suggest a likely answer to that question.

While literacy was hardly universal in Yorkshire by the mid-seventeenth century, the levels of reading skills and the availability of books and pamphlets increased dramatically as the population moved from countryside to town.[3] Parish teaching was generally confined to religious education and basic reading to lower grade levels. It was uneven in quality, but in Nayler's vicinity were several important grammar schools (a higher level form in English education than American usage of the term implies). Some of these grammar schools, with strong Puritan connections, functioned as preparatory schools for Cambridge University colleges. One such school was associated with the vicar in nearby Halifax, where we know Anthony Nutter had a connection with prominent clergy through his involvement in the Presbyterian Halifax conferences. Even closer than Halifax to Nayler's home was the school at Bradford attended by Joseph Lister, but equally convenient was St. Elizabeth's Grammar School, located on the western outskirts of Wakefield. Among the founding supporters of this school was George Savile of the Wakefield branch of that prominent family. The school accepted a limited number of boarders who typically came from the more affluent classes, so that sufficient places could be available to accommodate promising local students of lesser means, students of the yeoman class, for example, like James Nayler. The school statutes of 1607 declared that "... *this schole is principallie a seminarie for bringing up of christian children, to become in time ambassidours of reconciliation from God to his Church* ..." and the schoolmaster must be "... *an enemie to popish superstition* ..." and deliver a strong religious education. Among the required subjects to be taught were Latin and Hebrew. Greek and Rhetoric may have been offered as well.[4]

Nayler's minister, Anthony Nutter, was Chaplain to the Thomas Savile family of Howley Hall, cousins of the Saviles connected with St. Elizabeth's Grammar School. Sir John Savile of Lupset, seat of the Wakefield Saviles, was a governor of St. Elizabeth's School from 1625 to 1650, beginning his term when James Nayler was about nine years old. His connection as well to Sir Thomas Savile of Howley Hall is supported by the fact that soon after the outbreak of war, John Savile was a leader of the Parliamentarian forces fighting to protect Howley Hall, and that when he died in 1660 he was buried at Horbury, where Thomas and his father also came to rest.[5] Clearly Anthony Nutter had the connections with the Savile family to see that his student was accepted at St. Elizabeth's. This school also had connections to Cambridge University. Nutter may or may not have been to university. All we know of his education is that he was "bred in the schools."[6] What is clear from James Nayler's writing and army resume is that he had a high level of literacy as well as rhetorical skills. He must have obtained a far better than average level of education somewhere. His scorn for university educated ministers suggests, however, that he did not get beyond local schools, such as St. Elizabeth's.

Since 1629 King Charles I's personal rule had been a thorn in the side of the nobility and gentry. People from these classes were long accustomed to holding seats in Parliament that gave them a say in furthering their own interests. When the King wanted to raise money, the propertied class felt they had a right to be consulted, to consider, and even to accept the imposition or reject it by means of their voices in Parliament, but after that body had opposed him in 1629 on matters of religion and raising money by import duties, the King had refused to call Parliament. He ruled without Parliament until 1640. During this period Charles I, by Royal prerogative, had called for a forced loan from the gentry, "ship money" taxes from all towns whether or not they enjoyed the benefits of a port, and duties on a variety of imports. Much of this revenue was used to fund unwanted military adventures with failed outcomes. The present King's father, James I, had involved England in costly wars on the continent. Inheriting these conflicts in 1625, Charles I sought to end them and save his relatives in Europe by dramatic means, sending large contingents of troops abroad under his own orders, but without sufficient funding or resources to carry out their campaigns. The result was one disaster after another with the loss of many English lives, some of them reportedly due to starvation abroad in winter for want of supply from home. People from all classes, not just the wealthy, began turning against their monarch over his arbitrary rule.

The King's policy toward his northernmost subjects on the island of Britain was no more successful than his foreign policy, nor was it less costly to his reign. In 1633 Charles made a brief tour of Scotland, during which his long-delayed coronation was held in that Kingdom. Later that summer William Laud was raised to the head of the Church of England as Archbishop of Canterbury. The King and Archbishop now undertook, openly and ambitiously, to restore order in the Church of England under strong episcopal control, administered by consistent discipline. Reaffirming The Book of Common Prayer as canon, the King sought as well to bring Scotland's Church, largely Presbyterian, into conformity as nearly as possible to the English prayer book under episcopal rule. A Scottish prayer book was prepared along very similar lines to The Book of Common Prayer, written in England in consultation between English clerics and those chosen from Scotland who were thought to be most favorable to the English Church. Although it was attributed popularly to Laud himself, he and the bishops worked largely under the guidance of the King to accomplish his reforms.[7] When the product of this work was presented by Charles I to the Church in Scotland in 1637, not only was it rejected, but the people of Scotland answered with a Covenant of their own, asserting Scottish Presbyterian independence in Church matters. Meeting with Scottish recalcitrance equivalent in his view to rebellion, Charles I proposed to enforce his rights over that kingdom by military means. Again without English popular support, and without sufficient financial means to conduct war, he raised arms against Scotland in 1639 and again in 1640. Long known as the Bishops' Wars, this series of conflicts is called by more modern scholars the Prayer Book Rebellion and placed as the opening engagements of The War Between The Kingdoms.[8]

The Scots repulsed the King's army twice and in 1640 took up military occupation of the northern three counties of England, holding them hostage to monetary reparations for the unsuccessful invasion of their country. Charles I was forced to make treaty, at Ripon, with his own kingdom of Scotland. The English people held the purse strings, and their Scottish Presbyterian neighbors, by bold resistance to the King, had empowered them to act in their own behalf at last. Parliament had to be called by sheer financial necessity, for the King was without sufficient funds to cover the embarrassment of his debt to the Scots, the arrears due his troops, or the amounts due to the citizens who had and continued to billet and supply the army.

The West Riding of Yorkshire experienced threatening local effects. Scottish occupation, when the King's campaigns failed, came to within about 60 miles of Wakefield. Among the King's negotiating team for the treaty at Ripon was the notorious and certainly corrupt Lord Thomas Savile of Howley Hall. No doubt, some around Wakefield must have watched him closely to see that their own interests were not sold for a price either to the King or the Scots. With both armies at a near standstill in the north, waiting for money that Charles I could not deliver, unrest grew on both sides, with threats and occasional outbreaks of violence by the troops on local residents and each other.[9] This condition concerned not only people near the border. In 1640 angry army conscripts waiting for their pay in Wakefield became unruly, went on a rampage, broke into the House of Correction and released prisoners into the town in a riot.[10]

In 1639 James Nayler had moved to Wakefield, 5 miles from West Ardsley, after his marriage to Ann. Disorder spread over his homeland, just as Mary, his first daughter, was born.

Joseph Lister's vehement description shows how at least some of the King's subjects from around Bradford saw their condition:

About this time, that is, about the years 1639, 1640, and 1641, many good ministers and christians amongst the puritans (as they were called at that time) reflected upon the times, and with many sad and foreboding thoughts, concluding that Popery was like to be set up and the light of the gospel put out, many ministers were silenced, and great numbers for these three or four years past were posting away to New England, and many of these, both men and women, that I myself knew, and sad apprehensions remained with those that stayed behind.

Horse and foot soldiers were posted in the towns, he continued, swaggering, unruly, threatening men, "like so many bloodhounds."

Lister described the brief war as the Scots' effort to save England from ruin, by which he made clear that he meant take-over of the country by Popery. He declared the Scots' endeavor a success, in that the outcome of the war was to force King Charles I to call a Parliament at last. The Prayer Book Rebellion, or The Bishops' Wars, was not only a regional concern, but truly a national political event. Involved were lofty constitutional principles: the establishment of religion, the prerogative of the King to impose taxes by royal decree alone, and to conduct war without concurrence of the people. Interwoven between these principles was a network of perceived threats leading back to the source of virtually all fears, Rome. King Charles I was suspect of collusion in these pending disasters. With him stood his French Catholic wife, who welcomed recusants to her apartments for Mass. With the King also stood Archbishop Laud, now openly accused of introducing Papist secrets and rituals into the very Prayer Book of the Kingdoms. In London John Pym stirred Parliament with more and more evidence of papist plots everywhere in the kingdoms and in Europe. In the clothing towns in the north, and in port towns on both coasts, fear grew of a Catholic invasion to take over England.

Within a year Yorkshire was abuzz with fear of the next, still larger military adventure, spreading around them like a fire, before the Scottish issue was settled. Rumors circulated of the massacre of thousands of Irish Protestants. Some of the rumors held that the murderers were Irish Catholics. Other versions charged the killings to the King's own troops, and maintained that they were led by Papists in league with Charles I. Foremost of these was the King's minister in Ireland, Thomas Wentworth, made Earl of Strafford at the end of 1639, whose family and the Saviles had been at odds in Yorkshire for generations. Strafford, notorious for his ruthless financial and land dealings, was suspected of taking sides with Catholics in Ireland in order to take control and manage an invasion of Britain, supported, some claimed, by Rome and their allies in Catholic Europe. So the rumors went.

Lister wrote,

> ... many thousand protestants of all ages, sexes, and degrees, were put to death with great inhumanity and cruelty; and great fear came upon the protestants in England, these villains giving it out, that what they had done there [in

Ireland] was by the king's commission, and that in a little time the English protestants (or heretics as they called them) should drink of the same cup . . .

Notice here a strange turnabout. If this account were the story of a twelve year old, we might say the child had got it confused and somehow had put the villains on the wrong side. The Catholics of that country, in revolt, were dealt with harshly by the King's minister, Strafford, but then under his leadership had turned against their Protestant countrymen in a widely rumored massacre. When the Irish Catholics turned toward the Protestants of England, the people around Bradford in Yorkshire attributed their rumored attack on the English people to their own English King! Bizarre indeed, but this was not the belief of one confused boy. In London the rumors were augmented credibly by one of the foremost leaders of Parliament, John Pym, whose story was that Strafford planned to bring an army of 10,000 from Ireland into England, and of that number 8,000 were known papists. Further, the Earl of Worcester was preparing a papist army in Wales to march and join the force from Ireland.[11]

Strafford had returned to London in 1639 to aid the King's campaign against Scotland, adding fuel to the anti-papist fire. Scots called him and Laud their greatest enemies, and now he brought that fire ever closer to the King. The Queen acted first, for she was no friend to either Strafford or Laud. She gathered her own counselors, and of course, as she was, so were they Catholic. The Queen was Antichrist, and so must be the King.[12]

A story went about in the West Riding of Yorkshire that a force of as many as five thousand Catholic Irish had invaded Lancashire and was marching down the road toward Bradford, eight miles from West Ardsley. Joseph Lister heard this story while at church with his family on a feast day in Pudsey, near Bradford, when a man burst in on the service and gave alarm. Lister's family went home to Bradford, expecting to find "Incarnate Devils and Death" waiting for them. When Death did not come, the people of Bradford sent riders to Halifax to see if Death were there, but they found only a band of Irish ". . . protestants that were escaping out of Ireland for their lives in England."

So, we see the low level to which the King's repute had sunk. Charles I had subverted the very morality the men of God were trying to maintain. The King had bankrupted his monarchy in his adventures. He had made war against the people of Scotland who were trying to uphold their conservative religious practice, and those Protestant neighbors had come to the aid of England against her King and his papist archbishop. By the King's commission, papist villains had been given leave to massacre not only the people of Ireland, but also the men of God in England. Articles of Treason were brought in Parliament against the King's minister, Strafford. The Archbishop himself was arrested as a traitor and sent to the Tower of London.[13]

The papists, Lister wrote, were "... desperate, bloody men; and those that were put in offices and places of trust were such as would serve the king and his design." King Charles I

> ... did by the constant solicitation of the bloody Queen, together with the swarms of Jesuits and evil affected Councillors, Bishops, and men of great estate, place, and trust, all put their heads together to destroy Christ's interest in the nation ... to cut off the lives of all Protestants, and so to have enslaved this land to Rome, the mother of harlots.

The Prayer Book Rebellion in Scotland and rebellion in Ireland were soon followed by the outbreak of war between the King and his subjects on English soil, with organized opposition to the monarch represented now by Parliament as an adversary body. A fight in three intervals, like a great stage drama, the prolonged conflict following the Scottish rebellion has been called three separate wars, all of them together known as The English Civil Wars. Taken together the larger complex of conflicts in Scotland, Ireland, and England are known as The War of the Three Kingdoms, a more comprehensive terminology which seems to describe more accurately what the people must have witnessed.[14]

The Naylers' second daughter, Jane, was baptised in the year 1641, just before war commenced in England.

By the next year King and Parliament, belatedly called into session in 1640 in order to fund his campaigns, were themselves in direct military confrontation. In January, 1642 the King, in an unthinkable breach of constitutional separation, had personally entered a sitting session, accompanied by armed men of his guard, and attempted to arrest Members of Parliament, including Pym, having drawn Articles of Treason against the five leaders of Parliamentary opposition to his rule.[15] His Majesty met with no cooperation or success. Losing control of London, where "Trained Bands" of militia had made it impossible for his own army to maintain security, the King moved his capitol to York and commenced to gather forces around the core of his small command. Yorkshire's response at first was significantly in the King's favor, but this was short-lived.

Parliament sent troops, answering to its command and not the King's, to seize supplies of arms at Hull in the East Riding of Yorkshire. King Charles I, having stockpiled those weapons and ammunition to be used in defending his kingdom, attempted to take the arms and the fortified city by force in early April. Governor Hotham, serving Parliament, flooded the surrounding lowlands and slammed shut the gates of Hull in the King's face. The gauntlet was thrown down.

While at York the King concentrated on accreting his power in regions thought to be loyal to him. Early steps involved establishing commissions of array charged with raising troops for the King from the communities. This was a cumbersome process and not sufficiently productive. The King took a bold step at York in order to hasten the process of raising an army. Using the established social structure of noble landowners, gentry, clergy, and substantial farmers, the King called for a meeting of regional leadership at Heworth (or Hepworth or Heyworth) Moor, just outside York, in early June.[16] His belief in the willingness of his wealthier subjects to join him to put Parliament back in its place, however, turned out to be overly optimistic. The propertied people of Yorkshire and many of their puritan ministers remembered all too well how badly they were used by the King during his years of personal rule. The division between the King's supporters and Parliament's was just forming and was unpredictable even to some of the community members present. The King accomplished little to bring the community together in his favor.

The meeting was held at a field adequate in size for perhaps thousands of men and their horses to gather. Among them were James Nayler's neighbors, his landlord, some members of his church and friends of his former minister, as well as the man who would command the armies in which he later fought. Two reports from among those listed above will give a sense of what happened.

Thomas Savile, in correspondence with his friend, Lady Temple, reported that he himself went not to take either the King's side or Parliament's, although he had standing as a member of the King's household and as a member of Parliament. Savile wrote a long justification in which he characterised himself as peacemaker between factions. Having resolved to ". . . not contribute to anie of the fatall evils which must follow . . ." he approached community leaders he knew to try to get them to moderate the conflict with the King and withhold the confrontational petition they had prepared. It is significant that the men he approached at Hepworth Moor bore the names of clergymen from Woodkirk and nearby churches who had been charged several years earlier with nonconformity with rules of the Church of England—John Reyner, Mr. Todd, and Mr. Ridgeley.[17]

Savile's mediation was ignored, according to his own account, and the Yorkshire petition was carried forward toward the King, who was riding through the crowd, greeting those assembled and personally delivering his call for loyalty and allegiance. The gathered crowd was far too large for the King to address them all and be heard. Sir Thomas Fairfax was chosen by his neighbors to deliver the petition to the King. The petition he carried was outspoken about the King's avoidance of Parliament's wishes, his persistent taxing of the country to make war, and his interruption of the region's livelihood through billeting of troops and closing the clothing trade. Nevertheless, who better could be chosen to get it a fair hearing from the King than young Fairfax, the grandson of a prominent member of the King's Council of the North, son of a member of Parliament, cousin of the Mayor of York, and recently the commander of a company of dragoons who had fought for the King in Scotland? Yet the King refused the petition, and when Fairfax pursued him through the crowd and tried to press the paper into the King's hand, his monarch spurred the horse, whether intentionally or not is uncertain, and appeared to be riding Fairfax down. In that gesture, the prior loyalty of an influential subject and many who stood with him was spurned and turned away.

Soon all Yorkshire was in an uproar. Both sides were attempting to raise troops and to establish territorial battle lines. The King's forces aimed to control York and to slice Yorkshire north to south, cutting off access to the supply port of Hull from the primary source of Parliament's manpower in the clothing towns of Leeds, Bradford, Halifax, and Wakefield. Lord Ferdinando Fairfax, leading Parliament's troops with his son, Thomas, while building his base of power in the clothing towns, attempted to establish a line against the Royalists through Pontefract and Tadcaster, east of Wakefield, from which he could break through to York and Hull. Late in the year 1642 Lord Newcastle, taking up leadership of the King's northern forces, succeeded in taking the clothing towns from the Fairfaxes. Royal troops occupied Bradford, Leeds, and Wakefield.

Late in 1642, at the age of 24, James Nayler became a soldier against the King.

CHAPTER 5

The Outbreak of War

... by single persons they got to the water-side, and hid them in a little lane (James Nayler one of the dragooners being first) ...

—The Rider of the White Horse and his Army

*I*n January, 1643 Thomas Fairfax wrote to his father and commanding General that the people of Leeds and Wakefield were impatient with him to get rid of the occupying Royalists,

... for by them al traid & provisions are stopt so that the people in these clothing townes are not able to subsist ...[1]

The Royalists had established what amounted to an economic blockade, and something had to be done. For some time Fairfax and others had been recruiting troops for a northern army to march for Parliament under his father's command. Now the son moved to free the clothing towns from occupation. After liberating Bradford, Thomas Fairfax led an attack against Royalist forces occupying Leeds.

The account of these battles is found in an unsigned pamphlet published at London within a few weeks of the events and titled, *THE RIDER OF THE WHITE HORSE And His Army, Their late good successe in Yorkshiere.*[2] The title reference is to Revelation, 6:2 (Geneva Bible, 1599), the prophet John's vision of the first of the four horsemen of the Apocalypse, the irresistible conqueror of the end times:

Therefore I beheld, and lo, there was a white horse, and he that sat on him, had a bow, and a crown was given unto him, and he went forth conquering that he might overcome.

Here was a popular vision of the new civil war, the army of the righteous led by godly heroes marching out against the Antichrist King's forces of evil Papism. Note the image of the heavenly crown of conquest, here imagined by the journalist on young Fairfax's head. Later, as we shall see, James Nayler would mention the same crown of conquest as being laid before Cromwell, but Nayler would remind him that this crown belonged to no man.

No one was a better choice to lead the men of Yorkshire at the beginning of this heroic revolution than Thomas Fairfax, under his father, Ferdinando Fairfax's command. Thomas, age 30, had been taught the arts of horsemanship by his namesake grandfather, just as his father had been taught before him. He was sent down to Cambridge and London to learn leadership, then to Europe's Thirty Years War for military skills. Fairfaxes had been leading citizens of York for hundreds of years, always before for the King, but now for their neighbors and countrymen against a King turned wrong.[3]

The Royalists at Leeds were commanded by Sir William Savile, cousin of the Howley Hall Saviles, a man of civil stature and lineage comparable to that of the Fairfaxes. At Leeds Savile's forces occupied a town spread across a hill overlooking the River Aire, as it flowed eastward to its meeting with the River Calder, flowing northeastward from Wakefield. Royalists numbering some 2,000 men, including cavalry and dragoons, had two cannons positioned on high ground and had dug themselves into fortifications overlooking the river crossings.

Fairfax approached with fewer foot soldiers, but more cavalry and dragoons (mounted infantry), augmented by a great many "clubmen," crudely armed and ill-trained volunteers, full of enthusiasm, ready for anything, and by no means dependable without firm leadership. Fairfax's force included three troops of dragoons, James Nayler among them. These played a key role, utilizing their advantage in mobility and quick deployment.

Near the town center, prominent on a hill facing southward, was a new church, which still stands as a landmark in the city. Dedicated to St. John, the Evangelist, it was known locally as Mr. Harrison's church. Harrison, a wealthy wool merchant of the new gentry, was the uncle of Vicar Robinson of Leeds Parish church, which occupied a smaller, older building, made inadequate by the growth in population of the clothing town in the first quarter of the 17th Century. The vicar had persuaded John Harrison to build this new edifice to better house the congregation. It was completed a decade before the battle, about the time of Anthony Nutter's death at Woodkirk.

Royalist troops fortified the hilltop around Harrison's church, and their trenches ran down the hill toward the south bridge over the River Aire, protecting the way toward Wakefield. Fairfax's main force on the north side of the river attacked these defenses, but were unsuccessful in breaking the Royalist lines. Nor were they much hurt by Royalist fire aimed rather blindly from the high trenches down the hill toward the Parliament men. A smaller force of Parliament dragoons led by Captain Mildmay had crossed the River Aire to the south side and approached the defenses at the south bridge. There the two sides engaged and fought, but again unsuccessfully. Mildmay's troops saw an opportunity to advance a small force close to the river under the sentry position on the end of the bridge and there attack them, dividing the enemies' attention and breaking the impasse. If this could be accom-

The Outbreak of War

plished quickly enough, the cannon above might not be turned on the small group of attackers,

> ... whereupon by single persons they got to the water-side, and hid them in a little lane (James Nayler one of the dragooners being first) whither they had no sooner got, than the Demiculverin [cannon] from the bridge plaid about them....[4]

This daring move turned the battle against the Royalists. Those on the bridge fled north into the town, as Fairfax's forces in the town broke through to push the defenders back toward the river. A long street fight ensued, ending with the Royalist forces breaking away to escape toward Wakefield. Lord Savile and others were pushed back against the river, and some had to swim their horses to safety, in a January snowstorm. A few men drowned, including, the reporter declares, Vicar Robinson. In this, however, he was mistaken, as the vicar was apprehended later, jailed for a time, and lived to practice his ministry in a small country church for some years after, dying in 1663.[5]

Nayler's appearance at Leeds is plausible, but somewhat historically uncertain. Only this anonymous account of the fighting located him there, but, republished and cited many times, it has become the primary authority on the battle at Leeds. Publication came well before Nayler or almost anyone else involved except Fairfax was famous. Several other participants on Parliament's side were mentioned as well, soldiers named Forbes, Lee, Brigg and others, each cited for his role in the combat, and in some cases for unusual bravery. No one, including Captain Mildmay, was named because he was famous, for none of them were at this time. Perhaps they were locally known and were named for that reason. Clearly someone named James Nayler was there, boldly taking the lead in a dangerous situation. The only reasonable question is whether this James Nayler was *the* James Nayler. Most likely, he was. Though many men named Nayler from around Wakefield and the Ardsleys took part in the war, no other has been found named James.

Among those charging the Royalists was the vicar of Halifax, who led the men in singing a rallying cry, the first verse of Psalm 68;

> Let God arise, and then his foes will turn themselves to flight: his enemies then will run abroad, and scatter out of sight.

Here was an early example of the active role played by chaplains and preaching laymen in Parliament's revolutionary army. Commonly, before a battle, chaplains would lead the men in prayer or would read from selected Biblical passages. Singing Psalms in meter had long been practiced in church services, and it served well in battle to focus the motivation of attacking troops. The Geneva Bible was still commonly in use despite the publication in 1611 of the Authorized or King James version.

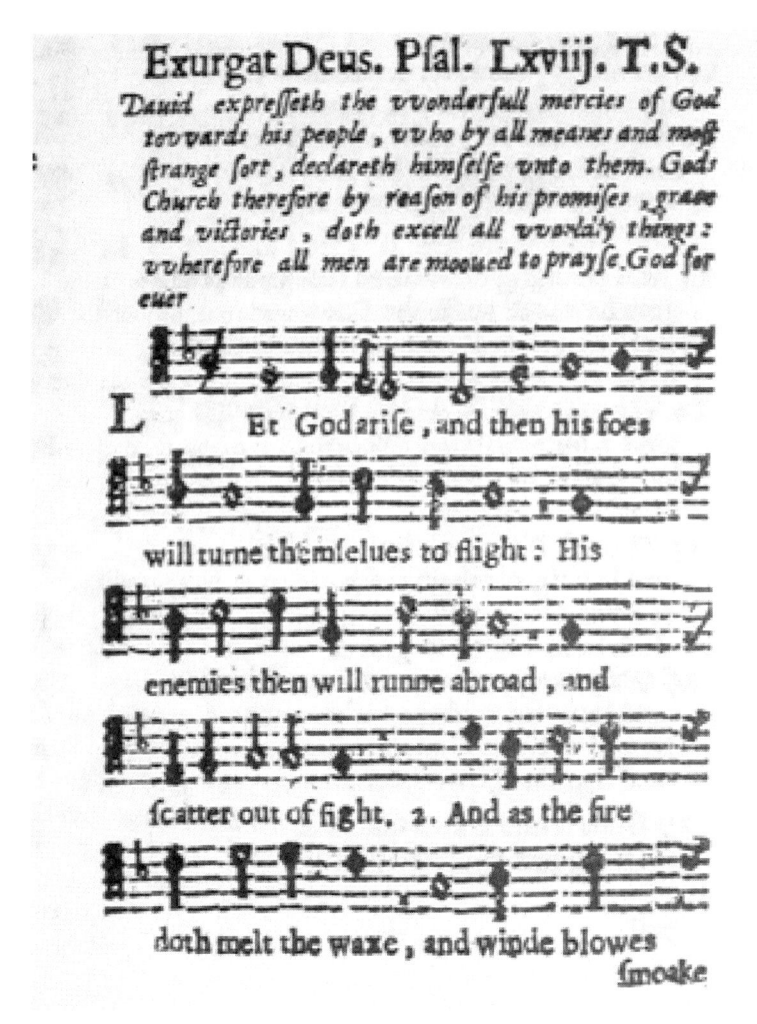

A 1599 edition of the Geneva Bible contained as an appendix, "The Booke of Psalmes: collected into English meeter . . . with apt Notes to sing them withall."

After the victory at Leeds it was not necessary for Fairfax to pursue the Royalists toward Wakefield, as the Royalist garrison at that city and the remaining defenders of Leeds and Bradford were quickly withdrawn to Pontefract, then to York, Lord Newcastle's stronghold. There they stayed through the remainder of the winter. In the spring they came again in great numbers, and this time it was an easy task for the Royalists to reoccupy Wakefield. It would take a major, well organized attack to dislodge them. However invigorating the Bradford and Leeds liberations

The Outbreak of War

may have been for the people of the clothing towns, however exciting a few see-saw cavalry skirmishes along the roads to York may have been for Parliament's forces, it was at Wakefield in May of 1643 that the real war between armies for the control of Yorkshire was engaged.

From Wakefield we can begin to trace James Nayler's commitment to the cause from original records, leaving little doubt as to where he was during the long course of his involvement in the wars. He testified in 1652[6] that he had been in the army between eight and nine years, and we will see in the pages that follow where he was during most of that time.

Recruitment of troops for Parliament had continued in the West Riding through the winter and spring of 1643, led not only by Thomas Fairfax, but also by Christopher Copley and other gentlemen from the area. Copley's family had property in several towns around Wakefield and the Ardsleys. Christopher was known as an agricultural innovator, and he had interests in iron works, which became useful suppliers to Parliament.[7]

Captain Christopher Copley raised a troop of horse (cavalry), under Thomas Fairfax's command in February of 1643. James Nayler enlisted at the age of twenty-five with the rank of Corporal on May 20, 1643, the eve of the Battle of Wakefield, which was fought on May 21, Whitsunday.[8] Enlisting at the same time and place, as a trooper, was William Nayler, Jr. of East Ardsley, who may have been a relative. This enlistment was recorded in Copley's own hand, and Nayler can be followed by means of troop payroll records and a variety of other battle accounts from May 20, 1643 all the way through the wars to Dunbar in 1651.

A few minor errors have been passed down from one Nayler biography to another. While they confuse the story only a little, it is worthwhile correcting the errors here to prevent further misunderstanding. Nayler did not serve for seven years as an infantry soldier.[9] He can be placed with confidence at the Battle of Wakefield, but that battle did not take place at Wakefield Castle, properly known as Sandal Castle.[10] Only the very end of his service was in Cromwell's army. (Nayler was not a Quaker at the time.) Until Cromwell took over, Nayler was under the high command of Lord Fairfax, but it is more proper to name his immediate superior officers as Christopher Copley and John Lambert.[11] When Nayler enlisted with Copley, Thomas Fairfax was Copley's superior, but he was not Lord Fairfax. Thomas, in turn was under the command of Lord Ferdinando Fairfax, his father, during the early years of the war. As if that were not enough confusion, Thomas Fairfax also commanded infantry of his own, in addition to Copley's cavalry.

An unrelated question arises here. Why did Nayler appear at first as a dragoon at Leeds in January under Mildmay's command and now appear in May at Wakefield, enlisting under Copley's cavalry command? No clear answer is known, but the most likely possibility is that Copley arranged to recruit some experienced men from other units in the area to form the core leadership of his own troop. This is supported by the fact that Nayler enlisted with Copley not as a common trooper, but as corporal. A man named Briggs also appears in Copley's enlistments, perhaps the one named at the battle in Leeds.

Raising a troop of horse meant not only recruiting men to serve, but also horses. Gentlemen and members of titled families often served in cavalry, because they owned horses and had been trained since childhood in horsemanship. Such was the case with Thomas Fairfax, who had served King Charles I in the Bishops' Wars by raising a troop of dragoons and by leading them in a number of skirmishes. During this time he corresponded with his grandfather, discussing horses the elder Thomas had provided for his use. When the grandfather died, he willed his best horse and some arms to the younger Thomas, with a rather curious life estate in them running to Ferdinando, young Thomas's father.[12] Horses were a major part of a noble estate, and so their owners were naturally inclined toward cavalry service, but more troops and horses were needed than the noble families could provide. Which brings us to Christopher Copley's raising of a troop of horse in the area around Wakefield and West Ardsley. No particular mention of this point is found in Copley's notes, but it seems clear that rather common folk in this locale had horses and knew about how to use them. Probably West Ardsley's trade fair, the ancient Lee Fair, had something to do with Copley's choice of where to find his recruits. If James Nayler lived almost directly across the road from the site of the Lee fair when he was growing up, and that Fair was a trading place for selling horses to gypsy horse traders, then it seems very likely that Nayler and many of his neighbors would have raised horses.[13] They may have lacked skills in warfare, but probably they could mount good horses, and perhaps bring a few extra animals to the troop as well. As Copley was wealthy and had money to buy horses, service with him may have provided financial as well as idealistic opportunity.

That Nayler fought in the Battle of Wakefield on Whitsunday, May 21, 1643 is reasonable to assume, though undocumented. No account names Copley or anyone under his command. The principal authority on the battle is the report from Thomas Fairfax, who seldom in his battle accounts named his junior officers and the nature of their involvement.[14]

On the night of May 20, 1643 Fairfax assembled Parliament troops recruited from Bradford and Leeds with troops raised from the Wakefield area. Their meeting place was Howley Hall, Lord Thomas Savile's elegant manor, well known to anyone from the Ardsleys or the neighboring clothing towns. Leaving Howley Hall in the predawn hours to attack from three entrances to Wakefield, north, west, and south, Fairfax had some element of surprise in his favor, but he commanded only 1100 troops against 3000 Royalists under General Goring. Speed and coordination were essential in capturing the city. Fortunately some Royalist officers were playing at bowls on the church lawn. Others, including Goring, were asleep after a night of Whitsun revelry. Parliament's forces were able to strike quickly, capture the Royalist cannon, turn them on their owners, and capture the town, along with General Goring and 300 Royalist soldiers. Fairfax, in his report, called it a miracle rather than a victory, for his poorly trained volunteers were ill-matched against the Royal Army.[15] Recruits from the day before had virtually no time to train between their enlistment and the battle. Nayler and a few others would have been valuable for their prior experience, however limited it may have been.

Although many were wounded, only seven of Fairfax's men were killed, among them his Clerk of Stores and his Quartermaster.[16] Here is evidence that the Quartermaster, today sometimes considered a noncombatant rank, was in the 17th Century a soldier who could well be exposed to mortal risk. Nayler became Quartermaster of Copley's troop a year later.[17] In this capacity he was responsible for arranging and assigning quarters for soldiers in otherwise private homes. Written records, or billets, were exchanged, which the homeowner was supposed to be able to redeem for payment by the army at daily rates that related to the rank of the soldier accommodated and presumably the quality of the lodging assigned. The quartermaster's responsibility obviously required respect, fair-mindedness, firmness in negotiation, and skills in recordkeeping and accounting. The incentive for corruption was equally obvious, and the newly organized army of Parliament inherited much ill will over the old practice, known by the unfortunately all too accurate term, free quarter.

> The practice of quartering or billeting soldiers on private citizens and the abuses and hardships which it occasioned were of old standing. As far back as April, 1628, the House of Commons had petitioned the King to reform the system.[18]

After the victory at Wakefield, the next major fight had quite the opposite outcome. On June 30, 1643 Thomas Fairfax joined his father and substantially all of Parliament's forces in the North in an effort to defend Bradford and Leeds. A much larger Royalist force under Lord Newcastle faced them at Adwalton Moor, near Bradford and within easy walking distance of the Nayler home at West Ardsley.[19] Captain Copley's troop this time was mentioned, ingloriously, in Thomas Fairfax's account of the battle. During the heat of the fight four of Copley's troopers dismounted and stripped the Royalist Colonel Herne "naked, as he lay dead on ye ground . . ." Shortly, a Royalist cannon shot fell and killed two of the four Copley troopers, which Fairfax says, ". . . gave me a good occasion to reprove it, by shewing the Soldiers ye sinfulnesse of ye Act, and how God would punish wn (sic) man wanted power to do it."[20] Late in the day, facing Royalists who held higher ground, Fairfax's troops were cut off by hedgerows from observing the rest of Parliament's army in retreat, leaving them on the field without support. Fortunately, local people in Fairfax's regiment knew that Warren Lane led from behind their position toward Oakwell Hall and the Halifax Road, which offered a way to escape. The day was lost. Bradford and Leeds were lost. Most of Parliament's forces had to retreat across country to Hull, where the fortified city could be defended until help came from the south. Copley's troop went another way.

From late that July through September, Copley's troop held a base at Barnsley in southern Yorkshire, as Hull was besieged by Royalists[21] In October Copley moved to capture Lincoln and Gainsborough, then to the Battle of Nantwich in Cheshire, January 26, 1644, where Parliament's troops, led again by Fairfax, prevailed. At one point, cavalry of John Lambert and (now) Major Copley were in danger close to the town, but forces "came to their succor in good time."[22]

During much of May and June, 1644 Copley moved about the Don Valley in southern Yorkshire guarding roads to prevent relief from reaching York, where Parliament's forces held Royalists inside the city under siege.[23] Until reinforcements could reach both sides, a stand-off continued. These reinforcements, when they came, led to the enormous battle at Marston Moor. The entire northern army of Parliament fought there, including Thomas Fairfax's cavalry, of which Copley's troop was a part. James Nayler had been promoted to Quartermaster of Copley's troop on May 27.[24]

Parliament had made a Solemn League and Covenant with the Scots, promising Presbyterian governance of the Churches of England and Scotland in return for enough troops to help defeat the Royalists. (We focus here on the military importance of this pact, but the political and religious impact was even more significant.)[25] In an effort to counter the Scots alliance Prince Rupert, the King's nephew, brought men from Lancashire and from Ireland into the battle on the Royalist side. When the two armies met on the field at Marston Moor, they numbered over 46,000 men and stretched between two villages almost two miles apart, 28,000 Parliament and Scots soldiers facing 18,000 of Prince Rupert's Royalists. It was perhaps the largest battle ever fought on English soil, before or since.[26]

Copley's command spent the night before the battle at Hessay Moor, between Marston Moor and York with the rest of Fairfax's cavalry. There, a Copley troop captain records in his journal losing three men in a skirmish with a Royalist patrol. Early on the morning of July 2, 1644 Parliament's army withdrew southward toward Tadcaster, with Fairfax's cavalry guarding the rear, for the Royalists had broken out of York. It was thought better not to fight them back into the city but to regroup elsewhere.

Prince Rupert's arrival from Lancashire soon forced a change in that plan. Parliament's forces turned in their tracks to face the Prince at Marston Moor. This placed Fairfax's cavalry, formerly the rear guard, now among the advance units. The supply wagons, which had been at the rear, were gathered behind the only hill of note on the Parliament side of the field, a ridge, marked by a clump of trees on a knoll, a feature of the landscape since known as Cromwell's Plump. As Quartermaster, Nayler may have been one of those responsible for this position, but no documentation confirms that proposal.

The Outbreak of War

The two armies took position by midday, but neither attacked, aside from a few testing skirmishes. By dinner time the Prince assumed that no attack would take place that day and allowed his men to eat their meals, while remaining alert. About seven in the evening Parliament's attack began. In early July in this latitude darkness comes after ten P.M. following a long twilight. Even so the battle went on until the combatants could hardly see one another.

On Parliament's side things went badly from the start. Royalist General Goring, restored to his command in an earlier prisoner exchange, faced his former captor, Thomas Fairfax once again. This time Goring prevailed, and the entire Fairfax cavalry on Parliament's right crumbled. Ferdinando Fairfax, leading infantry in the center, was beaten as well and could not assist his son. Thomas Fairfax, with few cavalrymen remaining to muster, removed the white feather from his hat, by which he was identified, and dashed across the field to get help from his counterpart cavalry officer on the left, Oliver Cromwell. Together Fairfax and Cromwell's forces fought their way back around the center lines and turned the tide against the Royalists. Goring's cavalry had wasted time and lost their advantage, by breaking ranks to plunder the Parliament supply train behind Cromwell's Plump.[27]

James Nayler's position, if it were so, was almost utterly destroyed. Parliament soldiers here sustained heavy losses. Many fled, and they were not alone in doing so on either side. Even Lord Ferdinando Fairfax gave up the battle for lost when darkness fell, and headed for home, about fifteen miles away. Soldiers from both sides of the battle were reported on roads the next morning as much as thirty miles distant, still in retreat.[28] Yet on the battlefield it became understood by midnight that Parliament had won, for they could find no more Royalists to fight. Only next morning was it possible to learn the extent of losses to both sides. The number killed was never reliably recorded, but it was surely far into the thousands.[29]

The Royalists withdrew to the south, and Parliament's army occupied York, where Lambert was assigned to save York Minster from possible damage or destruction by rebellious soldiers motivated to ruin papist symbols.

Copley's Case to Parliament,[30] a document attempting to justify payment of money due him later in the war, indicates that his command was busy soon after Marston Moor reducing remaining Royalist strongholds in the North. Pay records show that he and Nayler were at Whixley, near Knaresborough, in August and at Halifax in November.[31] Lambert and Thomas Fairfax took Knaresborough Castle in November, capturing much money and silver. Fairfax was wounded at Helmsley Castle, then again while besieging Pontefract Castle near Wakefield. Lambert took over and brought the siege to a successful conclusion, entering the castle on Christmas day, 1644.[32]

With Lambert were both Copley and Nayler. A list numbering "143 gentlemen volunteers" who entered Pontefract Castle on that day (supported, no doubt, by many common soldiers) includes Major Coppley (sic), Captain Laybourne (probably Robert Lilburne, of whom we shall hear more, along with his brothers, John and Henry) and Cornet Nayler.[33] Cornet is a rank lower than Quartermaster. Correct statement of his rank soon followed, however, as three days later, on December 28, Quartermaster James Nayler was paid £1 16s.[34]

In February, 1645 Thomas Fairfax went to London to take command of the New Model Army for Parliament. Most often attributed to Oliver Cromwell, the object of the New Model was to create a professional army, in which rank and leadership were based on military merit, not on family standing and class. Military office had long been assigned by royal prerogative, but that could hardly continue to apply to leadership of a revolution against the King. Fairfax smoothed the rough revolutionary edges of the New Model, as he carried the traditional standing of knighthood, as well as a distinguished record of military campaigns both at home and abroad. His choice of the rebellion was exemplary to his troops, and he embraced the reorganization of command.

Revolutionary as it was, the New Model Army was not a universal amalgamation of Parliament's armies. The Northern Army leadership was not cluttered with ineffective dukes and earls who lacked military experience, so it needed less reorganization. Furthermore, with the Scots rebels on its borders, it was too busy to be reorganized. As the New Model Army was being established in London, the Northern Army, consisting of about 10,000 men, was maintained separate from it.[35]

Quartermaster James Nayler remained under the command of the Northern Army. John Lambert was made Commissary General in charge of cavalry in the Northern Army under General Poyntz, headquartered at York.[36] Christopher Copley, having expanded the cavalry troop that James Nayler joined in 1643 at Wakefield into a full regiment during 1644, was made Colonel of the West Riding Regiment of Horse.[37] Lambert maintained, as he had from the beginning, close ties to his fellow Yorkshireman, Fairfax, who appeared always to be Cromwell's friend, but who remained also his potential rival for control of England's armies and its post-revolutionary government, the Rider On The White Horse.

CHAPTER 6

Nayler As Officer in Councils of War, The End of Charles I

I was struck with more terror before the preaching of James Nayler than I was before the Battle of Dunbar, when we had nothing else to expect but to fall prey to the swords of our enemies.

—third hand report from a witness after the battle

The period between the battle at Marston Moor in June 1644 and the end of 1645 was a fulcrum in English history, on which the leverage of power turned from monarchy toward democracy. Marston Moor had given Parliament control over the North, as long as Scotland would hold against King Charles I. Army reorganization under Cromwell's New Model promised to institutionalize Parliament's control over the whole national army, as long as its officers held for Parliament. William Laud, formerly Archbishop of Canterbury, having been imprisoned since 1641 in the Tower, was executed in 1645 after a long trial, charged with leading the English church toward Rome, or what amounted to treason. Parliament rejected the Stuarts' prayer book and replaced it with a new Directory of Worship, enacting with these two steps the church's release from Arminian control under a king believed to be in thrall to Rome, no matter that any possible help from Rome had so far failed to reach him, or that his Archbishop was no papist.[1] Hereditary alliance of the military with the King was broken, the discipline of the state church overthrown, and the King's prerogative to use his chosen bishops to govern religious life in his kingdoms all were taken away by Parliament. Freedom of Conscience was not a hollow rallying cry. While some urged that Puritan Presbyterianism be made the state religion, replacing Episcopacy in the Church of England, here the edges of the advancement of ideals were shown to be ragged. The country was not ready to accept a Presbyterian Church of England. Furthermore, Parliament was far short of the funds and social support to carry out all of its newfound powers, and the King was not finished being king. In 1645 the end of the first civil war may have been in sight, but the War of the Three Kingdoms was far from over.

Pontefract Castle was recaptured by the Royalists on the first of March, 1645, then besieged for almost five months and retaken by Parliament in July. During this second siege of Pontefract Castle, James Nayler was again present, but this time on the outside looking in. When he was paid on April 19 and May 4 at Pontefract, he must have been billeted in the town, not inside the fortress.[2] In July Colonel Copley, Nayler's commander, helped handle the surrender negotiations, which returned the castle to Parliament's control at not too great a cost.[3] Between negotiations he continued active nearby, with cavalry victories at Worksop and Sherburn-in-Elmet.[4]

Nayler's and Copley's part, if any, in the pursuit of the King in 1646 has not been discovered. Lambert's role is instructive, however, as we will soon see Nayler's and Lambert's paths converge in an association that lasted through the end of the war, and beyond that to Nayler's trial before Parliament in 1656. Lambert, along with his notable military successes, had a special talent for negotiation and conciliation. He was assigned repeatedly by Fairfax, after victories in pursuit of the King at Dartmouth, Torrington, Exeter, Barnstaple and Oxford, to settle the factions left behind in defeat. In most cases Lambert accomplished this work in the company of Henry Ireton, Oliver Cromwell's son-in-law.[5]

After the king fled Oxford for Scotland in the Spring of 1646, Lambert was assigned, as he had been at York after the battle of Marston Moor, to preserve the city, its treasures, and in this case, the university. During the occupation much preaching was done at Oxford by army officers, chaplains, and by common soldiers, described in one account as "Presbyterians, Independents, and worse," a pejorative which may have referred to Levellers.[6] As we have seen, the war against the King was also a war against his Church and the social order that supported it. Lambert encouraged free expression of religious beliefs by his troops, much as Fairfax and Cromwell did in the New Model Army at the same time. This expression expanded to include sociopolitical differences as well as religious debate, opening the way for the long-simmering Leveller dissent to come to a boil.

The Levellers had been an observable and troublesome presence In England, off and on, since at least the time of King James I. In June, 1607:

> Sir Anthony Mildmay and Sir Edward Montague went out to Newton where a 1,000 riotous persons who call themselves levellers were busy digging, but were furnished with half pikes, long bills, bows and arrows and stones . . . Using all their persuasion to make the rioters desist; but when nothing would avail, they charged them both with horse and foot. . . . There were slain some 40 or 50 and a great number hurt . . . This rising grew so fast out of Northamptonshire where it began that, but for lack of a leader, it would soon have become a rebellion, and it is suspected by some that great ones must have encouraged them. There is great vigilance in the city where the watch has been strengthened and all suspected persons, especially Catholics, closely observed.[7]

During the first part of the civil war especially, Leveller leadership helped to feed defiant energy into Parliament's army. After the capture of the King a better organized Leveller faction would attempt to play a major role, potentially rebellious within the ranks, in the political settlement of the country by the army and Parliament.

Early in 1647 King Charles I was handed over to the English by Scotland, which also was divided between pro- and anti-Royalist factions. The Royalists had lost in both kingdoms, Scotland and England, for the time being.

Now Parliament had to deal with the disposition of the King's person, with the institution of the monarchy itself, and with its own largely disaffected army. The troops had not been paid. Citizens who had quartered troops or sold supplies to them were owed as well. Thomas Fairfax called on Lambert's talents again to settle the restive troops and civilian population in the north.[8]

Late in 1647 Christopher Copley's command was consolidated under Lambert.[9] On January 26 Colonel Copley and Quartermaster Nayler were paid at York,[10] the headquarters of Lambert's command. Later in the year both began serving directly under Lambert, who testified nine years later at Nayler's blasphemy trial after the Bristol ride, "He was two years my quarter-master, and a very useful person."[11]

Readers of Nayler's tracts will be aware of his clear, logical discourse. His intense, yet good-natured debates with clergy and his trial testimonies suggest a quick-witted, persuasive style.[12] Furthermore, having served as troop quartermaster for Copley in Yorkshire, he was intimately familiar with quartering arrangements, persons who had supplied the army, and the locations where this had taken place. He was certainly qualified to assist Lambert in his work during the second half of 1647, attempting to settle discontent among soldiers and citizens in the North.

This work included dealing with the aftermath of Major General Sydenham Poyntz's command in Yorkshire and Lancashire. Prior to his downfall, Poyntz had been field commander in the North. Lambert had been under his command, and so therefore had Copley and Nayler, as well as Colonel Robert Lilburne, the elder brother of John, the famous Leveller leader. Robert Lilburne's soldiers and others were rebellious, demanding payment of arrears. Poyntz sent a letter, dated July 3, 1647, to the Speaker of the House of Commons, advising of impending mutiny. Only five days later the General was in fact captured by his troops and delivered under guard to imprisonment at Reading. Fairfax took charge, released Poyntz, and directed Lambert to take over command of the Northern Army.[13]

Lambert's orders required him to decrease the size of the army, reducing both costs and the threat of mutiny. Some soldiers refused to disband without satisfaction of arrears and indemnity against claims for crimes they may have committed under orders. Lambert made repeated efforts with Parliament to get the soldiers paid and in the meantime persuaded many to return home if they were no longer needed. Copley took charge of Pontefract Castle, now an important Yorkshire headquarters. Nayler and Copley became members of Lambert's council of officers.

Nayler was probably at Pontefract in December, 1647, engaged under Lambert's command in the efforts to settle the army's grievances. His consistent appearance at Pontefract prior to and following this date, together with his minuted attendance at meetings of Lambert's Council of Officers within a year, inform this judgment. The nature of the work under way at Pontefract and York further support the conclusion that here is where Lambert would have found Nayler most useful.

An example of the work in process is found in "Parliamentary Army Council of War Minutes 1647–1648," which includes a transcription of a paper dated December 1, 1647, called "Concerning Inequality of Quartering."[14] Published later in January with Lambert's approval, this policy statement sets standards of quarters to be provided, along with daily allowances, for the various ranks of cavalry soldiers, staff, and general officers. Additional disciplinary problems are addressed under the title "Against the Disorders of Soldiers," signed, as it was published, by "Thomas Margetts, Advocate."[15] Margetts was Lambert's secretary and treasurer, but the matters discussed are in Nayler's area of responsibility as Quartermaster. Soldiers in Poyntz's command had mutinied over matters including pay and quartering. Lambert's success in settling these differences depended on clear policy and discipline. Nayler, remarkable for his fluent writing and speaking, must have been a necessary participant in the process of restoring order in the aftermath of Poyntz's command.

At the end of 1647 the King escaped, and the Second Civil War was on, which could be seen as the second act of the great stage drama that was The War of the Three Kingdoms. The King signed an agreement with his Scots supporters, promising, for his part, to deliver a presbyterian form of governance of the Churches of England and Scotland. At last he had backed away from his support of the episcopacy. His favorite bishop after all, William Laud, was dead, and Parliament had already established in the Church of England what the King proposed to extend to Scotland. Neither kingdom's population would ever be unanimous in accepting a state religion. The King could offer allies what they wanted and worry out the consequences later.

Royalist uprisings spread in England and in Scotland, and Lambert gathered his Yorkshire forces to secure the North against a Scottish invasion. From Spring, 1648 onward, activity all over the North reached a hectic pace. The climax of the war was at hand. Royalist general Marmaduke Langdale was sent north in April, 1648 to consolidate his forces with allies from Scotland as they invaded England. Lambert was assigned, with insufficient forces, to hold back this attack until Cromwell, engaged in a two-month struggle at Pembroke Castle, could assist.

During the summer of 1648 Scottish troops under Lord Hamilton, allied with British Royalists under Langdale, tested Lambert's resistance in Westmoreland around Appleby, Kirkby Stephen, Brough, and Barnard Castle.[16] On arrival of Cromwell's reinforcements, both sides moved southward, toward a major battle near Preston. Atrocities against civilians were charged against the Scots during this campaign. English feelings against the Scots ran high for some time after the Scots and Royalists were defeated. Cromwell was able to reach settlement with the Kirk Party in Scotland, who opposed Hamilton's Royalists. Parliament's army, led by Cromwell and Lambert, rode into Edinburgh unopposed, took charge of the city, and received a letter of commendation to Parliament for the humane conduct of their occupation.[17]

Meanwhile, the situation at Pontefract had reversed itself again. In a surprise takeover, the castle stronghold had gone over to Royalist hands. Former Parliamentarian governor of the castle, Morris, had changed sides, declared for the King, and led a party of traitors to secure the castle from within. Lambert had to send a powerful force back to Pontefract to besiege the castle for the third time.

Copley and Nayler could have been near Carlisle with Lambert, or at Pontefract, or at one and then the other, which seems the more likely case. Parliament forces that had been assigned to hold Pontefract Castle against the Royalist siege could have been diverted to the north to assist Lambert in warding off a Scottish attack. That could have weakened the defense of the castle sufficiently for the takeover to occur, and troops would have been sent back to retake Pontefract. No documentation has been found, however, to clarify Copley's and Nayler's whereabouts until late in 1648, when we can be sure that they were both at Pontefract.

When Royalist troops took the castle in June, 1648, they were let in by turncoats. Prisoners were taken, but few lives were lost on either side. The siege began in remarkably good nature. Shots were exchanged. Royalists sallied forth into the countryside from time to time. Despite Parliament's attempts to tighten the siege, the Royalists inside remained confident that starvation was not to be their downfall. Indeed Cromwell wrote to Parliament in the fall that up to 240 head of cattle were in the castle, along with provisions and water sufficient for a year. He requested the largest siege guns available to batter down the walls, and ample supplies of ammunition.[18] Colonel Copley, meanwhile, was assigned to make periodic visits inside the castle to keep up a good communication, although he had no authority to negotiate terms.[19]

The siege might have been resolved more favorably for the Royalists but for a bold adventure late in October. Colonel Thomas Rainsborough, one of the most respected figures in Cromwell's army, known as the first officer to advocate trial of the King when he was in custody, was scheduled to be a witness against Royalist general Langdale, on trial for the atrocities committed around the Battle of Preston.[20] Rainsborough set up headquarters at Doncaster, twelve miles from Pontefract, to assist in taking the castle. Royalist soldiers inside Pontefract Castle, concerned that Langdale would be hanged, undertook to capture Rainsborough as hostage to gain Langdale's release. The adventurers succeeded in making their way to Doncaster by ruse. When they entered Rainsborough's quarters, however, he resisted capture so strongly that the Royalists killed him and returned to the castle.

Various accounts have from twenty to forty men leaving the castle, though only six attempted to seize Rainsborough.[21] Five of the six returned to Pontefract Castle. One was killed.

According to one account, among the murderers was one John Nayler, of Wakefield.[22] Although not the soldier named as killed in the action, he seems to have disappeared at the end of the siege of Pontefract, and escaped punishment that others received. Whether this Nayler was in any way related to James has not been discovered, nor do we know whether he was one of the former Parliament soldiers who changed sides, or was originally a Royalist. Nayler was a common name in Wakefield. Joseph Nayler, also listed among the Royalist defenders of the Castle, was from Flanshaw, a village in Wakefield parish, three miles from West Ardsley.[23] Records also show that four Naylers served with James in Copley's troop, namely John, from Batley, just on the other side of Howley Hall from Woodkirk (thus, only five miles from Wakefield), Robert from Billingley, near Barnsley, east of Wakefield, William Junior from Altofts, a village adjacent to Wakefield, and another William Junior from East Ardsley.[24] Either William could be James Nayler's brother.[25]

James Nayler by this time had become a regular member of General Lambert's Council of War, the committee of officers who met regularly to discuss and decide on policy for the Northern Army. On Friday, December 12, 1648 Nayler voted with the majority of Lambert's Council to try the King of England, Scotland, and Wales as a criminal.[26] It was the most radical act he took as a soldier. It had been one thing for Nayler and the rest to struggle at the beginning to resist the King's repression of the people of Yorkshire. It was far more grave by the end of six years of rebellion across the country to charge and try the King as if he were any other man, culpable of great crimes. The charge, if any could be brought against the monarch, must be that he had committed treason against his own realm, punishable by death. Anything less surely would degenerate into a petty squabble among malcontents. The vote in Lambert's Council showed, in the words of Professor Ingle, "that the Council was strongly in favor of killing the King, God's only anointed in the kingdom!"[27]

Charles I, on the other hand, must then argue before Parliament that no trial was possible. He was King by divine authority, against which laws of human society had no standing. Literally, no matter what he may have done, none of his subjects could touch him.[28] The King could not be tried, let alone punished, by anyone. This ancient assertion of the divine right of kings was his only argument, and it was lost before it was uttered.

Nayler and his peers, as officers of the Northern Army meeting at Pontefract, voted to affirm what the New Model Army, meeting at London, had already decided, and to join in the Army's Remonstrance, in which the status of the King as criminal was stated, preliminary to his charge and trial before Parliament. Lambert's Council took action because they felt it was in their own interests to declare that they stood with the greater army; the two forces were of one mind, acting together for the kingdoms. Nayler and his fellow officers knew that the outcome of the trial would be the King's death warrant, and one of their number, Robert Lilburne, went on to sign it in due time at London.

Absent from the December 12, 1648 meeting was Colonel Copley, the Yorkshire cavalry officer under whom Nayler had served, and commercial supplier of horses and metals to the Northern Army. Although he appeared at council meetings earlier, by late 1648 he was no longer listed. The reason had more to do with his falling out with Cromwell than with debts due him for his supplies. Copley later stated in his case to Parliament for payment of compensation due that Lt. General Cromwell had Copley's name taken off the list of regimental commanders because Copley wouldn't become subservient to Cromwell's ". . . ambitious ends . . . then under the curtain, since discovered . . ."[29] With benefit of hindsight, Copley declared that he had known of Cromwell's subversive plan to dispatch the King and take over his power, and Copley would have none of it, though that meant paying a dear price in terms of the loss of his command and pay, as well as compensation for bullets and iron he had sold to Parliament from his metals business.

Cromwell had stopped in Pontefract on his way south from Scotland until about the first of December, 1648. Although Lambert seemed quite in control of the siege at Pontefract, Cromwell delayed his departure, perhaps in order to avoid the struggle between the army and the Parliament then engaged in London. The Presbyterian majority in Commons had attempted for some time to reach a negotiated settlement with the King, by now in the form of the proposed Treaty of Newport, an agreement which could only lead to restoration of Charles I as monarch. The army, having had enough of the King's broken promises, sought to end negotiations and impose its will on the settlement. A Remonstrance to this effect and more had been sent to Parliament, that same Remonstrance that Lambert's Council voted later in the month to affirm and to join in support.[30] Cromwell, an Independent and therefore of the minority party, maintained a judicious (or perhaps indecisive) remove from the controversy as his son-in-law, Ireton, acted as leader of the radicals in both army and Parliament. Cromwell delayed returning to London much longer than necessary. On November 28, Fairfax sent him a direct order to proceed to Windsor with all possible speed.

Parliament tried to ignore the army's Remonstrance and persisted in negotiations with the King. Fairfax, supreme commander of the army, issued a warning to Parliament on November 30 to cease trying to interfere on matters regarding their prisoner. A demand for immediate payment of £40,000 arrears due the army from the city of London followed. The army began moving toward London the next day, and by December 5, the military takeover of the city was complete. On the morning of the 6th members of Colonel Pride's regiment met the members of Commons at Whitehall and began arresting Presbyterian members and removing them under guard. The Purge took close to 140 members out of the House, leaving the radical

Independents and their followers in charge of legislation under the direction of Fairfax, Ireton, and the army leadership. Only as these moves were being completed did Cromwell arrive from the north, expressing surprise, but general approval, that all this was happening.[31]

General Lambert had been kept in the North for two reasons.[32] One was military necessity, the other the radical army leadership's concern (certainly Ireton's, possibly Cromwell's also) that Lambert might put his considerable forces behind Fairfax in London, acting in favor of moderation and eventual restoration of the King with some agreeable constraints. While both Fairfax and Lambert were, first and foremost, military leaders in Parliament's cause, they were also careful moderates in regard to the monarchy. Both men appeared to align with the Independent political party in Commons, and both therefore stood for the removal of Charles I. Whether that meant the end of the monarchy, or even the end of the King's life, was not clear, and both Fairfax and Lambert avoided irrevocably declaring themselves, a prudent policy during a revolution that could change direction abruptly. So, Lambert and his officers of the Northern Army were kept ill-informed until Pride's Purge was in effect and the army in the south was firmly in control of a reduced Parliament, which was already drawing up charges to bring the King to trial.

The December 12, 1648 meeting of Lambert and his officers was held in the midst of this complex situation. Lambert spoke in favor of moderation in proceeding with the King. Other officers favored alignment with the army's Remonstrance to Parliament, treating the King as a criminal, and laying out required democratic principles for remaking the government as a republic. Despite this split, an effective compromise was possible within Lambert's Council. The officers sent a report to General Fairfax, which supported the Remonstrance and practically named as traitors any who would deal with the King as if he were still their monarch.[33] Only two of Lambert's council voted against the officers' report to Fairfax, namely Colonel Bright and Captain Westby. Their negative votes are noted in the margin of the Minutes. The rest of those present, including Nayler, supported the Remonstrance, which is to say, the army's revolution against the King, at least as far as it had gone at that point.

Lambert attached a letter of his own to Fairfax, to the effect that the officers in the North had established a committee to meet weekly and consult on "public affairs," sending their recommendations to Fairfax for his information, via Captain Baynes. In response to these communications, Lambert asked Fairfax to report in like fashion on just what was going on in London. While Lambert aligned himself with Fairfax in this communication and thus reassured Fairfax of his own moderate intention, he was at the same time advising Fairfax that the junior officers were more radically inclined. The chairman of the newly established officers' committee was to be Robert Lilburne, recognizable to Fairfax as the possible organizer of formidable army resistance to moderation in the north. The officers' report, though rendered official by Lambert's signature, was without his wholehearted support.

Further revealing possible concern about Lambert's moderation, Thomas Margetts, Lambert's secretary, sent a letter of his own to Baynes, advising him to make a strong case for the commitment of the Northern Army to the Remonstrance and the revolution. Afraid they had already missed the chance to join their support with the rest of the army's, he expressed concern that the northern troops would, ever after, come last in consideration, including when it came to getting paid.[34]

James Nayler's vote had aligned him with Robert Lilburne in support of the Remonstrance, seeking removal of the King.[35] Lilburne shortly was to go to London himself, in place of Baynes. There he sat on the commission of judges in the trial of the King, and when the verdict was given, Lilburne was one of fifty-nine men to sign the King's death warrant.[36] Fairfax and Lambert both, although they were named by others to the commission, declined to attend its meetings. Lambert never attended, Fairfax only once.[37]

With the King's execution the Second Civil War was effectively ended, but England was not settled. Army discontent, government and economic collapse at home, the threat of continuing Irish revolution, Royalist efforts in England and Scotland to restore monarchy in the person of Charles II, all combined to threaten the country. Woven through these great issues was a persistent dissent among sectarians in many parts of the country and among more radical political elements within the army. The army debates held in 1647 at Putney over the future of government had generated a series of declarations of popular dissent that continued and became more insistent after the dispatch of Charles I. Any moderate in Parliament must have felt threatened.[38]

Prominent in dissent were the Levellers, and since Nayler was accused in his trial at Appleby in 1652 of having been among them, they deserve mention here.[39] John Lilburne, middle brother of three, the most articulate Leveller, became a Quaker at the end of his life.[40] Although he admired Nayler's writings and commended them to his wife, he never mentioned meeting Nayler, nor did Nayler refer to Lilburne. Nayler, however, was often in proximity to John's older brother, Robert, who, as we have seen, was another prominent leader among army radicals. While Robert had seemed for a while to take a more moderate position than the Levellers with respect to the monarchy, Parliament's Presbyterian majority nevertheless had good reason to fear him as an incendiary to their delicate structure of power.[41] Some troops under Lilburne's command, after all, had mutinied against General Poyntz. The same Parliament, however, saw fit to release John Lilburne from the Tower on August 1, 1648. Cromwell was seen to have his eyes on the monarchy, even at this early date. Some in Parliament argued that John Lilburne might be able to speak effectively against that threat.[42] Henry Lilburne, the youngest brother, heard a different story—that the Levellers were plotting to murder King Charles I.

Although he was governor for Parliament of Tynemouth Castle, Henry was a moderate when it came to the monarchy and could not be part of such a thing. He declared for the King, just as the governor of Pontefract Castle had done, but Henry met with swifter retribution. Within twenty four hours he had been killed by his own soldiers, and the castle was in Parliament's hands again.[43] Henry did not live to see the King's execution in January, 1649.

By May of 1649 the Leveller movement had gained such a following in the army that numbers of Leveller soldiers revolted in at least two places.[44] One such group of mutineers marched toward London and were apprehended at Burford, with severe punishment ordered by Cromwell. It was with this group that Nayler was accused, three years later, of associating. He denied it, claiming he had been "in the North"[45] which probably meant Pontefract. No one at either the Appleby or the London trial asked Nayler if he were ever associated with any of the Lilburnes. The answer to that question would have had the same effect, guilt by association with individual rebels and mutineers, as an admission of involvement with the Levellers as a group.

Ironically, the charges against James Nayler of being with the Levellers were probably a case of mistaken identity. Quartermaster John Naylier (note the slightly different spelling) in the command of Captain Bray, under Major Reynolds of Kent, signed a petition to Parliament in April, 1649 which, among several other issues, supported John Lilburne.[46] Naylier then published his own tract protesting ill-use of his troop by Major Reynolds, blaming him for their twenty-five weeks of arrears in pay (a common complaint in the army at the time), and accusing him of trying to sell his soldiers for service in Ireland for £4 a man and a promotion to Colonel for himself. In this, his only discovered tract, "*The Newmade Colonel, or Ireland's Jugling Pretended Reliever,*" John Naylier mentions that he has been accused of being a Leveller, but he righteously denies it.[47] Due to his petition for Lilburne and his controversial publication within a month of the Leveller mutinies, it is easy to see that John Naylier's name might be remembered and later confused with James Nayler's.

Levellers notwithstanding, the next important national problem to be addressed, the greatest immediate threat, was Ireland. James Nayler very nearly went there. If he had, he would have become involved in Cromwell's relentless massacre of the Irish opposition, which resonates even today. What would have been the course of his spiritual leading if he had been ordered to give no quarter to trapped civilians? As it turned out, he was spared. Although Lambert's command was among those chosen by lot to go with Cromwell to Ireland, an exception was made.[48] Lambert's troops were needed in Scotland, for the peace there had not held. The young Charles II was gathering Royalist support for invading England to regain his father's crown.

The deciding battle was at Dunbar in September, 1650. Cromwell had been called back from Ireland and given command of all the English armies only a few months before, replacing Fairfax, who had reservations about invading Scotland. Cromwell usually gets full credit for the victory at Dunbar, but Cromwell himself gave major credit to Lambert and his cavalry, both for the winning strategy and for winning the fight.[49] A story of James Nayler's inspired preaching to an assembly of soldiers after the battle is told in his several biographies.[50] Though this description is secondhand reporting from years after the fact, it has become the cornerstone of the assertion suggested by Brailsford's title, that Nayler was "A Quaker from Cromwell's Army." Dunbar was Nayler's first battle under Cromwell's command. He was not yet a Quaker, but he had served in the military for about eight years already. Regrettably, however, no record exists of Nayler's ministry at Dunbar or anywhere else before 1652.

Nayler's army career ended sometime after Dunbar, but this is not documented. We have only the information that he was released in Scotland and went home too sick to fight any longer.[51] Consumption or tuberculosis has been mentioned, but Nayler lived a very active life for several years after his recovery.[52] Pneumonia and influenza are additional possibilities. The winter in Scotland between 1650 and 1651 was wet, cold, and unusually harsh. Food and shelter were scarce. Both armies suffered deeply. Cromwell himself reported that he was so severely ill that his life was in danger.[53] So many soldiers died or were disabled during the winter that both sides needed considerable reinforcement in order to resume fighting in the spring.

The Scots and Charles II, in danger of being trapped at Inverkeithing in July, 1651 by Lambert's cavalry, made a desperate turn and went toward England. Lambert gave chase. Cromwell followed. Holding at Worcester, a well fortified city, half encircled by a river with few bridges, Charles II stood against Cromwell and Lambert but was defeated on 3 September, 1651, ending this chapter of the war and making way for the establishment of the Commonwealth and Oliver's Protectorate.

Whether Nayler went as far as Worcester is doubtful. No evidence that he did has been discovered. Taken literally, his own description of serving "between eight and nine years" means that he left the army after January, 1651, the eighth anniversary of the Battle of Leeds. We are told that he left the army when he was too ill to continue in service, which information is consistent with what we know of conditions in Scotland in the winter of 1650–1651.[54] Probably that is where he mustered out of the army. If so, it seems highly doubtful that Nayler would have returned to be with Lambert's cavalry in their hot pursuit of Charles II and the subsequent battle at Worcester in September, 1651.

Later that year, in winter, Nayler met George Fox for the first time at the Roper's home in Stanley, a village adjacent to Wakefield. Although the two met there again the following spring, Fox described Nayler as being convinced after their first meeting at Stanley.[55] This is consistent with Nayler's description of hearing the voice of God calling him while he was at the plow planting barley,[56] which is planted as early as possible in the spring.[57] The second meeting with Fox seems to have taken place in May (Ingle says March), well after barley planting. In any case, and whether or not he fought at Worcester, it appears that Nayler began his association with Fox and the other Quakers of the early itinerant ministry after he had left the army, apparently with no intention of returning to military service.

CHAPTER 7

From Epiphany to Arrest, the Itinerant Ministery Begins

... Get thee out of thy country, and from thy kindred, and from thy father's house, unto a land that I will show thee ...

—Genesis 12:1

Nayler's account of the calling in his field, as he was planting barley, comes from his testimony in a court trial at Appleby, given in response to a question of how he came to be there. Nayler told the court, "... suddenly I heard a voice, saying unto me, *Get-thee out from thy Kindred and from thy Father's House ...*"[1] The words are an almost exact quotation from the Lord's word to Abraham as written in Genesis, with the notable omission of a direction that Abraham also leave his country. (The 1599 Geneva Bible, in common use in Nayler's time, and the 1611 Authorized or King James version, read exactly the same in this passage.) Nayler continued to testify that he had rejoiced to hear the voice of God that he had professed since he was a child, but had never heard before. He failed at first, however, to follow the direction. Immediately he fell so seriously ill that those around him doubted that he would survive. When he did recover and return to his field work, he heard the same voice a second time, telling him to go out into the west. He did so and when he had gone some way, there came a promise, much like the promise to Abraham, that God would always be with him. Thereafter until the present day, Nayler said, he never wanted for sustenance and never felt alone.

Rather than offering the court a progressive account of how, physically, he had come to Appleby, he chose to describe a turning point, after which everything in his life was different. Nothing mattered before God addressed him. Only his adherence to this divine direction mattered afterward. It was by God's leading that he came here. What more could the Justices ask?

We can say that Nayler's itinerary toward Appleby started from Woodkirk, not Wakefield, where he and Ann had moved after their marriage, because the voice said to get out from his father's house. Ann may have moved back to the Nayler family farm when James went off to war, or they may have taken up farming there on James's return after Dunbar. Saying that he left home with no more than the

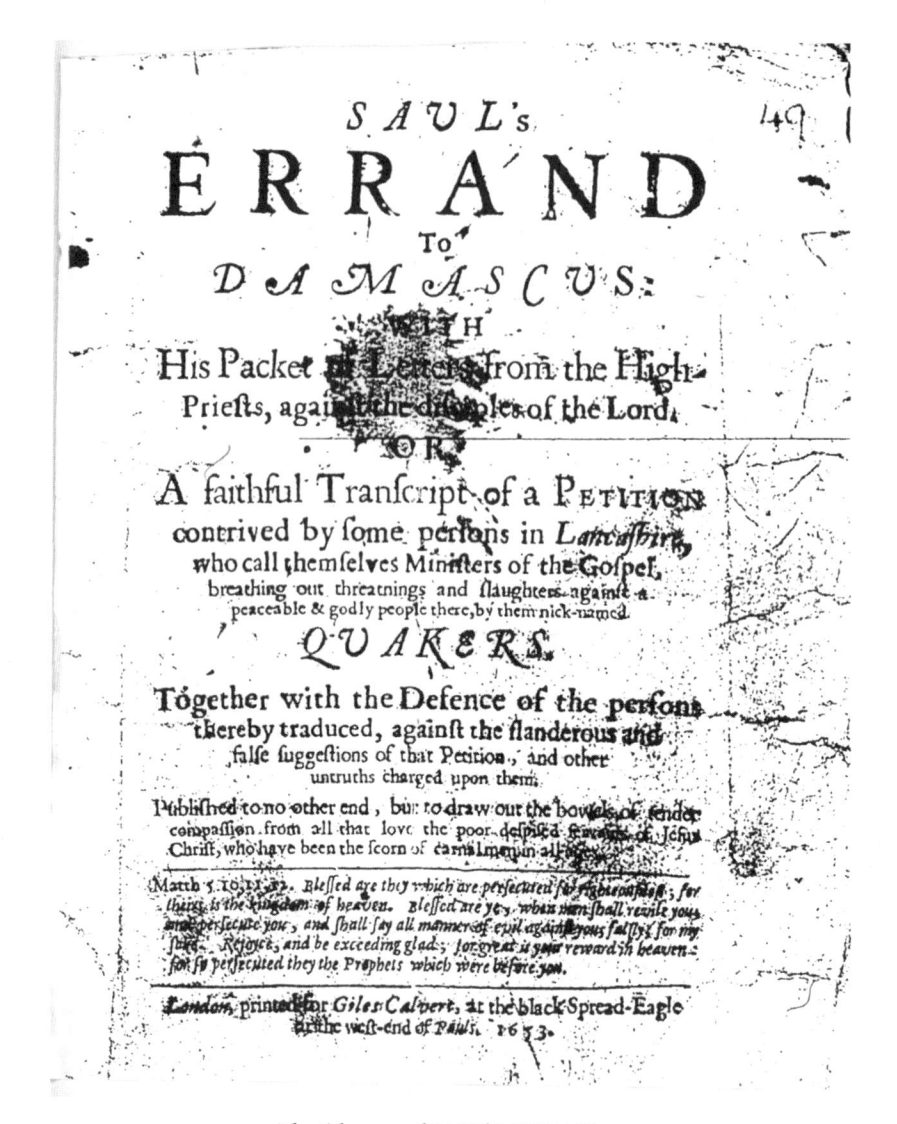

> *SAUL's*
> # ERRAND
> To
> *DAMASCUS:*
> WITH
> His Packet of Letters from the High-
> Priests, against the disciples of the Lord.
> OR,
> A faithful Transcript of a PETITION
> contrived by some persons in *Lancashire*,
> who call themselves Ministers of the Gospel,
> breathing out threatnings and slaughters against a
> peaceable & godly people there, by them nick-named
> QUAKERS.
>
> Together with the Defence of the persons
> thereby traduced, against the slanderous and
> false suggestions of that Petition, and other
> untruths charged upon them.
>
> Published to no other end, but to draw out the bowels of tender
> compassion from all that love the poor despised servants of Jesus
> Christ, who have been the scorn of carnal men in all ages.
>
> *Matth.* 5.10,11,12. *Blessed are they which are persecuted for righteousness, for
> theirs is the Kingdom of heaven. Blessed are ye, when men shall revile you,
> and persecute you, and shall say all manner of evil against you falsly, for my
> sake. Rejoyce, and be exceeding glad; for great is your reward in heaven:
> for so persecuted they the Prophets which were before you.*
>
> *London*, printed for *Giles Calvert*, at the black Spread-Eagle
> at the west-end of *Pauls*, 1653.

*The title page of SAUL'S ERRAND...
printed in 1653*

clothes on his back, Nayler did not tell the court where he went. Correspondence suggests that for a time he did some local ministry near his home, sometimes in the company of Thomas Goodaire (or Goodyear, to use Fox's spelling) and at other times with Richard Farnsworth.[2] He may have waited for an invitation to join Fox farther north.[3] Eventually, accompanied by Farnsworth, he traced Fox to the Fells' home at Swarthmore Hall near Ulverston, west of Lancaster, and caught up with him there. Farnsworth had come from Tickhill near Balby and Doncaster, where he was a leader of a group that has been called the Balby Seekers, radically conservative puritans who sought a way to move religious practice back toward primitive Christianity. George Fox had met at Balby and won converts to his movement shortly before he visited Wakefield and West Ardsley.[4]

Margaret Fell's papers describe Nayler's intercession with Judge Fell to speak in Fox's behalf.[5] The judge had been traveling in Scotland and returned to be greeted by irate neighbors who warned him that Fox had bewitched his wife. Older and apparently more stable than the intense young evangelist, Nayler, with Fox and Farnsworth, who was even a few years younger than Fox, spoke with Judge Fell after dinner, both as to their ministry and with an offer to leave his house if he desired. They calmed the situation, and the judge retired quietly for the night. The next day Judge Fell offered Swarthmore Hall as a meeting place for Friends. It remained so for nearly four decades thereafter, until 1690, functioning as a center for correspondence and administration for the fledgling religious society.

Fox and Nayler visited nearby Walney Island, where Fox thought there were some who wanted to hear the Quaker message.[6] The interest was limited to a few, and others attacked the visiting ministers, beat them badly, and chased them away from the island aboard separate boats. After several more confrontations with ministers and parishioners around Swarthmore Hall, Fox was charged before the quarter sessions court in Lancaster for blasphemy. Nayler traveled to Lancaster with Fox and Judge Fell, their recent host. Fell sat as one of the three judges, and the arguments of Fox's accusers were dismissed as biased and fabricated.[7] Reporting this event in a letter to Friends at Yorkshire from Kellet was James Nayler, who apparently did not play a major role in the court testimony.[8]

Shortly after Fox's Lancaster trial, Nayler and other Quakers started out for a tour of ministry toward Kendal, a market town with a small knitting industry, and beyond into rural Westmoreland. They may have intended also to visit the other two principal towns in the region, Kirkby Stephen and Appleby, but of this period Nayler said that he did not know from one day to the next where he would go, or how his needs might be provided.[9] If there were a plan to his itinerant ministry, Nayler did not refer to it in writing or in testimony. If there were a human leader guiding the effort, we might assume that it was Fox, but making this judgment tempts us to miss the point entirely. The charges later brought against Nayler, as well as against Fox and other Friends, included blasphemy. Part of their blasphemy was the assertion that Christ was present in them, and that they were guided by Christ directly, without intercession by any other. Nayler said it was Christ who sent him. He spoke for himself and made no claim that anyone else had a part in his being there, or that he had a plan for his efforts.

Nayler and some others left Kendal and made their way into the hills north and east toward Orton. In this case they went by invitation, but the names of their hosts were not given in the account.[10] Apparently their destination was known to the ministers from Lancaster and Kendal who opposed the Friends, as a number of them went on ahead, intending to lay a trap, which would result in the Quakers' arrest.

Orton is a remote town that has maintained many of its ancient features into the present day. All Saints, the medieval village church, still stands on the hill at the northerly edge of the village. Below it two becks, or streams, run nearly parallel courses southwestward through the village. Alongside the smaller of the two is the main road, lined with a few shops, an inn, and a large hall with attached grange, parts of it dating to before Nayler's time. Beside the wider stream, Chapel Beck, another street runs, lined with houses. Between the becks is a long, flat field, believed to be the same town field on which Nayler spoke three and a half centuries ago.

All Saints Church was affected by religious hostilities during the Civil Wars. Like Woodkirk in West Ardsley, Orton's church dated from the 12th century monastic period. Like Woodkirk, All Saints in effect had been sold into private hands during the dissolution of the monastic properties under Henry VIII. In Orton's case the little church's advowson, or the patronage right to nominate its vicar, was sold to a couple of London speculators. However unlikely this seems in modern times, it did happen in the 16th and 17th Century. In the more common case, what we might call institutional investors, most often endowment funds of the colleges of Cambridge or Oxford, would buy the advowsons and the accompanying right to collect tithes as income-producing investments, but affluent individuals did so as well. Some impropietors, as they were called, unlike the Saviles of Woodkirk, had no particular interest in the community, only in the income from the tithes. For the local congregations the effect was often to impoverish the churches. Tithes were intended to support the physical upkeep of the property, as well as the vicar's living, but the absentee owners of the patronage had little interest in spending their income for that purpose. Further economies could be gained by employing uneducated clergy or so-called "reading ministers" who could not deliver a sermon of their own making, but must read it from books prepared for the purpose, such as the Book of Homilies, which dated to the time of Elizabeth. Dissatisfied parishioners occasionally bought back the patronage rights of their village church so that they could manage their own affairs, and this was the case with Orton. Somehow the people of Orton raised £570, a shockingly large sum, to buy their church advowson in 1618, about the year of Nayler's birth. From that time onward, through a representative system of feoffees, or electors, the congregation chose their own vicar, who was then approved by the bishop after certifying the nominee's qualifications. Normally this was not a controversial process, but when civil war polarized the population along Royalist and Parliamentarian lines and their related religious affiliations, the election became hotly contested. In fact, even prior to the outbreak of war it had become all too common for the feoffees of towns like Orton to control the choice of vicars or lecturers so that the local congregation could favor their own particular political persuasion. Neither the King nor the Archbishop were happy with this practice, the Archbishop writing in his journal in 1632 that the feoffee system was "the main instrument(s) for the puritan faction to undo the church."[11] In the election for the vicarage of Orton in 1643, the two candidates were identified by political as well as religious affiliation. Orton's modern, informal town history calls them, Episcopal and Parliamentarian. The Episcopal or Anglican candidate stood for the established state Church of England and was therefore a Royalist, while the so-called Parliamentarian may well have been an Independent. The Church of England candidate won by a majority of 145 votes, but the Parliamentarian candidate defied the process and took physical possession of the church, holding it for 9 weeks. In the end the bishop interceded and established the Episcopal vicar. It was this man, George Fothergill, who had held the living for nine years by the time of Nayler's visit.[12] When a new threat to the old order appeared in Orton, in the person of a former Parliamentarian soldier turned Quaker, long simmering ill will was stirred afresh. Fothergill joined Francis Higginson from Kirkby Stephen to engage and oppose Nayler on the town field in front of the townspeople. Higginson had been one of those ministers who had pursued Nayler from Lancaster and had filed petitions against him and Fox.

This part of Westmoreland and neighboring Cumberland (both now combined into modern Cumbria) had been greatly affected by the campaign in 1648 in which General Lambert of Parliament's army was sent to the north to hold off the invasion by Scottish Royalist troops until reinforcements from Cromwell's forces could arrive. For about four months the English and Scottish Royalists had clashed to and fro over most of Westmoreland with Lambert's Parliament army forces, coming at least as close to Orton as Appleby and Kirkby Stephen, only ten miles away. The countryside had been stripped bare by the two armies, scouring every village and farm for enough food and fodder to maintain their forces[13] If Nayler were with Lambert for all or part of this campaign, which does seem likely but is unproven, then as quartermaster he would have been part of the quartering and provisioning effort and would be recognized when he returned to the country. Even if he were not part of the battles in Westmoreland, nevertheless he would carry the reputation of a recent member of that occupying army.

According to the account of events in "*Saul's Errand . . .*," Nayler's opponents at Orton tried to entice him to the church, where, they argued, the audience could sit down and listen with greater attention. It was a ruse. Speaking without authority to a crowd in a public place such as a church was a violation of law, for which Nayler could have been arrested. Nayler declined this invitation, apparently aware that it was a trap. He said he would speak in the field. Then it was argued that the town field was also a public place, and his speaking there was likewise illegal. While some of those present in the audience called for Nayler to be heard, the dominant faction was openly hostile. Violence would have ensued very shortly if Nayler had not broken off his discourse and retreated into a nearby house, perhaps one of those sturdy stone dwellings that still stand adjacent to the lane by Chapel Beck.

Nayler and his traveling companion, Francis Howgill, continued to visit communities nearby during the following days, staying where they could find hospitality and speaking to small groups of neighbors. They held a large meeting at Ravenstonedale, east of Orton, and then another at the home of John Knewstub at Shoregill in the Mallerstang Valley.[14] No doubt Howgill, an active minister in Westmoreland before he joined Fox and Nayler, would have known people who would receive them.

Several days later Nayler had another encounter in which those who came to hear him were outnumbered, or at least overcome, by the rough lot that tried to do him physical harm. This debate led to Nayler's arrest. A brief and highly prejudiced trial was held in the back room of an alehouse near the house where Nayler was taken into custody A justice was brought from twelve miles away to preside. Nayler then was taken to Kirkby Stephen, where he was held overnight in a private home. Howgill held forth outside the house until he, too, was arrested and locked up with Nayler.[15]

Higginson published his own account of the events described here, in which he describes the accounts in "*Saul's Errand . . .*" as largely untruthful and exaggerated.[16] Higginson wrote from a position of security, confidence in what he was sure he knew, and respected high standing not only in his parish and town, but also throughout the region. Educated, the vicar of a stable living, and welcome colleague among peers as far away at least as Lancaster, Higginson could reveal and humiliate Nayler as a vagrant interloper, endowed with none of his own attributes. In Higginson's version of the Orton encounter, he and minister Fothergill of Orton were both quite civil, and put reasonable questions of theology to Nayler, who was unable to answer convincingly, or even coherently. Nayler instead became rude, according to Higginson, but none of the townspeople, and certainly neither he nor Fothergill did. Higginson's account made the itinerant look foolish, but even in the favorable, unsigned record in "*Saul's Errand . . .*" Nayler did not come off very well. Given the violent crowd arrayed against him in that account, how could he have conducted an effective debate and given a ministerial message? That he maintained his composure when someone knocked his hat off with a pitchfork and another threatened to dash his brains against a stone wall is remarkable enough. Higginson contradicted "*Saul's Errand . . .*" and denied that there was any violence in the encounter. Clearly, one version or the other was untrue.

The account of his arrest in "*Saul's Errand . . .*" does not say explicitly where Nayler was taken into custody, but the inference can surely be drawn that it was at Orton. *First Publishers of Truth*, a collection of first- and secondhand accounts of events of the period, has a different account of the arrest. According to this source, both men were arrested at Mallerstang by order of Justice Burton at the request of Francis Higginson and taken directly to Kirkby Stephen.[17] Higginson's account confirmed that the arrest took place at Mallerstang but denied that he had anything to do with it, or that Burton was there. Justice Burton could well have been brought from Kirkby Stephen to Orton, which is about twelve miles away, or to Shoregill in Mallerstang, which is just a few miles closer. In either case Nayler and Howgill were jailed overnight at Kirkby Stephen, and then were taken to Appleby to await the quarterly sessions.[18]

On the way back and forth across the hills during his ministerial visits, or in custody en route to Kirkby Stephen, Nayler would have passed close to Sunbiggen, only a short walk from Orton. George Whitehead lived in this tiny settlement. About sixteen years old when Nayler and Howgill took their ministry to the countryside where he lived, Whitehead did not meet Nayler at that time, but much later in London. Whitehead did, however, become an active Quaker minister soon after Nayler's visit to Orton. He was to become recognized and respected as a leader, close to both Nayler and Fox, eventually basing his activities in London. After Nayler's death Whitehead gathered and published what until recently has been the only definitive volume of Nayler's writings.[19] He died in 1723, " the last survivor of the first generation of the Publishers of Truth."[20]

George Fox probably expected that they all would encounter rough treatment. He was already accustomed to violent encounters in his ministry. When Nayler and Howgill went off into Westmoreland, Fox went straight north toward Carlisle. Some logic appears in the way they divided their labor in the region. Nayler may have been familiar with Westmoreland from the war. Howgill, who came from near Kendal, was already a well-known minister in the area. Fox, more experienced by now in bringing the word to communities for the first time, went north toward the Scottish border and its market town. One locale was no less hostile than the other. Fox had to be protected by soldiers, when he went to the church to speak in Carlisle, and soon he was arrested and jailed there under unusually harsh conditions.[21]

Appleby must have been an attractive target for evangelism, just as Kendal had been. Appleby was also a market town. In June a noted livestock fair was held there, and as they did to the Lee Fair in West Ardsley, gypsies came to Appleby to trade horses. On market days vendors' wagons and stalls congested the main street around the Moot Hall, where on the second floor, in what is now the Council Room, the Assizes court held its quarterly sessions to hear cases. Down a side street was the shambles, or meat market, where the butchery was done in the street. A butter and egg market was held in front of the 14th Century St. Lawrence Church at the foot of the hill below the Moot Hall. Inns, shops, and ale houses lined the streets. The town had two jails, and at the top of the main street stood a castle, visible for miles around.[22]

Appleby Castle, along with castles at nearby Brough and Brougham, the legendary one called Pendragon in the Mallerstang Valley (Uther Pendragon was father of the King Arthur of Mallory's tales.), and others more distant, belonged to one of the most prominent Royalist sympathisers in the area, Lady Anne Clifford (1590–1676), who stood only about four and a half feet tall, but had challenged General Oliver Cromwell. She had vowed that if he laid waste her castles, as he

The Moot Hall at Appleby-in-Westmoreland. Nayler's trial before the Assize Court was held on the second floor.

threatened to do in 1648, she would build them all up again until her last penny was spent. He did as he threatened, and so did she. That was what she was about when Nayler and Howgill came on their ministry into Westmoreland. Sections of Appleby Castle were being rebuilt after being laid waste during the recent war, though the main part of the reconstruction was done later, starting in 1657. The Church of St. Lawrence, her family church in Appleby and resting place of her mother, had lain nearly in ruins, neglected for generations before she came into her fortune. Lady Anne funded the work to restore it, which was completed in 1655. She also caused housing to be built for poor widows, of whom there were more than a normal number after the war. Begun in 1651, the cottages opened for the winter of 1653. Lady Anne at this time was about sixty years of age and was energetically overseeing similar projects at several other of her properties.[23]

Appleby was a lively place when the Quakers came, full of people, markets, and jobs. A sizeable audience could be expected to gather to hear them speak, as it had at Kendal. Some would be curious enough to listen to the message; others might be hostile. In this predominantly Royalist territory Lady Anne was not the only influential citizen who felt that the army of Parliament had murdered the King, and that people like Nayler had blasphemed in the Church and on the streets. For some, no punishment for blasphemers and regicides was too harsh. No one from Cromwell's side could expect justice or even safe conduct here. Yet, dissenters could be found. Westmoreland, in fact, had a greater number of those called Seekers than were present around Balby, farther south. Nayler and Howgill, however, would not be speaking to the crowds in the streets of Appleby on market days. They were jailed for many weeks prior to the arrival of the circuit court of Assizes.

During this period of waiting Ann Nayler came to visit and support her husband. She made the trip, "with two brethren," which seems to indicate persons from the Friends' community around Wakefield and West Ardsley.[24] The distance from West Ardsley to Appleby is over one hundred miles on today's roads. One of two routes may have been used. In the first case the travelers could have gone by Leeds or Garforth toward the Great North Road, the former Roman road, which in places roughly followed the current route of the M1 Motorway, passing Wetherby, Knaresborough, and Ripon on its way north toward Richmond. They would have turned northwest up one of the valleys into the upper Dales and across the Pennine ridge down into the Vale of Eden and Appleby. The other route would have gone more westerly from the start, through Bradford toward Lancaster, turning north to Kendal and thence through Westmoreland into Appleby, roughly along the route James Nayler took to Orton. By either way, the trip from West Ardsley would have taken many days of rough travel crossing hilly terrain over poor roads. In those times the care of roads was the responsibility of local parishes at their own expense. In peacetime care for little used roads through rough and open country was often neglected. During the recent war, with taxes from both sides imposed on the communities through which the armies passed, and with manpower drawn away for service in the armies, or worse yet, reduced by casualty and death, many roads had fallen into ruin.

It has been widely accepted that Ann never saw James after he joined the army, except when he was at home in 1651 and during her visits at Appleby and London, when he was in jail. Historian Christopher Hill described the Naylers' marriage as "divorce by removal." Nayler biographer Emilia Fogelklou described Ann as a pillar of faithful support and understanding for James. Dorothy Nimmo extended that portrait in a wonderfully graphic narrative poem to reveal the pains of endurance Ann must have undergone, working a small farm alone. There is room for conjecture on all these interpretations, but the evidence is scarce, either to support or refute any of it.[25]

The view of Nayler's nearly complete absence during the war period is supportable, if at all, only by the absence of any account of the couple spending time together. There is no evidence that they did not. All of Nayler's military service, as it can be reconstructed, with the exception of time in Scotland and perhaps Westmoreland, took place within no more than a day or two's ride of West Ardsley. As we have seen, he spent a great deal of time at Pontefract, only about a dozen miles from home. Other soldiers visited home to see to their farms and families. Why not he? In fact, Fogelklou's research suggested that in addition to the three identified daughters born before the Battle of Wakefield, the Naylers may have had more children, including a son born during the war. Conjugal visits, while they may not have been frequent, should not be ruled out for lack of records that they happened, nor should Nayler be judged for abandoning his wife. How must it have been for the other soldiers from around Woodkirk, and for the other hundred or so who became Quakers after having been in the wars? Hard times for the wives and families at home? Certainly, but the case cannot be sustained for abandonment of his family by Nayler, or for very many others.

The occasion of Ann Nayler's visit to Appleby did produce the only tender acknowledgement of their relationship that we have from James. He wrote to George Fox:

> ... I myself had great refreshment by her coming, for she came and returned with much freedom and great joy, beyond what I in reason could expect, but I see she was sent of my Father and fitted not to be a hinderer, but a furtherer of His Works.[26]

In the same letter Nayler also said:

> The coming over of my wife was very serviceable and hath stopped many mouths and hath convinced them of many lies they had raised and was believed in the country. . . .

From this Fogelklou concluded that Ann had "gone before the judges" and assured them that Nayler had not been involved in adultery with Mrs. Roper.[27] The account of the trial in "*Saul's Errand to Damascus*" does not take note of her doing this, but Ann must have been outspoken on this subject in some way that James found "serviceable" and effective in stopping the rumors.

The stories about Nayler's conduct seem to have a lot to do with George Fox's visits to Stanley and West Ardsley. During the Appleby trial in the winter of 1652–1653 Colonel Brigs, one of the judges, asked Nayler if he were not excommunicated by the Woodkirk Independents for his blasphemous opinions. Nayler answered that he had not been excommunicated while he was still at Woodkirk, but he did not know what they had done since he left. He did not seem to express surprise or outrage at Brigs's question. Nayler had taken up Quaker ministry around Woodkirk before he left. Furthermore, he was associated with George Fox, who after one of his visits to Stanley created a terrific disturbance at Woodkirk, directed toward Christopher Marshall, the vicar. Fox was thrown out and beaten in the church yard. Feelings seem to have run high enough to justify Nayler's expulsion.[28]

John Deacon's story of Nayler's removal from Woodkirk was published in London after the trial at Appleby, and just before Nayler's London trial in 1656. Clearly the story had currency in the North four years earlier. Deacon reported that he received the adultery story in a letter from his friend, Marshall.[29] Deacon also stated that Nayler was expelled from a Baptist congregation in London after leaving Woodkirk, again for adultery. While Colonel Brigs did not say where he got the story on which his trial examination was based, one suspects that Marshall was again the source, having been approached for information on Nayler by someone who had an interest in the case at Appleby, such as Higginson. Marshall, no friend of Quakers, was quite capable of spreading slander. George Fox went to challenge him in his own church because Marshall had called him a sorcerer on a black horse, who could be in more than one place at the same time, who bewitched his audience with potions, and turned them to follow him for money.[30]

Francis Higginson, like Marshall, had been in Massachusetts before war broke out in England. Higginson's father, also named Francis, a graduate of Cambridge, had been a Puritan dissenter in England and was ejected from his parish during the Laudian disciplines. He had emigrated with his family and taken up ministry in Salem, Massachusetts. He died in 1630. His second son, Francis, went back to England at some point. He was educated at Leyden in Holland, one of the foremost universities in Europe, before beginning his tenure at Kirkby Stephen. Higginson and Marshall would have met during their time in Massachusetts, as Marshall took up his ministry in churches north of Boston in the immediate vicinity of Salem, where the Higginsons lived.

Examined on the accusations of adultery at his trial in London after his Bristol ride in 1656.[31] Nayler confirmed that he knew Mrs. Roper of Stanley. They had been familiar in the way that was customary among the close group of Friends at that time, but there had certainly been no adultery. She was the lady at whose home Fox gathered the meetings at which he and Nayler became acquainted. The village of Stanley, the Ropers' home, borders Wakefield to the north along the road to Leeds, and is walking distance from Wakefield or Woodkirk. If James knew Mrs. Roper, who lived there, probably Ann Nayler did too. Surely she would have heard the stories Marshall was spreading around. She came to her husband's side at Appleby to deny rumors about his infidelity. She would have been much less likely to travel so far to stand up for him, if the stories had been true. If the stories were true, it is likewise inconceivable that George Fox would have overlooked them and allowed Nayler to become a leading example for the Children of the Light. No corroborating evidence has been found that Nayler had an adulterous affair with Mrs. Roper, that he went to London after leaving Woodkirk and before arriving at Swarthmore Hall, or that he ever had any involvement with Baptists, other than to oppose them in challenging debates and published exchanges during his London ministry some years after the Appleby trial.

Nayler and Christopher Marshall had known each other for some time before the flare-up at Woodkirk. Two years older than Nayler, Marshall had emigrated to New England after graduating from Cambridge in 1632. There he studied with John Cotton and served some local congregations.[32] Cotton was one of the foremost, perhaps the single foremost founder of the Independent churches in New England. Though invited to return to England and take a leadership role there, Cotton preferred to remain at a distance, teach, and write.[33] Marshall, however, did return to England in 1642 to take part in the Puritan revolution. Acting as Colonel Copley's chaplain he served together in the same troop with James Nayler for at least a year at Pontefract, from November, 1644 to November, 1645.[34] They may have been together longer than that. We have no evidence to the contrary. Marshall appeared as vicar of Woodkirk in 1650, about the same time that Nayler returned. Nayler wrote to the congregation in about 1654, after being informed of his expulsion, to declare his reasons for making his own choice to leave that church. He cited, among page after page of differences with their practices, their habits of ". . . backbiting . . . false accusing . . . slandering . . ."[35]

Marshall is memorialized at Woodkirk on the same plaque on which Anthony Nutter's tenure is shown. Marshall's 1650 arrival date is also noted in a rather interesting short biography of Nayler by John Greenleaf Whittier, written in the 1850's. In the Whittier account Nayler is recorded as returning to Woodkirk in 1649, which conflicts with the widely quoted story of Nayler's preaching in Scotland after the Battle of Dunbar in 1650.[36] George Fox in his *Journal* relates his challenge to Marshall at Woodkirk, but does not give the date.[37] By deduction, we can say that this meeting probably took place in early 1652, which is the date Whittier uses.

The account of Nayler's trial for blasphemy at Appleby is brief, only less than six pages. Probably it is an incomplete presentation of what went on there, but even if it is, it reveals much about the man. All we know about Nayler's epiphany is here. For such a short exposition it paints a vivid portrait of a man shaken and bewildered, but nevertheless acting on a leading he wanted to believe, and feared not to believe, was spoken in the very voice of the Almighty. We also get a glimpse of Nayler as a gentle, humble man, concerned to apologize to one he may have wronged. He said to Priest Higginson, "Friend, I had not accused thee, had I not been asked what was the difference between the ministers and me: for I am not come to accuse any." Here we see a difference in character between Nayler and George Fox. Fox is never shown as apologizing to anyone, though he accused many, including ministers, publicly embarrassing them on their pulpits. So did Nayler, but here, he showed a kinder side of his nature as well, easing the harsh truth, both in a spirit of humility, and in the hope that it could be heard.

Two threads of questioning appear in the trial record. The first was by Colonel Brigs, one of three judges on the panel. Nayler also mentioned a jury.[38] Brigs was an antagonist. Functioning as a prosecutor, he attempted to discredit Nayler by association. When Nayler answered concerning his profession that he was a husbandman, Brigs pressed him. Had Nayler not been a soldier, and had he not been with the Levelers in their revolt against army authority at Burford, Brigs asked? Cromwell had dealt with the Leveler demonstrators as if they were mutineers and had the instigators hanged. How had Nayler come to be here in Appleby, Brigs continued? No doubt he hoped to bring out a story of an unsavory exit from the Army leading to Nayler's association with George Fox and the troublesome dissidents who had recently been charged and tried unsuccessfully at Lancaster, some of whom had come up into Westmoreland to commit more blasphemies and disruption of order. Brigs proved inept; he could not get Nayler to admit any of these accusations, nor association with any other notorious person or group of blasphemers. The frustrated Brigs asked, had Nayler not been excommunicated from the Independent church in his home town? Nayler admitted none of it. If he had, proof of repeated offensive behavior and association with known blasphemers, troublemakers, and political dissidents would have eased the way for the court to impose a sterner punishment. Indeed in later years, when Nayler's companion, Howgill, returned to Appleby, by then well-known as a Quaker firebrand, he was jailed again, this time for refusing to swear the Oath of Allegiance. He was held until his death in 1668. One of the Justices at Appleby, named Musgrave, had by that time been persecuting Howgill for years and was doubtless irritated by his wide reputation. He used Howgill's personal associations to attempt to implicate Howgill in a conspiracy plot against the King.[39]

While the first line of Brigs's questioning had focused on the objectionable character of Nayler as a wandering intruder into the community, the second, more serious line went toward the question of what he had preached and whether it were blasphemous. Nayler's interest was in telling of his own spiritual experience. He began with the voice in the field and stayed with that salient event, turning aside questions and insinuations concerning his past associations, so that the only evidence the court heard was his own testimony about his own faith. He was charged with having said that, "Christ was in him and that there was but one word of God."[40] Charged by whom? At least one of his accusers, Francis Higginson, was present, but consistent with legal practice of the times, no one was mentioned in this account as stepping forward to bear witness. The accusations were pressed by the judges. It was up to Nayler and Howgill to defend themselves, both as to law and as to fact. Nayler was imprisoned on the basis of his ministry and spiritual experience, but oddly, he was not convicted on the charge of which he was accused.

Nayler and Howgill (his part, if any, in the trial was not included in the account) were jailed for twenty weeks in Appleby without a finding on the blasphemy charges against them.[41] Their case was not put to the jury.[42] They were held on charges of being wanderers, or vagabonds, notwithstanding that Nayler named at least one in the crowd who had been in the army with him for years, and Howgill was known and recognized in the petition against them as a local minister. To be convicted as a wanderer, the law required, among other tests, that the offender be unknown to anyone in the local community. These offenders were known, but their defenses were ignored by the Appleby court, according to the account in "*Saul's Errand . . .*" Once they were imprisoned Howgill and Nayler were aware of a continuing effort on the part of their clergy accusers to investigate and amplify every rumor that was adverse to the prisoners' character and behavior. Knowing the case to hold them was weak, their accusers sought better evidence of real crimes. The prisoners were directed by the court, apparently as part of the effort to get them to incriminate themselves, to answer in writing to the charges against them in the ministers' petition. By this directive, however, the court effectively invited Nayler and Howgill to prepare written material for publication. Seeing no restriction against using their written responses for other purposes than satisfaction of the court's order, the prisoners proceeded with the intent of making their cases public, and somehow, in Nayler's case, the papers promptly got to London publishers.

CHAPTER 8

One of England's Prophets

How is your judgment failed you, to think that all this shaking and overturning hath no further end but to set up flesh and exalt one man to rule over the conscience of another by his own will, where Christ should reign as king forever!

—A Lamentation (By one of England's Prophets), James Nayler

Nayler was held for about two months prior to the trial sessions, and then was imprisoned from January, 1653 until the following April. Far from breaking either his health or his spirit, imprisonment seemed to energize him to write down and publish his ministry. Deprived, scorned, though anything but repressed, he set to work to reveal not only his personal spiritual discovery, but also the state of Christian practice and persecution in the English community. As he had done for a time at Swarthmoor Hall and as he would do again in later years at Exeter jail and London, Nayler applied himself to the discipline of surviving the effects of persecution and incarceration by fasting outwardly and turning to the Spirit of Christ within. Fasting was not uncommon among Quakers and those broadly described as Seekers.[1] In a more formalized way the practice had also been used among Puritans and, of course, Catholics, for some time. It derives from historic Biblical and early Christian usage. Possibly some of the Quakers like Nayler had learned the discipline in their home churches before they became Friends, but while members of other faiths may have fasted as part of their ritual of outward repentance, Quakers did so to withdraw in times of trouble to their inner spiritual guide, where they found strength and even cause to rejoice. Given the force and positivity of his writing from the period, this surely must have been Nayler's experience of his fasting discipline.

Where, and under what conditions he spent his time of imprisonment at Appleby is uncertain. Whatever the conditions of his confinement, however, adequate light, writing supplies, and the means to pass the product of his work along to get it to London for publication were available. Some of his publications were issued during the time of his imprisonment, and certain others, which followed closely after his release must have been written in jail, either in whole or in part.

The Armorer's House at Appleby-in-Westmoreland, believed to be where Nayler and Howgill were imprisoned

Appleby's House of Correction was just across the river from the town, a few buildings upstream from the bridge. A chantry chapel stood over the bridge. In the chapel's basement at one end of the bridge was another, much older jail. Nayler and Howgill could have been incarcerated in one or the other of these. The newer jail, the House of Correction, still stands, now used as an antique shop. The lintel over the door is dated 1639. Though the building does not look much like a prison today, its stone floors and thick cell walls reveal its past. This jail just predates the outbreak of the civil wars, but was actually the product of a program of prison reform begun during the reign of Queen Elizabeth. The Queen called for Houses of Correction to be constructed in each county, intended to be places where the lesser miscreants, such as debtors, drunkards, and vagabonds, could be locked up to work for their keep in a somewhat constructive atmosphere, so that rehabilitation might be possible. Sentences to Houses of Correction were often short in duration.

The old chantry house jail, which stood much closer to the water, was used for felons guilty of serious crimes. Howgill died at the chantry jail at the end of his second imprisonment in 1668.[2] At that time he was suspected, rightly or wrongly, of involvement in treasons against King Charles II known as the Kaber Rigg and Farnley Wood plots. For such crimes, the chantry jail was used, but the House of Correction's purpose better suits the Nayler/Howgill imprisonment of 1653.

Three other possible sites for the imprisonment existed. In "*Sin Kept Out of the Kingdom*" Nayler signed himself as, "late a prisoner in Appleby Castle."[3] The castle, as one would expect, has a dungeon. This may seem to settle the matter, but it doesn't. Correspondence indicates that he was staying at the home of the jailer.[4] Higginson confirmed this. In cases of minor charges, sometimes prisoners were held this way. The jailers' wives found the practice was a means for them to make a little extra money, operating a sort of penal bed and breakfast. Local Appleby history, however, has it that the jailer for the House of Correction lived far out of town, and that Nayler's staying there would have made no sense. How can these conflicting accounts be reconciled? Did he stay at the Castle, or at the jailer's house? Perhaps the answer is, both. It could be that simple.

He did not stay at the castle dungeon, which also still exists, though it is pretty much a ruin. Typical of such 17th Century cells, it had no light at all for writing. It was more like a burial chamber or a cesspool. The castle was under reconstruction anyway. Lady Anne Clifford, who considered the castle at Appleby her primary residence, spent time there during Christmas, 1652, but then went away to live elsewhere until late summer 1653. She was not living there at the time of the Assizes, according to her diaries. She makes no mention of the Nayler matter, or of housing prisoners, even though she was, among her many offices and quite remarkably, the High Sheriff of Westmoreland. The castle officer in charge of the dungeon, however, would have been the Armorer. His house still stands as well. A veritable fortress in its own right, entirely secure, it functioned as a weapons depot in addition to being a home. It was capable of staunch defense by reason of its solid walls and doors, and its arrow slit windows, which also let in light. It is outside the castle itself, but nevertheless a part of the castle property. Now used as a private home, the Armorer's House is the only place in Appleby, which fits all the elements of the description of Nayler's jail. It is part of the castle, has enough light for writing, and is the jailer's house. Given that the dungeon may have been unavailable due to construction, why then was the castle used instead of the House of Correction? In addition to the opportunity for the jailer and his wife to make some money, here are two more possible reasons. First, the prisoners were not found guilty of a crime that called for imprisonment in the House of Correction. Second, the House of Correction may have been full. Doubtless, town population was unusually high because of all the construction jobs being done, and the quarter sessions had just been held, which could have produced a seasonal increase in the number of jail sentences.

Nayler clarified the matter somewhat in a letter to George Fox and Margaret Fell, believed to be sent in February, 1653.[5] He wrote,

> The woman of the house where we are is very tender, & a pure love is in her to the truth, & she is made to suffer much, with great patience from the tyrant & the rest of the town, but she is made to bear all & still own the truth, there is much inquiry if she do anything for us, but I am made to stand clear from all & keep out the accuser . . . We are much threatened with low prison & irons, but what God wills, the tyrant is much tormented with us, that we do not bow nor conform to his beastly practice. . . .

It seems that he and Howgill were at the jailer's house, that the jailer's wife was caring for them rather kindly and taking some abuse by rumor for doing it, and that the jailer, or tyrant, was asserting his own power and displeasure with the situation by threatening the prisoners with cruel punishment in a real jail. Nayler described his own and Howgill's fasting in this same letter, taken up after the Appleby trial and during the period in which the accusing priests were attempting to gather additional evidence of worse offenses to be added to the charges against the Quakers. It is in this letter as well that Nayler described the visit from his wife.

Nayler's first major publication came that March and may have been written entirely or in part during his imprisonment. The pamphlet contains cornerstones in Nayler's biography and in the history of the beginnings of the Quaker faith. We have called this collection of works by an abbreviated name, "*Saul's Errand . . .*" In full the title reads, "*Saul's Errand to Damascus With his Packet of Letters from the High Priests against the Disciples of the Lord.*" Written in sections by George Fox, James Nayler, and Joseph Lawson, the purpose for its publication was stated on the title page as follows:

> Published to no other end but to draw out the bowels of tender compassion from all that love the poor despised servants of Jesus Christ, who have been the scorn of carnal men in all ages.

The collection begins with three introductory epistles, each unsigned and in a somewhat different style from the others. Then follow the charges and petition made by ministers of Lancaster the previous summer. Entries by Nayler, Fox and Lawson (whose piece is printed at the end of the collection, as if added after the rest had been assembled), answered the charges made by the ministers. Fox responded, in three groups or sections of text, in specific detail to some thirty objections and queries addressed to him by the petitioners. Nayler's "Answer and Declaration" formed a summary of Quaker beliefs in seven key subject areas: the nature of Jesus Christ, the Scriptures, Baptism, the Lord's Supper, Resurrection, Magistracy, and the Ministry. Then followed detailed sections describing what happened to Nayler and others at Kendal and at Orton, and the account of his trial at Appleby. These sections of the pamphlet are unsigned.[6]

Segments of "*Saul's Errand . . .*" have appeared separately for various purposes over time. Fox's and Nayler's contributions have been published separately and in the collected works of each man. The account of the events at Orton has been referenced in Nayler biographies by Bittle, Damrosch, and others, to describe the hostility visited on Quaker ministers and the circumstances under which Nayler's arrest and imprisonment took place. The Nayler trial record at Appleby appears in several publications. Lawson's answer to the petition has been largely ignored, as have been the three anonymous introductory epistles. The entire collection "*Saul's*

Errand . . ." in fact, has been referenced by various authors as source for the use of only parts of it, just as has been done in earlier chapters of this book. Yet each segment of "*Saul's Errand . . .*," the testimonies, persecutions, and trial, was part of a coherent reference to the title and the stated purpose of the collected work. While some pieces may have been written so that they might stand alone, they were published in this work for the purpose stated on the title page and quoted above.

Saul of Tarsus, (Acts 9–13) was a persecutor of Christians and an opportunist. En route to Damascus carrying papers that might be used as authority for the arrest and punishment of Christians found along the way, he was struck by a blinding light, led by hand into Damascus and left to wander for days without food and drink until he was prepared for instruction by the risen Jesus. Saul was restored and reborn into a new vision and witness. Along with the gift of prophecy, he was assigned the responsibility of ministry. Delivered with these were Christ's assurance of threats, torture, and suffering, which all attend the revelations the Prophet brings. Saul was transformed to a life of prophecy, in which he became known as Paul.

"*Saul's Errand to Damascus. . . . ,*" then, was published to direct the reader to appreciate the Scriptures not just as historical documents, in this case describing events in the life of the apostles, but as a metaphorical account of the living story of the faithful in the present time, that is, in 1652. Not only could Nayler and Fox witness to the presence of Christ, spiritually, within themselves, they could also witness to the words of God in Scripture as being fulfilled presently in life all around them. Fox and Nayler each had known that presence for some time, though at first only tentatively. For each man it had taken something like a blinding flash to get his attention; in Nayler's case, a divine voice in a field, in Fox's case a voice as well, and a vision on a mountaintop. Now they could expand from those events into the wider account, indeed into contemporary prophecy. What they told of their own experience was like Saul's. Indeed, it seemed to be almost the *same* experience as Saul's, for the source, the end of it, and the lesson, were the same for all, Saul, Fox, Nayler, and some others of the faithful. The way to the new life was through, as they wrote, "the bowels of compassion," that is, passage through a personal awareness of suffering to the very source of love.

If "*Saul's Errand . . .*" were a bit crude and self-promoting, it was also at its best controversial and inspiring. That was part of its intent, and its style was in keeping with the discourse in its time. Fox and Nayler seemed to agree that no public indictments against the Friends should stand unanswered. Neither could their ministry be slighted as just another malcontent outpouring against state and church. Unlicensed, uncensored writing had been published and widely available to the public since the early days of the revolution, when in 1640 the monopolistic control of the printed word in England was let go of the King's grasp. News sheets and pamphlets came out on every imaginable subject, and of the popular subjects, religion and the conduct of war, in that order, were probably at the head of the list in readership. Publications of books and pamphlets like "*Saul's Errand . . .*" could now be taken up as tools in delivering Quaker prophecy. Such discourse invited controversy. Rebuttals, like Higginson's, commonly extended the verbal exchange between Quakers and many of the leading clergy of the established church in England, as well as between other large nonconformist denominations such as the Baptists and the Quakers. It was a rough process through which the weaknesses and excesses of the participants could all be revealed, often quite fiercely and fearlessly. The publishing duel that developed has been called by later observers "the pamphlet wars."[7]

The justices at Appleby had inadvertently assisted Nayler, providing the opportunity for him to reach a wider audience, to their own disadvantage and potential embarrassment. Publication of *"Saul's Errand . . ."* when Nayler was still imprisoned at Appleby, revealed oppression of the new Quaker ministry by means of blasphemy charges, adversarial public arguments arranged against them by the incumbent clergy, tactics of violence, arrest, imprisonment, and biased courtroom processes. At the core of this pamphlet was an abbreviated version of Nayler's response to the charges made against him by the ministers of Lancaster. As part of the outcome of his trial Nayler was required by the court to write answers to all the charges against him. The material in *"Saul's Errand . . ."* could have been used to answer this requirement, but it appears to have been written before the court order was issued. Further explication was required by the order, which Nayler (and Howgill) were pleased to provide, and to publish. The justices of Appleby could have restricted distribution of the offender's responses and his other writings, at least while he was in their local jail. They could have prevented his access to materials he could have used to produce any other papers. They did make it difficult for both Nayler and Howgill to obtain court records needed for their response to the charges, but no effective means were taken to limit the extent of their writing, or its publication even during the prisoners' incarceration.

The court's arrogance was not unanimous. Justice Anthony Pearson, convinced by Nayler's testimony, absented himself shortly after he was outvoted. Justice Gervase Benson did not sit at all in Nayler's trial. Benson was already a Friend, had hosted Nayler in his home, and quite properly recused himself. That did not, however, restrain him from presenting a petition to the court regarding the Nayler charges. In remarkably few words Benson characterised the biased nature of what he called, the sessions of the peace.[8] He noted that although the words the accused spoke did not violate the blasphemy law, or any law, two of the Justices said they would risk being fined themselves by the Assizes court rather than let Nayler go free. The allegations in the ". . . petition of divers Ministers and other Inhabitants . . ." of Westmoreland was sufficient for them, even though, as Benson pointed out, the Ministers' allegations were not properly sworn to be true, as any court evidence ought to be. Benson stated that one of the Justices had been in arms against Parliament. In other words, he was a Royalist soldier in the recent civil war, and he had nothing more to say to Nayler in the proceedings than to rail against "the people of God, whom by way of reproach he called Quakers." It went without saying that some of those Quakers, certainly Nayler, had been in arms for the Parliament. Justice Pearson, Benson stated flatly, without further characterisation, had told Benson that he had commitments in Newcastle, and thus removed himself from the ongoing affair in Appleby. The removal of Benson and Pearson obviously left the court biased and incapable of a fair decision. The outcome of the trial was just as Benson stated it must be. Without legal standing the decision of the court went off into abuse of its powers, prejudice against the accused, and no conviction on any breach of law.

Howgill might have been dismissed with no more than an admonition that he "abide . . . at . . . home, . . . be quiet, do [his] own business, and not wander up and down the country as seducer . . ." That was all that the ministers' petition asked of the court in his case.[9] Howgill was known by people in the area and was described as "of better deportment." However misguided they thought he was, he was not the ministers' target. The petitioners sought especially to drive Fox and Nayler away. The easiest legal tool for this purpose was to have them charged as wanderers, vagrants without means of support and known to no person in the jurisdiction. This proof was part of what Justice Brigs had tried, ineptly, to establish in his questioning. The petitioners also charged Nayler and Fox (who was not present) with horrid blasphemy, the same charge Nayler would later face before Parliament in 1656 after the infamous Bristol reenactment of Jesus's entry to Jerusalem. The Appleby court, however, could find no blasphemy in Nayler's testimonies, far from it, let alone the more aggravated level of offense or the "damnable heresies" the petition alleged. Being a wanderer and a troublesome person would have to suffice, so the court ignored Nayler's attempt to point out one person in the audience who knew him. Howgill was known locally and therefore not a wanderer by legal definition, but apparently he refused more favorable treatment than Nayler. Both were held in prison until they answered the petitions against them. During the time they were held, more petitions were filed and the defendants had to answer these additional charges in their turn. However arbitrary the court's solution may have been, it was an explicit invitation for the prisoners to publish in their own behalf.

Perhaps the Justices thought Nayler a simple Yorkshire farmer who would be ineffective in answering his charges. If so, he might be held in prison at their pleasure. They should have anticipated that he could respond at least as effectively as he had testified before the court. They hardly seem to have imagined that he would reply point by point, even clause by clause, to every part of every allegation against him, and then have the paper published in London immediately after his release from jail.

"*Several Petitions Answered . . .*" was published in London in June, 1653.[10] The justices at Appleby must have already seen the parts of this paper that were addressed to them answering the conditions they had set for Nayler's release from their jail.

In addition to those sections, the published collection of works was introduced by Richard Farnsworth and closed with an exhortation by George Fox.

In his answers to the priests' petitions Nayler's tone was much more combative than it had been in the testimony recorded in "*Saul's Errand . . .*" Asserting at the outset that, "*The ministers of God never put up a petition to an outside magistrate to maintain the church of God,*"[11] Nayler challenged the standing of these ministers to represent God's church in any way. "*Your ministry is of man,*" he wrote, "*and must be upheld by an earthly power . . . [your] church is carnal and must be maintained by a carnal weapon . . .*" Which is, of course, exactly what the ministers were trying to accomplish by taking their differences with Nayler and the Friends to the courts. "*You shame your profession,*" Nayler scolded the petitioners,

> . . . for where the truth is springing, the pure seed arising, you cannot suppress it with your carnal weapon the letter; then you run to a magistrate without to suppress it. While we all lived under your ministry, and what you spoke we took for truth, . . . being . . . naturally blind . . . God now . . . according to his promise hath gathered us . . . and we witness the Scripture fulfilled; there do you hate us and seek to persecute them in whom Jesus Christ is made manifest, but it is that the Scripture might be fulfilled: he that is born after the flesh persecutes him that is born after the Spirit . . . and if any man live godly in Christ Jesus he must suffer persecution . . .[12]

The priests, who lived on the tithes of their parishioners, were no more than thieves, Nayler continued, who resold the stolen word of god for money. It was they who were corrupt, whereas the Friends had come to proclaim the coming of the Lord. As God's people, Spiritual people, they must be persecuted. Scripture told them so, and they expected it, but Scripture also said they could never be taken, because as God's own saints, they were of a different world, where carnal law did not apply. That was as close as Nayler came to denying the power of the civil magistracy, but he made a fine distinction. Earlier in the text of "*Saul's Errand . . . ,*" he had argued that magistracy was a part of God's plan and was to be honored.

> . . . where justice and righteousness is the head and ruleth without partiality, that land is kept in peace; and those that judge for the Lord, I honor as my own life . . .[13]

To honor the magistrate who judged for God's order, however, was not to honor him as a man in high station, for this was contrary to Jesus's teaching in Scripture.

The second petition in the set Nayler answered came from ". . . several gentlemen, ministers of the gospel and others . . ." most of whom, the petition claimed, had risked in the recent civil wars ". . . lives, liberties, estates, and relations . . . in the defense of religion and liberty, in concurrence with, and maintenance of the just proceedings of our Parliament." The petitioners had ". . . expected, the settlement of the grand ends of our engagement, and so much more, as being the promise of Parliament ..." They approved of acts of Parliament intended to restore order to the country, but now, here came these dangerous dissidents.[14]

The Appleby petition against Friends, specifically Fox and Nayler, made claims potentially as threatening in 1653 as those abroad in London and elsewhere several years later, when Friends were confused with the Fifth Monarchists, who advocated overthrow of the government in preparation for the second coming. The Quakers taught that Christ had indeed come and was doing battle with the Antichrist, but they did not preach violent overthrow of the government. Nevertheless the petitioners at Appleby accused them of fomenting rebellion and a new civil war. They must be stopped, before worse chaos developed.

Nayler responded with the same words Fox had used while in the house of correction at Derby in 1651.[15] Fox refused to fight for Parliament at Worcester because he "lived in the virtue of that life and power that took away the occasion of all wars." Nayler said it was truth that took away the occasion of all wars.[16] Here we find precursors from both leaders of George Fox's Epistle to Friends of 1659 and the declaration to King Charles II after Cromwell's death and the Restoration of the monarchy in 1661, which together describe what is often called by modern Quakers, the "peace testimony."[17]

Nayler took the allegations seriously, resisting what must have been a strong temptation to argue ad hominem against the self-righteous petitioners. It seemed now that everyone had fought for Parliament. There was not a Royalist to be found, although that had not been so at Orton, or on the bench at Appleby. The unidentified petitioners supported Parliament's recent laws protecting conservative stability in the church. They supported laws against "... promoters of heretical doctrines, Ranters, and blasphemers ..." Fox, Nayler and their "proselytes" had encouraged interruptions of worship services, blasphemous public outbursts promoting violence, and disturbance of the peace. "Their main drift," the petitioners complained, " is to enrage the people against the ministry by reason of tithes, crying out for ... the necessary overthrow ... of the laws ... tending to stir up sedition in the people ..." The Quakers, they charged, practiced sorcery, corrupted children, and consorted with the devil. In the case of George Fox, they said, it was known that he had been doing this for some time before he came to these parts. Quakers professed no difference between peoples (i.e. declined to remove their hats and use customary terms of deference) and refused subjection to magistrates. "To see such people unrestrained creates discontents and lays a clear foundation for civil wars ..."[18]

While other petitions had been based on religion and godly life in the community, this one went further. It made claims against Fox and Nayler of subversion of the family, of promoting the beliefs of the Levellers, of satanic connections, of using the tactics of the Antichrist. It suggested treasonous support for foreign interests, namely the Dutch and French, recently in arms against England. (Some Friends had, in fact, emigrated to Holland to avoid persecution.) The Quakers were fomenting rebellion and civil war. The petition read as if 17th Century political consultants had been enlisted to write a brief touching all the tender wounds of a country just now recovering from a painful war. The Quakers were blamed for all of it.

Nayler turned the argument back on his accusers as a group, naming no one individually. Calling them of the generation that persecuted Christ, he said they called truth blasphemy and preached as if they had never read the prophets. Quake and tremble, of course we do, he admitted, and so did Daniel, Habbakuk, and Isaiah. So also did Moses and Job.

> Truth ever stirred up confusion where it was, though it lay close till truth came as you read in the Scriptures. Christ came to put fire to the earth; (Luke 12:49) and the apostles where they came in the markets or synagogues, who witnessed forth the substance, to draw people to it, to serve the Lord in the newness of life, to come up into the everlasting truth and peace, then everyone stood up in his own imaginings and thoughts, as you do now to oppose the truth, and said they would turn the world upside down.

Nayler did not mean that the Quakers were here to turn the world upside down. They were not here to foment revolution. They were here to prepare Christ's way with the fire of their testimony. It was the corrupt men of the old life who feared change and would turn the world upside down to stop it. Nayler said he and his friends came with the truth, but

> The intention of your mind is to have the truth restrained, [truth] which takes away the occasion of all wars and brings into love and true heartedness, and there is nothing discontent with us but that which doth not abide in the truth. . . . whereas you speak of laying a foundation of new war . . . it is your own interest you fear, . . . if the Parliament should take away your tithes and your means . . . you are the men that raise up civil wars against them that live peaceably and love peace and go about to take away the occasion of all wars. . . . If you were the ministers of God you would go about to bring people from under all law, up to God: but you show yourselves to be of that generation which shut the kingdom of heaven from men, which kingdom is a kingdom of peace, this we witness. (Matt 23:13) . . . You need never fear them who live in the power of truth to raise up an outward war, . . . it is your false suggestion, to incense people to make them believe lies; but God hath raised up a light in people and in magistrates, which discerns all your intents.

During the period of Nayler's passage from Yorkshire, through Lancashire into Westmoreland, and his imprisonment at Appleby, Quakers were jailed elsewhere in the North of England in considerable numbers. Shortly after meeting with Fox and Nayler at Stanley, Thomas Aldam was imprisoned in 1652 at York for a year and a half for refusing to pay tithes amounting to 11£ 10s, and goods were confiscated from him worth five times that much. Soon after he was released, Aldam was imprisoned again. Justice Gervase Benson's wife was jailed at the same time at York.

Thomas Goodaire, with whom Nayler had traveled in the ministry, was jailed for ten months in 1653. George Fox was jailed at Carlisle under the most horrible conditions. Like Nayler's at Appleby, Fox's charges of blasphemy were not put to a jury trial before the Assizes, for if he had been convicted of repeated offenses, he should have been put to death under the blasphemy law of 1650. As unpopular as Fox was, execution for his religious beliefs would have backfired and sparked a public outrage.[19] William Dewsbury, who was listed with a residence at Stanley and Fox said was convinced there at the home of the Ropers along with Nayler, was jailed in 1654, the first of nearly a lifetime of sentences for him. Mary Fisher was given sentences in 1652, 1653, and 1654. Elizabeth Hooten was sentenced with her at York in 1652 and later found her way to the Caribbean colonies, where she died at Jamaica. Each year many other Friends, whose names are now less familiar, went to jail for the same sort of infractions.[20] The case of James Nayler's reception by the citizens and his treatment by the magistrates, judges, and jailers in Westmoreland was mild by comparison with what Quakers endured in some other places. What he would endure in London four years later in 1656 was far worse,

Peace and freedom of worship were not to be won by gentle insistence and reproach in 1652. Nayler was past expecting that. Eight years of civil war for the right to choose and act on his faith had hardened him and driven away any fear of man, leaving only the fear of God. He knew beatings and jail first hand. They held no fear. He had Scripture, all of it, in his head, and it told him that he had been on the right course. He had God's own words spoken to him in his field, directing him to go out and be with God in the things he was told to do. Prophecy was his responsibility. Scripture was fulfilled in him so far, and what lay ahead could be predicted by Scripture. Nayler had begun to frame his own vision in the imagery of Revelation. If some of that story were exaggerated metaphor, it was nevertheless the truth, and it was near. It was an image of war and chaos, of cosmic fire, justice, suffering and salvation. Against a background of 17th Century Puritanism, this was sobering stuff, but not any more terrifying than other common ministerial fare of the times.

If Nayler's struggle for religious freedom had ever been distinct from the political motives for the civil wars, surely that had not been so for many years. It will be seen in his writing from "*Saul's Errand . . .*" onward that Nayler felt that the only reason for fighting the war was to relieve religious oppression and bring forward a godly nation. Violent protest was caught up in the fulfillment of prophecy. There was no escaping it. The whole purpose of the former was to achieve the latter. In the ninth month (November) 1653 the following paper was published from York:

A Lamentation
(By one of England's Prophets)
Over the Ruins of
This Oppressed Nation
To be deeply laid to heart by Parliament and Army
And all sorts of People, lest they be

> Swept away with the Besom of Destruction
> In the Day of the Lord's fierce wrath and Indignation
> Which is near at hand
> Written by the movings of the Lord in James Nayler[21]

The title page is quoted here to give emphasis to the role Nayler saw for himself in doing the work God had called him from his field to undertake. No evidence has been found that he ever saw himself as a prophet during the course of the war. In fact his visceral resistance to God's call after the war was over is convincing evidence that he did not think anything of the sort. How or when exactly he first witnessed the change in his role in the work of revolution cannot be found in his discovered writing. Perhaps it was revealed to him spiritually. Perhaps a Friend like Fox or Howgill observed the Prophet in Nayler and named it for him. By whatever means he came to know, by late 1653 he was certain enough that he could call himself in writing to the world, Prophet, and having done so, he could revisit the war he had left behind and renew his work in its unfinished business.

Nayler wrote in the "Lamentation . . ."

> Oh England! How is thy expectation failed now after all thy travails? The people to whom oppression and unrighteousness hath been a burden have long waited for deliverance, from one year to another, but none comes, from one sort of men to another . . . power . . . hath been turned into violence, and the will of men is brought forth instead of equity . . . and this is not done by an open enemy, for then it had not been so strange unto thee, but it is done by those who pretend to be against oppression; and for whom under that pretense thou hast adventured all that is dear unto thee to put power into their hands; and now thou criest to them for help but findest none that can deliver thee. Oh foolish people, when will ye learn wisdom? When will ye cease from man, who is vanity, and the sons of men who are become a lie?
>
> . . . Woe is me for you rulers, how are you fallen from what you professed when you yourselves were sufferers under such bondage? . . . and how is it that that which Christ doth command and the saints did practice is now become so heinous offenses that nothing will serve but perpetual imprisonment in close holes without hearing or trial! and that you may see for what these despised ones do suffer under you, consider their crimes . . . some of them are moved to go into the idols' temples to dispute and reason with them . . .
>
> Others suffer . . . though the Scriptures saith they "respected no man's person," nor did they bow down nor give worship to the creature . . .
>
> Others suffer for confessing the name of Christ and witnessing him in their measure . . . and this is called blasphemy . . .
>
> Others suffer for denying to swear . . . , when Christ sayeth, "Swear not at all . . ."
>
> Others . . . because they are moved to go into the streets and markets to declare against . . . sin . . . and to call for repentance . . . and they suffer as disturbers of the peace . . .

> Others whom the Lord hath called to leave houses and land, wives and children, fathers and mothers, and hath in love [gone] out to declare his love to the world, and the glad tidings of the gospel freely. These are taken under the name of wanderers and strangers . . .
>
> . . . some of them by your law you imprison . . . whip out of your towns . . . and thus you entertain strangers, contrary to the practice of all the saints . . . and the commands of God and the apostles . . . but as the men of Sodom did compass Lot's house, who had entertained strangers, so do these compass the houses where these are, threatening to pull down the houses and dash their brains against the stones in the wall . . . and for such offenses as these do the poor despised little ones of Christ suffer the worst sort of imprisonment that can be invented, in dark holes, under tyrants. . . .

Nayler spoke from his personal experience. The similarity of these descriptions to those in "*Saul's Errand* . . ." is inescapable, but the treatments at the hands of the law are equally similar to those experienced by others, Howgill, Fox, Hooten, and many more. This was, after all, no plea of brutality against himself used in his own behalf. This was Nayler's protest against policies similar to those of Charles I and Archbishop Laud that he and Cromwell had fought together to overthrow, which now were visited on godly people by the government of the Commonwealth.

Nayler asked,

> How are you deceived who have sometimes been the wisdom of the nations . . . How is your judgment failed you, to think that all this shaking and overturning hath no further end but to set up flesh and exalt one man to rule over the conscience of another by his own will, where Christ should reign as king forever!

Although this paper clearly, if not explicitly, challenged Oliver Cromwell and the governing Council, it seemed to express no carnal threat to any of them. Nayler acknowledged where the power rested and the inability of any dissident individual who disagreed with the government to stand against its persecution. Yet it should not be so, he argued. These are the men in whose hands the people fought to place power, following their representation, certainly Cromwell's, that he would lead the way to a Godly nation and freedom of conscience. Now the power was in Cromwell's hands, and the only threat Nayler posed was to warn him and his government that they risked their spiritual lives if they persisted in locking down the godly in dark cells. The timing of this publication was not coincidental. Probably the fact that it was printed in York, not as usually happened, in London, is also no coincidence. It is no coincidence that the paper is addressed to the Parliament and the Army, and to no single individual, but there was a certain individual in whom Nayler may yet have had some faith. The "*Lamentation* . . ." came out in November, 1653. On December 16 Oliver Cromwell, heavily guarded by soldiers, marched through London's streets to Whitehall to take the title and honor of His Highness the Lord Protector.[22] Nayler wrote only days or weeks before:

> And now a word to the wise amongst you, forasmuch as the Lord hath showed me that there is a seed amongst you whose hearts are not wholly hardened, nor have willfully stopped your ears against the cry of the oppressed, nor have been consenting to the cruelty that hath been acted and is intended against the innocent: to you I say arise and deliver yourselves from the guilt of oppression and cruelty of these men, and humble yourselves before the Lord that you may receive wisdom from him and boldness to declare against all violence and injustice, and set yourselves to deliver the oppressed to the utmost, that you may be hid and have a sure house and be established.[23]

"*A Discovery of the First Wisdom from Beneath and the Second Wisdom from Above*" was published in April, 1653, the month of his release from jail. Nayler signed it, ". . . prisoner for the testimony of truth at Appleby in Westmoreland . . ."[24] This was a very different kind of work from the answers to petitions and the accounts of persecution. Here was Nayler the preacher, delivering a long epistle, or in part at least, a sermon.[25] The arguments are more fully developed than what he is reported to have said at Orton and Appleby, and much more fully developed than his testimony to the magistrates in "*Saul's Errand . . .*" The first chapter[26] is notable as one of the clearest expressions ever written of the basic Quaker principle now called the "inner light." Nayler distinguished between the Spiritual light and the light of man's wisdom.

> And if you abide in the pure light within, you shall see that whatever the light of Christ makes appear to be evil and cast off; the other light, which stands in man's wisdom, makes a covering for it that it may abide still, and thus the flesh lusteth against the Spirit, and that wisdom which ariseth out of the earth opposeth that which is from above, and calls evil good and good evil; and the woe being upon that nature you can have no peace while that stands . . . abiding in that light it will show you a path which leads to purity and holiness, without which none shall ever see the Lord; and it will let you see a law written in your hearts, even the righteous law of the new covenant, which is a book sealed to all the wisdom of the world, and none can read it but by the pure light that gave it forth; which light, as it rises in you, it will open all the parables and read all the Scriptures within you, in your measure, and so you will come to unity with all the saints in measure . . .

Here is a piece of writing as gentle, hopeful, and accommodating of human frailty as can be found in Nayler's inspirational literature. It reveals a side of him quite distinct from that represented in his answer to the second petition, discussed above. Here one could savor the peace testimony with no fear of the sacrifices involved in reaching it. Yet the writer did not leave us wandering in a rosy spiritual fog. Nayler went on to discuss the necessity of sacrifice as crucifixion, writing a gentle introduction to the hardest reality of Christianity.

> . . . here is your true teacher, whereby all shall be taught of God, as saith the Scripture; and minding this light it will show you a cross to be daily taken up, whereby all unruly nature must be crucified . . . for the cross is to the carnal, wild, heady, brutish nature in you, which lies above the seed of God in you, and oppresseth the pure. Now giving this up to be crucified makes way for that which is pure to arise and guide your minds up to God, there to wait for power and strength against whatever the light of God makes manifest to be evil, and so to cast it off, and so you shall see where your strength lies and who it is in you that works the will and the deed, and then you shall be brought into a possession of what you have had but a profession, and find the power of what you had but in words, which is hidden in all professions in the world and is revealed in no other way but by the pure light of God dwelling in you, and you in it.[27]

Nayler wrote this as a formula for daily Spiritual practice. Implicit in what he said was a leap across the end of carnal existence into eternity. He described the sacrifice of giving up everything to daily crucifixion. What could be more fearsome? Yet he offered the most calm reassurance. You can do this, because Christ is in you and shows the way.

This first chapter of "*A Discovery of the First Wisdom* . . ." was signed as if it were an epistle written for a separate delivery. It reads as if it were an intimate advice to a small audience of loved ones. The following chapters, generalized to suit the low station to which man had fallen, worked their way deeper toward a final exhortation to repent and turn toward Christ, to accept living crucifixion of the brutal, carnal ways of life. He left no room for intimacy there.

Even the suggestion that feelings of intimacy could have been expressed in any of these intense, directive writings may be hard to accept. It is easier to identify such feelings in Nayler's letters to Margaret Fell and others near his home. Indeed a great many Nayler letters are available either at Friends Library in London or on microfilm elsewhere. The addressees, for the most part are Margaret Fell, George Fox, and a few others of the original early Friends. Expressions of love and personal details connect them. For example, Nayler wrote to Margaret Fell in or about July, 1653, when he was a guest at Justice Benson's house, "*Thou art sealed in my heart, my sister . . . My dear love to Margaret [her eldest daughter] & the rest of thy family . . .*"[28] Later in 1653, from Appleby jail, he wrote a pastoral letter, "To Several Friends about Wakefield," presumably those he had left behind when he answered his call in the field. To the short sermon in this letter he appended a paragraph of greetings from his companion, Francis Howgill, with a bit of detail about how they fared in prison and a request for prayers.[29] Nayler was not impersonal or stingy with intimacies, given the writing style of the times, but readers will note that something was missing. There are no letters between James and Ann Nayler or their daughters. It would be tempting to ascribe this to some sort of estrangement between them, were it not for the fact of Ann's coming to visit and speak for him, and his comment on her visit to George Fox, which was a very personal sharing with a dear friend in its own right. Rather than concluding that Nayler never wrote to her, it is much more credible to suggest that none of their letters has survived, in part because they never came into the possession of Margaret Fell. And why should they? The remarkable thing about the correspondence among early Friends is that Margaret Fell saved, and organized with George Fox's help later, nearly every letter between Friends that came her way. Her work in that respect is uniquely and immeasurably valuable, but we are unwise to make judgments about the absences in her collection.

Nayler wrote to Friends in Yorkshire about how to survive the abuse that was their portion in society:

> Dear Friends, dwell in patience and wait upon the Lord, who will do his own work. Look not at the man in the work, nor at man who opposeth the work, but rest in the will of the Lord, that so ye may be furnished with patience both to do and to suffer what ye shall be called unto, that your end in all things may be his praise. And take up his cross freely, which keeps low the fleshly man, that Christ may be set up and honored in all things, and so the light advanced in you, and the judgment set up which must give sentence against all that opposeth the truth, that the captivity may be led captive and the prisoner set free to seek the Lord, that righteousness may rule in you and peace and joy may dwell in you, wherein consisteth the kingdom of the Father to whom all praise be forever! Dear Friends, meet often together, and take heed of what exalteth itself above its brother; but keep low, and serve one another in love for the Lord's sake. Let all Friends know how it is with us, that God may have the praise of all.[30]

More intimately, he wrote to Margaret Fell, when she was having trouble managing elements of her little congregation at Swarthmore Hall,

> Dear sister wait for a death to thy carnal wisdom, that thou mayest have that single eye open by which the whole body shall be full of light.[31]

In that same letter, believed to be dated late in 1652, before he so publicly named his own work prophecy, Nayler very directly warned against taking on falsely the name and role of prophet.

> ... Richard Myers, thou gets above thy condition. Mind the babe in thee, and it will tell thee so. And, friend, thou that calls thyself a prophet art run up into the air. Lowly consider it ...
>
> There is true prophecy, but thou that calls thyself a prophet, & speaks with thy own will, thy words comes not to pass; therein thy shows thyself a false prophet; & the vials of God must be poured upon that false prophet within ... O friends, your runnings out causeth others to stumble. I charge you by the Lord that you read this amongst the people ...

In his letter, "To Several Friends About Wakefield, " Nayler borrowed language and references from Genesis to Luke in order to encourage Friends to go forward. The pathway from sin through struggle and suffering to salvation is laid out in the Bible. One can find one's place in the story in the Scriptures, and know from that reference where to go forward. He reminded his audience of this, which he believed they already knew. In this one ebullient paragraph the reader can find at least a dozen Scriptural references or partial quotations, from at least five books of the Old Testament and three from the New Testament. Likely there are more than that. The emphasis is on the Old Testament Prophets, Isaiah and Jeremiah, probably Nayler's favorites, and they were to him just as relevant in his own time as they had been in theirs. Prophecy was being fulfilled. Hope and promise were alive and present before their very eyes. They should greet this deliverance with joy and faith, but the ancient risk was just as real now. Those who looked back would be lost now just as surely as in the time of Lot's wife.

> And now take heed of consulting with your old master: hath the Lord been so merciful unto you as that he hath set your faces out of Sodom and Egypt towards the promised Land? Oh take heed of looking back, lest you be taken captive and led back again, and so you come short of redemption, and your faith fail you, and so you come short of the promise; for unbelief cannot enter into the rest. But you, dear Friends, put on resolution, put on strength, be valiant for your freedom, cast off every weight, follow your captain, the Lord Jesus Christ, who, for the joy set before him, endured the cross, despised the shame, and so entered into rest and glory. Take heed of halting between God and the world: what agreement can there be, or what peace while you are married to the world? Your thoughts turn in thither, and you are adulterated from God, who gives you all good things, as so many tokens of his love. Hereby is the broken language brought forth, and you cannot speak the pure language of rest. And while you give way to that in you which leads you back to what is behind you, you keep yourselves in the wilderness and darkness, and lose your way, and know not where you are, grieving the holy Spirit of the Lord which hath appeared unto you to guide you. But O friends! Mind your Guide, and follow him; arise, shine, your light is come, and the glory of the Lord is risen upon you; the night is far spent, the day is at hand, even the day of Zion's deliverance. Arise, come away, all you that love her; come off from the world and worldly things, come into the life, lie no longer in death and dead things. Awake, thou that sleepest, and stand up from the dead, that Christ may give thee light: come forth, come forth of all created things, witness your redemption from the world that you are redeemed from the earth up to God, out of all kindreds, tongues, people and nations, to reign as kings and priests forever, above the world, sin and death, triumphing and treading upon all that you would take captive. This is the day of your deliverance, own it with the loss of all fading pleasures, make it appear to all the world. This is the day you waited for, even the day of your joy, but of the world's sorrow: a day of blackness and gloominess, a day of fear and trouble to them that oppress you, a day when the kingdom of Jesus

Christ shall be exalted and all the kingdoms and powers of the earth shaken, a day wherein the Lord will avenge the power of him that is too strong for you. Rejoice, rejoice, ye meek of the earth; shout for joy ye poor despised ones whom your brethren have trodden upon, and have cast you out, and you have been made their mocking stock for the truth's sake; sing and rejoice, the voice of a king is amongst you, and he will marry you to himself in righteousness, purity, and holiness, and will rejoice over you as a bridegroom over the bride, and you shall be for a crown of glory in the hand of the Lord, and a royal diadem in the hand of your God.[32]

CHAPTER 9

Traveling Ministry in the North

... I am brought much into silence within myself. And a willingness there is to be nothing ...

—James Nayler letter to George Fox, August, 1653

Nayler's advice to his friends at home applied no less to himself on the road in the North, that obedient adherence to one's spiritual calling required patience, faithful expectation, and attention to one's own leading, no one else's. God would do His own work, which would be revealed to the faithful along with the means to take up their own parts.[1] What a challenging exhortation that proved to be. What energy it would take for Nayler himself to follow that discipline. He would need help to keep to his own high standard.

No better source can be found for a sense of where he turned for this spiritual support, or for his intimate personal feelings of friendship, than Nayler's correspondence with George Fox and Margaret Fell during the early years of his prophetic ministry. He had no time or interest, apparently, in writing a personal journal. In fact, to do so could have been inconsistent with his responsibility to God. His divine leading was that he should undertake prophetic ministry. Even his letters to his closest friends, Fox and Fell, were ministerial in nature, and he expected them to minister to him.

In November, 1652 he wrote to Fox, "*Dear brother, my heart is much with thee. Thou art still more near me. I am much refreshed when I hear from thee; the Lord keep thee out of the hand of them who wait for blood. My spirit have been much troubled these two days, yet I am kept subject to his will whose I am, & in his work I desire to be found. Oh my heart, cease not to pray for me that all that would join with the enemy may be kept under & subject, that whatever come I may be found in his will. I stand only in faith . . .*"[2] Nayler was at Appleby when he wrote this, under arrest and awaiting trial, for what crimes he was not even sure he knew. He described the conspiracy of priests and accusers who, during his pre-trial confinement, were encouraging all comers to step forward to testify and bring out additional evidence of transgressions in any places where he and Howgill had been before arriving in Appleby. Though Nayler did not admit to any fear of the power arrayed against him, nevertheless, he pleaded for prayers in his behalf.

Fox would know just exactly what he meant, and not only because Fox had plenty of practical experience with false accusations and jail. Nayler expressed his certainty that Fox and he were guided and protected by God in the same work. It was vitally important that they keep in close touch in the work so as to support each other and keep close to God's leadings. Though Fox was eight years his junior, Nayler ranked him as at least equal, and at times perhaps the earthly leader in the work they shared.

He wrote:

> My dear brother, my heart, I have received thy letter, I rejoice to hear of the increase of truth where thou hast been, amongst my dear ones. . . . We are in the midst of Sodom for envy & wickedness. Dear Brother cease not to pray for me, that I may be kept serviceable to my Father till death. . . . Thou art dear to me, & all thy family (*the Fells*); the mighty God keep you all pure to himself forever. My brother, let me hear from thee. I am refreshed by thy letter . . .[3]

In July, 1653, after his release, he mentioned receipt of another letter from Fox, and requested in a conventional way, "*Dear brother, let me hear from thee, & pray for me . . .*" A few weeks later he asked twice in one letter for Fox to write to him, "*. . . as you are moved*" and, "*. . . as often as may be.*" On the last day of July, 1653, following a lengthy description of his own visits and ministries to several meetings in Westmoreland, Nayler included yet another plea for a letter from Fox, but eased its weight with this poignant acceptance of the separation he felt, "*It is my desire to see my way & be obedient. Let me hear from thee as soon as thou canst conveniently, & how all is with thee, & my dear friends with thee, to all whom I desire to be remembered, with whom I have more communion and fellowship than when I was present in the flesh, for they are near me in my heart without respect of persons, & that which before did draw me out from them in the flesh doth now draw me to abide with them in spirit. Oh how dear is the love of the Lord where it is manifest; dear friends, let nothing take your affection short of it, but grow up to live and abide in his love forever, where there is no separation.*" [4]

Note well in the passage above use of the phrase, "*. . . without respect to persons . . .*" This familiar reference to the Epistle of James, Ch. 2, was used often by Quakers as grounds for their refusal to remove their hats and use conventionally proper forms of respectful address to honor people in high station, such as magistrates in court. It was part of their argument with contemporary society over use of titles, stylish clothing, and any kind of ostentation as a means of separating people by their worth. Here Nayler applied the concept of separation of people in a different, less obvious way. In this correspondence his dear ones are bound by loving friendship certainly, but he seems to recognize as well that they may feel bound by their enthusiasm for the work of ministry and the successes they share. They may feel part of a specially gifted missionary body. Theirs is a joyful affiliation, when they are close enough to share it, and an association, which seems to suffer from distance and separation. Nayler says, no. We are gathered by Scripture into God's way. The closer we stay to that guide and the voice of the spirit within us, the smaller our differences become, until in the perfection of love, there is no difference between us, and no separation. The spiritual companionship into which Nayler would have had friends grow was not affected by distance or place, by their thriving new organization, or by the status of persons who led it. They were all, equally, children of God, bound together in that spirit. They were not so many separate persons, scattered about the country in their own individual lives. They were together in one life.

Although he mentioned recently having been with Fox, still Nayler struggled with his own feeling of isolation. He asked repeatedly for Fox's letters, but only seldom did he mention receiving answers. In addition to the personal and spiritual friendship Nayler once enjoyed, still longed for, but now found less and less forthcoming from Fox, there were practical ministerial needs as well, for which he looked to Fox for assistance. In the same letter cited above, in which Nayler can be seen as passing along a farewell message to those friends around Swarthmoor Hall from whom he was physically distant, he asked Fox for some help in ministry.

> Dear brother I see many got up into words & vain janglings, which lead them out of their conditions. If thou be moved to write anything to friends on this side of the sands in Westmoreland,[5] thou mayest put them in mind of it, for I see a necessity that they be warned of it. Some have lost themselves abroad by it; for minding words neglects the power by which they should grow, & while they think they grow up the simplicity is betrayed.[6]

Consider what Nayler meant by this request to Fox. The problem was too much talk and rhetorical posturing among the attenders of his meetings, too little deeply centered silent worship. A newfound freedom to preach their own testimonies fostered competition for the chance to utter the well-turned phrase. That very freedom obscured the simple truth of the spirit which could be found in silence. If Fox would write to Quakers and seekers in Westmoreland, warning them that simplicity of speech and practice was required to achieve a deepening life of faith, his ministry would carry important weight. For Nayler to speak to this issue was not enough. It was not that Friends needed a central ministerial authority to govern their practice. The need was for an effective elder ministry, in the sense of spiritual guidance from beyond their little congregations. The risk of putting words above simplicity was hard for Nayler to address, as he was at the same time the well-known spiritual leader whom people had gathered to hear. Concerned that his own verbal gifts might lead him astray along with the others, he needed Fox's ministry to help keep his own discipline. Nayler knew he could be as subject to "vain janglings" as any man.

Fox must have been tempted in much the same way in his own meetings. Perhaps he did not see this subtlety behind Nayler's repeated pleas for support, but how could he have missed the obvious in the postscript to the same letter:

> I shall be at a meeting this Monday at Sleagill. Dear heart, pray for me that I may be kept in the power of the Lord & humble before him, that all may be his praise alone to whom it is due; here is great wondering at the work of God & great rage in the priest & some others.

Fox did not see that letter until long after Nayler wrote it. He had troubles of his own in Carlisle, which appear to have been unknown to Nayler at the time. Engaged in a particularly contentious dispute in that city, Fox was jailed the day after Nayler wrote the long letter described above. His incarceration lasted nearly two months, at times in an unspeakably filthy dungeon. His treatment was so harsh and irregular that word of it reached London, and a letter was sent from Parliament to the local authorities expressing concern over their treatment of this religious prisoner. Under the circumstances Fox could not have received and read any mail from Nayler, or responded with letters of his own, until he was released in late September. At that time he returned to Swarthmoor Hall.

In mid-August of 1653, Nayler wrote another letter to Fox, this one including the most poignant and succinct statement of the stress under which he was working and the standard of self-discipline the work required.

> Dear brother, cease not to pray for me, the work is great, & many temptations, & a burden there is upon me; and I am brought much into silence within myself. And a willingness there is to be nothing, that all may be closed up in the will of my Father, & I see it good it should be so.[7]

Provocation called for response, or so it seemed. Whenever he stood up he was apt to be physically abused by ruffians or vilified by local vicars whose livings by tithes he threatened. More and more often he found himself alone among men, answering challenges from all sides, his only partner the voice of the spirit speaking through him. He gave it voice, in local ministry, public speaking, and on paper. On the one hand he met throughout the countryside with the sort of rough farmers and unlettered ministers he had known all his life. On the other hand he was drawn to engage the literate and powerful. Already he had challenged educated clergy in print and had publicly, if obliquely addressed Cromwell on the future of law and government. Much the same could be said of George Fox.

Nayler prayed and asked for Fox and others to stand with him and be his counsel in discernment, knowing that he needed consort and judgment on his utterance, so that he could be sure that what he did say was truly guided by the Spirit. Nayler was becoming famous, and if he proceeded as he was led, there was no way he could prevent that. It was not for him to tone down the power of what he was given to say. Fear of strong reactions could not relieve him of the burden of truthful testimony. Indeed, as the public light shone on him, the burden of his words became heavier, and that burden sometimes was unwanted. If he could, he would withdraw, or so he felt on some days at the least. He could not stop. He could hardly moderate his tone. As a seasoned soldier he knew the battle was already engaged. More to the point, grounded as he was in the Biblical accounts of Prophecy, he could see more and more clearly his place in God's plan. He expressed, ruefully perhaps, his willingness to let go of everything and be truly nothing in the eyes of the Lord, but that did not mean he could indulge in anything like monastic retreat. He was given much more work to do than he could imagine doing without others to share the burden. He called out for Friends' help. Though he knew that in a spiritual sense he was not alone, that God was the guiding Presence, he feared that nearby lurked the devil. Nayler could feel the power of his own utterance closing in around him, as if it were Satan's trap.

His need was seldom answered. In his letters to both Fox and Margaret Fell, Nayler appealed for Fox to write to him, which Fox did on rare occasions; and to come to work with him, which Fox could not often do. After he was freed from Carlisle jail and had spent some time at Swarthmoor hall, Fox went north and then east toward where Nayler was working. Around Strickland in Westmoreland their itineraries came together briefly. Fox very soon turned around and returned to Swarthmoor Hall after finding that warrants for his arrest were still outstanding, and men were abroad in the countryside looking for him.[8] The petitions for Nayler's and Howgill's arrest and trial at the Appleby Assizes had included Fox as well, but by some means he had escaped arrest then. Now, only less than a year later, he must hurry away in order to escape again.

By early 1654 Nayler was opening new territory to Quaker ministry in the north and east, using Anthony Pearson's home, Rampshaw Hall, near the present town of West Auckland as a base. Nayler wrote to Fox in late March[9] from Rampshaw Hall, reporting great attendance at several meetings he had held in the area, including a particularly successful one at nearby Barnard Castle. He noted that a general meeting had been appointed for Easter Tuesday and invited Fox to attend, if only briefly. Fox did attend. He reported in his *Journal* a large meeting at Pearson's house, which the editor dated "about March 1654."[10] Fox would not have made reference to Easter, or any other holiday or feast day by name, but the date is a close match. Easter fell on April 5 in 1654. Nayler had written that after the Easter Tuesday gathering he planned to go toward Tynwater, or Newcastle, just over the county border into Northumberland. Fox may have decided to take up that ministry, because his *Journal* relates going into Northumberland and visiting meetings along the River Tyne between Newcastle and Derwentwater. Nayler mentioned in a letter to Fox one large meeting in Northumberland, but clearly the two men were not traveling together. Nayler continued working hard in Durham, and then he went toward the coast.

He asked Fox and Fell to send others to help, as the work was great and the distances long. More people should visit Northumberland, where he found great interest at the large meeting he attended. He mentioned specifically Francis Howgill, John Audland, and Thomas Goodeaire, all three men he had ministered with not long before. Howgill he knew best, having spent time in Appleby jails with him after they had traveled in Westmoreland together. Howgill was the only one who was Nayler's age. Fox was several years younger. The firebrand John Audland was closer to the ages of Nayler's children. Probably he could not be effective counsel to Nayler, but his energy could be put to work in the grueling task of itinerant ministry, simply getting to the villages and delivering the message, a task rather similar to a modern political campaign as regards the physical demands it placed on the minister. Goodeaire was equally tireless. All three were, like Nayler and Fox, recently hardened by imprisonment. Howgill could have been more important than the others to Nayler. He could have stood with him in the way Fox might have, as a peer, an elder in the spiritual sense, perhaps also an editor and co-author. He was a good writer. But what Nayler needed more than anything else was strength and energy. He wrote to Margaret Fell from Durham in mid-April 1654,[11] however:

> I had hopes that John Audland or some friends would have come; I see not such fruit in any place, but the will of God be done. I desire that friends would deny themselves & come forth while the day is, for the powers of darkness . . . is returned back . . . and none is . . . but myself . . .

He was greatly fatigued. His loneliness and discouragement were palpable.

CHAPTER 10

No Protection Under the Law

. . . for the Punishment of Rogues, Vagabonds, and Sturdy Beggars
—from the title of the law used against itinerant Quakers

Nayler's host and guide to the countryside around Durham was one of the justices from his trial at Appleby, Anthony Pearson. A recently convinced Friend, he described his sudden conversion experience in a letter dated May 9, 1653, only about a month after Nayler's release from Appleby jail. Pearson had visited Judge Fell's home, Swarthmoor Hall:

> . . . but now, alas! I find my work will not abide the fire. . . . Oh! how gracious was the Lord to me in carrying me to Judge Fell's, to see the wonder of His power and wisdom,—a family walking in the fear of the Lord, conversing daily with Him, crucified to the world, and living only to God. I was so confounded, all my knowledge and wisdom became folly . . .[1]

George Fox, James Nayler, and Francis Howgill, Pearson said, knew his condition better than he did himself, and he felt he had made many great errors, not only in the field of religion, but also in his professional responsibility.

> I am afraid lest the orders we made at Appleby, cause some to suffer, who speak from the mouth of the Lord; I heartily wish they were suppressed or recalled.

Pearson was highly placed and respected in civil matters, unusual among Friends at the time. He held office in three counties, according to Fox, and had been one of those who had written to Parliament, alerting the Members to Fox's abuse at Carlisle. Nayler's regard for him was growing, but he still looked to Fox for deep spiritual counsel.

Reporting to Swarthmoor Hall, Nayler described not only his success in reaching large crowds at several meetings near Rampshaw Hall, but also the serious trouble he got into soon after. An overly earnest adolescent boy, convinced by Nayler's ministry, had stood with his sisters against their father. He, a local priest, gathered twelve of his peers, who sought unsuccessfully to bring the young ones back from the Quakers. Frustrated in that effort, one struck the boy, another urged that he be beaten and whipped. That night, overcome by what he understood to be the divine presence within himself, and hearing a voice telling him to get up and go out, the boy followed this direction, but then found nothing more, so he returned to his room. There he was visited by the tempter. He became sure that some spiritual power would protect him from injury. To prove it he plunged his hand into a boiling kettle, holding it there for a quarter of an hour, according to the account Nayler received. The result, of course, was a bad burn. In the morning Nayler was held responsible by an outraged crowd stirred up by the boy's father. Feeling that it was the devil's work, not his own, and that he was protected against harm in this by God, Nayler went out of the house to speak to the crowd. Many more were present than would have gathered to hear him if the boy had not been hurt. Many of those present listened and were convinced, Nayler thought, though the priests were still enraged and sent messengers to London to promote trouble for Nayler and his followers.

In his report to Swarthmore Hall Nayler laid responsibility for this disaster to the devil and his temptation. The priests were mad, cruel, and conspiratorial, but Nayler declared that events were ordered against them, to their torment. Whether he, himself, had any part in misleading the boy, Nayler did not even address. Rather, he was shaken by the intensity of the madness in this place and the power the devil held over so many of the people. He added in a thankful postscript that the boy was recovering well from his burn, which Nayler accounted one of God's wonders.[2]

Despite much help from Pearson, when he went on to the coastal towns and the large market town of Cleveland, Nayler realized that without more help, the effort required of him in this large unfamiliar area was just overwhelming. He began to work his way south toward his home county, Yorkshire. Correspondence with Fox mentioned visiting villages around the periphery of Bradford, only ten miles from Woodkirk, where he had grown up, then Pontefract, a town he knew very well from the war.

We can speculate about why Nayler left Westmoreland and Durham to carry on his ministry in the Yorkshire towns. Perhaps he felt he had outrun his leading in the north after the incident in which the boy was hurt, or after he had struggled alone in towns to the east where he knew no one. In the West Riding of Yorkshire he had friends. William Dewsbury, with whom Nayler had visited with Fox at Stanley, was working around Bradford and Halifax accompanied by Thomas Taylor. Nayler probably knew that they had supported establishment of meetings in those and smaller nearby towns.[3] On the other hand, Nayler also would have known that those communities were as unsettled as the ones he had visited in the North, with respect to religious tolerance under the new Commonwealth. Bradford may have stood out as a place where freedom of conscience did not flourish, where indeed the recent conflict, largely based on religious differences, was not yet over, and he was needed. Whether or not hostility was what he expected, it is what he found. Clearly, Bradford was waiting for Nayler and his party, to handle them roughly when they came. The challenge seemed to restore Nayler's confidence and energize his ministry.

When he entered Bradford from the country towns he had been visiting, Nayler and his companions met with a brutal reception, which gave occasion for a short epistle, addressed to the local ministers, town officers, and residents.[4] This writing stands apart from the more widely published debates with ministers, such as that between Nayler and Higginson in Westmoreland. The Bradford epistle addressed only a local audience, and was probably intended to be posted around the town to be read by and for the members of that community. Since it was not published, the Bradford epistle was not included in Whitehead's 1716 collection of Nayler's writings. It has been overlooked in Nayler's biographies. The letter provides important commentary on political conditions after the war, legal matters affecting Quakers, and the status of women. While many Nayler writings of the period were temperate and persuasively argued, this one is rough, not too closely edited, and presumptive of local knowledge of what happened and who took part. It was downright angry in tone. Still, it was subtle, forceful, and concise writing, full of nuance characteristic of Nayler's intellectual depth.

His account described the following events. He went to a private home, where others were present, and a meeting for worship was held. In the midst of the meeting townspeople, some of whom were drunk and violent, entered the home, accompanied by a constable, and dragged those present out of the house and off to the stocks, where they could be publicly displayed, humiliated, and punished. Along the way the worshippers were beaten and stoned. Blood was shed. Women worshippers were physically and sexually abused. Once they reached the public stocks, Nayler's party was held and further mistreated until responsible officers came to decide what should be done with them. No call was made for magistrates or justices of the peace, but rather members of the clergy took the officers' part. Nayler identified three priests by name, who arrived with a fourth priest, called only, a Cavalier, that is, a Royalist. He had been plotting with the other priests on an arrangement to stir up the crowd against the Quakers. The priests, or ministers, urged the crowd on, while the constable stood by and did nothing to stop the violence and disorder. When the worshippers inquired why they were being held, what laws they had broken, they were told they were held because the ministers wished it so, no other reason. When it became clear that there were too many to be put into the stocks, the worshippers were confined for a time in a nearby private home as if it were a jail. There they were subject to continuing abuse. Again no good answer was given as to why they were held. Finally they were released, but only after the man and woman of the house personally beat them on their way out.

Addressing ministers of the town by name, Robinson, Leake, and Waterhouse, Nayler wrote:

> ... for in your town where the people of God did meet to wait upon the Lord for his salvation now in these troublesome times—in your town we was stoned wicked & beaten & shamefully ... treated by your hearers who, some of them like fed horses in their beastly lusts, shamelessly in the midst of your own Sodomlike abused the women, men's wives, offering uncivil carriage by force with others of our friends reproving was threatened to be hewed to pieces & in our meeting place beaten & threatened, not one of us resisting, & all this not satisfying your envy by your means under the pretense of law was we haled out of the house even while we was at prayer, beaten & our blood shed by drunken men, & violently haled to the stocks, & there commanded to stand until the order came from you what should be done with us, & when your time was, seeing the stocks would not hold us all, we was commanded to be put prisoners into a house & there kept with much rude carriage, beating & threatening; & when some in meekness desired to know by what law you did it, it was answered it was your wills, & you would do it.

More followed. He attacked the ministers on moral, religious, political, and civil law grounds. The young constable was singled out for misinterpreting several laws and exposing himself to financial liability as well. On its surface a diatribe, the epistle was also a subtle expose of subversive disregard for the new Commonwealth, and a fairly learned legal argument for several charges of violation of law. Certain basic facts and details were omitted from the epistle on the apparent assumption that the readers would have a good enough idea what happened and who did the heinous acts. Nayler went to a higher purpose than accusing petty rowdies.

> And now see with that of God in your consciences (which condemneth all such practices) what sort of ministers you are & what fruits you minister forth such as none of Christ's flock was ever found in, & with the Scriptures you are tried and found to be of that generation chief priests who ever stirred up rude people (of their own washing) who knew not God, against the innocent, & see if you exercised a good conscience to God or man herein or done as you would be done by, or been subject to the law of the nation, but in your own wills have acted against it, imprisoning the people of God &commonwealth's friends ...

These victims were not dangerous radical elements. They were law-abiding and Commonwealth law protected them, ensuring the right of peaceable religious meetings.

Nayler went on to say,

> ... you priests was justly taxed with *[accused of]* your plots and prayers against the army & your false prophecies of the ruin of it, & that God would curse it, which we have heard both in England and in Scotland for divers years.

That is, these ministers long had been known Royalist sympathisers. They had been on the wrong side in the civil war in England, and they had supported the exiled Royalist factions in Scotland. Now they were acting in open conspiracy to subvert the laws of the peoples' new Commonwealth.

He singled out Waterhouse as a false accuser of the Quakers as plotters against the peace. If such were true and he could prove it, Nayler said, then Waterhouse was required to go the authorities and charge the offenders, but of course he did not because he had no proof. Waterhouse was falsely stirring up the people in disunity with God. No follower of Christ was he, and furthermore Waterhouse didn't know his Scripture and was preaching falsely from his ignorance.

Robinson was worse. He was a bad example to an already unruly people, by calling the Quakers wicked and telling the people to laugh at them, because the wicked were to be laughed at. That leadership was the devil's work,

> . . . which the saints mourns for, & such unsavory expressions shows thy unsavory spirit from whence they come . . .

Here Nayler generalized his charge against the lot of them, in an accusation that those readers would recognize who understood the purpose of the war just fought, and would know on whose side these priests still stood:

> Nay, you exceed the bishops in this thing who ever had some show of authority to imprison and shed blood by, which they would bring the people of God before. But you have none but your own wills, & though we have none amongst you that will take notice of your unjust dealings, yet know that those expressions and violence are laid up with the Just One to whom alone we look; & our cause he shall plead & doth clear our innocency who is our peace in the floods of ungodliness that would flow over our head, who is blessed forever. And now behold your practice & the practice of your people aforementioned with much more unchristian carriage—swearing, cursing and evil speaking—acted then in your town; & let the wise judge if such a people stand in need of deceiving or can be deceived worse than they are, or have aught to be deceived on but their wickedness. Seeing you accuse us for deceiving them. Nay they are deceived by you; their leaders cause them to err, etc, & their blood is upon you forever who own such begettings under the name of believers. Be ashamed of your fruits; what you have sown is now reaped before the sun, & you are ripe for the sickle of the Lamb's wrath & for the fire. Is such fruits find such a church in Scripture or such a ministry hired or maintained by such a people, or walking in such a way? You call yourselves ministers. Else stop your mouths for shame; your fruits hath made you manifest.

On the face of it this is pure fire and brimstone, a sermon on the rewards sure to be delivered by God against the wicked. Yet in these few lines there is more for sinners than the fire. The first sentence is half indictment and half history lesson. In the old days the bishops were empowered by the force of law to do what local clergy have done today outside the law. When you deal out punishment that should only be done under the law, you act in great peril. God's wrath will follow, surely, but Godly citizens may act as well. Even though today there are none with the courage to stand against you, once there were. Where are the bishops now? Where is Archbishop Laud? Where is the wicked Popish King? Who rose to take them down? Nayler suggested such questions by subtle implication. He did not spell out the answer. He had no such need, for he was in a town that knew him as a soldier, along with others who had stood with him. Perhaps they might again. Imagery of the Lamb's wrathful sickle, the fire, and the threat of chaos that must ensue from this kind of behavior is a favorite Nayler theme, straight out of the Book of Revelation. Like others abroad in England, both Quaker and Fifth Monarchy men, he spoke and wrote as a prophet of the day of judgment.

Here was Nayler on the cusp. Few could express the right place of law in a religious society as subtly as he, and here was an example. Though he would not lead a fight for secular vengeance, he had a clear sense of what he had already fought for, which was a country under God's law. He had just recently reminded Cromwell and the Major Generals what they had fought for and should now uphold. Law did matter to Nayler, as it did to other Quakers. While lecturing the priests on God's law, which they should have known better than their townspeople, now he reminded them that not only had they led their people in disregard for God's laws, but in violation of man's civil law as well. They had no right nor standing to treat people of any faith this way, and the priests should know it.

When he turned to the young constable, his tone changed. He took the role of teacher, for none of the town's leaders had taught the constable how to conduct himself. Charged with enforcing the law, the young fellow had made a mess of his work. Those leaders of the town who put him up to it should have given him some better idea of how to do his job.

> And thou, young man, whom they call constable, who came into our meeting & without the fear of God violently haled us out when we was at prayer & down to the stocks & in thy company, some of our blood was shed by men that was drunk by strong drink, & another drunken man came in scorn, offering strong drink to wash the blood off. Three there was so drunk could scarce speak to be understood nor go upright, & these was not counted offenders by thee nor their teachers, though it was in open street in the midst of your town, but served to make others' sport; & this wickedness is but laughed at as your teachers saith it should be. And thus you follow fools in their folly as you are taught, like priests like people. And at thy command was we kept prisoners, for other officer I know none present, though it was by the priest's order. Now with the light in thy conscience which leads to justice see if thou was executing the law either of God or man when thou put the innocent in prison that were beaten & did not resist, but set drunkards, fighters, and bloodsheders free.

Furthermore, Nayler informed him that there was a law against unlawful imprisonment, which this surely was, which law provided for recompense of the offended parties. The constable could be out a lot of money, if anyone were inclined toward revenge at law, but worry about that next time. Nayler was not after revenge. That was God's affair.

Probably the officers of Bradford hoped to apply the *Act for the Punishment of Rogues, Vagabonds, and Sturdy Beggars*. This old Elizabethan law had long been useful in moving undesirable elements out of towns. Its punishments included whipping, expulsion of the offender to his home parish, or commitment to a house of correction. It was this law which had been used against Nayler at Appleby. He had written against its unchristian practice in "*A Discovery of the First Wisdom . . .*"[5] He knew its provisions well, as must most of the itinerant Quaker ministers, for this law was often used against them. In the Bradford case, however, worshippers were hauled out of a private home. Interruption of public worship was bad enough, but how could people be charged as vagabonds when they were guests in a private home? It was insupportable. To be a vagabond required by definition that no one in the town know the offender, which clearly was not the case with invited guests. Incorrigible and unreformable the Quakers may have been in their zeal to spread the truth, but vagabonds surely they were not.

Connecting what happened to his gathering at Bradford with Royalist sponsored unrest and discontent with the Protectorate, Nayler reminded the Bradford community that civil law held its authority ultimately under Scripture. The rebellion, from its earliest days was identified with Puritan religious reform. The people had removed both King and bishops in favor of freedom of conscience, establishing the current Commonwealth. They ought not now to give back to the Royalists what had been won from them. His argument was subtle, not explicit, but Nayler's purpose could be seen. He did not write simply to rail against more petty abuse of Quakers. Rather he reminded those who had suffered revolution that all the noise they had endured was about the freedom to have, among other things, silence in which to hear the spirit within each person, to be reminded of Scripture, and to reform their ways toward a Godly place in which to live.

In addition, Nayler's epistle emphatically described public, apparently sexual, abuse of women worshippers. While this behavior was nothing new, it was and long remained unusual for a prominent male leader to name the problem as boldly as Nayler did here, albeit in very few words. Those words were chosen for their suggestive implication, ". . . like fed horses . . . beastly lusts . . . shamelessly in the midst of your town . . . Sodomlike . . . abused . . . men's wives" Need he say more? The picture was clear enough to a readership, some of whom had been present, no doubt, and had seen what happened.

The account is puzzling in one respect, however, that none of the Quakers present were mentioned by name. The offending clergy were certainly named, but the victims of all this violence were not identified. Many of them, of course, were residents of the town where these charges would be posted. They would have to continue living there, and to the extent possible, ought to be protected from further abuse. If some of them were women who had been violated in public, all the more reason to keep their names out of the press. These were not common street walkers. They were respectable wives.

One of those wives could well have been Ann Nayler. She lived less than a day's ride from Bradford. At the very least, James must have visited her and their daughters when he was nearby. He was in the vicinity for several weeks. It is quite likely that Ann would have gone to meeting with him on occasion. Indeed, what about their daughters, the eldest of whom was 14 years old at the time?

Nayler and his companions could have brought charges, for all the good that would have done, but he made no such threats. Though he was uncommonly angry, he kept his head, presenting his case with logic and subtlety, however emphatically. His message had to do with redemption, even here. If he seemed to pass lightly over the outrage of abuse of the women, it was not because he considered it any less serious a breach than interruption of worship and violence against those who attended. Crimes against God's law were equally heinous, all of them taken together, or any one such sin taken individually. Nayler's indictment against Bradford encompassed all those who participated or condoned what happened. Both the acts against the worshippers and the allowance of such acts were sinful in his eye. Similarly, the victims, whether men or women, whether stood up in the stocks illegally, or raped, whether unnamed neighbors, or even Ann Nayler, were no greater or lesser prey to the crimes of sinners. In this way, too, God was no respecter of persons. Nayler's prophecy did not admit shades of gray. The burden of his message was equal for all, the consequences of transgression always the same. The Godly life was as if black and white.

CHAPTER 11

The Low State of Morality

... therefore hath Satan kept his seat amongst you who with the light hath often been resisted, so that there was no hope for him openly who now hath prevailed in darkness to such a height of wickedness amongst you ...
—James Nayler, Epistle To Friends about Scalehouse

The first two years of prophecy had brought immediate and tangible results. Fox found "a great people to be gathered." Nayler found the promise he had been given made good every day, that God would always be beside him. Their ministry was attended by more and more people, many of whom were called "convinced." Their congregation was called by some, Children of the Light. Nayler expressed feelings of family love for them in his work. Fox seemed to have acted, and perhaps to have seen himself, as a prophet from the beginning, when he stood atop Pendle Hill and "sounded the day of the Lord." He kept up that sturdy enthusiasm as he continued personally to deliver that message from village to village. So did Nayler. They seem to have had a wonderful time at first, robust in going forward when released from their prisons, careless of their beatings, sure of what they were given to speak out, and secure in giving over self to the Spirit.

The message they delivered, joined by more and more fellow evangelists, was clearly God-sent, at least as they understood their gift. They could only call it the Truth. The name of their movement, Friends (or Friends of the Truth), found in the Gospel of John, became favored over the name used earlier, Children of the Light, found in the Epistles of Paul. Either name connotes discipleship intimately informed by an immediate communication with the Spirit of Christ, a profound concept, no less abstract under one name than the other. In fact, abstraction became part of the problem. Little notice was taken of the distinction between the names, Children and Friends, because of the focus on turning the common public pejorative, Quaker, into some kind of communicable identity, which recognized how the sect were guided by an inward and awesome spiritual power. Beatings and imprisonment, rage from the priests, every manner of legal and extra-legal opposition, while exhausting, provided stepping stones to higher ground. The lineage of the Biblical prophets reached through the ages to these first ministers. Their own experience was like that of the Apostles. For a time, the harder their ministry became, the more certain they could be of its rightness, but they were human. That famous certainty could be their weakness as well, more visible to others than to themselves.

There came a time toward the end of 1654 when Fox could say, the Northern churches were settled, and he could turn toward the south.[1] Joined with him in the work now were some seventy ministers, fulfilling Biblical precedent (Luke, Ch. 10). They spread out to do their work with an energy and endurance that would not be restricted. If the Northern churches were settled, the midlands, the centers of population, the cities, London and Bristol, were not. There they must turn. Yet the great city was so very different from the North. As many as 375,000 people lived in London,[2] although other estimates suggest closer to 200,000.[3] Could a prophet thrive in a place so large and complex, ten or twenty times the size of the next largest settlement by population in all of England? If the devil were at home anywhere in the country, it was in London, with all his powers of temptation and corruption spread around him, glowing and inviting in daylight, seductive in the dark. This was no place for the naive or the weak.

The wise former Justice, Anthony Pearson, wrote to George Fox in July of 1654, eight months before Fox went into the city,

> Oh! That none might come to London, but those who are raised up in the life of Truth, who dwell in the living power of God, whose words may have authority: for there are so many mighty in wisdom to oppose and gainsay, that weak ones will suffer the truth to be trampled on; and there are so many rude savage apprentices and young people and Ranters, that nothing but the power of God can chain them. Dear heart, let none go to London, but in the clear and pure movings of the Spirit of Life; that the blessing may rest upon them. And great is the harvest to be in that city; hundreds are convinced, and thousands wait to see the issue, who have persuasions that it is the Truth.[4]

A great turmoil stirred the countryside as well. Fox was working through Yorkshire, Derbyshire, Lincolnshire, Nottingham, toward his old home near Leicester, and everywhere he found the same sort of excitement and instability, along with the potential, as Pearson observed, for a great harvest. England was ready, whether to be gathered up raw to be turned into a new world, or to be reaped by the tempter's scythe and cast into the fire. Nayler worked much of the same territory and with similar concern for the immediacy of both the opportunity to turn people toward God, and the likelihood that many of those, if not turned, would follow the devil into the flames.

About the time he visited Bradford he wrote on this very concern to the people of Scalehouse, a remote meeting about twenty-five miles to the northwest of Bradford. This place had been a worry to Nayler and other visiting Friends for some time, he said, because of the divisions within its congregation. The way Nayler put it, the devil had got into their midst and was tearing them apart. He warned,

> . . . you . . . have been ready to make party out of the life of God, in words & imaginations, whereby the spirit of life hath been veiled in you & burdened in others, though few of you even yet have laid it to heart: therefore hath Satan kept his seat amongst you who with the light hath often been resisted, so that there was no hope for him openly who now hath prevailed in darkness to such a height of wickedness amongst you as ever yet he could in this generation of the people of God, neither is this laid to heart amongst you, but many of you are puffed up with the world, whispering & slightly talking of the thing, not knowing that the pollution is spreading amongst you & the devil is making havoc in the darkness who when he hath further seated himself amongst you will manifest his power in several other things as he sees his advantage by your several inclinations. Therefore I warn you stand up clear out of the darkness & that you every one in the particular search yourselves & also the whole body, that with the spirit & power of the Lord Jesus that wicked one may be cast out from amongst you & that you henceforth presume not to eat & drink with him but clear yourselves in the presence of the Lord & all his holy ones lest you ease your own damnation & the wrath of the pure God (who cannot endure that unclean one in his presence) break out upon you & he cut you off from himself & all the children of the light . . .[5]

Unlike the Bradford epistle, the Scalehouse message was not an angry diatribe, but more of a warning to family members, offered in a sprit of love. So, too, was a third epistle, To Them of the Independent Society.[6] Though the date is uncertain, this piece suggests that it may have been written for delivery to Nayler's former Woodkirk congregation of Independents. The subtitle reads, "*Some grounds why I deny you to be a church in Christ, though in times of ignorance I walked with you in these things, worshipping I knew not what.*" He did not name Woodkirk or go so far as to mention serving briefly as one of its ministers, as evidence suggests, but he did admit that for a time he was a member among them, for reasons that made little sense to him now. Perhaps in light of his own prior involvement and friendships in the Independents, he did not really unsheath his verbal sword. His criticism was direct, matter of fact, and at the very last paragraph, gently loving, as if it were a letter to the family, explaining why the author felt he had to leave home, and would not come back.

From his earliest adult years at Woodkirk Nayler had struggled toward a moral community, organized under Christ's direction as understood from Scripture. He did not engage this task alone. The struggle had divided his village church from the national church when he was still a boy, and had further divided his local church into its conservative Presbyterian and liberal Independent elements as he became a young man and participated in the split. Eventually Nayler and those who discovered and followed their inward guides toward the Children of the Light divided from their previous alignments, whether Independent or otherwise. Nayler's quest for religious unity took place not only in a local venue, but also simultaneously within a grander struggle for a national moral unity reaching into government, law, economic systems, and all the organizing principles of society. He wrote of this vision in *A Lamentation (by one of England's Prophets) Over the Ruins of this Oppressed Nation*,[7] addressed to the leadership of the country at the time of Cromwell's elevation to Protector under the Instrument of Government, a limited form of constitution for a country which still struggled to emerge from martial law. From Durham in the spring of 1654 he wrote *To The Rulers of This Nation*,[8] again reminding Cromwell, the Council, and Parliament of promises made in the course of revolution for, among other things, freedom of religious conscience, and lifting the burden of tithes. He would find it necessary to address Cromwell again on these subjects, as would Fox and others of the Quaker leadership.

Cromwell, having recently taken hold of the national government, continued to act in ways that prolonged and aggravated factional divisions left over from the rebellion. In the spring of 1653 the Rump Parliament was dismissed. Exercising power in concert with the Governing Council, controlled by army officers, he arranged seating of another Parliament, this one called, pejoratively, the Nominated Parliament. Cromwell had selected acceptable members and dismissed about one hundred others. Predictably, his arrangement failed; the effort toward a republic failed with it. In December Cromwell took up the ill-defined position of Lord Protector, an appointment for life, but short of monarchy. His task, in part, was to hold a strong center between army factions and a new, weakened Parliament, eventually seated the following September. Arrayed against order were elements of confusion originating from all quarters. General Monck was trying to put down another Scottish rebellion. From elsewhere within the army came an assassination plot against Cromwell. The radical Fifth Monarchist movement promoted overthrow of the government in preparation for the imminent Second Coming. Secret cells of Royalists plotted insurrection. Abroad, desperate naval battles were fought, with grave consequences. Victory could end the Dutch war, but defeat would allow invasion of the island of Britain itself. The treasury was, understandably, in ruins. Along with the Royalist threat, which was certainly real, all manner of religious sects raised their voices, among them Baptists of at least two sorts and Quakers. Which, if any, of these were of lasting significance, Cromwell had little time or patience to try to ascertain. Religious toleration was severely restricted, and by late in 1655 local peacekeeping was put into the hands of a committee of the Council, which became known in fear and loathing by the Quakers and others, as "the major generals."

There were those who would make of Cromwell a new King, for monarchy was what they knew, while others wanted rid of the Protector in order to restore legitimate monarchy in the person of Charles II. Cromwell eventually refused the crown for himself, but he ruled with much of the pompous ceremony associated with royalty. Acting with singular decisiveness when he had the backing of the Council, and therefore the army, he could be equally uncertain when caught between Council and Parliament without firm support. Though his course was often

The Low State of Morality 117

unclear, this much was certain. To be a Royalist during the Protectorate was subversive to the new government.

Nevertheless, presence of the Royalist movement was evident in places such as Bradford, where Nayler had taken public notice of it in his epistle, and in England's then third largest city, Bristol,[9] where Royalists openly held control of the civil government. Royalists, though their armies had been defeated, remained a strong presence in society. They constituted an opposition element within the national government as well, where little effort was made to conceal their presence.

In Bristol, another former soldier for Parliament in the civil war, George Bishop, was turning to Quakerism.[10] Formerly a Captain in the New Model Army, closely associated with the high command around Bristol, Bishop had continued working for Cromwell's government as the war wound down. His primary concerns involved developing intelligence information to secure the new Commonwealth against secret Royalist elements, who were allied with supporters in France in the effort to restore Charles II to the throne of the English kingdoms. Having been a successful brewer and merchant, he combined skills of financial acumen and management with military discipline and was also employed in administering sequestration of assets of propertied Royalists after the war. Bishop's reasons for engagement in the War of the Three Kingdoms were not entirely political and economic. Like Nayler, even the pragmatic Bishop was moved in large part by religious objectives. He, too, had aligned with the Independents in favor of religious toleration. He ran for and lost election to Parliament and wore out his welcome in the new national government with his frequently repeated purpose, which was ever to hold Cromwell to their original cause, freedom of conscience.

In Bristol, as in London by 1654, an outpouring of nontraditional religious ministry attracted larger and larger crowds, the sheer size of which sometimes threatened stability in the community. One such group, more vocal than they were numerous, The Fifth Monarchists, did in fact openly advocate uprising and overthrow of all government in preparation for the real restoration as they anticipated it, the Second Coming of Christ, the reestablishment of His kingdom, the Fifth Monarchy, and the last. They saw that the great battles of the end times depicted in Revelation were about to be on them. Fear of the apocalypse was a great motivator to seek salvation. It was a view widely, if not always so literally, appreciated by the religious sects. Returning home to Bristol, somewhere around the time of Nayler's visit to Bradford, George Bishop met with religious radicals of this and other dispositions, most of whom stood, as Bishop did, against the Royalist powers who had retaken Bristol's government affairs after the war. Finding the Fifth Monarchists too radical for his taste, he then joined with the Quakers and soon became active in ministry and publication. Bishop was much like Nayler in background, beliefs, and writing skills. He became a prominent figure in the Quaker community of Bristol, which constituted a significant minority of the population. The two men might have grown into a constructive service together, if they had met sooner and under different circumstances, but as circumstances would have it they only crossed each other's paths in conflict.

Nayler did not turn westward from Bradford to visit Bristol in 1654. He had no leading in that direction. John Audland went there with John Camm and others, attracting both enthusiastic attendance at their meetings, and antagonistic resistance from established clergy and royalist elements. Nayler, although he knew, respected, and had wanted to work with Audland, apparently had no connection with people in the Bristol area as early as 1654. He went in the direction he knew better, eastward toward Pontefract, Chesterfield, and Nottingham, working, as he had around Bradford, from the small, outlying farming settlements eventually toward the market or county towns.

This pattern invites a practical question. How did Nayler, as well as Fox and other itinerant ministers, support themselves in their ministerial work? With all their preaching against ministry for hire, it is impossible to believe that they were paid for their appearances. Nayler did not mention working for money during his travels, though he may have done so. Fox had family money, as well as a portable skill, shoemaking, which he mentioned using to this purpose occasionally.[11] Nayler was a farmer. Though separated from his farm, surely he had the skills to be useful in agricultural work, not to mention his experience with animals. He recorded in his correspondence with Fox and Fell meetings he held at tiny farming villages, such as Thornton and Brighouse near Bradford and Pinxton, Skegby, and Mansfield clustered near Nottingham. In these places he must have been invited to stay as a guest at the homes of people interested in hearing and helping him to spread his message. He would have traveled under the guidance Jesus laid out, as recorded in the Gospel of Luke Ch. 10, 4-7:

> Carry neither purse, nor scrip, nor shoes: and salute no man along the way,
> And into whatsoever house ye enter, first say, Peace be unto this house,
> And if the son of peace be there, your peace shall rest upon it; if not it shall turn to you again.
> And in the same house remain, eating and drinking such things as they give:
> For the labourer is worthy of his hire. Go not from house to house.

Such a ministry would not have taken much money. He may have behaved as any normal guest between meetings, pitching in to help around the house or farm as needed. Or, he may have been welcomed for his ministry, and that was labor enough. In this way, he could have progressed from place to place with introductions from one family to another. As his reputation spread around the places where he gathered meetings, so would his welcome. As he railed against ministers who accepted payment for uttering God's word, he would have lived his own ministerial life by the plain Scriptural alternative.

When he went from the Bradford area toward Pontefract, Nayler was following a familiar path, well-known from his experience during the war. In addition, the town, though smaller and more distant than Bradford or Wakefield, had an ancient church connection to the area between Wakefield and Bradford, including Woodkirk. For generations Woodkirk, along with other nearby churches and parishes had come under the Deanery of Pontefract in regional Church of England administration. Gatherings of Quakers in the area formed loosely from personal acquaintanceship from parish to parish along similar geographical lines. Later, meetings connected with their neighbors and organized more formally along similar lines.

Progressing southward from Yorkshire, Nayler's path and Fox's crossed in the vicinity of Chesterfield, and perhaps at several other points. Nayler wrote to Fox about 7 November, 1654[12] asking for a location at which they could meet the following week. Each mentioned in correspondence, or later journal entries in Fox's case, vigorous ministry in locations from the border of Yorkshire toward the eastern coast near Holderness and into Derbyshire and the Nottingham area, with visits and meetings in late 1654 or early 1655 at a number of towns along the way, including Balby, Skegby, and Chesterfield. Neither man mentioned that the other traveled with him, and they may not have been together very often. They did, however, cover much of the same ground during the same period, and on at least a couple of occasions they did meet in the course of their work.

Nayler visited Chesterfield more than once after leaving Bradford and Pontefract. He began a correspondence with ministers there by writing a letter on December 20, 1654, taking them to task for allowing without reproof the rustic entertainment of bull-baiting. In this popular sport, usually accompanied by lewdness and drunken brawls, a beast was tied to a ring embedded in the ground in the market square, where it was tormented by dogs and men. The game had long been assailed by conservative Puritans, but at the same time it was allowed as an acceptable and harmless entertainment in farm country. An excellent example of a bull-baiting ring is still visible in the pavement of the market square at Appleby, just in front of the Moot Hall, where Nayler's trial was held. He could have witnessed the sport as well in almost any other market town he visited. The clergy at Chesterfield, he charged, while bound to be teachers of divine peace, instead allowed their parishioners to mistreat God's creatures and each other, promoting violence and the seeds of war. His letter of reprimand drew bitter response. The vicar, John Billingsley, publicly declared that Nayler ought to be hanged for such an affront to the clergy, and he urged seriously that this be done. Failing that, he invited Nayler to a public dispute on a list of provocative questions centered on commonly argued differences with Quakers. The battle was joined, running on into several exchanges of public letters between Nayler and Billingsley, who was joined in the invitation to debate by about twenty of his peers, by Nayler's account. The exchange was printed and published in London in 1655, one of the early battles of the Pamphlet Wars.[13]

The Chesterfield dispute provides an important insight into Nayler's decision process in his ministry. He described becoming aware of the bull-baiting by way of a commotion outside the house where he was staying. Alerted by noise and profanity, he did not need to go outside to see what was going on; he knew it was a bull-baiting.

> ... whereat being much troubled in spirit I waited to know the will of God, what he would have me do; whether I should go and declare against their ungodly practice. But after I had waited a while I was moved to write him that is called their teacher and was showed that I must lay the thing upon him, being the cause why the people knew no better but perish under him for want of knowledge ...

The obvious response, addressing the rowdy, probably drunken crowd, exhorting them to correct their behavior, was not the right one. Nayler viewed them as innocents, ill-served by their clergy, as the people of Bradford had been. The problem lay with the priest, who had failed in his responsibility to teach them to follow God's way in the world. What would God have Nayler do with that person? Write a rather simple letter? That might have seemed at first to be the least effective response, but it opened a hornet's nest, and much more came out of it than an address on lax teaching about profane sports. The process Nayler took to his action was routine, and modern Friends will not find anything remarkable in it. One notable feature, however, is the fact that Nayler described the process in a public writing. Seeking spiritual guidance, "the will of God," was not uncommon in the 17th century, either among Quakers, or people of many other religious traditions. It was uncommon to write out the process so clearly, revealing to readers how a prominent Quaker worked within his own life. More important than that example is the fact that here at the end of 1654, only months before he moved into the spiritual maelstrom of London and became caught up in its intensity, it was Nayler's practice to pause, center into his spiritual guidance, and seek God's will before taking his next step. In reading of his misfortunes less than two years later we may look for something like it again and wonder if the practice still held.

From Chesterfield, Nayler went to nearby Nottingham, an important county town. He sent for Rice (or Rhys) Jones to visit him. Nayler knew of Jones by reputation, no doubt from Fox, but they had not met before. An early respondent to Fox's ministry, Jones was counted a Quaker, but he disagreed with Fox and Nayler in significant and public ways. To him, the historical Jesus was not the divine Christ. The apostles had suffered spiritually, but not necessarily physically. Furthermore, it was not necessary that Friends lead lives of simplicity in material ways.[14] Fox named Jones and his followers, Proud Quakers, and for years after their first meeting in 1651, he and Jones were at odds. Fox had met with Jones recently as well. Jones had been sending papers attacking Fox to many local communities, and though in his *Journal*, written later, Fox dismissed him as "false prophet,"[15] he had answered

The Low State of Morality 121

Jones in print at the time. After their Nottingham meeting Nayler reported to Fox[16] a discussion of not much consequence. Jones was confused, easily persuaded, unsure of his own argument or the logic of his assertions.

Nayler apparently thought that Jones and his followers, if any, were unworthy of the kind of arguments in print that he was having with the ministers. He did not mention Rhys Jones again, but instead continued in the public arena, answering challenges against the Quakers from prominent and respected learned clergy. The lifting of access to a free press in the early 1640s, a product of the overthrow of the monarchy for which Nayler had fought, expanded the opportunity of ministry into written as well as spoken levels of communication. Quakers used the easy publication of books and pamphlets as an effective way to spread the news of their discovery of the personal, inward guidance of the Light of Christ. Print on a page lasted and circulated in ways that spoken testimony could not, but publications also invited and fueled challenge from opponents with equal access to the press. Everything in print, it seemed, became a volley in a battle with an array of differing churchmen. Nayler wrote dozens of such exchanges over the few years between his own epiphany and his disgrace in 1656, contributing to "almost one in five of all Quaker publications between 1652 and 1656 . . ."[17] Many of these were laboriously constructed theological papers founded in dispute with ministers from both the established church and those from other substantial nonconformist denominations, such as the Independents and the Baptists. Pamphlet disputes were a regular feature of religious life. Tiresome to read, sometimes shockingly rude and abusive, these works can be studied for the points of theological difference between the national church, the sects, the Baptists, Independents, and Quakers. Fortunately the bookseller Thomason acquired and preserved everything of this nature that he could find, leaving what are now known as The Thomason Tracts, one of the most valuable historical collections of this period. Nayler, Fox, Higginson, Baxter, are all represented.

Public morality was at such a low state that it seemed necessary to address its condition headlong and at the source. While the Quakers were accustomed to go into the churches, they now had to go beyond the parish clergy to the learned leadership and take on those who were respected for their writing and rhetoric and had standing in the city. This part of the campaign was engaged in late 1654, and from there widened well into the time when Nayler was established in London, a period of about two years. There is no evidence that Fox ever assigned the pamphlet controversy to Nayler, or that they had any agreement between them as to who should undertake it. Neither is there any reference in Nayler's writing that he undertook this work, as he did his first ministry, because of a sense of leading delivered to him inwardly as a spiritual experience. It may well be that as the controversies grew and multiplied, they carried Nayler along without any deep consideration on his part of what he was doing.

To suggest that Nayler was now above the endless fray with lesser lights in the countryside would be an overstatement. Men like Rhys Jones, an early disputant with Fox who became a tavern-keeper,[18] John Billingsley, a local pastor in Chesterfield who condoned bull-baiting, and four clergy petty-tyrants in Bradford who harbored left-over attachments to the old King's prejudices, had been easy enough for Nayler to uncover before their congregants, surely. He could have gone on with such a ministry and found no end to it, but the one great city in all England was ever nearer physically, and ever more attractive of his attention. What is missing in his removal from the countryside and his refocusing on that prodigious task in the city, is any account of what spiritual experience turned him to go there. We have at least a few allusions in his letters to spiritual leadings to visit this place or that, but we find no mention of a spiritual leading toward London.

CHAPTER 12

Quakers in London

... the work of wickedness is set on foot and not restrained ...
—James Nayler, Letter to Margaret Fell, July, 1655

Quaker ministry in London was not introduced by George Fox in person, or by any of the well-known men engaged in Friends evangelism in the North. According to an account by William Crouch, a contemporary of Fox and an early host of Friends meetings in the London area, the first ministry in the city and its close environs was carried out by two women, only one of whose names he could remember when he wrote his account decades later.[1] Isabel Buttery came from Yorkshire where she probably knew of Nayler and had become convinced after meeting Amor Stoddard, a captain in Parliament's army. He appears to have served with Nayler in Lambert's cavalry and laid down his arms about the time Nayler did.[2] He had first met Fox as early as 1648.[3] In early 1654, Isabel Buttery and her forgotten companion received copies from Stoddard of a Fox epistle, *To All Who Would Know the Way to the Kingdom,"* and began distributing them around the outskirts of London, accompanied by invitations to meetings. Their ministry was productive of a growing attendance at meetings held at the homes of two brothers named Dring, who lived near, but outside, the walled limits of London city.

Buttery may have shared the connections which facilitated publication in London of tracts by Fox, Nayler and other early Quakers. The publisher of these works was Giles Calvert, who issued not only religious tracts, such as those by Quakers, but also works of political and social radicals, including Lilburne, the Leveller and Winstanley, the Digger. Thomas Aldam, one of those Quakers imprisoned early on in York, took up an active sponsorship of Quaker writing and publishing even from jail, and was frequently in touch with Fox and Fell over getting Quaker works into print and distributed. He was acquainted, through Amor Stoddard, with Giles Calvert, and paid for some of the early publications.[4] Margaret Fell sent some of Nayler's writings, as well as others, to London with her husband, Judge Fell, to be published by Calvert. Included were "*Saul's Errand to Damascus . . .*" and "*Several Petitions Answered.*" Published in 1653, these works by Nayler were among the earliest Quaker writings to be circulated in London.[5] Another publisher who favored

Quaker works after the London ministry had begun was Thomas Simmonds, who was related by marriage to Calvert. Calvert's sister was Simmonds's wife, Martha, who was to be indicted along with James Nayler for blasphemy in their reenactment at Bristol in 1656 of Jesus's entry into Jerusalem. By that time she, too, had some published writing to her credit. It is not a great leap of conjecture to suggest that Martha Simmonds and Isabel Buttery were acquainted, and that through the efforts of Buttery and others to assist in the publication of Quaker tracts by her brother, Giles Calvert, Martha Simmonds first encountered Nayler in his written works.

Soon, Fox did arrive in London, though not entirely by his own plan or choice. Fox was in Leicestershire in early 1655, gathering large meetings and confronting many whom he called Ranters. Oliver Cromwell had at the same time some serious concerns about possible subversion of his government and threats to his own person. These threats came not only from Royalists, but also from within the army itself, in particular from its long-established Leveller elements. A meeting at London in late 1654 was attended by prominent Quakers, along with Levellers and a Fifth Monarchy leader. Suspicion grew that the meeting involved a possible plot against the government and Cromwell himself. Leadership of those gathered included John Wildman, a radical Leveller theorist, and Robert Overton, an army officer and Fifth Monarchy man formerly close to Cromwell but recently turned publicly against him.[6] Quakers involved included Anthony Pearson and George Bishop. The publisher of religious and radical tracts, Giles Calvert, was also present. George Fox was elsewhere, but he had been a guest in Overton's home only a couple of years earlier. He and other Friends who had associated with the Leveller and Fifth Monarchy leaders became suspect themselves in a wide investigation into security matters of great importance. Soon after the London meeting, in January and February, 1655 Quakers including Fox, Camm, Aldam, Farnsworth, Burrough, Audland, Howgill, and again the publisher, Calvert, but not including Nayler, met at Swannington with attention to organizational matters and planning for extending the ministry into London. An army intelligence report brought attention to the gathering. Quakers intending to challenge the new government to improve toleration of dissidents now came under scrutiny for a potentially dangerous alignment with radicals threatening to Cromwell's new Protectorate. On the face of it, such a concern did not grow out of far-fetched speculation.[7] Overton and Wildman were soon arrested and locked up in the Tower, under suspicion of plotting subversion.

It is significant that Nayler was not among the Quakers attending the meetings in which army officers suspected of radical intent were present. He certainly had a wide acquaintance within the army, which he gained from actual participation in military affairs, unlike Fox, who had become acquainted with his army contacts outside of any military service. The fact that Fox did not involve Nayler in meetings with army men he knew suggests strongly that Nayler may not have been friendly with the officers Fox found worthwhile in his efforts, and that Nayler was not in accord with the Leveller agenda that apparently attracted Fox. Nayler had rejected assertions that he was associated with Levellers when questioned on the subject at Appleby, and he would do so again in his London trial. His disinterest in Leveller politics seems clear and consistent.

After the Swannington meeting a Colonel Hacker arrived at Whetstone, near Leicester, to take Fox into custody. Fox's traveling companion, Alexander Parker, insisted on staying with him, so the Colonel respectfully but firmly escorted them both to London.[8] In this way Fox entered the city for the first time in his adult career. He had been in London when he was wandering in search of his spiritual course as a very young man but he had not been back to the city since.

Understanding that Cromwell may have been unclear about the Friends' goals with respect to the government, immediately on his arrival in London Fox sent the Protector a letter, urging him to live in the spirit of peace. Cromwell responded promptly, calling Fox to meet with him, but first directing him to put in writing a denial of any violent intentions on the part of Friends. Fox responded with one of the early iterations of what has come to be known as the Quaker Peace Testimony. Cromwell conducted his own inquiry into Fox's and his followers' intentions. According to Fox their meeting was cordial and relaxed. Cromwell found Fox was not a threat and released him without further restrictions.[9]

The Protector had met earlier with Francis Howgill and John Camm who had traveled to London to petition for relief of religious persecution. Howgill returned to London in July, 1654 accompanied by Edward Burrough, sixteen years his junior but already a powerful minister, the most articulate and energetic, perhaps, of all the earliest Friends. Together they undertook to entrench and stabilize Quaker ministry in the greatest city of England.

Burrough and Howgill could not manage the London ministry by themselves. The two men wrote to Margaret Fell:

> We have three meetings or more every week, very large, more than any place will contain, . . . which we can conveniently meet in. Many of all sorts come to us, and many of all sects are convinced—yea, hundreds do believe. . . . Many begin to consider us, and think there is something in it more than bare notion; at the first, they looked upon it to be no more: but it sinks deep inward in many; for to that we speak, which brings us in remembrance when they see us not.[10]

They called for help, and much help came, but for a time it seemed no one stayed very long. In a letter to Margaret Fell in the spring of 1655, is this accounting of the Friends who visited London briefly and moved on to other places. Fox, Parker, and Lancaster were gone away to Bedfordshire, Cleaton and Bond toward Norwich and Suffolk, Stubbs and Caton toward Dover, Halhead and Salthouse toward Plymouth, Audland and Camm toward Bristol, and the sturdy Hubberthorne was in prison. Burrough and Howgill held on, preaching the message of Christ come to teach His people, addressing a fast-growing London audience, sometimes helped by Friends passing through and sometimes without their support in leading new meetings. So many people came to hear them that Friends acquired part of a property called The Bull and Mouth, an inn or tavern with a hall that could hold a thousand people. "The great place," as Howgill and Burrough called it, was always nearly full, and the meetings were often disrupted by rowdy elements who created havoc and pulled them down from their platform. They arranged meetings divided among several locations, some large venues for morning meetings, smaller gatherings at private homes in the afternoons and evenings, and still the numbers grew, and people were convinced.[11]

At least one writer has suggested that the reason Nayler came to London was to help Burrough and Howgill with their burden of ministry.[12] Many of those listed above as having been in London and then gone out to other towns could not, for the time being, come back to London if they would. They were in jail. Letters from Parker and Howgill to Fell, dated in May, 1655 list several Friends who were incarcerated.[13] Some of them showed up again in a short time, so their sentences were light, but nonetheless, the threat of jail hung over them all.

Fox himself did not stay in one place for very long, but he did come to join in the London ministry several times. He and Nayler spoke at the Bull and Mouth, where according to Burrough and Howgill, Fox had held forth alone earlier and had hardly been able to make himself heard over the din. Fox was certainly not regarded as reticent or soft-spoken before crowds. One wonders how anyone could have managed an audience of a thousand in a place like that. Worship in the manner of Quakers today is characterized by silent waiting for the working of the inner voice of the spirit, but surely there could not have been much quiet centering at the Bull and Mouth. To hold the crowd's attention must have taken inspired, loud, and probably insistent testimony. How different it was from the house meetings held in sober farming villages, where quiet was as much an ambient state as noise was in the city.

The Quaker message that there was in each person an accessible presence of Christ, what they called a seed or an inner light, was received with such enthusiasm in part because it spoke to the an ideal of responsible perfectibility that could govern a society near the edge of chaos. But the message could be twisted to serve those chaotic contributors to 17th Century life as well. The belief in a personal, unmediated experience of the Divine within oneself was an attractive idea to many people, who found in it an opposite motivation to that preached by the Quakers. While the followers of Fox and Nayler were led toward liberation of the Godly spirit within from the false constraints of prideful self-identity, others found their way, through claims of personal divinity, to another kind of liberation, that of the self from the constraints of an unwanted adherence to strictly limited morality. God's presence within them was a notion they found easy to accept, because it seemed to mean that they were, by nature, divine in all their natural behavior. Carnality and sin were vindicated, for the divine presence was without sin. Redemption, if indeed it were necessary at all, was here and now, so they need not fear Satan or being held to account in the end times. Certainly they could dismiss concern about election to walk on the streets of Heaven.

These were the Ranters. Notwithstanding that modern historians have questioned whether such a random and ill-defined sect could even be said to have existed,[14] there can be no doubt that individuals were identified as Ranters by their contemporaries. According to usage of both their Quaker neighbors and much of the rest of Puritan society, Ranter was a term as ill-defined and pejorative as the name Quaker, but the Quaker leaders saw and identified Ranters all around them. Rhys Jones "developed Ranting tendencies."[15] Ranters heckled Fox and Nayler all through the Midlands, and London was full of them. Anthony Pearson warned in his early letter from London that the city held three types dangerous to any but the strongest Quaker ministers. They were the smart, sophisticated, and quick urbane wits, skilled in debate; the rash, impressionable, energetic young people; and the Ranters. Of all of them, he seemed to feel the Ranters presented the greatest threat.

Nayler gave them short shrift. While his personal ministerial meetings had to address the obstreperous part of the population, and he possessed the energy and skills to do that effectively, his attention and best efforts were directed at a higher level. Little survives in the way of accounts of his meetings with the London crowds. As is the case with all the Friends ministers, his words and conduct of the meetings very seldom were recorded. We have no account of him before a crowd at the Bull and Mouth, for example. We do have accounts of Nayler meeting with prominent citizens in several situations, some of which were organized debates on religion, as with well known Baptists, a sect well established among the educated and gentry classes. On other occasions Nayler met on what seem to be social occasions with people of high station. He described one such event in a letter to Margaret Fell dated November, 1655.[16]

> I had a meeting at a house called Lady Darcy's; many were there from the Court, some called lords (as it is said,) divers ladies, divers officers of the army, some of the ... priests of the city, how many I know not ... Two or three of Henry Vane's brethren were there all the while, and he himself kept behind [*a dividing screen*], came after all was ended: he is very loving to Friends, but drunk with imaginations.

Nayler knew, and assumed Margaret Fell would know, that this was Henry Vane, the younger. His father, of the same name, had died recently. Lady Darcy was the widow, mother of the Henry Vane Nayler met. She was of a long noble lineage, probably wealthy in her own right, and certainly independent. She not only hosted this prominent Quaker in her own home, and invited him to debate Baptist ministers there, but also she was among those who visited the millennialist Anna Trapnel, who issued mystical prophecies sympathetic to the Fifth Monarchists from her sickbed in Whitehall in 1654. Margaret Fell's husband, Judge Fell, was also present at some of those meetings, accompanied by William Sydenham, who would be one of the few who would speak in Nayler's favor two years later at his trial before Parliament for Blasphemy.[17]

Vane, the elder, Lady Darcy's husband, had been King Charles I's secretary of state, among other more lucrative patronage offices, but changed his allegiance before the King was deposed. Vane, Sr. became a supporter of Parliament's cause. His son achieved much greater prominence in government. Having been part of the Puritan emigration to Massachusetts for freedom of conscience, he had briefly served as governor of that colony. Returning he took up the cause against the King in Parliament, joined with Cromwell to introduce legislation eliminating the episcopacy, and supported elimination of the state church. Henry Vane, the younger, led Parliament's delegation to the Scots which negotiated their alliance and made possible Parliament's victory in the civil war. More recently, as Navy secretary he had supported the naval defeat of Holland.

As an administrative official and Member of Parliament, he had met and worked with George Bishop, before Bishop was a Quaker, to bring the city of Bristol into the Commonwealth fold after the war, reconciling Royalist and revolutionary factions.[18] Lately, however, he had opposed Cromwell in the restructuring of the republic, advocating the primacy of Parliament over the army, whereas Cromwell's favor leaned toward the military. They split in 1653. It was over this point, too, that the Levellers clashed with the Protectorate, and so to some in power, Vane was among the liberal elements suspected of subverting Cromwell's government. While his prominent friends and his unblemished record defended him against harassment, nevertheless he was watched and reported on. Hence his concealment behind a screen as he listened to Nayler at Lady Darcy's soiree. By 1656 he would be imprisoned briefly for opposing Cromwell in writing.

Vane was also known for his religious essays. The acerbic historian, Clarendon, wrote "His religious writings, apart from his constant devotion to toleration and dislike of a state church, are exceedingly obscure both in style and matter. While his enthusiasm and fanaticism in speculative doctrine combine curiously, but not perhaps incongruously, with his exceptional sagacity and shrewdness in political affairs . . ."[19] We can see why Vane would have been interested in Nayler, but we cannot tell whether Nayler knew Vane's religious principles, or indeed, if anyone did. It is clear that Nayler took more than passing interest in the man, and was not alone in his judgment about Vane's active imagination. It is also clear from this encounter that Nayler had at least occasional access to some of the most prominent people in London, in particular those on the liberal or progressive edge of society, to many of whom new religions, such as Quakerism and millennialism held a kind of exotic fascination and must have been the subject of much high-sounding conversation. Perhaps it would be revealing to see the other names on Lady Darcy's guest list, and to consider who among them Nayler would have found promising candidates for convincement to the Truth.

His report to Margaret Fell of the meeting at Lady Darcy's also suggests a hint of levity, unusual amidst all the grave and righteous reports of ministry that flowed back and forth in Quaker correspondence. Whereas Fox was inclined to be a contentious, even difficult guest in social contexts, Nayler seems to have had a more gentle style of discourse, at least until he was rudely engaged. Each man, in his way, seemed clearly to enjoy the verbal sparring. Each man also liked to report his successes with a crowd, or with someone who was swept into convincement by his ministry. These reports were not entirely self-congratulatory. They were a way of recording names of those who might become noteworthy members of the movement. Often those touched by the ministry made a corresponding entry in their own diary records.

One of Nayler's most loyal friendships developed out of a similar social encounter in London about this same time. Rebecca Travers, a well educated woman in her forties, met Nayler at gatherings in which he debated respected Baptist ministers. She had been seeking a spiritual home for some time, including recent study of Baptist teaching. Nayler, however, turned her toward Quakers, and she wanted very much to learn more. She reported sitting beside him at dinner and asking probing questions. Some modern readers of her account have taken Nayler's response as patronizing toward women generally. Travers apparently took him at his word, which came explicitly from the Genesis account of mankind's Fall from Grace. (Genesis 2:17) He put his hand on Rebecca's and said, *"Feed not on knowledge, it is as truly forbidden to thee as ever it was to Eve: it is good to look upon, but not to feed on: for who feeds on knowledge dies to the innocent life."*[20] Travers understood Nayler's ministry, according to Whiting, to mean that the only way through toward God's will was by way of humble denial of self.

This was in 1656. Nayler had been in London for some time, and he was no more innocent than anyone else. All sorts of distraction swirled about in the city, much of it luring him toward challenges to his ministerial skills or debating gifts that he found hard to resist. Fox worried, he recorded in his *Journal* decades later, about Nayler's situation, about something he thought he saw in Nayler's eyes when they were together. Fox wrote with the benefit of hindsight. In the mid-1650s, while Nayler was under great stress in London, so, doubtless, was Fox, but his *Journal* records little of this. In what way the two might have helped each other to cope with their temptations at the time is a deep question. Nayler had asked many times before for Fox's prayerful support. His letters almost all contained such pleas. Whether he did so in London goes unrecorded, just as we have no record of Fox asking for or feeling upheld by any prayers of Nayler for him.

The task of ministry on an urban, indeed on a national level, was far greater than simple evangelical preaching to country meetings, for the obvious reason of the great size of the gatherings, but also because of the wider requirement of public debate and writings in support of theological tenets and practices still new and formative. Nor were these disputes confined to printed tracts. Much of the debate was carried on in public meetings before enthusiastic and vocal crowds. Fox, Nayler, and the Quaker ministry described faith and practice as they understood it to be revealed not only in Scripture, but in personal, inner experience. Anyone interested in paying attention to Scripture and to their own inward spiritual guidance could find the same Life within themselves, with no need for paid clergy to provide the words. (The capitalization follows Nayler's practice with these words.) The professional clergy, however, fought to hold their ground, demanding more answers from these interlopers from the North, to whom so many of their own congregants went off to listen. Whether by choice or not, their sometimes strident accusations of bad faith and theological ineptitude had to be answered if the Quakers were not to be made foolish in the public eye. Quaker ministry became, for a time, as much about answering debating questions as it was about setting out a form of Scriptural interpretation, beliefs, and personal practices of faith.

Nayler excelled as much in this rough debate as he did in vocal ministry and writing tracts. He was well begun in all these forms before he arrived in London. His notoriety preceded him into the city. Certainly Burrough and Howgill were glad to see him. They seem to have taken his arrival as their relief. As soon as he was settled into the work, the two men who had held the ministry together from the start left London as others had done before them. They departed for Ireland, leaving Nayler to carry on without much help. In their correspondence with Margaret Fell reporting conditions in London, they had named the same problem that had undermined Nayler's efforts from the earliest days after his release from Appleby jail, that is, isolation from the support and intimacy of his closest friends and colleagues in the faith. The work of ministering to those they called "the rude multitude" took up almost all the time and energy Burrough and Howgill had. Necessarily they divided their efforts, one going to this huge meeting, the other to a similar gathering in another part of the city. Howgill put it this way, near the end of 1654, "... *our burthen is great, we cannot get any separation* [from] *the multitude, and so Friends do not much know one another and we cannot conveniently get any place to meet in, that Friends may sit down.*"[21] Ironically, Nayler had last enjoyed the freedom of prolonged intimate time with a peer when he was confined at Appleby with Howgill, but not since he was released back into the world. Once he settled into London, this absence opened the space in his heart for the tempter, whom he called, The Adversary, to begin tearing him apart.

CHAPTER 13

Enter the Adversary, Nayler Weakens

... for the Cross is to the carnal, wild, heady, brutish nature in you ...
—James Nayler, A Discovery of the First Wisdom ...

In the summer of 1656 Nayler's prophetic course took him down from the station of shining example and guide for his religious society into the mire of disunity. The meaning of the symbolic act he undertook, beginning in that season, took years to clarify in his own eyes, and even longer in the understanding of his peers in the faith. Here began Nayler's trial by humiliation, his muddy road toward crucifixion.

He had written before he ever came to London:

> And all those enemies that will not that Christ should reign over them, bring them before the judges that they may be slain, even upon that cross that is daily to be taken up, for the cross is to the carnal, wild, heady, brutish nature in you, which lies above the seed of God in you, and oppresseth the pure. Now giving this up to be crucified makes way for that which is pure to arise ...[1]

It was in the nature of London, the city in which he worked, to be carnal and brutish. From its population stepped a class of admirers rightly described as wild and heady. The adulation of some of his followers overtook him during that summer, offering a variety of temptations. His closest supporters in London were the handmaidens of the devil's own scheme of ego and pride, that which Nayler had written years before was to be given up daily for crucifixion, for it would not simply be laid aside. This he knew, but did not yet truly understand by experience. He was about to learn what such sacrifice meant. The London ministry was his cross.

In January of 1656 George Fox, who had briefly joined with Nayler in ministry to large crowds in London, was imprisoned in Launceston, Cornwall for vagrancy and miscellaneous charges intended to interrupt his preaching in that district. At first confined in a relatively decent space, Fox was an uncooperative prisoner. Soon he was moved to another part of the jail and locked up in one of the most dire holes he had so far had to endure. He was left there for some months, much of the time in darkness with his feet fouled with the urine and stinking excrement that flooded the floor. He wrote that he thought the stuff had been there for years. Unstoppable, Fox maintained contact with and directed Quaker affairs by way of visitors who came out from London and a secretary or amanuensis who assisted with his correspondence.[2]

During that spring, feeling overwhelmed by the ministerial work in London, Nayler wrote to Burrough and Howgill in Ireland, appealing for help. Burrough arrived in April. Howgill and Hubberthorne soon followed.

In early May Nayler wrote an epistle to Friends at Lincoln, which contained this advice "*. . . take heed that ye be not shaken in your Minds at the appearance of Satan's Wiles and Temptation, who must be revealed (at the Brightness of the Lamb's Appearance) . . .*"[3] He saw the two figures, of evil and salvation, working in the same space, the one to tempt and deceive the weak from a position both concealed and close at hand, the other to nurture and redeem them, revealing the devil's work by shining on it the bright light of Truth. That was only one, poignant example of his many writings during the period, to which could be added dozens of meetings at which he spoke or was supportive. Demands on his energies continued to grow, and as shown by the address of this epistle, they came not only from London, but from elsewhere in the country. His colleagues were similarly burdened. Exhaustion was evident in Howgill's letter to Margaret Fell, written after he and Burrough had returned from Ireland at Nayler's urging and taken up their ministry again. Howgill wrote:

> We have about twenty meetings in a week in this city; and ten or twenty miles about, great desires; and if we can, we go out; but we cannot stay: great is our care. . . . E.B. salutes thee—he is almost spent: few know our condition.[4]

E.B. was his colleague, Edward Burrough, seventeen years younger than Nayler, probably just as talented, relatively unattached to family and property, also a gifted writer, and though inexperienced, as Nayler was experienced in war, a born fighter for a cause. Burrough, at the age of 22, was almost spent. Did Nayler still appear robust by comparison, having kept in London, while Burrough and Howgill had endured the trials of Ireland together? Or was Nayler's fatigue already so well known that Howgill, who was about Nayler's age, could only add his own experience as endorsement to Burrough's with their accounts of London's demands?

Fox was kept informed and found reason to respond from his prison, asking Nayler to go to Yorkshire for a short visit.[5] He could find time during the trip to visit his wife and children. Nayler went on this mission, but he didn't stay long, as there was much to be done in London. He wrote from Wakefield "*To All Friends in London*" that while he was away they were very much in his mind,

> . . . take heed to your spirits, and keep your Dominion in the Life of Christ; and therein feel your authority over all that would shake off the Yoak, and can-

not Joy in the Cross. Hearken not to unprofitable things, neither lend an Ear to the Wicked; stand you still armed in the Covenant of Promise, til the Mystery of Iniquity be revealed against the workers thereof . . . *Surely I see the eyes of the beloved ones in the Nation turned towards you, and your fame is spreading as a child of Beauty . . .*[6]

The epistle seems to have been written in a spirit of unification and encouragement, perhaps intended to have been used as a pastoral message, a short sermon, for delivery in his absence. It could be what Nayler might have wished to say to the congregation if he were among them, but this is no simple and mercifully brief homily. It is almost the same length as Paul's second letter to the Thessalonians, which is in fact the model on which Nayler's piece was written. It was unashamedly borrowed. Nayler's purpose here was just the same as the apostle Paul's. The clue is in the tension set up between the Covenant of Promise and the uncovering of the Mystery of Iniquity (2 Thess. 2:6–2:12)

In both Paul's time in Macedonia and Nayler's time in London, it was believed that the Apocalypse was at hand. The Second Coming of Christ was imminent. The Quakers preached that it was both imminent and immanent, that is, that Christ was coming and had come to teach His people. Divisive elements in both Paul's and Nayler's societies threatened the cohesion of small bodies of believers who struggled to follow Christian teaching in chaotic times. In London millennialist extremists like the Fifth Monarchy men preached something between rebellion and anarchy. They were not alone. Friends meetings were not isolated from this influence. Even the most secure among their ministers, including Fox and Nayler, admonished that the day of the Lord was at hand. Sinners would be called to account, but they urged sobriety and what they called lowness, an inward focus on spiritual guidance. The need to reform was urgent, yes, but the nature of the work to be done required humility, not exaltation and self-promotion. Some in their meetings, however, rose to be heard in a strident ministry which prepared for the immediate arrival of Christ, or in a few cases they spoke out to name the Messiah already in their midst. In this *Epistle to All Friends at London* (not to all *people*; his admonition was specific), Nayler addressed the very division that was widening during his brief absence, as if it were the Biblical account of the Thessalonians repeated. Friends must mind the measure of Christ that was in themselves, be humble to the righteousness that was in them, and do their own work, as God did His. Only if they held to this instruction would God preserve them from the wrath that was to come for those who disbelieved His word, and Paul was his messenger.

In his letters to the Thessalonians, Paul reminded them that Satan would appear to deceive the people before the true Christ appeared to them. That test was happening indeed as he wrote. ". . . *the mystery of iniquity doth already work* . . . (2 Ths. 2:7). The people must discern between truth and lies, before the day of Christ would come to them.

Paul wrote: (2Ths. 3:7–12)

> For yourselves know how ye ought to follow us: for we behaved not ourselves disorderly among you;
> Neither did we eat any man's bread for nought; but wrought with labour and travail night and day, that we might not be chargeable to any of you:
> Not because we have not power, but to make ourselves an example unto you to follow us.
> For even when we were with you, this we commanded you, that if any would not work, neither should he eat.
> For we hear that there are some which walk among you disorderly, working not at all, but are busybodies.
> Now them that are such we command and exhort by our Lord Jesus Christ, that with quietness they work, and eat their own bread.

We needn't wonder whether Nayler knew of the widening split in London. Surely he did know what was going on with the zealous crowd who were challenging the established Quaker ministry in the city, dividing the body of the meeting between two projected factions. He had agreed to Fox's request to go to Yorkshire, saying that he must not stay long because he had much to do in London. He wrote the Epistle because he could not be present in person to say what must be said. Judging from his choice of the 2 Thessalonians text as model for his epistle, Nayler knew that an excited misinterpretation of the end times in Revelation was the problem. It went beyond an argument over who should have leadership of the London Friends, Fox and his followers, or Nayler. If Fox thought the building furor was all about his own leadership, which is doubtful, he was wrong. Fox was only in the way. Adulation of Nayler as if he were something he was not would tear at the unity of what all the ministers, Fox, Nayler, Howgill, Burrough and the rest, had been trying to build—a community of humble, spiritually strong people focused on the word of the Lord, not on the human figure of some presumed Messiah. If the meeting split, and some followed a person such as the charismatic Nayler triumphantly down the road toward some millennialist vision of the apocalypse, those Friends who went that way could be lost. Fox, Nayler, and the rest would be made out fools, vulnerable to any sort of outrage, and their ministry would have failed. Nayler knew that if his readers in London recognized the obvious reference he had made to Paul's second letter to the Thessalonians, then they would take up their Bibles to reread Paul's direction as to how to deal with those who were falsely carrying on Satan's work with ". . . *signs and lying wonders . . .*" (2 Thess 2:9).

Paul wrote:

> And if any man obey not our word by this epistle, note that man, and have no company with him, that he may be ashamed. Yet count him not as an enemy, but admonish him as a brother. (2 Thess 3:14, 15)

If the problem could be handled this way, then Nayler's understanding of faith could help bind up Friends into unity again. He wanted no part of adulation. The way to Christ was through simplicity, humility, honesty. Paul called it work, and so did Nayler. Its reward was backed by God's Promise.

Who, if anyone in the London Friends community, saw Nayler's epistle, or how it was taken is unknown. His admonition may not have arrived in time. It could well have been lost in the spreading confusion. One thing is clear, Nayler did not get back to the city in time to head off the chaotic breakdown that was about to ensue.

Around this same time, May or June, 1656, two of the most respected leaders of the London Friends wrote harsh letters to Martha Simmonds, a prominent member of that congregation, declaring her out of fellowship, misguided, and in jeopardy of salvation at the final judgment.[7] Edward Burrough's letter was addressed to "Martha Simmonds & Others," indicating that he acknowledged that she had a following whose conduct was as objectionable as hers. William Dewsbury's shorter letter addressed Martha alone, although when he predicted that God would throw her down for her deceit, he included with her in that retribution, "all that depart from the truth." Burrough's outrage was just as firm as he declared her, "out of the truth, out of the power, out of the wisdom, & out of the life of God." Both accused her of blasphemy and of following her own will, not God's, but neither named specific offenses she had committed, nor did they quote back to her anything she had said.

Howgill and Burrough described the scene in the London Friends ministry in a letter to Margaret Fell, written a few months later, but in part relating events of the early summer. Howgill wrote, "About a month ago or upwards Edw. Burrough and I went out of the city . . . and James Nayler was left in the city . . . soon after my departure two women of this city . . . run out into the imaginations and lying wonders, and James let them in and harkened unto them, and was quite overthrown, and lost all taste & savor, and was brought totally under the powers of deceit; and set these women on the top of all, although they manifested both him and them; yet he went out of this city and left all under the power of darkness & the enemies do rejoice, and so all our sore travails and labors like to be made void in a day . . ."[8] Richard Hubberthorne, another of the most respected of the original Quaker ministers though still under the age of 30, began a correspondence to Margaret Fell and George Fox over the state to which the ministry in London had fallen. Matters had gotten quite out of hand. An undisciplined contingent led by Martha Simmonds and Hannah Stranger had taken to outrageous behavior in meetings, including interruptions, singing, and disputes with Howgill and himself in the midst of worship and ministry. Though Quakers were accustomed to disturbing other congregations' church worship by disputing with their priests, such behavior was seldom heard of in their own meetings. The reason was based more on widely agreed spiritual discipline than on stern control by the leadership. Spoken ministry was (and remains in Quaker worship today) intended to consist only of words authentically moved by the Spirit through some speaker to be uttered as a message from God. By some this ministry, faithfully delivered, meets the definition of prophecy. No such sanctity was believed to pertain to sermons preached by a paid clergyman. Interrupting speakers of the standing of Howgill or Hubberthorne was considered, not only by themselves, but by many in attendance at their meetings, to be an insult to the Spirit moving in that chosen person.

By her own account, Simmonds had been a seeker for spiritual leadership and community for at least fourteen years prior to finding the Quakers. In recent times she had become accustomed to challenging ordained ministers in their own churches and to carrying on publicly in her own voice and in print. She had offended her targets and had spent time in jail. Her ministry was apocalyptic. She had enacted signs before she ever attached herself to Nayler in London, or ever met George Fox and his ministers. She had dramatized her ministry in enactments of Biblical origin, and so had Fox. For him it was walking into Litchfield barefoot in winter, proclaiming the day of the Lord. Martha Simmonds had appeared on the streets of Colchester in sackcloth and ashes, uttering prophecy of the end times, before she encountered Fox or Nayler or the London Quaker ministers.[9] By the time she did come under their influence she had already attracted a small following of both women and men. No wonder that when he met her, Nayler found her worthy of attention. While it seems unlikely that she gave him any choice but to listen to her, that did not mean that he agreed with what she said.

Martha, born in 1623, was almost the same age as George Fox, about eight years younger than Nayler, fervid in her faith, articulate, sister of Giles Calvert, printer of the Quakers' tracts, and married to and spiritually supported by a man who stood close to her in her ministry and her excesses. Thomas Simmonds also had a printing press and the courage to use it to promote prophetic ministry. Like his wife, he respected Nayler as, at the very least, a prophetic minister. Martha wrote three pamphlets, which have survived, one of which her brother published together with work by Nayler, Hannah Stranger, and William Tomlinson. The style and substance of what she wrote was similar to Nayler's most ardent appeals. Both made fluent allusions to Old Testament prophecy fulfilled in the New Testament. Simmonds's writing was distinguished by even more vehement warnings than Nayler's that the end time, the day of judgment, was upon them all. She wrote as insistently as he about the consequences of the sin and corruption to be found on every hand. England's time had run out, she warned, with none of Nayler's occasionally hopeful exhortations that the national leadership, either on their own or by the force of popular insistence, could turn the course of English life into a godly model.[10]

When Nayler returned from the North, he was asked to rebuke Simmonds, which he did when she came to him seeking, as she said, Justice. Simmonds and

Hannah Stranger together assailed him, asserting that he, like the other men, was dismissive of Martha's ministry having any spiritual authenticity. She had been moved to speak in meeting, and Howgill had attempted to silence her. Now Nayler seemed to her to be doing the same thing.

Part of the problem, no doubt, was the fact that these were women disrupting the ministry of men of recognized standing among Friends. It was not the case, however, that their witness was considered without value. James Parnell, another of Fox's early circle of ministers, had written to William Dewsbury in 1655, praising Simmonds's fearless and powerful ministry. His was the account which favorably described her going in sackcloth and ashes at Colchester. The problem now was that Simmonds and Stranger had taken the figure from Revelation 11:3 of Christ's two messengers a step farther. They had named the unbelievers who were threatening the establishment of the New Jerusalem. Simmonds had called Hubberthorne himself "the head of the beast," meaning the Antichrist rising from the pit, a common insult at the time, but aggravated within the close society of the Meeting. Not enough that he be Satan, she was, in the imagery of Revelation, calling him out in their faith community as her own murderer.

It is not incidental that Martha Simmonds and Hannah Stranger had become notorious and offensive at least in part because they were women in a religious body led by men. Clearly their chief adversaries were the male leadership of the London meetings, Howgill, Hubberthorne, and Burrough, who wanted to silence these two because they were talking out of their wills, as was said of the irreverent who spoke in meeting. Their ministry, the men argued, was not led by the Spirit within them, quite the contrary. That outrage by itself effectively masked what the men and their absent leader Fox may have believed about whether women had the standing to utter ministry in meetings. Nayler, however, not only believed, but also behaved as if the spirit of Christ were present and powerful in all people. It was to this expectation of him that Simmonds appealed when he returned to London. He would support her standing to speak, she seemed sure, as if her utterance were truly from God, that is, prophetic. With his support she could deliver her ministry, which went beyond the question of validity of women's ministry and beyond her objection, soon made explicit, to the personal authority over all Friends assumed by George Fox and upheld by his coterie of elders. Nayler would surely hear her apocalyptic message, as it so closely paralleled his own, or so she thought.

Simmonds and her companion, Hannah Stranger, undoubtedly knew the passage in Revelation in which John wrote:

> But I will give power unto my two witnesses & shall prophecie a thousand two hundreth and three score dayes clothed in sackcloth. (Rev XI:3)

Probably they read it as quoted above, from the 1599 Geneva Bible, widely used in the 17th Century, and popular with serious readers for its copious marginal notes.

The notes accompanying Revelation, Chapter XI suggest reference to 2 Thessalonians, 2:8, which reads:

> And then shall that wicked man be revealed whom the Lord shall consume with the Spirit of his mouth, and shall abolish with the brightness of his coming.

This is part of the passage which Nayler had just recently used as the model of his Epistle *"To All Friends in London."* That *"wicked man"* is also called *"the Man of Sin"* and his presence represents the *"mystery of Iniquity"* which must be revealed before the Day of Christ can be fulfilled. If Simmonds ever saw Nayler's letter to Friends in London, she would likely have seen that he touched on her same text from Revelation. She might have concluded that he agreed in casting the deceptive man of sin as Hubberthorne, just as Hubberthorne, if reading the same drama into the Scripture, may well have said, no, it was she who was the deceiver.

The support Simmonds expected from Nayler turned to an uncertain rebuke. He seemed to think that her outrage was less spiritually grounded than she asserted, and more self-serving. Hannah Stranger tried to reason with him that he had unfairly judged the innocent. Martha Simmonds fairly exploded, shaking him hard by turning the prophet, Isaiah on him, whose words Nayler knew very well:

> For the vineyard of the LORD of hosts is the house of Israel, and the men of Judah his pleasant plant: and he looked for judgment, but behold oppression; for righteousness, but behold a cry. (Isa. 5:7)

The Lord told the people that he had made a great vineyard, full of wonderful produce, which was their vaunted Israel, now become the focus of their pride and corruption. He would show that he could just as easily destroy it. He called for them to acknowledge that his power was wonderful, not their worldly harvest, but that was not mens' woeful response to their loss of material gifts.

Simmonds suggested that Nayler's judgment must be as misguided and unfaithful as that of the other men who led the London meetings, if he would silence her when she spoke the truth to them. The greatness of this city, the greatness of the congregation Friends had brought together in faith within it, were nothing if the leaders could no longer humble themselves before the Lord. It was Nayler's own ministry that she turned on him, as well as on the hierarchy of leadership she saw taking hold under George Fox. Nayler, of all of them, should have understood the soundness of her ministry, however threatening it may have seemed to the others. She had preached from his own favorite Scriptures. Now she had looked for Nayler's righteousness for support, and all she got was weakness at the prospect she envisioned, the coming of the Lord in wrath. All she heard from him was a cry. Perhaps she had expected too much of him.

Nayler was overcome by doubt. He was said to have retracted his rebuke and apologized. Unsure of his own discernment of what was truly the spirit moving him to act, he was unable to do anything. Martha Simmonds took him under her care at her home. In acute emotional distress and all but incapacitated, he is described as lying on a table in her house for days thereafter, fasting, immobilized.[11]

Suggestions that Simmonds and Nayler were carnally involved, however frequently alleged at this point in the story, have no more substantial evidentiary support than similar allegations of his involvement with Mrs. Roper in Yorkshire during the earliest days of his ardent ministry. Indeed, if Fox and Fell had heard from London Friends that the relationship between Nayler and Simmonds was adulterous, they would have denounced the two of them abruptly, emphatically, and probably publicly. No such explicit denunciation occurred, though Fox soon began expressing abundant disapproval of Simmonds and Nayler's involvement with her.

Simmonds was among those who thought that the best cure for Nayler's depression after his return from Yorkshire would be a dose of public attention and renewed recognition of his principal standing in Quaker ministry. The energy generated by getting up before a great crowd would, as it always had, advance the truth, but it would also revive Nayler's vigor. It was summer, and no greater crowds were to be found in England than those gathered in Bristol to hear the Quaker word spread by John Audland and John Camm. Their audiences had grown far too large for any building to contain, so their meetings had been moved out to a field, which reportedly held thousands. Those crowds would certainly come to hear Nayler, who would rise to an opportunity to minister to them.

Friends in London came up with a plan to get him there, likely endorsed by Fox. Simmonds came to the same plan, apparently independently of the others and certainly without any support from Fox. She was not, however, responsible for actually getting Nayler to Bristol. Somehow he was whisked away from Simmonds's own house, leaving her behind. Finding him gone without her, she hastened after and caught up at Bristol, where she was, she said, forcibly and roughly restrained from being with Nayler. Local accounts, principally George Bishop's, contradicted her accusations. While Simmonds claimed she was pushed down the stairs of a house, Bishop said she was never roughly handled, and in fact, the house in question was of a single story and had no stairs.

The civic occasion was a large summer fair. A grand crowd gathered, but the effort to get Nayler back into his former public self was a failure. Though thousands may have come to hear him, he was not moved to speak. He sat in silence, his mind and spirit apparently far from the almost festive scene. Whether he knew Simmonds was being kept from him is unclear. He was described soon after as, ". . . a man who is not."[12]

Fox wanted Nayler to stop at Launceston jail on his way back to London, notwithstanding the fact that to go to London via Launceston would add roughly 160 miles to the trip, as compared with returning to London directly from Bristol. Nayler was reluctant to make the trip, but others urged him to go. If anyone could help Nayler recover his spirit and judgment, surely it would be Fox, but helping

Nayler in his distress was not all Fox had on his mind, and Nayler surely knew it. Fox had received reports of the "turbulent women"[13] around Nayler, who brought chaos into the London meetings and acted as if Nayler were their leader. While it was hard for Fox to believe that Nayler could have accepted their behavior, it was clear that he had not put a stop to it. Fox was concerned that great harm could be done not only to the London ministry but also to Friends' reputation in general if Nayler could not be got to end this business. All too often Friends were called Ranters by their debating adversaries in the formal clergy. Here was a case of people who called themselves Friends, attaching themselves to the most well-known Quaker leader under Fox himself, and acting the part of Ranters and worse. To Fox this was not only outrageous but dangerous.[14] Nayler vacillated as he was urged to visit Fox, but eventually he set out with a few Friends toward Launceston. He didn't get that far. He and his party were arrested near Exeter and jailed. Major Desborough, the military officer for the district and Oliver Cromwell's brother-in-law, was aware of the interdiction, could have intervened and freed Nayler, but let the arrest proceed with scant, if any, legal grounds. By now it was simply a matter of policy to restrict the well-known Quakers from free movement around the countryside.

Not long after Nayler's exit from Bristol and his subsequent arrest, Martha Simmonds took action. She went first to Desborough, whose wife, Cromwell's sister, was seriously ill. Simmonds undertook to be her nurse in exchange for Nayler's release once the sick woman recovered. Then, while Nayler was still incarcerated, Simmonds with Hannah Stranger went to Fox at Launceston prison, where they attacked him in a fury.

Fox's letters and *Journal* are the primary source of what happened. Simmonds did not write about any of this, or if she did, her record was lost. According to Fox, Simmonds came to him to challenge his entire assumed authority over the Friends and to assert that if anyone ought to be recognized for his leadership, it should be Nayler. She said Fox had put himself up as if he were king of the Quakers, but his heart was rotten. He supported his usurpation by giving authority under himself to lieutenants like Howgill to control the meetings and keep down the people who spoke up for the truth. There was more of this "filth" as Fox called it. Hannah Stranger joined in, challenging him to try to silence them. It was not she and Simmonds who spoke with the voice of the devil, but Fox and his lot who were false and ungodly.[15]

Meanwhile, for Nayler, as had been the case four years earlier at Appleby, jail at Exeter was not all bad. His release was slow in coming, which gave him time to rest, reflect, worship, and restore himself. Following his earlier practice, he spent much time fasting, only sipping a little water or dilute wine, until after about two weeks he began taking meat again. Visitors found him quiet, withdrawn, reflective, but notwithstanding his prolonged fast, in better health than he had seemed in London. He was surrounded in his prison by several Friends who had been arrested either with him or on the road in Cornwall. One, Thomas Rawlinson, wrote to Margaret Fell suggesting that she not believe everything she must be hearing about Nayler, that he had foreseen much earlier that there must be suffering, but in what way he could not foresee. Rawlinson reminded her that she knew this because Nayler had written to her about it before the trouble began. Some of his London adherents paid visits, carrying on too much about his near-divine standing, which influence, one visitor reported, did him no good at all.[16]

Soon, the simmering bitterness between Nayler and Fox came to the boiling point. Some doubt is advisable in reading the accounts of what happened between them at Exeter. Part of what passed between Fox and Nayler was witnessed and reported, but for other key exchanges only the two principals were present. One side of the story is included in Fox's *Journal*, written decades later. Hubberthorne, who was present for most of the encounter, promptly related what he saw and heard in a letter to Margaret Fell. Nayler's account was recast into print by others after his death.[17]

Following is an attempt to summarize the break between Fox and Nayler as its elements can be pieced together. The reader is advised that the author's bias is more toward the longevity and depth of this building estrangement than toward the specifics of what happened at Exeter, or who said what to whom.

During the time when Fox and Nayler had been together in and near London Nayler had occasion to benefit from Fox's advice and judgment. On one such occasion in 1655 they had converged to respond to active anti-Quaker ministry by an organized regional clergy in Derbyshire. Nayler received an invitation to meet with a delegation of ministers from the area in open, public debate. He discussed the proposal with Fox, seeking his advice. Fox prayed on the matter, and seeing how God would have it, advised Nayler to go ahead and engage the debate. It went well as Fox had foreseen, and Nayler came to him, "praising the Lord." Fox took some satisfaction in his own part, it appears.[18] His satisfaction was short-lived, however, for soon after as he was leaving Nayler in London, Fox saw something in Nayler's eyes that greatly worried him. He wrote, many years after the fact, and long after Nayler's fall, "*I cast my eyes upon him, and fear stuck in me concerning him.*"[19]

During the summer of 1656, while Fox was imprisoned at Launceston, he had received the letters from London describing how Simmonds and her followers were disrupting the ministry, and Nayler seemed to be their passive supporter at least, if not their leader. Fox had labored with how to address this problem with Nayler, but he seemed to find no opportunity, since Nayler had not visited him at Launceston. Finally came the visit and diatribe from Martha Simmonds. A short time after Fox was released, he went to visit Nayler, who was still incarcerated at Exeter.

Their visit spanned the better part of two days, as Fox roomed at a nearby inn and went several times to Nayler's confined quarters. They were also allowed release time in which to walk together outside the prison. Taken together, these opportunities appear to have amounted to the longest time the two founders of the Quaker faith had spent together in years. Apart from a brief, strained, arranged meeting at

Reading four years later, it was their last intimate time together, doubtless the saddest encounter of their entire friendship, and the end of it.

Nayler's traveling companions and cellmates, who had been arrested with him, seemed to be acquainted with Fox and his companions, including Hubberthorne. Fox decided all would join the First Day Meeting for Worship held by the prisoners. While he and Nayler could have attempted to come together again in the familiar silence of the meeting, that was not Fox's purpose. He preferred to have an audience for what he had to say. Speaking out in the meeting, Fox took Nayler to task. He blamed Nayler and his supporters for all the unruliness and disrespect Simmonds and Hannah Stranger had recently delivered, both to him in Launceston jail, and to Howgill and the other ministers in London. Nayler and his fellow prisoners put up with this as long as they could. Then apparently they walked out of the meeting. Fox said in his *Journal* years later that here began the practice that came to divide the Quaker movement in the years after Nayler's death, of expressing disrespect for prayer spoken in meeting by keeping one's hat on, rather than removing it when ministry was given, as was the custom. He counted this one of the principal breaks in Quaker discipline and laid it not only to Nayler's supporters, but to James himself.[20]

Now the tension between them was too great. Nayler felt Fox had come to accuse him for transgressions Fox had only heard about second hand, could not have witnessed, and still was willing to believe. That being so, it was impossible to hold meeting in a spirit of free seeking for unity in the truth. Fox had already decided the truth for himself, and Nayler saw his former dear friend use the respectful silence of the meeting for worship to speak out of his own will and humiliate Nayler before the others present. That was not acceptable. If Fox had things to say to him, he should say them. So, by arrangement with the jailer, they had a few private conferences at the inn where Fox stayed, and took a couple of walks together over the two-day visit. What was said between the two was blunt, angry, and lastingly hurtful. Fox declared that Nayler had completely lost his spiritual guide, and unless he removed himself from his entourage of followers, he would be overtaken by the devil. He related what had happened during Simmonds's visit to Launceston jail, and he went on to describe what he had heard of Nayler's carryings-on. He may have made allusion to possibilities of adulterous behavior. Nayler lost his temper and called the sources of all these stories liars. George Fox was as much a liar as the rest for repeating what he had heard. This Nayler shouted at Fox on a public street before passersby. Fox lost his temper as well. These were no petty charges between the two foremost Quakers in England. The two parted on the worst of terms. Back in his cell Nayler wept at what had passed between them.

Fox went away for a time and then returned to try to talk with Nayler. The anger between the two erupted in the most graphic depiction of the sad state between them. Hubberthorne witnessed and recorded the events in a letter to Margaret Fell.

Nayler's close friend and supporter, Robert Rich, later described Nayler's own version of the encounter, which substantially agreed with Hubberthorne's.[21]

The entrance to the cell was a step higher than the main floor. Fox stood at the upper level to greet Nayler, who was on the level a step below him. Nayler may have been kneeling, in great distress and tearful. He greeted Fox humbly, but after all that had been said between them, Fox was having none of it. Nayler is reported to have offered Fox an apple, which Fox refused, after asking Nayler if he were truly moved by the spirit to give him the apple and Nayler answering that he was not. Nayler grasped Fox by the hand and seemed to try to pull him down from the higher level to the lower, where the prisoners were. It has been suggested to this author by one student that Fox may have seen the symbolism of the apple being offered from the fallen one, in a low station, to the righteous one on high, who in this version of the Fall of Man refused the lure. It is probably just as likely that Nayler wanted to offer his visitor some kind of hospitality or good will, and an apple was all he had. He wanted to try to draw Fox closer to him somehow. Taken aback by Fox's rebuff, Nayler then asked if he might kiss Fox. Perhaps he stood as if to reach Fox, who nevertheless still stood at a higher floor level. Fox extended his hand toward Nayler to be kissed, but either Nayler refused it, or Fox withdrew it. Remaining aloof, Fox advanced his boot toward Nayler and said, "*It is my foot.*" Fox made clear in his abbreviated account of what happened between them that he meant to press Nayler into a humiliating capitulation. He wrote,

> . . . so the Lord God moved me to slight him and to set the power of God over him.[22]

CHAPTER 14

The Ride into Bristol, Blasphemy and Imprisonment

... I durst not resist it, though I was sure to lay down my life for it.
—Testimony of James Nayler

On an October afternoon in Bristol, Nayler took part in the tableau for which he is remembered. Accompanied by idolaters singing Hosannas, he took center stage as a figure on a horse riding into Bristol after the manner of Jesus entering Jerusalem. Beside Nayler were Martha Simmonds, no stranger to enacting prophetic signs in public, and her regular companion, Hannah Stranger. Another participant, Dorcas Erbury, had claimed that, just as Peter had raised her namesake, Tabitha (Dorcas in Greek translation), from the dead (Acts 9:40), James Nayler had raised her from the dead at Exeter jail. Though women were most often mentioned in accounts of this theatrical parade, men were just as much part of the cast of characters. Hannah's husband, John Stranger, as zealously devoted as she, took part, having expressed in writing the extravagant belief, held by others as well, that Nayler was Christ returned. Samuel Cater and Robert Crab were present. Timothy Wedlock of Devonshire led the rider's horse to help guide the animal along the rutted way. He went bare-headed before Nayler, as Friends did only in the divine presence when prayer was given in Meeting for Worship. Having no palm fronds, certain members of the entourage cast down their cloaks on the mud before the rider. Nayler wore a long narrow beard, it was said, as if he meant to impersonate Jesus as depicted in a popular portrait. He must have worn a hat too, unlike the Saviour in the portrait, for a cold autumn downpour soaked the little train and its spectators. He wore as well a great coat with pockets full of letters from some of his loving friends, which documents were taken from him when he was arrested and used as proof against him and them of blasphemous intent.[1]

At best the procession could be seen as a rude approximation of what some know as Jesus's triumphant entry into Jerusalem (Matthew 21, Mark 11, Luke 19, John 12), but surely no triumph was portrayed or intended by Nayler. That much is certain. What his companions meant by what they were doing is another question. Oddly, nothing much really should have come of this brief demonstration. It was an awkward thing. The re-enactors numbered only about eight. They came by a mired road normally used for freight wagons, not by way of the high road into the city. Their procession had no dramatic destination setting at which to conclude the show, nothing resembling the temple at Jerusalem. They gathered at the end of their walk in a low class tavern near the market cross. What they had done was not extraordinary. Enactments of signs with Scriptural origins were not uncommon and could be more startling. Both Quakers and those of other sects, for example, had "gone naked as a sign" of the need for repentance and cleansing of sin for the coming of the Lord. (Isaiah 20:3). Nayler and his group had performed their reenactment at least twice on the way to Bristol, with little notice taken or insult claimed, at Glastonbury and Wells. News of those events, however, alerted authorities at Bristol to prepare a hostile reception. George Bishop, reporting by letter to Margaret Fell, described, "multitudes following them (for the whole town was aroused)," If Nayler really did, as he testified later, feel he would surely lay down his life for this act, then he may have felt a twinge of recognition when he dismounted from his horse that here would be his end. He knew the loathing and contempt Quaker ministers could expect wherever they went. Recently he had experienced jail at Exeter, and he knew of Fox's confinement at Launceston. He knew that numbers of other Quaker itinerant preachers and prophets were locked up all over the countryside. He knew that outspoken, enthusiastic women like those in his troupe were targets for abuse and punishment to a greater extent in society at large than their modest state of disapproval in Quaker circles would indicate. In short, each time they rode into a town to present their sign, the response was likely to be aggravated, and if anywhere, Bristol could be the worst place to try it. Here the little band would stand out. In London their troupe might have been overlooked in the throngs, motion, and diversity of the inhabitants. Bristol was already tense, as the proportion of Quakers to the general population had grown to significant levels. The resident Quakers, many of whom were in business, had much to lose if their reputations were compromised by outsiders' offensive religious demonstrations. Martha Simmonds, however, might well have favored an audacious display at Bristol to defy local Quaker leadership who had so rudely dismissed her earlier in the summer, when she had tried to join Nayler. Even their coreligionists here would be turned against them. The reenactors were asking for trouble at Bristol, in a practical sense, and they found it.[2]

    The lot of them were promptly arrested, searched, interrogated, taken before magistrates and jailed. Here there was no question of charges of wandering vagrancy. These people were well known. According to Bishop's letter, they traveled with a "pass from O.P.," that is an official traveling permission over the signature of Oliver Protector, Cromwell. Some citizens argued that their charge should be blasphemy. A proper trial would give the offenders more notoriety, so here was a fine chance to start getting rid of Quakers by damning them all for the excesses of these few. Interrogation was conducted to try to establish what was the intent of the procession, an issue central to any ensuing prosecution, but no simple explanation was discovered. Confusion characterised the body of testimony taken as a whole. While Nayler denied he was Christ, and tried to distinguish that state from the presence of Christ in him, some of his company seemed clearly to put him on a divine pedestal. Personal letters Nayler carried were enough to cast doubt on his claim of innocence, as well as to incriminate some of their authors, who were part of the entourage. John Stranger, for one, had written a postscript to his wife's letter to Nayler, saying that in the final judgment days soon to come, or here now, his name would be no longer James, but Jesus.[3]

Now the question was, what was the worst the magistrates of Bristol could do to the demonstrators? Not enough, it seemed. While some leading residents of the town wanted down with all Quakers and a cruel example to be made of the whole party, that would not be possible. Prominent citizens of Bristol, though in the minority, were of that same faith. George Bishop was a member of a solid family, a man of property and credentials, a respected former military officer. He had a political following in the city, having only just lost election to Parliament for Bristol, yet he had turned Quaker. Bishop knew his neighbors and was concerned about how Nayler's procession would be taken. Nevertheless, in his letter to Margaret Fell he offered the opinion that not much would come of the scandal. Most of the resident Bristol Quakers had avoided both the reenactment and the subsequent judicial process. The magistrates had discovered in the letters he carried that Nayler was not in good favor with Fox and some other Friends. His isolation was already public knowledge. For local magistracy to attempt to set precedent for punishment of Quakers generally for a few demonstrators' enthusiasm was impractical, but the politics of the situation did present an attractive alternative to harsh local punishment. Halting the spreading disease, and some said threat, of Quakerism in all parts of the country might require a prominent case to be brought out of a local magistracy to the national government. Nayler's alleged blasphemy could be made into the cause for action by Parliament. His high standing in Quaker leadership could indicate that what he did was example for all of that sect to commit similar insults elsewhere across England. The whole business could be passed on for examination in London, where whatever might fall on all the Quakers for their errant leader's activities would not fall by Bristol's hand. A modest procession of eight sorry souls on a rainy fall day in that city could be turned into a national cause celebre, and while Bristol's people were witness, they needn't pass harsh judgment on their own neighbors.

The victor in George Bishop's failed contest for a seat in Parliament, Robert Aldworth, readily agreed to take the Nayler case before the national body in London. All the Members could have a part in a public display of force against the Quaker problem, but no one would come away with bloody hands. Not only that, but here was a great opportunity for the young Parliament as a body to prove its capability to manage the internal affairs of the country. Parliament needed an easy win in order to help define itself. They were still on uncertain ground between the two principal administrators of the Protectorate, Lord Protector Cromwell and the Council of State, which represented, effectively, the Army. The government was now established de facto in a three part constitutional form, but no one yet quite knew what Parliament's place could be in the scheme. The army's power was clear, potentially absolute, and dangerous. The Protector could be equal, if he could keep his place. By strength of will, alliance, and a naturally bold but careful character, Cromwell could, but where was Parliament? If they only held the purse-strings, would that be enough? They needed as well to take care of the law, extending it to fit the needs of the people. Here in the Nayler case was a chance to do that. Parliament's response was quick in coming. Nayler's ride took place on October 24, 1656. A committee in Parliament to investigate the matter was established by an action on October 31. Its charge was to address judicial action by Parliament against Nayler and his followers, as well as the possible need for stronger laws against blasphemy.

Sent from Bristol to London, Nayler and most of his companions were kept in custody at a house near Whitehall during the proceedings. It was not a harsh confinement. Visitors were allowed, and the attendants described rather cheerful conditions. While Nayler was quiet, contemplative, perhaps depressed, others sang and demonstrated love and camaraderie.[4]

Parliament's intent in the case became clear enough. Nayler was their target. One Member urged eliminating Nayler in order to eliminate the whole sect of Quakers.[5] People like Simmonds, the Strangers, and Dorcas Erbury were of no particular value. Their punishment would serve no great purpose, but if their testimony could be used against Nayler, it would serve high purpose indeed. Let them carry on if they would not be silent, but keep relating their testimony to Nayler. As to him, for a time there was no move toward requiring Nayler's testimony at all. George Bishop wrote to Parliament, calling for him to be given a chance to speak in his own defense. Others, including some Members, took up the call, and eventually Nayler was allowed to answer questions. The interrogation closely followed that of the Bristol magistrates.

Taken together, Nayler's testimony and that of his companions at Bristol served to confuse the committee rather than to clarify what the group had in mind in presenting their sign. A firm definition of their blasphemy became more and more elusive. It appeared that the message in their ministry was inconsistent. John Stranger affirmed in his writing that Nayler was surely Jesus returned, but under examination declined to explain what he meant. His wife, Hannah, using the words "Prince of Peace" and "Son of God," and admitting that she had kissed his feet, left little doubt as to how she saw him. Martha Simmonds, as well, called Nayler Lord, agreed with Hannah's appellations and said that she worshipped him because Nayler would be Jesus when the new life was born in him. Witnesses described the ways these two and others worshipped at his feet in the prison and sang him hymns of praise. The Strangers, Simmonds and Dorcas Erbury, herself a daughter of a radical preacher, all played on semantics in their testimonies to avoid proving blasphemy. Nayler himself claimed he was not Jesus Christ, but only that he was a man, moved by the Spirit to do what he did. He went on to elaborate what this meant, and where were the lines between what was God's and what was the Spirit in him. If the Members were confused, no wonder. If outrage were a Member's predilection, it was justified by what looked like efforts to obfuscate the miscreants' motives. If, on the other hand, a listener to this testimony were inclined toward objectivity, his path through the testimony would not be easy.[6]

Most Members could agree that blasphemy was one's assumption to her or himself of any of the attributes which belong to the Lord alone. While a few, listening to the distinctions he had drawn in his testimony, argued that Nayler had not done this, it became more convenient for the majority to agree that he had, but that was not enough. The Members debated and construed for days the nature and extent of Nayler's offense, whether it was truly a crime separate from simple blasphemy and somehow greater, and what should be its particular punishment. As the nature of blasphemy was reviewed and professed at length, many and verbose definitions were offered. Long-standing law offered the simplest sanctions.[7] At least one law already stood against blasphemy. Fox and others had been charged with its violation, with various degrees of successful and unsuccessful prosecution. Nayler's court in Appleby, it will be remembered, had been unable to agree that Nayler had committed blasphemy in their jurisdiction. If that same offense were the charge against Nayler for his Bristol appearance, it might have been prosecuted more successfully, but the matter should have rested with the magistrates at Bristol, who were fully empowered to deal with it. It should not have come to Parliament unless the offense amounted to something more than the law already addressed. Parliament was not a court, but a legislative body. Part of its committee's charge was to consider whether more comprehensive law was required to address the current excesses of the various sects, especially the Quakers. If their offense were greater than blasphemy, then what was it?

Some Members found support and precedent in Scripture for something called "horrid blasphemy." That crime, they understood, went to a more grave offense than blasphemy as broadly encountered. It was directly to offend or deny God. The punishment for horrid blasphemy found in Scripture was death, and the means of death was the ancient practice of stoning the offender to death in the streets. (Leviticus 24:16; John 10:30-33) No such thing was known in English law. No court had ever adjudicated such a sentence, but the offense was an affront to God's word in Scripture, and Scriptural law provided the answer. Members led by, among others, war hero Major General Philip Skippon argued for Nayler's execution, and by his death as its leader, for the death of the whole body of this threatening sect called Quakers.

Parliament, however, was not of one voice in agreement that it could make up, whether by judicial precedent or legislation, such a retroactive package of law and punishment. It seemed more than even the Nayler outrage could possibly justify. Surely, however, the case extended somewhere far beyond the limits of the conventional and long-standing definition of blasphemy. Crudely and publicly mimicking and mocking the Son of God went beyond all pardonable limits. Furthermore, Members argued that Nayler had long been setting himself up for the station of false Messiah, as proven by the growing adulation of his followers ever since he had come to London. One Member argued that his companions at Bristol were greater offenders than he, because of their idolatry. Extraordinary actions to stop this enlargement of insult against God were justified. On that the majority of Members agreed, if not on the extent of the sanctions.

Their most learned colleague, Whitelocke, argued at length the misapplication of the Biblical sanctions held out for Nayler's case, and probably saved his life. Fortunately for Nayler, the arguments for execution did not prevail, though he was spared by only 14 votes out of 178.[8] No doubt the political implications of such an action by the representative body had been simply too dark to invite. A terrible punishment nowhere found in law, for a crime extended from the existing law into some retrospective enactment without normal process and consideration, charged against no traitor but a misguided religious dissident, could have the effect of bringing down the Parliament once again, and reestablishing the army's martial law or the Protector as king, who were both, as yet, silent observers of this strange trial. No. There must be an appearance of judicious restraint. The crime they had reinvented, horrid blasphemy, could stand on moral authority, as if uncertain citation of Scripture were the source of such a thing. The crime called for harsh punishment, but that could be made up of existing legal elements, not some newfound and cruel means of execution. Stigmatization by means of public exhibition and humiliation were commonplace. Torture, in certain of its many forms, branding and mutilation for example, was a frequently applied sentence. So was lashing with a whip, just as was used aboard ship. An indefinite term of imprisonment was also acceptable, and these punishments could be used in any combination. The committee agreed, sent the matter to the House for even more debate, construction of a sentence, votes, and the notorious trial was concluded. Nayler, convicted of horrid blasphemy, was to be publicly humiliated in the stocks, branded "B" and his tongue bored through with hot iron. Then he was to be drawn through the city and lashed repeatedly. Then the public humiliation and lashings were to be repeated at Bristol, for the benefit of that city's offended populace. Thereafter the prisoner was to be locked away in solitary confinement at daily labor for a term extending to the will of the Parliament. He might die in Bridewell prison, for all the Members cared. It would be no political loss for anyone, and Parliament would have defended the faith and applied the righteous laws of England. Whether and how they might codify what they had done for the future protection of the people against the sects might be left for another day. In the end, how they tried to do that and whether they accomplished anything at all by their efforts would ever be controversial.[9]

Oliver Cromwell, though he avoided assiduously taking any part in Parliament's process on the matter, did write just before it was complete to question by what course of legal reasoning they had come to their conclusion on the Nayler case. Parliament considered whether the Protector had any standing to question its actions and decided after much debate to test the issue by ignoring his letter, making no response. Oliver took the challenge no further. The Council remained silent for the time being.

Silence may have satisfied George Fox as well. The extent of his support for his former companion in the faith, now in this time of mortal distress, was to write a letter to Parliament which offered two categories of unsolicited advice. The first was that Parliament must avoid punishing by death those who had committed offenses of religious acts of conscience. The second advice, by way of postscript, was to offer this bit of Foxian clarification:

> If the seed speak which is Christ he hath no other name, for the seed is Christ Jesus and is not blasphemy but truth; but if the seed of the serpent speak and say he is Christ that is the liar and the blasphemy and the ground of all blasphemy and is not the seed which is Christ, but the seed of the serpent is to be bruised which is the cause of all enmity, strife, and debate with the seed of the woman which is Christ.[10]

Fox's letter obviously spoke to the matter before the House, but he did not mention Nayler by name, or declare that Nayler had, or had not, said he was Christ. In fact, Nayler had denied in all his testimonies that he was, affirming instead that he, like all men, was the son God and had something of Christ within. Fox had argued that case many times. All the Friends ministers had, and for them it was no blasphemy. In Nayler's case, however, Fox seemed to say to Parliament, you may have the argument your way. If anyone had blasphemed, Fox would not stand with him, and let the Parliament do as it would. Only be advised, that if you kill Nayler, or any of us, you'll pay for it with your own high position and salvation. Fox didn't call Nayler a liar, as Nayler called him.[11] He rose above that, but said to Parliament, if they wanted to call him liar, here were the words to use. It was clear enough, and certainly was Fox's intention, that if he let James stand alone in his own defense, the Quakers as a body would avoid involvement as well. Thereby, they might avoid greater persecution.

From Nayler's uncharacteristic reticence between the time of his comeuppance before Martha Simmonds at her home during the previous summer, and the time of his examination before Parliament, some have concluded that whatever followed from his failure to maintain unity and prevent schism at London, Nayler was beyond being held responsible. He was temporarily insane, or was the sad victim of what in the first half of the twentieth century had come to be called nervous exhaustion.[12] Only in that condition could he have been party to the ride into Bristol.

His testimony may have confused the magistrates at Bristol, as the excesses of his companions diverted attention from his answers. All the Bristol testimony, the letters he carried, along with the foremost of his exuberant companions themselves traveled on to London, appearing before Parliament's committee before Nayler did. He was called to testify late in the hearing, almost as an embarrassed afterthought in the process. By this time Nayler was rested and quite lucid. Still, his testimony was difficult for some to follow, while others seemed to close their ears entirely to what he had to say. To Generals Skippon and Boteler, respected, hardened Puritans, here was the leader of all the Quakers, exposed at the most dangerous fringe of that sect's profession. The man's subtle distinctions about the natures of Christ and man were not persuasive. In Skippon's straightforward expression, religious toleration had become dangerous, and here was the place to make an example and stop it. Lord Lawrence, on the other hand, listened and accepted Nayler's argument for the presence of Christ within each person; that part of his profession was not blasphemy at all. The eminent General Lambert, Nayler's former commanding officer in the army, who so often has been cited for his character witness in Nayler's favor, in fact equivocated over whether his formerly respected subordinate, turned Quaker, had blasphemed the Lord. Lambert, ever the careful opportunist in politics, had his eye on Lord Protector Cromwell's job, and he avoided once again the appearance of support for unpopular causes. The other man on the committee who may have known Nayler well, Captain Baynes, spoke more clearly in his favor, though from a weak position. Baynes had served with Nayler under Lambert in the Northern Army. Though he was not convinced by Nayler's theological argument, that was not a crime, and he could find no other. He pointed out that Nayler was obviously a Christian believer, which was all that the Instrument of Government required for the extension of religious toleration. The hearing's public audience also differed on the effectiveness of Nayler's testimony. The young John Locke, freshly embarked from Oxford on his career in the sciences and philosophy, wrote to his father that he thought Nayler was mad and his party uncouth.[13] Anthony Pearson, respected Quaker leader and former justice of assizes courts, reported to Friends that Nayler testified as clearly and directly as anyone could, correctly stating Quaker convictions.[14] Yet, Nayler stood accused before Parliament among idolaters who claimed he was something quite different from what he claimed to be himself. While their guilt may have been as great, or greater than his, their purpose in the trial had been served. Nayler stood convicted alone.[15]

Was he incompetent to judge what he was doing at Bristol? Irrational in trying to understand what he had felt moved to do? Probably not. Bewitched by the women into acting beyond his own leading? If not, then misled into error and sin by devilish deception, by Satan acting against the Spiritual guide within the man? Or, did he know what he was doing and what he meant to be his ministry by doing it? Each of these proposed explanations were current in 17th Century discussion of why Nayler did the Bristol reenactment, except, probably, the last one. Almost no one, who was not a participant, seemed able to accept the idea that Nayler had a rational scheme in mind that supported the sign.

Thomas Simmonds, who had addressed Nayler in one of the condemnatory letters found on his person at Bristol, "*Thou King of Israel and Son of the Most High . . .*" did not accompany his wife in the Bristol sign. Unwilling to participate, he returned to London. He wrote to his wife after she had got into so much trouble doing it, reminding her that he had warned her that it would turn out this way.[16] She had got ahead of her guide (God's will), who surely would have sent her home, if she had listened, rather than to Bristol. Thomas left no doubt that the Bristol ride was Martha Simmonds's idea. He knew she was behind it, and he hoped she would not have to pay too dear a price for doing it. Then he added a curious and unexplained comment. He hoped it would not turn out as Burford had.

What had Burford to do with the Bristol demonstration? Burford was the place where in 1649 an incipient rebellion of Levellers from within the army, en route to London, was intercepted by Cromwell in a surprise nighttime raid. Some were killed in the church where they slept. The ringleaders were executed at dawn.[17] Martha Simmonds's brother, Giles Calvert, had published Leveller tracts and must have known some of the leaders of this faction, perhaps even some of those executed at Burford as ringleaders of the rebellion. Was her husband, by mentioning the fate of these rebels, trying to frighten his wife into ceasing her challenging behavior, or was there some closer connection between Martha Simmonds and the Levellers, political dissidents from whom James Nayler had insisted on distancing himself?

Fox, Fell, Bishop, Hubberthorne, Howgill, and Burrough, all feared that Nayler's outrageous public behavior would isolate the Quakers from society. Friends would be made out as no better than the worst of the Ranters. At every turn they would be threatened more than ever with grievous persecution. Fox and Fell thought Nayler had "run out" back in June, when he came under the influence of the women led by Martha Simmonds. Fox, Howgill, Hubberthorne, and Burrough had written letters about the womens' "filthiness." Fox's letters to Nayler after their split at Exeter described them in terms clearly associated with Ranters, as did Margaret Fell in her letter to Nayler written just before his Bristol ride, but withheld by Bishop from delivery, lest it might associate Fell too closely with Nayler. Fell published a book in 1656 attacking the Ranters and explicitly disassociating the Quakers from them, as if the Ranters were also a religious entity with a body of doctrine. Bishop also wrote of how the Nayler affair would endanger innocent Friends. Their fears were well-founded. During the trial, General Skippon classed "Quakers, Ranters, Levellers...." and certain others as groups to whom religious freedom and toleration must be denied, on the authority, as he claimed, of the Protector himself.[18]

Nayler had become a scapegoat figure in Quaker history, like the goat in Leviticus, on whose head the sins of the city were heaped on the Day of Atonement, and it was sent out into the wilderness. But that analogy goes too far. In Leviticus two goats were chosen: the one to be offered as a sacrifice of appeasement and slaughtered; the second, the scapegoat, to be no more than a convenient beast of burden. Both were victims. Nayler was not a victim. He came to be here as consequence to his own choice. It was not because of some kind of madness or witchcraft that led him astray, unless seduction qualifies for one of those. Nor was it because these leading Friends had tried to understand his ministry in the Bristol ride, had found that ministry opposed to Quaker principles, and somehow excommunicated him for proceeding anyway. He had never asked anyone in the leadership for their guidance, and they had no procedure anyway for judging another Friend's leading. Nayler was a potentially divisive figure in the movement, a prominent thorn in the side of Fox's style of Quakerism, before he ever left London. Whether he accepted them or not, a troublesome splinter group had broken off from the body of London Friends and put Nayler forward as their leader. When the Quaker leadership could not separate him from his most ardent supporters, they let him go and were not much surprised to see him appear the demented fool in front of the Bristol fiasco. He was no longer one of them, so Fox declared. The ride came in October, and Nayler had run out back in June. For all their great concern over the damage his act could do to them, the leading Friends all took refuge in the redemptive silence and let him stand up alone before all England's representatives, for good or ill. Fox wrote only when it appeared likely that Nayler would be executed. When he was not, but his punishment seemed likely to exceed the limits of human strength, a great many citizens, and not all Quakers by any means, petitioned Parliament for remission of the penalties. Fox and his leadership coterie were not to found among the signatories.

Though Nayler's punishment did not include execution, that absence only amounted to evasion of the likely consequence. If all the measures Parliament meted out had been carried off, he could well have fallen dead in Bristol. The worst of his punishment amounted to 312 lashes, applied as he was dragged behind a cart through London. Rebecca Travers, who nursed him during and after his ordeal, reported that there was not the breadth of a finger between the wounds. Surviving that beating, on the following day he was tortured by branding irons. Then he was taken to Bristol, where the aforesaid stocking, parade, and lashing was to be duplicated in every respect. Had the entire sentence been repeated, the people in charge at Bristol judged, probably correctly, that he would have died in their city, which was never their intent. They moderated the punishment by allowing a Quaker to hold the executioner's arm and partially restrain the delivery of each lash, so that fewer and lighter strokes were delivered than at London. This much, Nayler did survive.

He was returned to London to be imprisoned at Bridewell at the pleasure of Parliament, that is, indefinitely, and most likely, until his death. At Bridewell, the terms of his tenancy were defined as solitary confinement behind multiple doors with multiple locks, the keys to which were held by different jailers. He would have no visitors, no writing supplies, nothing to read, and like all the prisoners, he would work pulling hemp for cordage at a small rate of pay by the pound, which he could apply to buy his food. The cordage made from his hemp, presumably, would be used for such things as rigging naval warships, or for hangmen's ropes.

Unlike the buildings at Appleby-in-Westmoreland, where Nayler's trial and imprisonment were conducted four years earlier, which stand today in as good condition probably as they were in 350 years ago when Nayler was there, no landmarks of his London trial and incarceration remain. Bridewell was destroyed in the Great Fire of 1666. The Painted Chamber at Westminster Palace, where his trial was held, lasted longer, but was lost to fire in 1834. Formerly called The King's Chamber and decorated in keeping with its use by royalty, it had become the permanent seat of the House of Commons, and was counted a sad loss to England. Few would have missed Bridewell, though it had seen finer days as well. Bridewell, as it stood in Nayler's time, occupied a former royal palace, parts of which dated back hundreds of years. Henry VIII had lived there briefly with Catherine of Aragon. His son, King Edward VI, founded Bridewell Hospital in 1553 in the renovated building by the Thames at Blackfriars, to be used as a housing for the poor. Edward did not live to see the palace used according to his plan, and it went through various degradations, until by 1656 it had become a minor prison, more of a house of correction in practice than a lockup for hardened criminals. Still called Bridewell Hospital, its inmates were likely to be debtors, drunkards, miscreants of a minor sort, public and persistent nuisances, put there not for health care in the modern sense, but rather for reform of bad habits. Some of its recent occupants were religious troublemakers, such as John Reeve and his cousin Ludovic Muggleton, self-professed prophets of the end times who claimed to be the two messengers of Revelation, and who were charged with blasphemy. Anna Trapnel, the Fifth Monarchist who spoke prophecy from a trance, had also been there two years before Nayler. These undesirable sorts of people could be left in relative peace and anonymity, perhaps eventually to die.[19]

James Nayler's wife went to him there. Probably she did not travel alone, but nothing was said of any companion in accounts of her presence in London. She had made a journey of almost 200 miles from Woodkirk in Yorkshire. No record of how she traveled has been found. She was not wealthy, but she came from a place where there were horses. It may be that she rode, or she may have taken a seat on a private mail and freight wagon. The public post coaches did not yet exist. Her purpose was to hurry to London and care for a husband in very poor health. Had she not done so, Nayler might very well have died in Bridewell within a year of his arrival there. Ann Nayler saw to his immediate needs and then petitioned Parliament for medical care for her husband. Her petition, allegedly written in her own hand, showed that Ann was a literate, intelligent, and persuasive person. She petitioned Parliament twice and succeeded in getting medical attention. Some supportive Friends had also visited and appealed in his behalf. Doctors visited Nayler in jail and agreed that he was needy of care. Eventually he was moved to somewhat better quarters and was put under the care of an elderly Bridewell inmate named Joan Pollard, who had some common nursing ability.[20] Ann could not stay indefinitely, but had to return home. The youngest of the three known Nayler daughters was only fourteen, and there may have been a younger son. In addition, she had a farm to care for. After Ann returned home, it is uncertain whether she and James ever saw each other again.

Nayler was to have been denied access to any writing materials and kept from contact with the outside world. This stringent plan was relaxed enough that visitors were able to come and go, means to write were made available somehow, and some of his writing was got out of the prison and soon published. Nayler alluded to this benefit only briefly and obliquely so that the identities of his accomplices were not revealed. "*By a way unexpected did the Lord open a way to declare these words, all other means of writing being taken from me.*"[21]

Had his jailers followed the original plan for his confinement, much of Nayler's best work might have been suppressed. Included in his works done at least in part in Bridewell, were some of his most important writing. *The Lamb's Warre Against the Man of Sinne...*, *What the Possession of the Living Faith Is,* and perhaps, *Milk for Babes...* are examples. Also written in Bridewell were a number of articles and letters which, taken as a whole, go far toward explaining what Nayler attempted in performing the controversial Bristol ride, and distinguishing what he thought he was doing from what some of his companions thought he and they were doing together.

CHAPTER 15

Explaining the Events at Bristol

But this is the Evil in his Sight, and that which provokes his Pure Spirit, That vain man, in whom he thus delights, should be exalted in himself . . .
—James Nayler, Answer to a Fanatick History

Blasphemy, in contrast to Prophecy, is an inward looking indulgence. It attempts to glorify and serve the self, not God, and not God's people. Lust, as Nayler defined that sin and charged himself with its commission, is in the same category. Nayler recognized lust as a misdirection of that affection which belongs rightly and only to God. He called it spiritual adultery. It was the gravest offense for which he accepted guilt, an offense well known not only to Quakers and Christians generally, but to those of other religious traditions as well.

Nayler did not envision his ride into Bristol whole from the start. He came eventually to understand that the purpose of the Sign which God gave him to enact was not simply to alert and prepare the people for the glorification of the return of Christ. Probably he never did think it was that limited, but under examination before Parliament, he could say not much more about why he undertook the reenactment than that God had sent him to do it. He needed no explanation from God, only to do what he was told. He protested vehemently that he never meant to take on himself any of the attributes of God. He could not presume to know the divine purpose in what he was called to do. Neither did he accept the adulation, the hosannas, the glorification of his own person as the returned Messiah. He never meant that his presence in the Sign should justify any of that. What he thought was that his own presence was to represent the requirement that every person must submit personally to humiliation and an equivalent to crucifixion on the way toward salvation. Nayler's prophecy, even in this sorry tableau, was both political in its address, and deeply individual, inasmuch as while one must die alone and under judgment, one must live in a wide society of similar creatures, also under judgment, which if they did not point toward Christ, would wander far astray. That was what he believed he was demonstrating, and what he might have accomplished, but God, Nayler learned, had an additional purpose for the whole affair.

He wrote *A Testimony to Christ Jesus, delivered to the Parliament, who Persecuted him as a Blasphemer: written in the time of his imprisonment at Bridewell*. It seemed to be an effort to clarify, in the most straightforward terms possible, parts of his testimony to Parliament's committee which might have seemed convoluted or evasive. Nayler declared that he denied whatever was dear to his person so that he could be found in Christ and not in himself. He found Christ's Life and Virtue manifest in his mortal body daily, according to the Measure of Grace working in him. He was committed to suffering all that might come, including death, to serve Christ. *"But to ascribe this Name, Power, and Virtue to James Nayler, (or to that which had a Beginning, and must return to Dust) or for that to be exalted or worshipped, to me is great Idolatry, and with the Spirit of Christ Jesus in me it is condemned, which Spirit leads to Lowliness, Meekness, and Long suffering."*[1]

Elsewhere and more publicly, however, he expanded on misinterpretations of his words and outright false claims that he had recanted what he had testified. *His Confessions and Answer to Some Particulars, Printed,* 1659, was probably Whitehead's choice of title for the version of this response included in Collected Works, edited and published by Whitehead long after Nayler's death. The opening text, in italics below, in its entirety probably constitutes Nayler's title.

> Having heard that some have wronged my Words, which I spoke before the Committee of Parliament, concerning Jesus Christ, and concerning the Old and New Testament, some have Printed Words which I spoke not: Also some have printed a Paper, and call it James Nayler's Recantation, unknown to me: To all which things I shall speak a few Words, which may satisfy such as love the Truth, and he who is out of the Truth may proceed no further.

Opening with a restatement that Christ is an Eternal Spirit of Truth, to whom Nayler confessed all Power, Glory, Honour and Worship, he asserted that he never intended to offend the least part of that Spirit, though others attempted to use him to stir up enmity and division among the people of God, dishonoring the name of Christ. To the Power the name was given, he wrote, but not to James Nayler.

Apparently some had said that Nayler denied the suffering of Christ at Jerusalem. (Rhys Jones had made a claim of this sort earlier). Nayler declared that he had always believed literally the Scriptural account of Jesus's suffering, "... *and much more I am confirmed therein Daily, having found the Effect and Power of that Suffering Spirit to be all my Strength in all my Tribulations, who in all our Afflictions hath been afflicted, which whosoever abides in, seeks no Revenge, their reward being present with them; which Power and Spirit whosoever feels in the deep, cannot call Jesus accursed, nor undervalue his Sufferings, neither can any say (in Truth) that he is Lord, but thereby."*[2]

Nayler had argued long before that each must bear the cross daily. He had preached and behaved based on this belief. Yet here he said that notwithstanding what he had always believed, he never had fully understood what he professed and believed by faith until now, after he had himself gone through the suffering of crucifixion. Only in knowing one's own suffering spirit and by knowing the accompanying presence of Jesus, can one both begin to understand Jesus's suffering, and can one say that Jesus is Lord.

As to the Recantation paper, Nayler declared it was not written by him, nor with his knowledge, nor did he know who did write it. It had been used against him. He had heard of many wild, divisive actions taken in his name in the Quaker meetings. The result was confusion and dissention and the dishonouring of God's name. For this Nayler felt God's wrath directed at him for letting it happen. He said of the so-called recantation, "... *I own it not; for in the Patience and Tribulation of Christ Jesus, and with those who have the Power this Day to testifie therein, against all the Evils of this present World, I am one in Heart and Soul to the utmost of my Strength, till the coming of the Lord Jesus over all*. ..."[3]

He did not count the idolaters who conducted the Bristol Sign with him among those who stood in the Power. He wrote as follows in a paper titled, *And in the Day when my God lifted my Feet out of the Pit was this given forth*, published in 1659.

> Glory to God Almighty, who ruleth the heavens ...
> But condemned for ever be all those False Worships, with which any have idolized my Person in the Night of my temptation ... All their casting off of their Cloathes in the Way, their Bowings and Singings, and all the rest of those wild Actions ...[4]
> This Offence I confess, which hath been Sorrow of Heart, that the Enemy of Man's peace in Christ should get this Advantage in the Night of my Tryal, to stir up Wrath and Offences in the Creation of God, a Thing the Simplicity of my Heart did not intend, the Lord knows. ... And also that letter sent me to Exeter, by John Stranger, when I was in Prison, with these Words, *Thy Name shall be no more James Nayler, but Jesus*. This I judge to be written from the Imaginations, and a Fear struck me when I first saw it; and so I put it in my pocket (close) not intending any should see it: which they finding it on me, spread it abroad, which the Simplicity of my Heart never owned. So this I deny also, that the Name of *Christ Jesus* is received instead of *James Nayler*, or ascribed to him: for the Name is to the Promised Seed to all Generations, and he that hath the Son, hath the Name which is Life and Power, and the Salvation and the Unction, into which Name all the Children of the Light are baptized : So the Name of Christ I confess before Men, but not according to Men; which Name to me hath been a strong Tower, in the Night and in the Day.
> And this is the Name of Jesus Christ which I profess, The Son and the Lamb, the Promised Seed ... Head over all ...[5]
> And all those Ranting Wild Spirits, which then gathered about me in the Time of Darkness, and all their wild Actions and wicked Words against the Honour of God and his pure Spirit and People, I deny the Spirit, the Power and the Works thereof, and as far as I gave Advantage, through want of Judgment and Discerning where-ever it was: Which Darkness came over me through Want of Watchfulness and Obedience to the Pure Eye of God, and diligent Minding the

> Reproof of Life, which condemns the Adulterous Spirit: so the Adversary got Advantage, who ceases not to devour. . . . if the Lord of all my Mercies had not rescued me, I had perished, for I was as one appointed to Death and Destruction, and there was none could deliver me.[6]
>
> . . . yet was there many things formed against me at that Day to take away my Life, and cast upon the Truth, of which I am not guilty at all; as that Accusation, as if I had committed Adultery with some of those Women who came with us from Exeter Prison; and also those who were with me at Bristol the Night before I suffered there . . .
>
> Also that Report, as though I had raised Dorcas Erbury from Death; This I deny also . . . though that power that quickens Death I deny not, which is the Word of Eternal Life.[7]

James Nayler was no blasphemer. His arguments, which seem clear and unequivocal on that point from the perspective of three centuries time, may have seemed confusing at the bench to some of the lawyer politicians, but not all the Members of Parliament were convinced that he had made himself out to be Christ. Fox's definition, which spoke in a language they should have found clear enough, was not overtly used against Nayler. They found against him as much for the political expedience of convicting a leading Quaker as for hateful insult to their God. Quakers, on the other hand, did see sinful behavior in what Nayler had done. Fox never charged that Nayler had said that he was Christ. He must have known it was not so. He did charge Nayler with Lust, and Nayler so charged himself. Nayler also attributed his downfall in part to those who offered him Affection, but when we read his use of these terms, Lust and Affection, we must be careful to realize that he did not intend that they be read as we would probably read them in modern usage. Nayler was not talking about sexual seduction or physical desire. He specifically denied any such thing.

He wrote in *To The Life of GOD in All,* dated 1659:[8]

> And in this same Life and Dominion did he bring me up into this great City London, into which I entered with the greatest Fear that ever into any Place I came, in Spirit forseeing somewhat to befal me therein, but not knowing what it might be; yet had I the same Presence and Power as before; into what Place or Service soever I was led of the Spirit, in that Life I never returned without Victory in Christ Jesus, the Lord thereof.[9]

Feeling upheld in that state he became careless of standing ". . . *single and low . . . to be led in all things . . .*," and he gave way ". . . to the Reasoning Part." He was drawn little by little through things which by themselves seemed harmless, then into ". . . *Trifles, Vanities, and Persons which took the Affectionate Part, by which my Mind was drawn from the constant Watch and pure Fear, into which I was once begotten, and spiritual Adultery was committed against that precious pure Life which had purchased me unto himself alone . . .*" It was the same as looking on a woman with lust. "... *letting any visible Object into the Affections is Idolatry: Into that Life I was comprehended, and the Apple of that pure Eye was opened in me, which admits not of an Evil Thought; but is wounded and bruised with the least Appearance of Evil. . . . And this is the Son of God for ever, and into this Life and kingdom I was translated . . . I could feel him in Spirit lifting up his Witness against it.*

> But when I reasoned against his tender Reproof, and consulted with another, and so let the Creatures into my Affections, then his Temple was defiled through Lust, and his pure Spirit was grieved, and he ceased to reprove, and he gave me up . . .[10]

Note here that Nayler "... *consulted with another* ..." about his concern that he was overstepping his faith, and that he was assured somehow by that other person that he was not. His advisor could not have been one of the leaders of the London meeting; was it Martha Simmonds? Whoever he turned to for advice turned his head away from Christ with false affection and reassurance. So, the Temple was defiled, and he was given up. He therefore went forward with the Bristol demonstration unrestrained.

Nayler had lost his guide and the Adversary had got in. Confused, he let himself be led by others, whose purpose was to divide him from the Children of the Light, which was accomplished, though some friends, unnamed in Nayler's own accounts, tried hard to prevent it. People came to him to try to pull him out of it, and he rejected them, although secretly he hoped and had faith that God would somehow pull him out.

> Thus was I led out from amongst the Children of the Light and into the World, to be a Sign, where I was chased as a wandering Bird gone from her Nest, so was my Soul daily and my Body from one Prison to another, till at length I was brought in their own Way before a backsliding Power to be judged, who had lost their first Love, as I have done; So they sentenced me, but could not see their Sign, and a Sign to the Nation, and a Sign to the World of the dreadful Day of the just God, who is come and coming to avenge for that pure Life, where it is transgressed, and to plead the Cause of that precious Seed where-ever it is oppressed and suffers under the fleshly Lusts of this present World, and the Cup is deep and very dreadful that is seen and filling, and it hath begun at God's House, but many must drink it, except there be speedy Repentence.[11]

Almost in passing, he had declared that the widespread understanding of God's intention for the sign given to him and the others to enact was wrong. He had come to this conclusion as he reflected during his time in Bridewell, not having understood while it was happening to him what was God's purpose for his calling to do the Bristol sign.

The point was not that the party of demonstrators must emulate Jesus riding into Jerusalem accompanied by his adherents, as if Bristol were somehow the homecoming part of the Apocalypse. No, the sign was in the public outrage, the trial, the incarcerations, the continuing refusal of the people of England and their government to repent and prepare the way for their own Judgment, ignoring once again that it was not for humankind to judge the foolishness or veracity of prophets. Man's vanity was undiminished. The wrath of God would come on inevitably. Nayler was put forward to be crucified, as it were, to make clear that humankind still, despite all their pious protestations had not accepted Christ's sacrifice for them and repented of their continuing sins. In that respect, Nayler declared, even though he had been as blind to what was really happening at his trial as any other participant, the Sign, God's Sign in God's own way, was there for the whole nation to see.

Writing in *Answer to a Fanatick History*, Nayler explained, "*. . . when my Adversary was above, and wherein I was made a Sign to a Backsliding Generation, who then would not see or hear what now is coming upon them, but rejoyced against this piece of Dust, and had little pity towards him that was fallen into their Hands, wherein God was Just in giving me up for my Disobedience, for a little Moment, as a Father to correct . . .*"[12]

Ranters and wild spirits, using his name, continued to disturb and divide the Meetings. A few Friends came in pity to try to comfort Nayler, who had abused his power without knowing it. He had lost his self, he confessed, but still he was under the care of God. He had preached before about renunciation of self, but now that he had lost his own, it was not in the same way at all as what he thought he had meant. There is surrender on the one hand, and foolish abandonment on the other.[13]

> So I give all Glory to the Life for evermore, and to Him it is due, and all the Evil hath been from Self.
> This Life is the Root and Off-spring of all Heavenly Fruit upon Earth, and in whom this is planted, as it grows it will bring forth Truth and Righteousness toward God and Man . . .
> But this is the Evil in his Sight, and that which provokes his Pure Spirit, That vain man, in whom he thus delights, should be exalted in himself. . . .[14]

So he went down, and those with him went down the same way. He hurt others as well as himself. Still more were tempted in their own way. His story was a warning to all, from one who has "*. . . drunken a Measure of that Depth which cannot be measured.*"[15]

All but one of the above quotations are read from the introduction to the first publication of substantially all Nayler's writing, the 1716 *Collected Works. . .* , gathered and edited by George Whitehead. (*Answer to a Fanatick History* is printed in the body of the *Collection*, not in the Introduction.) The introduction is paginated in small Roman numerals, indicating that it is to be taken as a separate from the collected Nayler writings which follow, paginated in conventional Arabic numerals. The introductory material begins with, *An Epistle To The Serious Reader Containing An Impartial Account of the most Remarkable Transactions relating to James Nayler,* signed G.W., or George Whitehead. This 24 page account is undated, but is likely to have been written after Nayler's death in 1660, probably long after. The eight Nayler pieces included in the introduction were all written during or soon after Nayler's imprisonment in Bridewell and constitute his own explanation of what happened to him during the breakdown of his London ministry, his involvement with the Simmonds/Stranger group, and the Bristol ride. Also included are the clarification addressed to Parliament of his testimony at the trial, commentary and denial of the testimonies of some others, his disavowal of the fraudulent recantation published over his name, and apologies to Friends for his behavior and for his rejection of those who tried to help him.

Nayler, it was commonly believed, had fallen in with a bad lot, who had led him astray. Whitehead wrote:

> By a good measure of Divine Illumination and Inward Experience, he knew the Ministration of Judgment and Mercy, Law and Gospel, preferring the Ministration of the Spirit above that of the Letter; and accordingly preached to turn People's Minds to the Light, the Life, the Spirit and the Power of Christ in them, out of all empty Forms, carnal Observations, dead literal Preachings and Professions, where the power of Godliness was or is denied. In these Matters the said J.N. was in Measure Gifted, with Demonstration of the Spirit of Christ while the Light shined upon his Tabernacle, before he was clouded and hurt.[16]

Whitehead charged that hurt against Martha Simmonds and her followers, based on what he said was Nayler's personal account to him of what happened. This story was told to Whitehead by Nayler first hand as they walked "*. . . together in the Field at Great Strickland in Westmoreland, 1657 . . . this was after he was revived and restored to a Measure of good Understanding and Judgment . . . whereby his first Love was renewed in him towards his faithful Friends and Brethren in Christ.*"[17]

These words of Whitehead are the subject of considerable controversy. Damrosch has observed that the date of Whitehead's conversation cannot be right, as Nayler was imprisoned in Bridewell throughout 1657.[18] I have postulated that since Whitehead referred to a meeting with Nayler after his release from prison, it was probably in 1659, suggesting a simple typographical or transcription error, misreading a 9 for a 7. Braithwaite, however, accepted Whitehead's account and from it suggested that Nayler was temporarily released from Bridewell in 1657.[19] Braithwaite pointed out that Whitehead's diaries show that he was in Great Strickland in 1657, but not after that during Nayler's lifetime. No other evidence of a temporary release from Bridewell has been found, and Nayler's health during 1657 casts a great deal of doubt on the idea of travel to the north for any reason other than a return home to West Ardsley or Wakefield in expectation of death. These communities are far south of Great Strickland. Whitehead wrote his introduction as much as sixty years after the event he described. Although he asserted that he really had not been acquainted with Nayler until they both roomed at the Travers home after Nayler was released from Bridewell, he was a schoolteacher in Orton when Nayler was there in 1652, and had heard Nayler's preaching elsewhere in the North around 1653.[20] Nayler was in Great Strickland at that time. Possibly, Whitehead was confused in this relation of where and when he had heard Nayler's story. By the time his Nayler collection was published in 1716, Whitehead, aged over eighty, was the only survivor of the so-called "Valiant Sixty" of those early years of Quaker ministry. He had outlived George Fox, Margaret Fell, and all the others from that time, and soon Whitehead, too, would be gone.

We must consider also Whitehead's unnamed publication committee. One might be justified in calling them censors, for his selections of Nayler's works and no doubt his own introductory remarks had to meet the approval of the Quaker leadership, even as late as 1716. In order for this first collection of Nayler writings to be published, Whitehead had to answer the question of blame for what Nayler had done to bring scandal, insult, and further persecution to the already beset Friends. Laying the charge squarely against the Temptor, that is, Satan, and the women, seems to have been what was needed to get the job of publication done.

Nayler's own words told a subtly different and far more complete story, which was allowed in print. Nayler was dead, of course. The choice was either to publish what he wrote, or not to do so. His words could not be changed to any significant extent by honest men. Whitehead's editorial comments were appropriately limited, and they were written after the passage of years. Nayler spoke for himself in this introduction, but he had not chosen the words for the purpose to which Whitehead put them. His purpose in the works included in Whitehead's introduction to the collected Works was specific in the case of each paper, direct and contemporaneous. He apologized profusely to the many he had wronged, assigned and accepted blame where it was due. He laid out as well the reasons why this disaster could happen to a man of his level of faith, and accepted how a stern but merciful God had let him go down his careless path to be an example of what lay in that direction. Nayler did not mention, nor did Whitehead, what both of them surely knew, that in this dreadful experience Nayler found the material for the final chapters of his prophetic ministry.

CHAPTER 16

Possession of the Living Faith, the Last Great Works

... this is clear to me for ever without any more Controversie, That the faith that admits of sin is not Christ's Faith, nor hath any share or possession in him; that faith which came not from God and so cannot build up to God ...
—James Nayler, What the Possession of the Living Faith is

During Nayler's imprisonment, in September of 1658, Oliver Cromwell died. His son Richard took over the Protectorate, but Richard was not made of the same stuff as his father. The balance of power had tipped against him and the Protectorate. He could not overcome its bias. Within a year of his father's death Richard Cromwell was forced to resign. Military control of the country was established, first under General Lambert, and then under the strong hand of General Monck, who had met and defeated Lambert's armed opposition between Scotland and London. Parliament was dismissed briefly and later recalled. During their brief tenure the body saw to an amnesty and release of Quaker prisoners, including Nayler. Shortly there followed, in May of 1660, the Restoration of the exiled King Charles II. The great revolutionary experiment of the past twenty years was turned back on itself. A tender, hopeful order began to appear, but there were many debts to be paid. Those freedoms gained by regicide could not be allowed to stand by the executed King's son. More so, they could not be sanctioned by the military, which supported the new monarch.

General Monck was every bit a soldier and cared little for politics. By the end of the wars he had served both sides, bringing on Irish troops at the outset to assist King Charles I. Captured at the Battle of Nantwich, he was forgotten by his king as he lay prisoner of Parliament in the Tower. There he wrote a treatise on the subject of military structure and discipline. When the monarchy fell, he committed his allegiance to the victors and fought for the good old cause alongside Oliver and the rest until the Royalist cause was broken in Ireland and Scotland.

Monck had a firm standard of discipline, law and order. He held Scotland for Parliament during the Protectorate, refusing a veiled offer from a minority to come south and take over from Cromwell. Religion, among other subtleties was behind that treachery. He may have seemed to turn openly against Parliament, when he did come south from Scotland with his army after Cromwell's death. Brushing Lambert's forces aside en route he ousted the sitting Parliament, and took over rule of the country under military administration. He may have appeared to turn Royalist, but it was required by his soldier's notion of order. Monck saw the necessity to bring forward the monarchy once more in order to stabilize the country. The Protectorate, balanced against Parliament, clearly had failed, and few knew better than he the risks of an ungoverned army.[1]

Monck was no friend of Quakers, who could never, as he understood them, be counted on to follow the orders of officers in the army or at the head of State, for Quakers served only one high officer, who was not of any army or nation of the world. Monck was right in that. He distrusted Quaker leaders with political power as well. Bishop, for example, a soldier, had served Cromwell and Parliament as an intelligence officer, gathering reports on the Royalist elements who would restore Charles II to the throne. Bishop had become de facto leader of the Quakers when Fox was imprisoned, so if anyone could be in a position to lead a Quaker insurgency, it would be this man. Fox was rightly in prison and should stay there, for he would answer to no man, but only stir up his brethren, who in Monck's eyes resembled the mad Fifth Monarchists, who more and more threatened revolt (and in fact soon did rise up). Nayler had used to seem mad as well, after the Bristol affair, but Monck was in a position to know much of his army background as well. Here was a man to be watched now that he was free and rebuilding his standing among the Friends. Nayler had been close to General Lambert, who opposed Monck and had long held aspirations to head the government. Lambert was soon imprisoned, ruined as to his health and aspirations. He barely escaped execution. Nayler's health was broken too, that much was known. Monck was content to let him be for now, as nature took its course.

As to Nayler, his last few years were a sweet period, in their way, full of suffering and physical decline, yet productive of reconciliation, brilliant writing, and spiritual clarity. Having been imprisoned at Bridewell in January, 1657 and suffered deeply from his torture for months, he had begun to recover by the middle of that year and to write. He sent letters expressing grief and apology to Margaret Fell, to Friends elsewhere, and to George Fox. He was visited fairly often after his wife, Ann, had seen to remission of some his harshest treatment. Largely at the urging of his old friend, William Dewsbury, he began in earnest to seek reconciliation with Fox and other leading Quakers. Some of Nayler's conciliatory correspondence, as well as a letter of Dewsbury's acknowledging Nayler's recovery and correction of his errors, was chosen by Whitehead decades later to be included in the introduction to Nayler's collected works.[2] Nayler needed a respected sponsor in order to regain some of the esteem he had lost among Quaker leadership. Undertaking of that sponsorship was one of Dewsbury's great, though largely unnoticed, legacies to the Quaker movement.

By late in 1658 one of Nayler's most important works, *The Lamb's Warre Against the man of Sin,* was published and distributed by Thomas Simmonds. Later it was included in Whitehead's collection.[3] In it Nayler wrote in accessible detail of how God not only expected but had uniquely gifted humankind to follow the way of Christ toward Salvation. He wrote:

> First, That he may be just who is to judge all Men and Spirits, he gives his Light into their Hearts, even of Man and Woman, whereby he lets all see (who will mind) what he is displeased with, what is with him, and what is against him; what he owns, and what he disowns, that so all may know what is for destruction, to come out of it, lest they be destroyed with it, that so he may save and receive all that are not wilfully disobedient, and hardened in the pleasures of this World, against him; all who are deceived, who are willing to be undeceived; all who are captivated, who are willing to be set free; all that are in darkness, and are willing to come to light. In a word, all that love Righteousness more than the pleasures of Sin, that he may not destroy them, nor they fight against him, and know it not, but that he may receive them, to be one with him against that which misled and deceived them; and as many as turn at his reproof, he doth receive, and gives them Power in Spirit and Life to be as he is, in their measure, but all in Watching, and Wars against that which hath had them, and now has the rest of Creation in Bondage, that he may restore all things to their former Liberty.[4]

One could expect, Nayler argued, no jealous god who kept secrets of predestination and election. Rather, by a high standard and stern judgment, be sure of justice. Everyone had been given the Light needed to see what was expected in their life. This was a gentle father, accepting of no excuses, but who would admit all who had turned from deception and wrongdoing into righteousness. Quakers were not prone to sermons. Their ministries were called testimonies, and surely this was one. The war of the Lamb against the Man of Sin—Nayler called it also the war of the God of Spirit against the God of the World. Here rose the Antichrist, the fallen angel, Satan, the deceiver and adversary of each person on their way toward redemption or damnation, but Nayler said the way has been traveled for us already. The guide is written. You have the Light within you to follow the path. No excuses. The way led through crucifixion, but if one should boast of seeing it and perhaps enduring a suffering, that was deceit. Boasting was deceit.

> Now you that cry, The Kingdoms of this World are become the Kingdoms of the Lord and of his Christ; See that it be the Truth in you, and that you Lye not within your selves. The Lamb's War YOU must know, before you can witness his Kingdom and how you have been called into his War, and whether you have been Faithful and Chosen there or no. He that preaches the Kingdom of Christ in Words, without Victory, is the Thief that goes before Christ. . . .[5]

To some it would have seemed still to be abstract and uncertain to argue, as Nayler did, from a prison, where he stood sentence for horrid blasphemy, or if one did not accept that judgment against him, perhaps then he was held prisoner for his own foolishness. It could have seemed hard to accept that he said in effect, you may think you know what I mean about following Christ's way. You may think and be moved to say that you are righteous. But until you have been through the crucifixion, in the way Jesus knew, then you cannot meet the standard God requires.

For secular revolutionaries, closed to his real ministry, there was another way to read Nayler. He said that persecution is our lot. Those who truly follow Christ, are to be hated by the people, and he spoke of the whole progress toward salvation as a war in Christ. Many, and not just Friends, knew first hand about persecution. Many had fought in war against it. These were tender times to speak again of religious war. The Fifth Monarchists spoke of war in a very real sense. Revolution to overthrow the Royalists was very likely from that group, and others as well had not yet ended their fight. Where exactly did Nayler's Quakers stand? What was this holy war he spoke about? If one read *The Lamb's War* it was all there, and carefully read, it threatened no secular revolution. Yet, it did hark back to the one just concluded. Some would see the continuity.

> And thus the Lamb in them, and they in him, go out in Judgment and Righteousness, to make War with his Enemies, conquering and to conquer, not as the Prince of this World in his Subjects with Whips and Prisons, Tortures and Torment on the Bodies of Creatures, to kill and destroy Mens Lives who are deceived and so become his Enemies; but he goes forth in the Power of the Spirit with the Word of Truth, to pass Judgment upon the Head of the Serpent, which doth deceive and bewitch the World . . .[6]

The figure is familiar. It comes from Revelation 6, along with the image of the Lamb,

> And I saw when the Lamb opened one of the seals, and I heard, as it were the noise of thunder, one of the four beasts saying, Come and see.
> And I saw, and behold a white horse: and he that sat on him had a bow; and a crown was given unto him: and he went forth conquering, and to conquer.

(Nayler was using the language of the King James version, not the old Geneva Bible, which differs in the last line quoted above.)

The Rider on the White Horse had arisen sixteen years before, in the person of James Nayler's officer, Thomas Fairfax, leading the revolution in Yorkshire. In that war the Head of the Serpent was King Charles I's head. Such a double entendre in Nayler's writing was never accidental. It did not serve his purpose to deny or overlook the past. It was part of the same story. He wrote in *The Lamb's War* . . . :

> Now these are the Last times, and many false Christs there must appear, and be made manifest by the true Christ, with their false Prophets, false Ways and

false Worships, and false Worshippers, which though they be at Wars with one another, yet not the Lamb's War. Now seeing he hath appeared, who is from Everlasting and changeth not, here is an Everlasting Tryal for you all, all sorts of Professors, whether you Profess him from the Letter or from the Light; Come try whether Christ is in you, measure your Life, and weigh your Profession with that which cannot deceive you, which hath stood, and will stand for ever, for he is sealed of the Father.[7]

Still abstract? Perhaps, but only a little. Still possible to infer a revolution from *The Lamb's War* . . .? Yes, it was possible, but the revolution was not by arms against the government.

The Lamb's War is not against Creation, for then should his Weapons be Carnal, as the Weapons of the Worldly Spirits are, For We War not with Flesh and Blood, nor against the Creation of God, that we Love, but we Fight against the Spiritual Powers of Wickedness, which wars against God in the Creation, and Captivates the Creation into the Lust which Wars against the Soul, and that the Creature may be delivered into its Liberty, prepared for the Sons of God. And this is not against Love, nor everlasting Peace, but without which there can be no true Love, nor lasting Peace.[8]

Whether *The Lamb's War* . . . ever came to Oliver Cromwell's attention is not known. It was published before he died. Cromwell was concerned about what he heard of Nayler's condition in prison. Surely, the Protector must have realized, Nayler's death in Bridewell would have stirred much disapproval. In poor health himself, he sent a secretary to visit Nayler, but the report was not helpful one way or the other. Nayler ignored this visitor as much as possible, not even deigning to speak to him. It was clear enough that the prisoner was unwell, but to what extent his illness endangered his life could not be determined. At any rate, Cromwell soon expired, and whether he would have released Nayler or urged Parliament to do it will never be known.

1658 saw Nayler in reasonably good health, sufficiently so that he could resume his efforts at reconciliation and his written ministry. In addition to letters to Margaret Fell, he wrote at least six epistles to Friends, a letter to Robert Rich in which Nayler urged him to temper his outrage at the way Nayler was treated, also a letter to Independents in Massachusetts, and his published apology to Friends, all this in addition to *The Lamb's War* . . . By the spring of 1659 his health was again in decline, and he required medical and nursing care. Nevertheless, he continued energetic enough to write a discourse on his own spiritual journey and the place beside Christ to which it had brought him, a work which for the completeness of its discourse could have sufficed in the event that it were the last of his important writings. Written during Nayler's imprisonment at Bridewell and published by Thomas Simmonds in 1659, it provides a guide to Nayler's London and Bristol misfortunes with special emphasis on his failure to interrupt the demonstration. The full title reads:

> What the Possession of the Living Faith is
> And the fruits thereof, And wherein
> It hath been found to differ from the dead faith
> Of the World, in the learning and following
> Of Christ in the Regeneration
>
> With
> An Opening of Light to all sorts of
> People that waits for the Kingdom of God;
>
> And a Candle Lighted to give the sight
> Of the good Old Way of God from the wayes
> That now ensnares the simple.[9]

In describing his own passage through faith into Christ Nayler discussed blindness, even the self-deception, that flowed almost inevitably from one's initial, absolute acceptance of the Scriptural account of Jesus in Jerusalem. That acceptance and the ensuing fall into faith brought him, and he was sure others, to such a level of joy that he felt convinced that the secret of life had been revealed to him.

> The effect of which Faith when in the Light I first received it, did turn my mind out of all my sins' path, and took my mind out of them and turned me towards God, and holiness of life I then believed to attain in that faith . . .

But no, it was just the beginning.

> . . . then I see no less Faith could save me then {than} the perfect Faith of the Son {of} God, which before I had not received, but then received with such gladnesse of heart, that it set my face and delights out of all sin towards the perfection of Christ in which I then believed . . .

He might have stopped at that level and begun professing his great understanding, but that way led to self-deception, from which must follow false teaching.

> . . . I was turned from my sin, and so from condemnation, yet there was a great work to do in me before I could witness freedom from the body of death, and the root and ground of evil removed . . . And that glorious liberty of the new Creature, and all things to be of God in me, as the scriptures do witness; so this faith did not work in me into a conceit of myself, glorying in knowledge, and so to become a Teacher of others what I had conceived below the life, but it led me down into the obedience of the Spirit of Life, to wait therein for the Resurrection of Life, and I came to see in that Light that the motions of sin did still work from the old ground and root, and that must be removed by the power of Christ working in spirit, and my obedience and watchfulness therein was required, and that

without obedience to this faith, I could not come to perfect victory over the enmity, nor the glorious victory of the Sons of God; for though this faith had turned my heart towards Christ and given me hope to attain him, yet I had not then learned him, nor was he yet formed in me, so I was led in the Light of Christ to see what I had of this treasure in the earthen vessel, which I found to be in me very little, and that Seed the least of all Seeds, so I became little in that eye which told me the Truth, though I had been high in my own thoughts formerly . . . And then came I clearly to see Christ Jesus before me in all things that I was to go through, in that faith which I had first received, and that the attaining of him was the hope of glory, and no hope without him . . .

We have no markers along the way in this narrative of where in time these realizations took form, or to what specific events any of it relates. Nayler did not write that way, for it would have drawn the focus from Christ, where attention was due, to James, who was but a creature. The statement which immediately follows the above quotation, however, guides us to the conclusion that the above understanding of what he must do came into full force after his world fell apart in the London and Bristol disaster.

. . . and this hope was an Anchor in all hardships and temptations, which was not a few I was led through, but all was counted little while I stood in this Faith, for the hope was in me now to win Christ . . .

The clarity of hindsight surely brightens this picture. His eye was turned from Christ, Nayler admitted himself, when he gave in to the reasoning and the affectionate worldly temptations in London. When he fought with Fox that last time at Exeter, he had lost track of Christ. Even when he testified before Parliament, he could only obliquely, if at all, touch on the process of following and learning Christ, as he later laid it out in this writing. If he had the idea whole as he sat there accused and cross-examined, could he have told them? Few persons could have expressed such a ministry before the mighty. Yet, in that committee room Nayler knew full well that his life was in grave danger. If at any time he should have said what he said here, that was the place and the time. Clearly, he didn't quite have it. Instead, he looked back from Bridewell in 1659 and understood at last what he had been about, not only at Bristol, but during the whole course of his prophecy, from Woodkirk onward. He had been learning all along the way, yet the farther he progressed in his journey, the more he found he had to learn, and the deeper he had to reach to find the words to say it.

He wrote next of the end times and of the appearance of God in judgment. This was yet more difficult, for it went beyond the footsteps of Jesus into faith in Scripture and the limits, the physical limits, of the Creature, humankind. Here Nayler laid out, without attributing the error to particular persons, the fault in the idolatry his companions at Bristol focused on himself, and the greater fault of his own acquiescence to how they presented him. He could not excuse any of it.

> And this I found also, that this Son of God doth not appear in any within or without, but as he conforms them to his own Image . . . When he shall appear we shall be like him, who shall change our vile bodies and make them like his glorious body, from glory to glory by the same Spirit; And herein we have boldness in the day of Judgment, because as he is so are we in this present world; and this is not obtained with thoughts of believing without, but by a lively working Power, which works out the earthly image and nature, and conforms to the heavenly in that spiritual birth which is not of flesh and blood. . . .
>
> And this Faith which confesseth him present, is that which the world cannot bear nor receive, who will preach him themselves at a distance, what he was and will be, but this faith cannot reach his coming at present in any measure to grow to his appearance now, nor will this faith ever give an entrance into his Kingdom upon earth, nor the holy rest, nor is this the Faith of Christ (that puts him thus far off) . . .
>
> . . . this is clear to me for ever without any more Controversie, That the faith that admits of sin is not Christ's Faith, nor hath any share or possession in him; that faith which came not from God, and so cannot build up to God . . . but is deceiving faith which deceives the Soul, and suffers lust to defile it and destroy it, and so brings it under Condemnation, by believing lyes, and so letting in sin upon the Soul by consent, perswading that it cannot be otherwise; and so gives the Devil victory and the world victory, and the flesh victory and sin victory over the Soul, which should give the Soul victory over all; And what greater deceit can there be to the Soul than this is?

These lines were among the harshest that Nayler ever wrote. If one can see in them the address and dismissal they contain of what Martha Simmonds, the Strangers, Dorcas Erbury and perhaps others led him into, one can imagine the extent of Nayler's outrage. One can see as well that his anger is directed not only at these deceivers, but all the more so at himself. He did not come to the understanding written in this document entirely full blown at Bridewell in 1659. He had been working toward it for years. He understood as well as anyone could the difference between Faith in Christ and adoration of worldly figures, between worship and ceremony. He understood false profession of what were held out as direct leadings from God to enact some offensive sign. Certainly he understood flattery. Yet in the course of being drawn toward a ministry far deeper than any he had yet undertaken, he allowed those who attached themselves to him to practice flattery, deceit, and ceremony under the veil of a representation that these excesses were as much leadings from God as were the movements of Nayler's own ministry, which held that the way toward Christ at the time of Judgment led through crucifixion and denial of self for each person, just as much as the path of Jesus had done. Nayler had allowed himself to admit the possibility of divine inspiration at work in his idolaters as it was at work in himself, when in fact, if his wits had cleared, he could have seen the deception in all of it. Was he too ill to see what was going on? That was suggested by others, but he never made that excuse for himself. If some kind of sickness were the cause of his failing, he might have felt outraged and indignant that he had been used, when he weakened. Surely he held those feelings, and perhaps more. Anger seems to drive the last line quoted above, "*And what greater deceit can there be to the Soul than this is?*" Notwithstanding possible illness, Nayler felt he had let himself be taken for a fool by a troupe of extravagant people, just as he told George Whitehead at about this same time. Anger to him was no simple matter, for it was named in Paul's letter to the Colossians with the worst litany of worldly behaviors that must be laid aside before Judgment:

> Col. 3:5. . . fornication, uncleanness, inordinate affection, evil concupiscence, and covetousness, which is idolatry:
> Col. 3:6 For which things' sake the wrath of God cometh on the children of disobedience:
> Col. 3:7 In the which ye also walked some time, when ye lived in them.
> Col. 3:8 But now ye also put off all these; anger, wrath, malice, blasphemy, filthy communication out of your mouth.
> Col. 3:9 Lie not one to another, seeing that ye have put off the old man with his deeds;
> Col. 3:10 And have put on the new man, which is renewed in knowledge after the image of him that created him.

No doubt Nayler needed to write *What the Possession of the Living Faith is, and the Fruits Thereof* in order to move his feelings about the matters leading to his own imprisonment into a productive discourse at a general level about how such things could happen, be recognized, and be turned toward a right course. It served that purpose. The writing was not his best, being repetitive and somewhat crudely organized. Its shortcomings, however, were overcome in large part by driving energy and occasional, though inconsistent, forthrightness. Once it was done, he may have felt relieved of a burden so that he could move on. He would not have claimed that he had put on the image of the new man, not yet, but without attaining the clarity described in this piece of writing, he never would put on the new man, nor would the idolaters who for a time had held him up. In the spirit of love, he must let go the feelings he held about this worst period of his life, let go, and fall into Christ.

The great work of this period, also written at Bridewell, and probably the last of his long written ministries, was titled, "*Milk for Babes and Meat for Strong Men Treated of. That a Feast of fat Things and Wine well refined on the Lees, They may come to be Partakers of.*"[10] Taken together, two texts, *The Lamb's Warre . . .* , and *Milk for Babes . . .* , provide the most complete and mature of Nayler's statements regarding the way toward Christ and salvation. *The Lamb's Warre . . .* addresses the struggle to separate from things of the worldly spirit, the Adversary, and to stand instead with Christ, the Lamb. *Milk for Babes . . .* represents the closing chapter of this ministry, the explication of what salvation really is, its cost, and its reward. This is the work that deals with God's foundation of the new life, that ground onto which one finally sinks when all other false support is let go and the fall into Christ reaches bottom. The nature of all the sin and iniquity experienced on the way down through layer on layer of deception is described, expanded on, and repeated. A distinction is drawn between false grounding and a true foundation built of the stones chosen by God. The reward of leaving the self and all its deceit behind is shown, but it is no gentle, airy thing.

Milk for Babes . . . is a complicated teaching. The Scriptural references of the title must be explored for guidance into the content of the piece, two New Testament sources and one from the Old Testament. The source readings weigh against one another, as in Scripture, so that no one reference is left simply to stand on its own and limit the scope of the ideas presented. Nothing is that simple. Nayler did not sweeten the truth to make it easier to accept.

Milk and Meat; a feast with fat things and fine wine. The figure of "Milk for Babes" is found in two books of the New Testament, 1 Peter 2:2 and Hebrews 5:12-14. The "feast of fat things" appears in Isaiah 25:6. Peter's epistle, known as a most hopeful and practical set of directions for living the Christian life, was a popular text. John Cotton, the Puritan Congregational spiritual leader of the New England colonies, had used the title "Milk for Babes" in 1646 for a children's catechism that was widely used for generations. Nayler's application of Peter's words, however, was not for use by children. He meant by this phrase to suggest the state of innocence and unquestioning desire to which the faithful should have stripped themselves to prepare for the word of Christ. He added to his title the phrase, "Meat for Strong Men," which was not found in 1 Peter. Those words suggested the second text in which "Milk for Babes" was found, the Pauline letter to the Hebrews, in which the author expressed the sardonic view that many of the readers to whom his teaching was directed needed to be fed the harsh realties of faith as if they were children; they could not receive the truth in the form of strong meat, as if they were mature persons. Nayler did not intend sarcasm. He wrote that it was for the meek and humble to sink through persecution and suffering at the hands of the strong, the sinful, the lawless and godless.

> . . . There is the strong Man to be bound, before the Babe can reign; and strongly is he armed with all Manner of Wiles to save himself; and it's not Words and Thoughts that will cast out the Mother and her Son, which must not inherit: And this must be done, or all is in vain. He that is born of Flesh is in Bondage to things here below; this cannot inherit Immortality, for Sin hath Power in him; and die he must, that the Son of Righteousness may arise to Life in you, and bring your Light to Life with him, as he appears; and though the Light be above the Transgressor, yet the Son is lowly that gives it . . .[11]

He spoke of falling through levels where the foundations on which one stood were false and ultimately weak, to the true foundation, God's cornerstone. One fell through lust and persecutions, into a place where there was no more fear of falling, onto a foundation where every stone is everlasting.

> So with all Diligence, sink down to feel the election, not minding that which boasts in high Words before it be tried, but when it comes into the Fire will not stand patient in the Tryal . . .[12]

The election? Had the Quaker prophet softened during his imprisonment and accepted that notion of the churchmen, that the good people of the Lord would be singled out in the end times for their righteousness to walk forever on Heaven's golden streets? Not at all. Here he turned to the sense of Strong Meat, found in the text from the letter to the Hebrews, and in Nayler's title as Meat for Strong Men. Nayler's idea of election was a different thing altogether. It must not be a glorifying process to reach it, but a humbling one. Yes, there was joy at the end, but joy was to be had in suffering and resignation of all earthly things, to be upheld on God's foundation, where no man of sin could ever stand. The only true riches were to be found in utmost humility. Furthermore, Nayler's final plunge was unique and solitary. There was no notion in what he wrote of an earthly church to uphold anyone in their fall off the precipice of sin into the hope of salvation. One died alone, and what Nayler meant by the image of God's rock at the bottom of the fall was that one hit it hard, and it was death. Only out of death could there be salvation.

Weighty enough, but this much was only the beginning of the book. The second half of *Milk for Babes* . . . is like the working manual. It follows the example of the Pauline letter to Hebrews and lays out the task of being faithful, ever watchful, resistant to all temptations, and especially the temptation to look back with fondness to the times before.

> Wherefore stand fast in that which you have proved to be Liberty indeed, and by no means look back nor hanker to that which is behind, to let it overtake you again: Remember Lot's wife; and the Wrath of God will ever be upon that Mind which looks back into Old things, which are judged in the Light; and led out of with the Life: Wherefore stand single in your Minds to follow nothing New or Old, but what the Holy Spirit leads into; for the Work is a Work you know not, nor the Way do you know, but as it is learned in Obedience . . .
>
> And this Work will be darkened to your Understanding, if your Minds come not clear out of the Old, into the New: For Wrath will arise, and Confusion will be to that Mind which is double, where the Eye is not single, kept forward in the Belief of the Spirit only, but looks back into the loss, and to that which is dying and condemned; there is the Smoak, and Darkness, and Torment, and Temptations, being enticed back into the Old: But if the Eye be single, the whole Body is full of Light, and the Faith ariseth to endure to the end of the World, and to look to the beginning and finishing of the Work of Regeneration. And standing single to God herein, though the World pass away with Thundering and

Earth quakes, and a mighty Noise, yet shall ye not fear or faint, abiding in the meek, patient and suffering Spirit, and the leadings of that which endureth all things to win Christ: And coming out of Babel, you shall not fall with her, nor be darkened with the Smoak of her Torments, as all that abide in her must, and of her Plagues must partake; but the pure Mind rejoyceth over her in the midst of all.[13]

So ends *Milk for Babes* . . . The reference in Nayler's title, Isaiah's feast of fat things for the faithful, reads as follows:
Is: 25:6 –9

And in this mountain shall the Lord of hosts make unto all people a feast of fat things, a feast of wines on the lees, of fat things full of marrow, of wines on the lees well refined.

And he will destroy in this mountain the face of the covering cast over all people, and the vail that is spread over all nations.

He will swallow up death in victory; and the Lord God will wipe away tears from off all faces; and the rebuke of his people shall he take away from off all the earth; for the Lord hath spoken it.

And it shall be said in that day, Lo, this is our God; we have waited for him, and will be glad and rejoice in his salvation.

On his release from prison Nayler found housing at the home of Rebecca and William Travers in London. Also living there was George Whitehead, later publisher of Nayler's collected works. James seemed to be in good health. Thomas Ellwood, who was to become one of the foremost thinkers and writers of the next generation of Friends, met him only three weeks after Nayler left Bridewell. Ellwood found him remarkably sound in health and mind after three years in that place. Nayler and Burrough together had a great influence on the young Ellwood and his father, as they began a ministry together in London and environs.[14] During this time in mid-1660 Nayler answered some publications critical of him and Quakers generally. He also wrote for the last time to a public leader.

Prominent among the papers he answered was one called *A Fanatick History*, a diatribe against the Quakers put out and subscribed by a list of leading clergy, addressed to the new King Charles II, and naming Nayler as one of the leaders of what they described as a dangerous sect.[15] Nayler went to great lengths to debate every point in the paper, to assure its readers that there was no danger from the Quakers, and of course, to ridicule the authors of this attack. He did, however, take full responsibility for his own actions at Bristol and made no excuse for himself. (Part of his admission of fault has been noted in Chapter 15.)

After answering the priests, he wrote a public letter to the King on behalf of Quakers. This letter bears comparison with the earlier letters to Cromwell and the Parliament. In his earliest letter to Cromwell Nayler had urged the new head of government not to accept a crown for his victories, but rather to give that symbol to the real victor to whom it belonged, and to bring forth a country newly formed under God's rule.[16] It was a call to inspired leadership, and in this way rather like the 1660 letter to Charles II, but the letters Nayler issued in the intervening years challenged the Protector, the Parliament, and the army officers to renounce hypocrisy and persecution in order to deliver on their old promises of freedom of conscience. The letter to Charles II was a polite introduction to Quakers, their faith, and the persecution they had endured, but in no way did Nayler blame Charles II for what had gone on before his restoration to monarchy. He was careful to assure the King that the Quakers had no hostile intent toward him and his government or anyone else. In a straightforward, gentle, and unequivocal way, however, Nayler advised the new King that he could expect no support from Friends, nor special obedience either, for that matter, unless by the guidance of God. Friends only answered to one higher power, and that one without regard for conflicts with the rule of any other. The call for inspiration in this letter was not so much for the leadership of the nation as it was for the King to see to his own salvation. In the end, the letter expressed all good will and concern for the King as a man, but no political graciousness or understatement. Nayler had taken another step away from the process of political protest and toward prophetic ministry.

> O King, spend not thy time in Fleshly Pleasures, neither strive after that Glory which will fade away, but apply thy Heart to God, and wait to feel his Spirit in thee, giving thee Light and Understanding to guide thy Ways before him; for only Blessed is he who Rules by his Power, and who is Taught of God shall be established in Righteousness, and be far from Oppression; and only such shall be called the Blessed of God to all Generations: Read, and Remember the Righteous and the Wicked.[17]

This was written the 3rd day of 4th Month, 1660, that is in June. A month later in a letter to George Fox, Richard Hubberthorne mentioned an earlier letter from Fox to Hubberthorne in which Fox discussed sending Nayler to The Bishopric, the area around Durham, far to the northeast near the Scottish border. Nayler, said Hubberthorne, had not heard from Fox regarding this idea.[18] In October, 1660, his health failing again, James Nayler set out for the north, perhaps toward Bishopric, perhaps intending to return home, traveling on foot. His route is uncertain and the reason for its choice unknown. All that is known is the end of it. He was seen by witnesses early in the day looking poorly. Farther on he was found that afternoon, having been set on by parties unknown, beaten severely, and left by the side of the road.[19] If robbery were their motive, surely his assailants were disappointed. Near death, Nayler was carried to a house in Kings Ripton, near Huntington, the town where Oliver Cromwell had once lived. That place lay near a main highway, which did not lead toward Woodkirk. It led toward Cambridge and on northeastward. He may have intended to pass through York, farther north, perhaps to visit Friends in prison there, and possibly on toward The Bishopric. He may have been going from home to home of Quakers with whom he might stop. Such a one, physician

Thomas Parnell, lived in King's Ripton, and he was taken to the doctor's house. Whatever the circumstances, there James Nayler's life ended. His remains lie buried in a ground of typically unmarked Quaker graves in a private garden under fruit trees, down the hill from the village church and its formal graveyard. Quakers could not be buried in consecrated ground, nor would they have wanted any such ceremony or burial monuments.

A serene and deeply personal epitaph exists in print, published in one source as "*His Last Testimony, said to be delivered by him about two Hours before his Departure out of this Life; several Friends being present.*"[20] This, of all Nayler's writings, is the only one widely known, which is sad commentary, for the genius of his life's work is elsewhere. It is doubly sad, because the most common representation of these few words is misleading and probably incorrect. Even the most eminent Quaker historian, William C. Braithwaite, called this piece "his last words." This highly unlikely claim, now attached almost everywhere the piece is published, attracts attention disproportionate to that due the beautiful and lyrical text. Whitehead, stating that it came about two hours before death, did not claim these as "last words," as if their beauty were enhanced by some accident or spiritual coincidence. He could have, for it fell to him to make a title for this presentation in his Collection; Nayler gave it none. Whitehead described it as Nayler's "Last Testimony," which to a 17th Century Quaker was a very different thing. Testimony meant Prophecy.

> There is a Spirit which I feel, that delights to do no Evil, nor revenge any Wrong, but delights to endure all things, in hope to enjoy its own in the End: Its hope is to outlive all Wrath and Contention, and to weary out all Exaltation and Cruelty, or whatever is of a Nature contrary to it self. It sees to the end of all Temptations: As it bears no Evil in it self, so it conceives none in Thoughts to any other: If it be betrayed it bears it; for its Ground and Spring is the Mercies and Forgiveness of God. Its Crown is Meekness, its Life is Everlasting Love unfeigned, and takes its Kingdom with Intreaty, and not with Contention, and keeps it by Lowliness of Mind. In God alone it can rejoyce, though none else regard it, or can own its Life. It's conceived in Sorrow, and brought forth without any to pity it; nor doth it murmur at Grief and Oppression. It never rejoyceth, but through Sufferings; for with the World's Joy it is murthered. I found it alone, being forsaken; I have Fellowship therein, with them who lived in Dens, and desolate Places in the Earth, who through Death obtained this Resurrection and Eternal Life.
>
> J.N.

Notes

INTRODUCTION

1. The term Quaker began as a popular derogatory name. Members of this sect were an irritant to the established Church and its society. They were rude, loud, insistent, and when moved by the Spirit, they were sometimes inclined to tremble or quake. Fox liked to call them, the Children, Children of the Light. That name declined in usage as the name, Friends of Truth, became accepted. It seemed better to fit the gravity of their work, and it could be shortened to the same term Jesus used so often in the Gospels. The proper name of the religious body became The Society of Friends, and a Quaker is properly known as a Friend.

CHAPTER ONE:
A Sense of Place: Woodkirk and West Ardsley

1. Geographical features of West Ardsley have been located and identified with the help of Mr. Peter Aldred, using his private collection of maps, property documents, and photographs.
2. Norrison Scatcherd, *THE HISTORY OF MORLEY in the West Riding of Yorkshire*, Second Edition, (Morley, S. Stead, 1874), pp. 93, 98.
3. Emilia Fogelklou, *JAMES NAYLER, The Rebel Saint, 1618–1660*, (London, Ernest Benn Limited, 1931), p. 38.
4. William G. Bittle, *JAMES NAYLER, 1618–1660, The Quaker Indicted by Parliament*, (York and Richmond, Indiana, William Sessions and Friends United Press, 1986), p. viii.
5. James Nayler, *THE EXAMINATION OF JAMES NAYLER UPON AN Indictment OF BLASPHEMY AT THE SESSIONS AT APPLEBY, JANUARY, 1652*, contained in *SAUL'S ERRAND TO DAMASCUS, With his Packet of Letters from the High Priests, against the disciples of the Lord*, (London, Giles Calvert, 1653), p. 30.
6. Mildred Campbell, *THE ENGLISH YEOMAN UNDER ELIZABETH AND THE EARLY STUARTS*, (New York, Kelley, 1968), p. 24.
7. John Deacon, *AN EXACT HISTORY OF THE LIFE OF JAMES NAYLOR, with his parents, birth, education, profession, actions, and blasphemies, also How he came first to be a Quaker, etc*, (London, Elwood Thomas, 1656).
8. "Nayler Will," *Journal of Friends Historical Society*, x.23, quoted in Fogelklou, p. 290.
Mabel Richmond Brailsford, *A QUAKER FROM CROMWELL'S ARMY: JAMES NAYLER*, (New York, Macmillan, 1927), p. 197.
9. Scatcherd, *MORLEY*, p. 99.

10. Nicholas Pevsner, *THE BUILDINGS OF ENGLAND, Yorkshire West Riding*, revised by Enid Radcliffe, (London, Penguin Books, second edition, 1967), pp. 82, 188.

11. Peter Aldred, private collection and oral history.

12. Pevsner, *BUILDINGS*, p. 557.

13. Scatcherd, *MORLEY*, p. 105.

14. Janet Burton, *THE MONASTIC ORDER IN YORKSHIRE 1069–1215*, (New York, Cambridge University Press, 1999), p. 73.

15. Abbott Francis Gasquet, *ENGLISH MONASTIC LIFE*, (London, Methuen & Co. 1904), p. 295.

16. Tom Leadly, *LEE FAIR, WEST ARDSLEY, WAKEFIELD, the story of England's oldest charter fair*, (West Ardsley, Tom Leadly, 1994).

THE REGISTERS OF TOPCLIFFE AND MORLEY, William Smith, ed. (London, Longman's, Green and Co., 1888), p. 7.

17. Samuel Lewis, *TOPOGRAPHICAL DICTIONARY OF ENGLAND*, (London, E. Lewis & Co., 1832).

18. Scatcherd, *MORLEY*, p. 110.

19. Ibid., p. 121.

Web site of the West Yorkshire Archeological Service, "Tudors in West Yorkshire–Howley Hall," www.arch.wysj.org.uk/advsrv/Tudorweb/HowleyHall.html (accessed April 28, 2004).

20. George Edward Cokayne, *THE COMPLETE PEERAGE OF ENGLAND, Scotland, Ireland, Great Britain and the United Kingdom, extant and dormant*, vol. 5, (London, Alan Sutton, 1982).

21. *DICTIONARY OF NATIONAL BIOGRAPHY*, eds. Leslie Stephen and Stephen Lee, (London, Oxford University Press, 1917).

22. "Correspondence, Lord Savile to Lady Temple, active in politics and used as agent and messenger for Savile, November 1642" included in "Papers Relating to the Delinquency of Lord Savile, 1642–1646," ed. James J Cartwright, *The Camden Miscellany*, vol. Eighth, (Westminster, 1883), pp. 6–7.

23. "Papers Relating to the Delinquency of Lord Savile," pp. 30–33.

CHAPTER TWO:

Anthony Nutter and the Puritans

1. H. Larry Ingle, *FIRST AMONG FRIENDS, George Fox and the Creation of Quakerism,* (New York and Oxford, Oxford University Press, 1994) contains an excellent discussion of Anthony Nutter, pp. 13–16. The author is most grateful to Professor Ingle for the suggestion to investigate the connection between Anthony Nutter and James Nayler.

2. A.F. Scott Pearson, *THOMAS CARTWRIGHT AND ELIZABETHAN PURITANISM 1535–1603*, (Cambridge, Cambridge University Press, 1925) p. viii.

3. Patrick Collinson, *THE ELIZABETHAN PURITAN MOVEMENT*, (Berkeley and Los Angeles, University of California Press, 1967), p. 493.

4. Pearson, *CARTWRIGHT*, p. 239.

5. Alan G.R. Smith, *THE EMERGENCE OF A NATION STATE, The commonwealth of England, 1529–1660*, (London and New York, Longman, 1997), p. 426.

Collinson, *PURITAN MOVEMENT*, p. 245.

6. Ibid., p. 248.

7. Pearson, *CARTWRIGHT*, pp. 252–262.

8. Smith, *EMERGENCE*, p. 245.

9. Leonard W. Levy, *THE PALLADIUM OF JUSTICE, Origins of Trial by Jury*, (Chicago, Ivan R. Dee, 1999), pp. 43–44.

10. Pearson, *CARTWRIGHT*, pp. 260–261.

11. Ibid., pp. 313–334.

12. Ibid., p. 338.

13. T. Joseph Pickvance, *GEORGE FOX AND THE PUREFEYS*, (London, Friends' Historical Society, 1970), pp. 12–13 argues that notwithstanding views of Usher, Babbage and Marchant that "Nutter turned Queen's evidence . . ." it was entirely out of character for him to do anything more than speak the truth.

14. Smith, *EMERGENCE*, p. 427.

Henry Gee and William John Hardy, eds., *DOCUMENTS ILLUSTRATIVE OF ENGLISH CHURCH HISTORY*, (New York, Macmillan, 1896), pp. 508–511.

15. Stuart Barton Babbage, *PURITANISM AND RICHARD BANCROFT*, (London, S.P.C.K., 1962), pp. 178–179.

16. Collinson, *PURITAN MOVEMENT*, p. 452.

17. "*an abridgement of that book which the ministers of Lincoln diocese delivered to his Majestie, being the first part of an Apologye for themselves and their brethren that refuse the subscription and conformitie which is required*" (British Library Doc. STC 15646, Diocese of Lincoln, 1605, Reprinted 1617, 1638).

"*The Abolishing of the Booke of Common Prayer by Reason of above fifty grosse Corruptions in it,*" etc. Being the Substance of a Booke which the Ministers of Lincoln Diocesse delivered to King James the first of December, 1605.

"*Well worthy of the serious consideration of the High Court of Parliament.*" (London, Samuel Satterthwaite, 1643) Thomason Tracts, E178(2).

18. A marginal note on p. 3 of the 1643 edition states that this statement of the King was "Printed at London by Thomas Man, 1603."

19. Pickvance, *FOX AND THE PUREFEYS*, p. 15.

20. John C. Brandon, "The English Origins of Hatevil Nutter of Dover, N.H.," *The American Genealogist*, 72, Numbers 3–4, July/October, 1997.

21. Ronald A. Marchant, *THE PURITANS AND THE CHURCH COURTS IN THE DIOCESE OF YORK 1560–1642*, (London, Longman's, 1960), p. 42.

22. Pickvance, *FOX AND THE PUREFEYS*.

23. Babbage, *PURITANISM*, p. 178.

24. Elliot Rose, *CASES OF CONSCIENCE: alternatives open to recusants and Puritans under Elizabeth I and James I*, (London and New York, Cambridge University Press, 1975), pp. 213–218.

25. Marchant, *PURITANS AND THE CHURCH COURTS*, pp. 42, 108, 266.

26. Brandon, Origins of Hatevil Nutter.

27. Collinson, *PURITAN MOVEMENT*, p. 367.

28. Kevin Sharpe, *THE PERSONAL RULE OF CHARLES I*, (New Haven and London, Yale University Press, 1992), p. 279.

29. Marchant, *PURITANS AND THE CHURCH COURTS*, pp. 43–59. Sharpe, *PERSONAL RULE*, p. 366.
30. Sharpe, *PERSONAL RULE*, p. 282.
31. Brandon, Origins of Hatevil Nutter.

CHAPTER THREE:

Religious Dissent and Freedom of Conscience

1. John Wilson, *FAIRFAX, A Life of Thomas, Lord Fairfax, Captain-General of all the Parliament's forces in ther English Civil war, Creator & Commander of the New Model Army*, (New York, Franklin Watts, 1985), p. 20.

2. Ronald A. Marchant, *THE PURITANS AND THE CHURCH COURTS IN THE DIOCESE OF YORK 1560–1642*, (London, Longman's, 1960), pp. 52–58.

3. Kevin Sharpe, *THE PERSONAL RULE OF CHARLES I*, (New Haven and London, Yale University Press, 1992), p. 281.

4. James Nayler, *THE EXAMINATION OF JAMES NAYLER UPON AN INDICTMENT OF BLASPHEMY AT THE SESSIONS AT APPLEBY, JANUARY, 1652*, contained in *SAUL'S ERRAND TO DAMASCUS, With his Packet of Letters from the High Priests, against the disciples of the Lord*, (London, Giles Calvert, 1653), p. 32.

5. Portfolio number 36/116, Friends House Library, London.

6. Thomas Burton, *DIARY OF THOMAS BURTON, ESQ. MEMBER IN THE PARLIAMENT OF OLIVER AND RICHARD CROMWELL FROM 1656–59*, 4 vols., ed. John Towill Rutt, (London, Henry Colburn, 1828,) vol. 1, p. 24.

7. "Proceedings in the House of Commons against James Nayler, for Blasphemy, and other Misdemeanors: 8 Charles II, A.D. 1656 [Commons Journal]. 6 Harleian Miscellany, p. 399.}" in *COBBETT'S COMPLETE COLLECTION OF STATE TRIALS*, vol. 5, (London, Bagshaw, 1810) p. 802.

8. John Deacon, *AN EXACT HISTORY OF THE LIFE OF JAMES NAYLOR with his parents, birth, education, profession, actions, and blasphemies, also How he came first to be a Quaker, etc*, (London, 1656).

9. Sir Leslie Stephen and Sidney Lee, eds., *DICTIONARY OF NATIONAL BIOGRAPHY*, (London, Oxford University Press, 1917).

10. Norrison Scatcherd, *THE HISTORY OF MORLEY in the West Riding of Yorkshire*, Second Edition, (Morley, S. Stead, 1874), pp. 52, 100, 101.

William Smith, ed. *THE REGISTERS OF TOPCLIFFE, AND MORLEY*, (London, Longman's Green and Co., 1888) contains a history of the church, which, as to the Nayler story, repeats nearly verbatim the Deacon story about his ejection for adultery and subsequent removal to a Baptist congregation in London led by the rather famous Hanserd Knollys. The chronology of events surrounding Nayler in these source documents here becomes thoroughly insupportable.

11. James Nayler, "To Them of The Independent Society," *THE WORKS OF JAMES NAYLER (1618–1660)*, Licia Kuenning, ed. vol. I, (Glenside, Pennsylvania, Quaker Heritage Press, 2003). p. 319.

12. Marchant, *PURITANS AND THE CHURCH COURTS*, pp. 30, 266.

13. Ibid., pp. 108–109.
14. Smith, ed., *REGISTERS*, p. 3.
15. Scatcherd, *MORLEY*, p. 104.
16. Marchant, *PURITANS AND THE CHURCH COURTS*, pp. 111, 249, 272.
17. Ibid., p. 109.
18. Sharpe, *PERSONAL RULE*, p. 756.
19. John C. Brandon, "The English Origins of Hatevil Nutter of Dover, N.H.," *The American Genealogist*, 72, Numbers 3–4, July/October, 1997.
20. Sharpe, *PERSONAL RULE*, p. 321.
Marchant, *PURITANS AND THE CHURCH COURTS*, pp. 54–55.

CHAPTER FOUR:

Charles I and Abuse of Personal Rule, the Prelude to Revolution

1. Thos. Wright, ed. *THE AUTOBIOGRAPHY OF JOSEPH LISTER OF BRADFORD IN YORKSHIRE, to which is added a contemporary account of the defense of Bradford and capture of Leeds by the Parliamentarians in 1642*, (London, J. R. Smith, 1842.) All quotations from Lister which follow are from this source.
2. David Cressy, *BONFIRES AND BELLS, National Memory and the Protestant Calendar in Elizabethan and Stuart England*, (Berkeley and Los Angeles, University of California Press, 1989), pp. 35–38.
3. Ann Hughes, *THE CAUSES OF THE ENGLISH CIVIL WARS*, Second Edition, (London, Macmillan, 1998), pp. 63–67.
4. J.T. Cliffe, *THE YORKSHIRE GENTRY FROM THE REFORMATION TO THE CIVIL WAR*, (University of London, Athlone Press, 1969), pp. 67–70.
5. C. Sklinar, Wakefield Family History Society, www.wakefieldfhs.org.uk/Grammar%20School%20Governors%201-108.htm, accessed March 5, 2008.
6. Stuart Barton Babbage, *PURITANISM AND RICHARD BANCROFT*, (London, S.P.C.K., 1962), p. 178.
7. Kevin Sharpe, *THE PERSONAL RULE OF CHARLES I*, (New Haven and London, Yale University Press, 1992), pp. 783–785
8. Ibid., pp. 769–777.
9. Anthony Fletcher, *THE OUTBREAK OF THE ENGLISH CIVIL WAR*, (New York and London, New York University Press, 1989), pp. 19–30.
10. Mark Charles Fissel, *THE BISHOPS' WARS: Charles I's campaigns against Scotland 1638–1640*, (Cambridge, Cambridge University Press, 1994), p. 273.
C.V. Wedgewood, *THE KING'S PEACE, 1637–1641*, (New York, Macmillan, 1956), p. 338.
11. Fletcher, *OUTBREAK*, p. 4.
12. Sharpe, *PERSONAL RULE*, p. 842.
13. Fletcher, *OUTBREAK*, pp. 4–6.
14. Jane Ohlmeyer, "The War of the Three Kingdoms," *History Today*, November, 1998.
15. Fletcher, *OUTBREAK*, p. 178.

16. John Wilson, *FAIRFAX, A Life of Thomas, Lord Fairfax, Captain-General of all the Parliament's forces in the English Civil war, Creator & Commander of the New Model Army,* (New York, Franklin Watts, 1985), p. 18.

17. "Correspondence, Lord Savile to Lady Temple, active in politics and used as agent and messenger for Savile, November 1642," *PAPERS RELATING TO THE DELINQUENCY OF LORD SAVILE, 1642–1646,* ed. James J Cartwright, (Westminster, The Camden Miscellany, 1883) vol. Eighth, p. 3.

CHAPTER FIVE:

The Outbreak of War

1. John Wilson, *FAIRFAX, A Life of Thomas, Lord Fairfax, Captain-General of all the Parliament's forces in the English Civil war, Creator & Commander of the New Model Army,* (New York, Franklin Watts, 1985), p. 28.

2. Anonymous, *THE RIDER OF THE WHITE HORSE And His Army, Their late good successe in Yorkshiere.* (London, Thomas Underhill, 1643). Thomason Tracts, E88(23).

3. Wilson, *FAIRFAX,* Chapter One.

4. "A True Relation of the passages at Leeds, on Munday the 23 of January, 1642," contained in *THE RIDER OF THE WHITE HORSE.*

The same account was also published in: Thos. Wright, ed. *THE AUTOBIOGRAPHY OF JOSEPH LISTER OF BRADFORD IN YORKSHIRE, to which is added a contemporary account of the defense of Bradford and capture of Leeds by the Parliamentarians in 1642,* (London, J.R. Smith, 1842).

5. Ronald A. Marchant, *THE PURITANS AND THE CHURCH COURTS IN THE DIOCESE OF YORK 1560–1642,* (London, Longman's, 1960), p. 274.

6. James Nayler, *THE EXAMINATION OF JAMES NAYLER UPON AN Indictment OF BLASPHEMY AT THE SESSIONS AT APPLEBY, JANUARY, 1652,* contained in *SAUL'S ERRAND TO DAMASCUS, With his Packet of Letters from the High Priests, against the disciples of the Lord,* (London, Giles Calvert, 1653), p. 30.

7. J.T. Cliffe, *THE YORKSHIRE GENTRY FROM THE REFORMATION TO THE CIVIL WAR,* (University of London, Athlone Press, 1969), pp. 53, 107, 277.

"Colonel Christopher Copley, *HIS CASE,*" (British Library, Sloane manuscripts, Additional: Cole Manuscripts 5832.209).

8. Colonel Christopher Copley, "The Notes of the Entertainment and Continuance of the Officers and Soldiers of My Troop," April 6, 1649, collected in G.E. Aylmer, ed., *SIR WILLIAM CLARKE MANUSCRIPTS, 1640–1664,* (Oxford, Harvester Press Microfilms, 1977), vol. 4/2.

9. Mabel Richmond Brailsford, *A QUAKER FROM CROMWELL'S ARMY: JAMES NAYLER,* (New York, Macmillan, 1927), p. 34.

John Deacon, *AN EXACT HISTORY OF THE LIFE OF JAMES NAYLOR, with his parents, birth, education, profession, actions, and blasphemies, also How he came first to be a Quaker, etc,* (London, 1656).

10. Emilia Fogelklou, *JAMES NAYLER: The Rebel Saint, 1618–1660,* tr. From the Swedish by Lajla Yapp, (London, Ernest Benn, 1931), p. 39.

11. Deacon, *AN EXACT HISTORY.*

Nayler himself, in his London trial testimony, named his superiors as Lord Fairfax, in the first part of the war, followed later by General Lambert. Deacon's account and others were based on that testimony.

12. Wilson, *FAIRFAX*, pp. 13–15.

13. Tom Leadly, *LEE FAIR, WEST ARDSLEY, WAKEFIELD, the story of England's oldest charter fair*, (West Ardsley, Tom Leadly, 1994), pp. 1–5.

14. Thomas Fairfax, "A Short Memorial of the Northern Actions, During ye Warre there Fro ye Yeare 1642 til 1644," quoted in George Tyas, *THE BATTLES OF WAKEFIELD*, (London, A. Hall & Co., 1854).

Wilson, *FAIRFAX*, p. 31.

15. George H. Crowther, *A DESCRIPTIVE HISTORY OF THE WAKEFIELD BATTLES AND A SHORT ACCOUNT OF THIS ANCIENT AND IMPORTANT TOWN*, (London, W. Nicholson and Son, 1886).

Samuel R. Gardiner, *HISTORY OF THE GREAT CIVIL WAR, 1642–1649*, (London, Longman's Green & Co., 1901), Vol. I, p. 140.

Keith Snowden, *THE CIVIL WAR IN YORKSHIRE AND ACCOUNT OF THE BATTLES AND SIEGES AND YORKSHIRE'S INVOLVEMENT*, (Pickering, Castledon Publications, 1998), p. 18.

16. Fairfax, "A Short Memorial."

17. Copley, Notes, *CLARKE MSS, 4/2*.

18. William Harbutt Dawson, *CROMWELL'S UNDERSTUDY: the Life and Times of Colonel John Lambert and the Rise and Fall of the Protectorate*, (London, W. Hodge, 1938), p. 29.

19. Dave Cooke, *THE FORGOTTEN BATTLE, The Battle of Adwalton Moor, 30th June, 1643*, (Hammondwicke, West Yorskhire, Battlefield Press, 1996).

Colonel H.C.B. Rogers, *BATTLES AND GENERALS OF THE CIVIL WARS, 1642–1651*, (London, Seeley Service & Co., 1968), pp. 70–71.

20. Wilson, *FAIRFAX*, p. 33.

21. *CLARKE MSS.* 4/2, payroll records of Copley's troop, which show the date, location, amount paid, and to whom, including James Nayler.

22. Dawson, *CROMWELL'S UNDERSTUDY*, p. 31.

23. Courtesy of Mr. David Evans of Rotherham, an independent Civil War scholar who has helped me to trace Copley's movements

24. Copley, Notes, *CLARKE MSS, 4/2*.

25. For an excellent discussion, see Douglas Gwyn. *THE COVENANT CRUCIFIED, Quakers and the Rise of Capitalism*, (Wallingford, Pennsylvania, Pendle Hill Publications, 1995), p. 83.

26. Edward Hyde, Lord Clarendon, *THE HISTORY OF THE REBELLION and Civil Wars in England, a new edition*, (Oxford, Oxford University Press, 1843), p. 491.

Dawson, *CROMWELL'S UNDERSTUDY*, p. 34.

Rogers, *BATTLES AND GENERALS*, pp. 136–151.

Snowden, *THE CIVIL WAR IN YORKSHIRE*, pp. 24–36.

Wilson, *FAIRFAX*, pp. 47–54.

Peter Young, *MARSTON MOOR, 1644, The Campaign and the Battle*, (Moreton-in-Marsh, Gloucestershire, Windrush Pres, 1997), the most authoritative and complete study of this event, on which this account is based.

27. Wilson, *FAIRFAX*, p. 53.
Young, *MARSTON MOOR*, pp. 104–108.
28. Young, *MARSTON MOOR*, p. 120.
29. Ibid., p. 132, cites Captain Clarke's estimate of 3,500 killed on the Royalist side alone.
30. Copley, *HIS CASE*.
31. *CLARKE MSS.* 4/2, payroll records.
32. Dawson, *CROMWELL'S UNDERSTUDY*, p. 35.
33. George Fox (not the Quaker), *THE THREE SIEGES OF PONTEFRACT CASTLE*, printed from the manuscripts, compiled and illustrated, 1987, (Pontefract, John Fox; London, Longman's, 1987) (originally published as *HISTORY OF PONTEFRACT*, 1827).
34. *CLARKE MSS.* 4/2, payroll records.
35. C.H. Firth, *CROMWELL'S ARMY*, (London, Methuen; New York, James Potts & Co., 1902), p. 34.
36. Dawson, *CROMWELL'S UNDERSTUDY*, p. 38.
37. Copley, *HIS CASE*.

CHAPTER SIX:

Nayler As Officer in Councils of War, The End of Charles I

1. Kevin Sharpe, *THE PERSONAL RULE OF CHARLES I*, (New Haven and London, Yale University Press, 1992), p. 286.
2. *SIR WILLIAM CLARKE MANUSCRIPTS, 1640–1664*, G.E. Aylmer, ed., (Oxford, Harvester Press Microfilms, 1977), vol. 4/2, payroll records.
3. George Fox, *HISTORY OF PONTEFRACT*, (Pontefract, George Fox; London, Longman's, 1827), p. 225.
4. Edward Hyde, Lord Clarendon, *THE HISTORY OF THE REBELLION and Civil Wars in England, a new edition*, (Oxford, Oxford University Press, 1843), p. 578.
Colonel Christopher Copley, *A GREAT VICTORY OBTAINED BY GENERALL POYNTZ AND COL: COPLEY AGAINST THE KING' FORCES*, Thomason Tracts, 1645, E305(14).
5. William Harbutt Dawson, *CROMWELL'S UNDERSTUDY: the Life and Times of Colonel John Lambert and the Rise and Fall of the Protectorate*, (London, W. Hodge, 1938), pp. 40–41.
6. Ibid., p. 42.
7. G.B. Harrison, *A SECOND JACOBIAN JOURNAL, being a Record of Those Things Most Talked of during the Years 1607 to 1610*, (University of Michigan Press, Ann Arbor, 1958), pp. 30–35.
8. Dawson, *CROMWELL'S UNDERSTUDY*, p. 57.
9. Colonel Christopher Copley, *HIS CASE*, (British Library, Sloane manuscripts, Additional: Cole Manuscripts 5832.209).
10. *CLARKE MSS.* 4/2, payroll records.
11. Thomas Burton, *DIARY*, (London, Henry Colburn, 1828), Vol. 1, p. 33.
12. James Nayler, *SAUL'S ERRAND TO DAMASCUS, With his Packet of Letters from the High Priests, against the disciples of the Lord*, (London, Giles Calvert, 1653), pp. 15, 20, 29 for examples.

13. Samuel R. Gardiner, *HISTORY OF THE GREAT CIVIL WAR, 1642–1649*, (London, Longman's Green & Co., 1901), Vol. II, pp. 321–322.

14. "*Parliamentary Army Council of War Minutes, 1647–1648*," York and Pontefract, Document C469, West Yorkshire Archives, Wakefield.

15. John A. Lambert, "*A Declaration of the Northerne Army with Instructions concluded at a Councill of Warre, concerning the Northerne Forces also a Letter concerning the Countries resolution in relation to the Scots,*" (York, printed by Thomas Broad, 1648) Thomason Tracts, E421(31).

16. Dawson, *CROMWELL'S UNDERSTUDY*, p. 67 ff.

17. "*A True Account of the Great Expressions of Love from the Kingdom of Scotland unto Lieutenant General Cromwell and Officers and Soldiers Under His Command,*" (London, 1648) Thomason Tracts E 468(26).

18. Oliver Cromwell, *THE LETTERS AND SPEECHES OF OLIVER CROMWELL*, with elucidations by Thomas Carlyle, S.C., ed. 3 Vols. (New York, G.P. Putnam's Sons; London, Methuen, 1904), Vol. I, p. 383.

19. Richard Holmes, ed., *COLLECTIONS TOWARD THE HISTORY OF PONTEFRACT, THE SIEGE OF PONTEFRACT CASTLE, 1644–1648,* (Printed by the liberality of Thomas William Tew, esq., 1887).

20. Gardiner, *HISTORY OF THE GREAT CIVIL WAR*, Vol. IV, p. 232.

21. Clarendon, *THE HISTORY OF THE REBELLION*, p. 669.

Dawson, *CROMWELL'S UNDERSTUDY*, p. 83.

22. George Fox (not the Quaker), *THE THREE SIEGES OF PONTEFRACT CASTLE*, printed from the manuscripts, compiled and illustrated, 1987, (Pontefract, John Fox; London, Longman's, 1987) (originally published as *HISTORY OF PONTEFRACT*, 1827), p. 119.

23. Ibid, p. 42.

24. *CLARKE MSS.* 4/2, payroll records.

James Nayler died owing money to a William Nayler, as well as to a John Nayler, according to the accounting for his estate, found at Friends House Library, London, or in Mabel Richmond Brailsford, *A QUAKER FROM CROMWELL'S ARM: JAMES NAYLER*, (New York, Macmillan, 1927), p. 197.

25. Leo Damrosch, *THE SORROWS OF THE QUAKER JESUS, James Nayler and the Puritan Crackdown on the Free Spirit,* (Cambridge, Massachusetts and London, Harvard University Press, 1996), p. 15.

H. Larry Ingle, *FIRST AMONG FRIENDS, George Fox and the Creation of Quakerism,* (New York and Oxford, Oxford University Press, 1994), p. 322, n. 32.

26. *At a Genll Council of Officers mett at Pontefract on Friday the 12th of December 1648, Parliamentary Army Council of War Minutes, 1647–1648,* Wakefield, West Yorkshire Archives, Document C469.

27. In personal correspondence November 15, 2008.

28. Sharpe, *PERSONAL RULE*, p. 218.

29. Copley, *HIS CASE*.

30. Dawson, *CROMWELL'S UNDERSTUDY*, pp. 85–96.

31. David Underdown, *PRIDE'S PURGE, Politics in the Puritan Revolution,* (Oxford, Clarendon Press, 1971), contains a complete account of the events briefly summarized here.

C.H. Firth, *CROMWELL'S ARMY*, (London, Methuen; New York, James Potts & Co., 1902), p. 363.

32. Dawson, *CROMWELL'S UNDERSTUDY*, p. 91.

33. "*A Declaration of the Officers belonging to the Brigade of Col. John Lambert Commander in chief in the Northern Parts, now lying Leaguer before Pontefract Castle, At a General Meeting of them, to advise upon (and declare their sense of the present conditions of Affairs of the Kingdom.) To his Excellency the Lord general Fairfax and his General Councel. As also Col. Lambert's Letter concerning the same.*" Pontefract, 12 December 1648, signed Tho Margetts. (London, John Partridge, 1648) Thomason Tracts, E477(10).

34. Underdown, *PRIDE'S PURGE*, p. 182.

35. The appearance of Captain Lilburne on the attendance list raises an interesting question. Robert Lilburne was a Colonel at this time and often sat with Lambert's council. His cousin, Thomas, was a Captain, described in the Dictionary of National Biography (DNB) as a Cromwell supporter. He served in the Northern Army in proximity to Robert. Either or both Lilburnes could have been at the meeting, but it is certain that Robert emerged as chairman of the committee.

36. *A Catalogue of the Names of so many of those Commissioners as sate and sentenced the late King Charles to Death,* Thomason Tracts, 1017(7).

Samuel Gardiner, *CONSTITUTIONAL DOCUMENTS OF THE PURITAN REVOLUTION, 1625–1660,* (Oxford, Clarendon Press, 1906), pp. 379–380.

37. *A List of the Names of the Judges of the High Court of Justice for the Tryall of the King,* London, Jan 11th 1648, Thomason Tracts 669f13(70).

Dawson, *CROMWELL'S UNDERSTUDY*, p. 93.

38. For a compact account of these disorderly events, see Douglas Gwyn. *THE COVENANT CRUCIFIED, Quakers and the Rise of Capitalism,* (Wallingford, Pennsylvania, Pendle Hill Publications, 1995).

For the text of most of the debates, see A.S.P. Woodhouse, ed. *PURITANISM AND LIBERTY, Being the Army debates (1647–1649) from the Clarke manuscripts with supplementary documents, 2nd edition* (Chicago, University of Chicago Press, 1951).

39. Nayler, *SAUL'S ERRAND*, p. 30.

40. Pauline Gregg, *FREE-BORN JOHN, a Biography of John Lilburne,* (London, George G. Harrap, 1961), pp. 341–346.

41. Underdown, *PRIDE'S PURGE*, pp. 86–87.

42. Gardiner, *HISTORY OF THE GREAT CIVIL WAR,* Vol. IV, p. 179.

43. Cromwell, *LETTERS,* vol. I, p. 244.

44. John Wilson, *FAIRFAX, A Life of Thomas, Lord Fairfax, Captain-General of all the Parliament's forces in the English Civil war, Creator & Commander of the New Model Army,* (New York, Franklin Watts, 1985), pp. 156–157.

John Lilburne (by attribution), *The young mens' and the apprentices' outcry. Or an inquisition after the lost fundamental laws and liberties of England. 20 August 1649.* in *THE ENGLISH LEVELLERS,* Andrew Sharp, ed. (Cambridge, Cambridge University Press, 1998).

45. Nayler, *SAUL'S ERRAND*, p. 30.

46. "*The Foxe's Craft Discovered,*" 2 April 1649, Thomason Tracts, E549(7).

47. "*The Newmade Colonel, or Ireland's Jugling Pretended Reliever,*" 30 April 1649, Thomason Tracts, E552(10).

48. C.H. Firth, assisted by Godfrey Davies, *THE REGIMENTAL HISTORY OF CROMWELL'S ARMY,* (Oxford, Clarendon Press, 1940), pp. xxi–xxii.

49. Dawson, *CROMWELL'S UNDERSTUDY*, p. 115.

Colonel H.C.B. Rogers, *BATTLES AND GENERALS OF THE CIVIL WARS, 1642–1651*, (London, Seeley Service & Co., 1968), pp. 294–297.

50. Emilia Fogelklou, *JAMES NAYLER, The Rebel Saint, 1618–1660*, (London, Ernest Benn Limited, 1931), p. 42, quotes from an account in James Gough, *MEMOIRS*, (Dublin, 1782), reporting a conversation with an unnamed former Parliamentary army officer, which took place at an inn several years after the Battle of Dunbar, where the event described took place.

William G. Bittle, *JAMES NAYLER, 1618–1660, The Quaker Indicted by Parliament*, (York and Richmond, Indiana, William Sessions and Friends United Press, 1986), p. 5.

Damrosch, *SORROWS*, p. 83.

Brailsford, *QUAKER FROM CROMWELL'S*, p. 33.

All refer to the same source, Gough's MEMOIRS.

51. *COBBETT'S COMPLETE COLLECTION OF STATE TRIALS*, (London, R. Bagshaw, 1810), vol. V, p. 803.

52. Brailsford, *QUAKER FROM CROMWELL'S*, p. 36.

53. Peter Gaunt, *OLIVER CROMWELL*, (Oxford, Blackwell, 1996), p. 131.

54. James Gough, *A HISTORY OF THE PEOPLE CALLED QUAKERS, From their First Rise to the Present Time*, 4 Volumes, (Dublin, Jackson, 1789), vol. I, p. 233. His statement that Nayler, disabled by sickness, returned home about 1649 differs with Gough's brother's account of Nayler's presence at Dunbar in 1650.

55. George Fox, *JOURNAL OF GEORGE FOX, A Revised Edition*, John J. Nickalls, ed.(London, Religious Society of Friends, 1975), pp. 73, 100.

56. Nayler, *SAUL'S ERRAND*, p. 30.

57. From the author's personal conversation with farmers around West Ardsley, March, 2000.

CHAPTER SEVEN:

From Epiphany to Arrest, the Itinerant Ministry Begins

1. James Nayler, *THE EXAMINATION OF JAMES NAYLER UPON AN INDICTMENT OF BLASPHEMY AT THE SESSIONS AT APPLEBY, JANUARY, 1652*, contained in *SAUL'S ERRAND TO DAMASCUS, With his Packet of Letters from the High Priests, against the disciples of the Lord*, (London, Giles Calvert, 1653), p. 30.

2. William G. Bittle, *JAMES NAYLER, 1618–1660, The Quaker Indicted by Parliament*, (York and Richmond, Indiana, William Sessions and Friends United Press, 1986), p. 9, quoting a Farnworth letter, Swarthmore Mss. 3:72, (London, Friends House Library).

3. Mabel Richmond Brailsford, *A QUAKER FROM CROMWELL'S ARMY: JAMES NAYLER*, (New York, Macmillan, 1927), quoting Swarthmore Mss. Iii6I.

4. Richard J. Hoare, "The Balby Seekers and Richard Farnsworth," *Quaker Studies*, 8, Issue 2, March 2004.

5. "*The Testimony of Margaret Fox Concerning Her Late Husband George Fox . . .*" quoted in Isabel Ross, *MARGARET FELL, Mother of Quakerism*, (London, Longman's Green & Co., 1949), pp. 14–16.

Mary Garman, Judith Applegate, Margaret Benefiel and Dortha Meredith, eds., *HIDDEN IN PLAIN SIGHT, Quaker Women's Writings 1650–1700*, (Wallingford, PA, Pendle Hill Publications, 1996), pp. 236–237.

6. George Fox, *JOURNAL OF GEORGE FOX, A Revised Edition*, John J. Nickalls, ed.(London, Religious Society of Friends, 1975), p. 116.

7. Bittle, *JAMES NAYLER*, pp. 12, 13.

8. James Nayler, "To Friends at Yorkshire," in *THE WORKS OF JAMES NAYLER (1618–1660)*, Licia Kuenning, ed., vol. 1 (Glenside, PA, Quaker Heritage Press, 2003), p. 307.

9. Nayler, *SAUL'S ERRAND*, p. 31.

10. James Nayler, "*SAUL'S ERRAND TO DAMASCUS, With his Packet of Letters from the High Priests, against the disciples of the Lord*," in *WORKS*, p. 25.

11. Kevin Sharpe, *THE PERSONAL RULE OF CHARLES I*, (New Haven and London, Yale University Press, 1992), p. 312.

12. "*Election of Vicars, a Unique Tradition*," *MEMORIES OF ORTON, A Westmoreland Parish remembered*, (Orton, 1998), pp. 49–52.

13. William Harbutt Dawson, *CROMWELL'S UNDERSTUDY: the Life and Times of Colonel John Lambert and the Rise and Fall of the Protectorate*, (London, W. Hodge, 1938), pp. 67–77.

14. Norman Penney, *THE FIRST PUBLISHERS OF TRUTH, Being early records (now first printed) of the introduction of Quakerism into the counties of England and Wales*, (London, Headley brothers; New York, D.S. Taber; 1907).

15. Nayler, "*SAUL'S ERRAND . . .* ," p. 30.

16. Francis Higginson, "A Brief Reply to some parts of a very scurrilous and lying Pamphlet, called Saul's Errand to Damascus," (London, 1653), contained in *WORKS*, p. 537.

17. Penney, *FIRST PUBLISHERS*.

18. Bittle, *JAMES NAYLER*, p. 17.

19. James Nayler, *A COLLECTION OF SUNDRY BOOKS, EPISTLES, AND PAPERS, written by James Nayler, Some of which were never before Printed, with an Impartial Relation of the Most Remarkable Transactions relating to His Life*, (London, J. Sowle, 1716). This collection was republished in the United States in 1826. Both contain Whitehead's fine introduction, as well as his editing.

THE WORKS OF JAMES NAYLER (1618–1660), Licia Kuenning, ed., vol. 1 (Glenside, PA, Quaker Heritage Press, 2003) contains Nayler's writing as nearly in their original form as the editor has been able to locate.

20. Penney, *FIRST PUBLISHERS*, p. 252.

21. H. Larry Ingle, *FIRST AMONG FRIENDS, George Fox and the Creation of Quakerism*, (New York and Oxford, Oxford University Press, 1994), pp. 98–100.

22. Like the Lee Fair, Appleby's Fair is still held. The Moot Hall remains a local landmark, housing the town offices and tourist bureau. The Church of St. Lawrence and Appleby Castle are also in good repair.

23. D.J.H. Clifford, ed., *THE DIARIES OF LADY ANNE CLIFFORD*, (Stroud, Gloucestershire, Sutton, 1990), p. 101.

24. Letter from Howgill to Fox from Appleby, Journal of the Friends Historical Society 28, 1931.

25. Christopher Hill, *THE EXPERIENCE OF DEFEAT*, (New York, Viking, 1984), p. 138.

Emilia Fogelklou, *JAMES NAYLER, The Rebel Saint, 1618–1660*, (London, Ernest Benn Limited, 1931), p. 78.

Dorothy Nimmo, *A TESTIMONY TO THE GRACE OF GOD AS SHOWN IN THE LIFE OF JAMES NAYLER, 1618–1660*, (York, Sessions, 1993).

26. Bittle, *JAMES NAYLER*, p. 20, quoting Swarthmore MSS 3:66.

27. Fogelklou, *NAYLER*, p. 91.

28. Fox, *JOURNAL*, p. 101.

29. John Deacon, *THE GRAND IMPOSTER EXAMINED, or, The life, tryal and examination of James Nayler : the seduced and seducing Quaker : with the manner of his riding into Bristol*. (London, Henry Brome, 1656.) Microfilm. Ann Arbor, Mich. : University Microfilms International, 1982. (Early English books, 1641–1700 ; 1336:20).

John Deacon, *AN EXACT HISTORY OF THE LIFE OF JAMES NAYLOR, with his parents, birth, education, profession, actions, and blasphemies, also How he came first to be a Quaker, etc.*, (London, 1656).

30. Fox, *JOURNAL*, p. 101.

31. Deacon, *GRAND IMPOSTER*.

Deacon's record can also be found in William Oldys and Thomas Park, notes, *THE HARLEIAN MISCELLANY: or, a collection of scarce, curious, and entertaining pamphlets and tracts, as well in manuscript as in print. Selected from the library of Edward Harley, second earl of Oxford*. (London, Printed for J. White and J. Murray, 1808–1813), vol. 6, pp. 426–436.

32. A.G. Matthews, *CALAMY REVISED, Being a Revision of Edward Calamy's Account of the Ministers and Others Ejected and Silenced, 1660–1662*, (Oxford, Clarendon Press, 1934, 1988), p. 340.

33. Geoffrey F. Nuttall, *VISIBLE SAINTS, The Congregational Way, 1640–1660*, (Oxford, Blackwell, 1957), pp. 14–17.

34. G.E. Aylmer, ed., *SIR WILLIAM CLARKE MANUSCRIPTS, 1640–1664*, (Oxford, Harvester Press Microfilms, 1977), Vol. 4/2.

35. James Nayler, "To Them of the Independent Society," in *THE WORKS OF JAMES NAYLER (1618–1660)*, Licia Kuenning, ed., vol. 1 (Glenside, PA, Quaker Heritage Press, 2003), pp. 319–322.

36. John Greenleaf Whittier, *OLD PORTRAITS AND MODERN SKETCHES*, (New York, Hurst & Co., 185?), p. 72.

37. Fox, *JOURNAL*, pp. 100–101.

38. Nayler, "*SAUL'S ERRAND . . .*" in *WORKS*, p. 31.

39. Penney, *FIRST PUBLISHERS*, p. 158.

Hugh Barbour *THE QUAKERS IN PURITAN ENGLAND*, (New Haven, Yale University Press, 1964 and Richmond, Indiana, Friends United Press, 1985), p. 220, 227.

40. Nayler, *SAUL'S ERRAND*, p. 33.

41. Nayler, *A COLLECTION OF SUNDRY BOOKS*, p. 16.

42. Leonard W. Levy, *BLASPHEMY*, (New York, Alfred A. Knopf. 1993), p. 181.

CHAPTER EIGHT:

One of England's Prophets

1. William C. Braithwaite, *THE BEGINNINGS OF QUAKERISM*, Second Edition, (York, Sessions, 1981), p. 147.

Kenneth L. Carroll, "Early Quakers and Fasting," in *Quaker History*, 97, Spring 2008, No. 1.

Isabel Ross, *MARGARET FELL, Mother of Quakerism*, (York, Sessions, 1984), pp. 82, 100.

2. Hugh Barbour *THE QUAKERS IN PURITAN ENGLAND*, (New Haven, Yale University Press, 1964 and Richmond, Indiana, Friends United Press, 1985), p. 227.

3. James Nayler, "Sin Kept Out of the Kingdom," in *THE WORKS OF JAMES NAYLER (1618–1660)*, Licia Kuenning, ed., vol. I (Glenside, PA, Quaker Heritage Press, 2003), p. 166.

4. Letter from Howgill to George Fox from Appleby, *Journal of the Friends Historical Society*, 28, 1931, p. 53.

THE WORKS OF JAMES NAYLER (1618–1660), Licia Kuenning, ed., vol. II (Glenside, PA, Quaker Heritage Press, 2004), Letter from Nayler to George Fox and Margaret Fell, from Appleby, February, 1653, pp. 571–573

5. Ibid.

6. *SAUL'S ERRAND TO DAMASCUS, With his Packet of Letters from the High Priests, against the disciples of the Lord*, (London, Giles Calvert, 1653).

Note that the entire text of "*Saul's Errand . . .*," as printed in the original, is available in *THE WORKS OF JAMES NAYLER (1618–1660)*, vol. 1 (Glenside, PA, Quaker Heritage Press, 2003), p. 1.

The 1716 edition of Nayler's *A COLLECTION OF SUNDRY BOOKS, EPISTLES, AND PAPERS*, edited by Whitehead, does not include the opening epistles or the Fox and Lawson entries, and it does not use the title of the collection. Rather, it includes only a slightly different version of Nayler's answers to the priests' petitions, and the two sections titled, "Divers Particulars of the persecutions of James Nayler by the Priests of Westmoreland," and, "The Examination of James Nayler upon an Indictment of Blasphemy, at the Sessions at Appleby, in January, 1652." Neither of these pieces were signed by Nayler in "*Saul's Errand . . .*" The fact that Whitehead included them in the collected works, but not other unsigned material from the pamphlet suggests that he thought Nayler was the author of the account of the Orton persecutions and the Appleby trial record.

7. Rosemary Moore, *THE LIGHT IN THEIR CONSCIENCES, Early Quaker in Britain, 1646–1666*, (University Park, Pennsylvania; Pennsylvania State University Press, 2000), p. 101.

Nayler, *WORKS*, vol. II, p. iii.

8. "Some Pleadings that passed between Justice Benson and some of the Bench concerning James Nayler," contained in "Several Petitions Answered That were put up by the Priests of Westmoreland" in Nayler, *WORKS*, p. 114.

Also appearing at the end of the trial in Whitehead's edited, Nayler, *COLLECTION OF SUNDRY BOOKS*, 1716, p. 16.

9. "To the Right Worshipful the Justices of the Peace for the County of WESTMORELAND, the Humble petition of divers Ministers and other Inhabitants in the said County who earnestly desire the Glory of God, and the Peace of his Church, and this Commonwealth," in Nayler, *WORKS*, p. 78.

10. The year of publication shows on the title page; the month does not. Where a month is cited on a document from the Thomason Tracts collection, it is the month that Thomason noted on the title page of pamphlets as he acquired each item.

Notes

11. "Several Petitions Answered . . ." in Nayler, *WORKS*, p. 79.
12. Ibid, pp. 86–87.
13. *SAUL'S ERRAND* . . . p. 18, and Nayler, *WORKS*, p. 21.
14. "Another Petition put up by the Priests in Westmoreland," in Nayler, *WORKS*, pp. 93–109.
15. George Fox, *JOURNAL*, John L. Nickalls, ed., revised edition (London, Religious Society of Friends, 1986), p. 65.
16. Nayler, *WORKS*, "Another Petition . . . ." p. 105.
17. Fox, *JOURNAL*, pp. 357, 399.
18. Nayler, "Another Petition . . . ." pp. 92–109.
19. Leonard W. Levy, *BLASPHEMY*, (New York, Alfred A. Knopf), 1993, p. 181.
20. Joseph Besse, *SUFFERINGS OF EARLY QUAKERS IN YORKSHIRE, 1652 TO 1690.* (Facsimile of part of the 1753 edition, York, Sessions Book Trust, 1998), pp. 89–92.
21. Nayler, *WORKS*, p. 196.
22. Antonia Fraser, *CROMWELL, The Lord Protector*, (New York, Grove Press, 1973), p. 450.
23. Nayler, *WORKS*, p. 203.
24. Nayler, *WORKS*, p. 41.
25. It will profit the reader to take Chapters IV, V, and VI of this work (pp. 59–71) and the entirety of the answers to the second petitioners cited in the paragraphs above, find the speech cadences and emphases, the meter and the beat, and read the passages aloud in declamatory fashion as if they were part of a sermon delivery in a modern Pentecostal church. Read in this way, James Nayler's writing comes to life.
26. Nayler, *WORKS*, pp. 42–45.
27. Ibid, pp. 43–47.
28. Nayler, *WORKS*, p. 312.
29. Ibid, p. 313.
30. Ibid, p. 309.
31. Ibid, p. 311.
32. Ibid, pp. 313–314.

CHAPTER NINE:

Traveling Ministry in the North

1. Letter of James Nayler "To Friends in Yorkshire," *THE WORKS OF JAMES NAYLER (1618–1660)*, Licia Kuenning, ed., vol. I, (Glenside, Pennsylvania, Quaker Heritage Press, 2003), p. 307. (Earliest extant letter by Nayler, October, 1652).
2. Sw. Mss. 3.69, *THE WORKS OF JAMES NAYLER (1618–1660)*, Licia Kuenning, ed., vol. II, (Glenside, Pennsylvania, Quaker Heritage Press, 2004), p. 568.
3. Sw. Mss. 3.65, *WORKS*, p. 570.
4. Sw. Mss 3.64, 3.63, and 3.60, *WORKS*, pp. 573–576.
5. The sands in reference are the Cartmel tidal sand flats in Lancashire. To the west, across the flats lies Ulverston, where Swarthmore Hall is located. Westmoreland, where Nayler was conducting his ministry, lies to the east and north about thirty miles.
6. Sw. Mss. 3.60, *WORKS*, p. 576.
7. Sw. Mss. 3.59, *WORKS*, p. 578.

8. George Fox, *JOURNAL OF GEORGE FOX, A Revised Edition,* John J. Nickalls, ed.(London, Religious Society of Friends, 1975), p. 165.
9. Sw. Mss. 3.70, *WORKS,* p. 579.
10. Fox, *JOURNAL,* p. 166.
11. Sw. Mss. 3.192, *WORKS,* p. 580.

CHAPTER TEN:

No Protection Under the Law

1. A.R. Barclay, ed., *LETTERS OF EARLY FRIENDS,* London, Harvey and Darton, 1841, pp. 10–12.
2. Sw. Mss. 3.192, *THE WORKS OF JAMES NAYLER (1618–1660),* Licia Kuenning, ed., vol. II, (Glenside, Pennsylvania, Quaker Heritage Press, 2004), p. 580.
3. Hugh Barbour and Arthur O. Roberts, eds., *EARLY QUAKER WRITINGS 1650–1700,* (reprinted Wallingford, PA, Pendle Hill Publications, 2004), p. 57.
4. James Nayler, *TO THE PEOPLE OF BRADFORD,* Caton Mss. ii.35, *WORKS,* vol. II, p. 592.
5. James Nayler, *A DISCOVERY OF THE FIRST WISDOM FROM BENEATH AND THE SECOND WISDOM FROM ABOVE, WORKS,* vol. I, pp. 61, 66.

CHAPTER ELEVEN:

The Low State of Morality

1. George Fox, *JOURNAL OF GEORGE FOX, A Revised Edition,* John J. Nickalls, ed.(London, Religious Society of Friends, 1975), p. 177.
2. Christopher Chalklin, *The Rise of the English Town, 1650–1850,* (Cambridge, Cambridge Univ. Press, 2001), p. 1.
3. Peter Clark and Paul Slack, *English Towns in Transition 1500–1700,* (London, Oxford University Press, 1976), p. 63.
4. A.R. Barclay, ed. *LETTERS OF EARLY FRIENDS,* London, Harvey and Darton, 1841, p. 13.
5. James Nayler, *To Friends About Scalehouse,* Caton Mss, ii.39, *THE WORKS OF JAMES NAYLER (1618–1660),* Licia Kuenning, ed., Vol. II, (Glenside, Pennsylvania, Quaker Heritage Press, 2004), p. 591.
6. Nayler, *To Them of the Independent Society, THE WORKS OF JAMES NAYLER (1618–1660),* vol. 1 (Glenside, PA, Quaker heritage Press, 2003), p. 319.
7. Nayler, *A Lamentation (by one of England's Prophets) Over the Ruins of this Oppressed Nation, WORKS,* p. 196.
8. Nayler, *To The Rulers of This Nation, WORKS,* vol. II, p. 583.
9. Chalkin, p. 77.
10. Maryann S. Feola, *GEORGE BISHOP, SEVENTEENTH-CENTURY SOLDIER TURNED QUAKER,* (York, William Sessions Limited, 1966). The following references to Bishop come from this excellent work.

11. H. Larry Ingle, *FIRST AMONG FRIENDS, George Fox and the Creation of Quakerism,* (New York and Oxford, Oxford University Press, 1994), p. 23.
12. Sw. Mss. 3.74, *WORKS,* vol. II, p. 588.
13. *WORKS,* Vol. II, pp. 1–19.
14. Ingle, *FIRST AMONG,* p. 68.
Fox, *JOURNAL,* p. 63.
15. ibid, p. 178.
16. Sw. Mss.3.75 Nov. 1654, *WORKS,* vol. II, p. 589.
17 Kate Peters, *PRINT CULTURE AND THE EARLY QUAKERS,* (Cambridge, Cambridge University Press, 2005), p. 22.
18. William C. Braithwaite, *THE BEGINNINGS OF QUAKERISM,* Second Edition, (York, Sessions, 1981), p. 46.

CHAPTER TWELVE:

Quakers in London

1. Hugh Barbour and Arthur O. Roberts, eds. *EARLY QUAKER WRITINGS 1650–1700,* (reprinted Wallingford, PA, Pendle Hill Publications, 2004), p. 84.
2. Kate Peters, *PRINT CULTURE AND THE EARLY QUAKERS,* (Cambridge, Cambridge University Press, Cambridge, 2005), p. 52.
3. George Fox, *JOURNAL OF GEORGE FOX, A Revised Edition,* John J. Nickalls, ed.(London, Religious Society of Friends, 1975), p. 23.
4. Peters, *PRINT CULTURE,* pp. 50–52.
5. Ibid., pp. 53, 213–214.
6. Peter Young, *MARSTON MOOR, 1644, The Campaign and the Battle,* (Moreton-in-Marsh, Gloucestershire, Windrush Press, 1997), p. 143.
7. Peters, *PRINT CULTURE,* pp. 224–225.
Fox, *JOURNAL,* pp. 93, 182, 190–191.
H. Larry Ingle, *FIRST AMONG FRIENDS, George Fox and the Creation of Quakerism,* (New York and Oxford, Oxford University Press, 1994), pp. 119–121.
William C. Braithwaite, *THE BEGINNINGS OF QUAKERISM,* Second Edition, (York, William Sessions Limited, 1981), pp. 71, 113, 175, 177.
8. Letter, Parker to Fell 12 Feb 1655, A.R. Barclay, ed., *LETTERS OF EARLY FRIENDS,* (London, Harvey and Darton, 1841), p. 21.
9. Fox, *JOURNAL,* pp. 192–198.
10. A.R. Barclay, ed., *LETTERS,* p. 16.
11. Letter, Burrough and Howgill to Fell. 27 March 1655, A.R. Barclay, ed., *LETTERS,* pp. 26, 27.
12. William G. Bittle, *JAMES NAYLER, 1618–1660, The Quaker Indicted by Parliament,* (York and Richmond, Indiana, William Sessions and Friends United Press, 1986), p. 77.
13. A.R. Barclay, ed., *LETTERS,* pp. 34, 35.
14. Peters, *PRINT CULTURE,* p. 6.
15. Braithwaite, *BEGINNINGS,* p. 46.
16. A.R. Barclay, ed., *LETTERS,* p. 38.

17. Carola Scott-Lukas, "Propaganda or Marks of Grace, The Impact of the Reported Ordeals Of Sarah Wight in Revolutionary London, 1647–1652," in *Women's Writing*, 9, Number 2, 2002, p. 12.

18. Maryann S. Feola, *GEORGE BISHOP, SEVENTEENTH-CENTURY SOLDIER TURNED QUAKER*, (York, William Sessions Limited, The Ebor Press, 1996), pp. 27–28.

19. Quoted in Encyclopedia Brittanica, Eleventh Edition, 1910.
Oliver Lawson Dick, ed. *Aubrey's Brief Lives*, David R. Godine, Boston, 1999, p. 382.

20. Leo Damrosch, *THE SORROWS OF THE QUAKER JESUS, James Nayler and the Puritan Crackdown on the Free Spirit,* (Cambridge, Massachusetts and London, Harvard University Press, 1996), p. 75; quoting from John Whiting, *Persecution Expos'd in some memoirs relating to the suffering of John Whiting, and many others of the people called Quakers, for conscience sake* (1715), p. 177.

21. A.R. Barclay, ed., *LETTERS*, p. 27.

CHAPTER THIRTEEN:

Enter the Adversary, Nayler Weakens

1. James Nayler, *A Discovery of the First Wisdoms from Beneath, and the Second Wisdoms from Above*, 1653, THE WORKS OF JAMES NAYLER (1618–1660), Licia Kuenning, ed., vol. 1 (Glenside, PA, Quaker heritage Press, 2003), p. 43.

2. H. Larry Ingle, *FIRST AMONG FRIENDS, George Fox and the Creation of Quakerism,* (New York and Oxford, Oxford University Press, 1994), pp. 134–141.
George Fox, *JOURNAL OF GEORGE FOX, A Revised Edition*, John J. Nickalls, ed.(London, Religious Society of Friends, 1975), p. 254.

3. James Nayler, *A COLLECTION OF SUNDRY BOOKS, EPISTLES, AND PAPERS, written by James Nayler, Some of which were never before Printed, with an Impartial Relation of the Most Remarkable Transactions relating to His Life*, George Whitehead, ed. (London, J. Sowle, 1716), p. 704.
THE WORKS OF JAMES NAYLER (1618–1660), Licia Kuenning, ed., vol. III, (Farmington, ME, Quaker Heritage Press, 2007), p. 758.

4. A.R. Barclay, ed., *LETTERS OF EARLY FRIENDS*, (London, Harvey and Darton, 1841), p. 40.

5. William G. Bittle, *JAMES NAYLER, 1618–1660, The Quaker Indicted by Parliament*, (York and Richmond, Indiana, William Sessions and Friends United Press, 1986), p. 83.

6. Nayler, *A COLLECTION*, p. 705.

7. Nayler, *WORKS*, vol. III, pp. 530, 532.

8. Ibid. pp. 534–535.

9. Rosemary Moore, *THE LIGHT IN THEIR CONSCIENCES, Early Quaker in Britain, 1646–1666*, (University Park, Pennsylvania; Pennsylvania State University Press, 2000), pp. 37–39.
Kenneth L. Carroll, "Martha Simmonds, a Quaker Enigma," *Journal of the Friends Historical Society* 53, 1972–1975.

10. Kate Peters in *PRINT CULTURE AND THE EARLY QUAKERS*, (Cambridge University Press, Cambridge, 2005), lists the following works by Martha Simmonds: *A lamentation for the lost sheep of the house of Israel,* (1655) *When the Lord Jesus came to Jerusalem* (1655); *O ENGLAND thy time is come,* (1656).

Bernadette Smith, in "The Testimony of Martha Simmonds, Quaker," *QUAKER STUDIES*, 12, Issue 1, September, 2007 includes valuable biographical data on Simmonds, as well as excellent discussion of the Biblical references upon which her papers were built.

11. Hubberthorne letter to Margaret Fell, July 26, 1656, *WORKS*, vol. III, p. 538.

12. Ingle, *FIRST AMONG*, p. 142.

William G. Bittle, *JAMES NAYLER, 1618–1660, The Quaker Indicted by Parliament*, (York and Richmond, Indiana, William Sessions and Friends United Press, 1986), p. 86.

William C. Braithwaite, *THE BEGINNINGS OF QUAKERISM*, Second Edition, (York, Sessions, 1981), p. 245.

13. Whitehead used this vivid description of the women in his introduction to Nayler's works, long after the events took place. Whether it originated then with him, or earlier, is unknown.

14. Fox letter to Nayler, *WORKS*, vol. III, p. 542.

Fox, *JOURNAL*, p. 268.

15. Ingle, *FIRST AMONG*, p. 143.

16. William C. Braithwaite, *THE BEGINNINGS OF QUAKERISM*, Second Edition, (York, Sessions, 1981), p. 246.

17. An excellent, balanced summary of this encounter can be found in Bittle, pp. 96–100, drawn from Fox, Hubberthorne, and Nayler, as related by Robert Rich. Three errors in Bittle's account are noted in Ingle, p. 323.

18. Fox, *JOURNAL*, p. 223.

19. Fox, *JOURNAL*, p. 230.

20. Ibid., p. 268.

21. Bittle, *JAMES NAYLER,* pp. 98–100.

22. Fox, *JOURNAL*, p. 269.

CHAPTER FOURTEEN:

The Ride Into Bristol, Blasphemy and Imprisonment

1. William C. Braithwaite, *THE BEGINNINGS OF QUAKERISM*, Second Edition, (York, William Sessions Limited, 1981), p. 251 ff.

COBBETT'S COMPLETE COLLECTION OF STATE TRIALS, vol. V. (London, R. Bagshaw, 1810), p. 802 ff.

Both of these sources rely in part on original accounts by Farmer and Deacon.

2. Braithwaite, *BEGINNINGS*, p. 253.

Maryann S. Feola, *GEORGE BISHOP, SEVENTEENTH-CENTURY SOLDIER TURNED QUAKER*, (York, William Sessions Limited, The Ebor Press, 1996), p. 86

George Bishop, letter to Margaret Fell, October 27, 1656, reprinted in Hugh Barbour and Arthur O. Roberts, eds., *EARLY QUAKER WRITINGS 1650–1700*, (reprinted Wallingford, PA, Pendle Hill Publications, 2004), pp. 481–485.

3. *COBBETT'S*, p. 812.

4. Ibid., pp. 814–815.

5. Leonard W. Levy, *BLASPHEMY*, (New York, Alfred A, Knopf, 1993), p. 195.

6. *COBBETT'S*, pp. 805–816.

7 Levy, *BLASPHEMY*, pps. 120,156, 192.

8. *COBBETT'S*, p. 817.

9. Levy, *BLASPHEMY*, pp. 184–206.

10. Leo Damrosch, *THE SORROWS OF THE QUAKER JESUS, James Nayler and the Puritan Crackdown on the Free Spirit,* (Cambridge, Massachusetts and London, Harvard University Press, 1996), p. 231 quoting from George Fox, *JOURNAL*, 1911).

H. Larry Ingle, *FIRST AMONG FRIENDS, George Fox and the Creation of Quakerism,* (New York and Oxford, Oxford University Press, 1994), p. 149.

11. *COBBETT'S*, p. 835.

12 Emilia Fogelklou, *JAMES NAYLER, The Rebel Saint, 1618–1660*, (London, Ernest Benn Limited, 1931), p. 152 ff., interpreting Whitehead's account.

Braithwaite, p. 254.

13. Kenneth Dewhurst, *DR. THOMAS SYDENHAM (1624–1689), His Life and original Writings*, (Berkeley and Los Angeles, University of California Press, 1966), p. 25.

14 William G. Bittle, *JAMES NAYLER, 1618–1660, The Quaker Indicted by Parliament*, (York and Richmond, Indiana, William Sessions and Friends United Press, 1986), pp. 116–117.

Kate Peters, *PRINT CULTURE AND THE EARLY QUAKERS*, (Cambridge, Cambridge University Press, 2005), p. 240.

15. Excellent, detailed accounts of Nayler's trial and subsequent imprisonment can be found in other sources and need not be repeated here. For the trial itself Burton's diary is a remarkable effort:

Thomas Burton, *DIARY OF THOMAS BURTON, ESQ., MEMBER IN THE PARLIAMENT OF OLIVER CROMWELL AND RICHARD CROMWELL FROM 1656 –1659*, ed. John Towill Rutt, (London, Henry Colburn, 1828), vol. I.

The official record, however, is more complete and makes especially interesting reading for those trying to understand the varied ideas of what constituted blasphemy, as well as the political positions of conservatives and former revolutionaries as they met in an effort to govern. The record is condensed in *COBBETT'S COMPLETE COLLECTION OF STATE TRIALS*, vol. V.

Bittle's biography of Nayler uses the trial record and other sources to construct a fine narrative of the Parliamentary process in Nayler's case and records his imprisonment in detail. Levy's book on blasphemy is probably the best modern examination of the subject from a legal viewpoint and, with Bittle, provides some of the best explanations of the nuances of the Nayler case.

16. Braithwaite, *BEGINNINGS*, p. 255.

17. Antonia Fraser, *CROMWELL, The Lord Protector,* (New York, Grove Press, 1973), pp. 315–317.

18. Braithwaite, *BEGINNINGS*, pp. 260, 264, 269.

Feola, *GEORGE BISHOP*, pp. 90–91.

Isabel Ross, *MARGARET FELL, Mother of Quakerism,* (York, Sessions, 1984), pp. 105–110, 396.

19. Websites describing Bridewell include:
http://homepage.mac.com/philipdavis/English%20sites/3984.html
www.mkheritage.co.uk/nppm/bridewell.html
www.british-history.ac.uk/report.aspx?compid=45178
accessed July 3, 2008.

20. Bittle, *JAMES NAYLER*, p. 169.

Notes   199

21. James Nayler, *To All the Dearly Beloved People of God, Mercy and Peace*, an epistle included in the introduction to *A COLLECTION OF SUNDRY BOOKS, EPISTLES, AND PAPERS, written by James Nayler, Some of which were never before Printed, with an Impartial Relation of the Most Remarkable Transactions relating to His Life*, (London, J. Sowle, 1716), p. xxxi.

CHAPTER FIFTEEN:

Explaining the Events as Bristol

1. James Nayler, *A COLLECTION OF SUNDRY BOOKS, EPISTLES, AND PAPERS, written by James Nayler, Some of which were never before Printed, with an Impartial Relation of the Most Remarkable Transactions relating to His Life*, (London, J. Sowle, 1716), p. xxxv.
2. Nayler, *COLLECTION*, p. xxxvii.
3. Ibid., p. xxxix.
4. Ibid., p. lii.
5. Ibid., p. lii–liii.
6. Ibid., p. liii–liv.
7. Ibid., p. liv.
8. Ibid., p. xxxix.
9. Ibid., p. xl.
10. Ibid., p. xli.
11. Ibid., p. xliii.
12. Nayler, *In Answer to the Book . . .* , *COLLECTION*, pp. 650–651.
13. Nayler, *COLLECTION* p. xliv.
14. Ibid., p. xlv.
15 Ibid., p. xlviii.
16. George Whitehead, in James Nayler, *COLLECTION*, p. vii.
17. Ibid., p. ix.
18. Leo Damrosch, *THE SORROWS OF THE QUAKER JESUS, James Nayler and the Puritan Crackdown on the Free Spirit*, (Cambridge, Massachusetts and London, Harvard University Press, 1996), p. 118.
19. William C. Braithwaite, *THE BEGINNINGS OF QUAKERISM*, Second Edition, (York, William Sessions Limited, 1981), p. 273.
20. Whitehead, in James Nayler, *COLLECTION*, pp. xiii, xxi.
Hugh Barbour and Arthur O. Roberts, eds. *EARLY QUAKER WRITINGS 1650–1700*, reprinted Wallingford, PA, Pendle Hill Publications, 2004), p. 614.

CHAPTER SIXTEEN:

Possession of the Living Faith, the Last Great Works

1. Oliver Lawson Dick, ed., *AUBREY'S BRIEF LIVES*, (Boston, David R. Godine, 1999), pp. 204–208.
Peter Young, *MARSTON MOOR, 1644, The Campaign and the Battle*, (Moreton-in-Marsh, Gloucestershire, Windrush Press, 1997), p. 7.

2. James Nayler, *A COLLECTION OF SUNDRY BOOKS, EPISTLES, AND PAPERS, written by James Nayler, Some of which were never before Printed, with an Impartial Relation of the Most Remarkable Transactions relating to His Life,* (London, J. Sowle, 1716), p. xxvi.

3. Nayler, *COLLECTION*, p. 375.

4. Ibid., p. 377.

5. Ibid., p. 391.

6. Ibid., p. 379.

7. Ibid., p. 382.

8. Ibid., p. 393.

9. James Naylor, *WHAT THE POSSESSION OF THE LIVING FAITH IS, and the Fruits thereof, And wherein it hath been found to differ from the dead faith of the World, in the learning and following of Christ in the Regeneration.* (London, Thomas Simmons, 1659).

10. Nayler, *COLLECTION*, p. 664.

11. Ibid., p. 674.

12. Ibid., p. 669.

13. Ibid., pp. 690–691.

14. William G. Bittle, *JAMES NAYLER, 1618–1660, The Quaker Indicted by Parliament*, (York and Richmond, Indiana, William Sessions and Friends United Press, 1986), p. 171.

15. Nayler, *COLLECTION*, p. 643.

16. Letter of James Nayler to Oliver Cromwell, *THE WORKS OF JAMES NAYLER (1618–1660)*, vol. II, (Glenside, Pennsylvania, Quaker Heritage Press, 2003), p. 262.

17. Nayler, *COLLECTION*, p. 600.

18. Letter from Hubberthorne to Fox, London, 24th of 5th Month 1660, in A.R. Barclay, ed., *LETTERS OF EARLY FRIENDS*, (London, Harvey and Darton, 1841), p. 82.

19. William C. Braithwaite, *THE BEGINNINGS OF QUAKERISM*, second edition, (York, William Sessions Limited, 1981), p. 275.

20. Nayler, *COLLECTION*, p. 696.

Bibliography

LOCAL HISTORY

Burton, Janet. *THE MONASTIC ORDER IN YORKSHIRE 1069–1215*. New York: Cambridge University Press, 1999.

Gasquet, Abbott Francis. *ENGLISH MONASTIC LIFE*. London: Methuen & Co., 1904.

Leadly, Tom. *LEE FAIR, WEST ARDSLEY, WAKEFIELD, the story of England's oldest charter fair*. West Ardsley: Tom Leadly, 1994.

MEMORIES OF ORTON, A Westmoreland Parish remembered. Orton, 1998.

"Papers Relating to the Delinquency of Lord Savile, 1642–1646," ed. James J Cartwright, *The Camden Miscellany*, Vol. Eighth. Westminster, 1883.

Pevsner, Nicholas. *THE BUILDINGS OF ENGLAND, Yorkshire West Riding*, rev. Enid Radcliffe. London: Penguin Books, second edition, 1967.

THE REGISTERS OF TOPCLIFFE AND MORLEY. William Smith, ed. London: Longman's, Green and Co., 1888.

Scatcherd, Norrison. *THE HISTORY OF MORLEY in the West Riding of Yorkshire*, Second Edition. Morley: S. Stead, 1874.

HISTORY OF ENGLAND

AUBREY'S BRIEF LIVES, Edited from the Original Manuscripts and with a life of John Aubrey by Oliver Lawson Dick. Boston: David R. Godine, 1999.

Campbell, Mildred. *THE ENGLISH YEOMAN UNDER ELIZABETH AND THE EARLY STUARTS*. New York: Kelley, 1968.

A Catalogue of the Names of so many of those Commissioners as sate and sentenced the late King Charles to Death. Thomason Tracts, 1017(7).

Cokayne, George Edward. *THE COMPLETE PEERAGE OF ENGLAND, Scotland, Ireland, Great Britain and the United Kingdom, extant and dormant*, V.5. London: Alan Sutton, 1982.

Chalklin, Christopher. *THE RISE OF THE ENGLISH TOWN, 1650–1850*. Cambridge: Cambridge University Press, 2001.

Clark, Peter and Paul Slack. *ENGLISH TOWNS IN TRANSITION, 1500–1700*. London: Oxford University Press, 1976.

THE DIARIES OF LADY ANNE CLIFFORD, D.J.H. Clifford, ed. Stroud, Gloucestershire: Sutton, 1990.

Cressy, David. *BONFIRES AND BELLS, National Memory and the Protestant Calendar in Elizabethan and Stuart England.* Berkeley and Los Angeles: University of California Press, 1989.

Cromwell, Oliver. *THE LETTERS AND SPEECHES OF OLIVER CROMWELL, with elucidations by Thomas Carlyle, S.C., ed.* 3 Vols. New York,: G.P. Putnam's Sons; London: Methuen, 1904.

DICTIONARY OF NATIONAL BIOGRAPHY, Leslie Stephen and Stephen Lee, eds., London: Oxford University Press, 1917.

THE ENGLISH LEVELLERS, Andrew Sharp, ed. Cambridge: Cambridge University Press, 1998.

"*The Foxe's Craft Discovered*," Thomason Tracts, E549(7), 2 April 1649.

Fraser, Antonia. *CROMWELL, The Lord Protector.* New York: Grove Press, 1973.

Gardiner, Samuel. *CONSTITUTIONAL DOCUMENTS OF THE PURITAN REVOLUTION, 1625–1660.* Oxford: Clarendon Press, 1906.

Gaunt, Peter. *OLIVER CROMWELL.* Oxford: Blackwell, 1996.

Gregg, Pauline. *FREE-BORN JOHN, a Biography of John Lilburne.* London, George G. Harrap, 1961.

Harrison, G.B. *A SECOND JACOBIAN JOURNAL, being a Record of Those Things Most Talked of during the Years 1607 to 1610.* Ann Arbor: University of Michigan Press, 1958.

Hill, Christopher. *THE EXPERIENCE OF DEFEAT.* New York: Viking, 1984.

———. *ANTICHRIST IN SEVENTEENTH-CENTURY ENGLAND.* Oxford: Oxford University Press, 1971.

———. *THE WORLD TURNED UPSIDE DOWN, Radical Ideas During the English Revolution.* London and New York: Penguin Books, 1991.

———. *THE ENGLISH BIBLE AND THE SEVENTEENTH CENTURY REVOLUTION.* London and New York: Penguin Books, 1994.

Holdgate, Martin. *A HISTORY OF APPLEBY.* Appleby: J. Whitehead & Son, 1982.

Levy, Leonard W. *THE PALLADIUM OF JUSTICE, Origins of Trial by Jury.* Chicago: Ivan R. Dee, 1999.

Lewis, Samuel. *TOPOGRAPHICAL DICTIONARY OF ENGLAND.* London: E. Lewis & Co., 1832.

A List of the Names of the Judges of the High Court of Justice for the Tryall of the King, London. Thomason Tracts 669f13(70), 11 January, 1648.

"*The Newmade Colonel, or Ireland's Jugling Pretended Reliever.*" Thomason Tracts, E552(10), 30 April 1649.

Pickvance, T. Joseph. *GEORGE FOX AND THE PUREFEYS, a study of the Puritan background in Fenny Drayton in the 16th and 17th centuries.* London: Friends' Historical Society, 1970.

Scott-Lukas, Carola. "Propaganda or Marks of Grace, The Impact of the Reported Ordeals Of Sarah Wight in Revolutionary London, 1647–1652." *Women's Writing*, Vol. 9, Number 2, 2002.

Sharpe, Kevin. *THE PERSONAL RULE OF CHARLES I,* New Haven and London, Yale University Press, 1992.

Alan G.R. Smith, *THE EMERGENCE OF A NATION STATE, The commonwealth of England, 1529–1660.* London and New York: Longman, 1997.

Underdown, David. *PRIDE'S PURGE, Politics in the Puritan Revolution*. Oxford: Clarendon Press, 1971.

———. *REVEL, RIOT, & REBELLION, Popular Politics and Culture in England, 1603–1660*. Oxford, New York: Oxford University Press, 1985.

PURITANISM AND LIBERTY, Being the Army debates (1647–1649) from the Clarke manuscripts with supplementary documents, 2nd edition. A.S.P. Woodhouse, ed. Chicago: University of Chicago Press, 1951.

CIVIL WARS

Cliffe, J.T. *THE YORKSHIRE GENTRY FROM THE REFORMATION TO THE CIVIL WAR*. London: University of London, Athlone Press, 1969.

Dave Cooke. *THE FORGOTTEN BATTLE, The Battle of Adwalton Moor, 30th June, 1643*, Hammondwicke, West Yorskhire, Battlefield Press, 1996.

Colonel Christopher Copley, *A GREAT VICTORY OBTAINED BY GENERALL POYNTZ AND COL: COPLEY AGAINST THE KING' FORCES*, Thomason Tracts, 1645, E305(14).

Copley, Colonel Christopher. *HIS CASE*. British Library, Sloane manuscripts, Additional: Cole Manuscripts 5832.209.

———. "The Notes of the Entertainment and Continuance of the Officers and Soldiers of My Troop," April 6, 1649, collected in *SIR WILLIAM CLARKE MANUSCRIPTS, 1640–1664*, G.E. Aylmer, ed. Oxford: Harvester Press Microfilms, 1977, Vol. 4/2.

Crowther, George H. *A DESCRIPTIVE HISTORY OF THE WAKEFIELD BATTLES AND A SHORT ACCOUNT OF THIS ANCIENT AND IMPORTANT TOWN*. London: W. Nicholson and Son, 1886.

Dawson, William Harbutt. *CROMWELL'S UNDERSTUDY: The Life and Times of Colonel John Lambert and the Rise and Fall of the Protectorate*. London: W. Hodge, 1938.

"*A Declaration of the Officers belonging to the Brigade of Col. John Lambert Commander in chief in the Northern Parts, now lying Leaguer before Pontefract Castle, At a Genral Meeting of them, to advise upon (and declare their sense of the present conditions of Affairs of the Kingdom.) To his Excellency the Lord general Fairfax and his General Councel. As also Col. Lambert's Letter concerning the same.*" Pontefract, 12 December 1648, signed Tho Margetts. London: John Partridge, 1648. Thomason Tracts, E477(10).

Firth, C.H. *CROMWELL'S ARMY*. London: Methuen; New York: James Potts & Co., 1902.

Firth, C.H. assisted by Godfrey Davies. *THE REGIMENTAL HISTORY OF CROMWELL'S ARMY*. Oxford: Clarendon Press, 1940.

Fissel, Mark Charles. *THE BISHOPS' WARS: Charles I's campaigns against Scotland 1638–1640*. Cambridge: Cambridge University Press, 1994.

Fletcher, Anthony. *THE OUTBREAK OF THE ENGLISH CIVIL WAR*. New York and London: New York University Press, 1989.

Fox, George (not the Quaker). *THE THREE SIEGES OF PONTEFRACT CASTLE*, printed from the manuscripts, compiled and illustrated, 1987. Pontefract: John Fox; London: Longman's, 1987 (originally published as *HISTORY OF PONTEFRACT*, 1827).

Gardiner, Samuel R. *HISTORY OF THE GREAT CIVIL WAR, 1642–1649*. London: Longman's Green & Co., 1901.

At a Genll Councill of Officers mett at Pontefract on Friday the 12th of December 1648, Parliamentary Army Council of War Minutes, 1647–1648. Wakefield, West Yorkshire Archives, Document C469.

COLLECTIONS TOWARD THE HISTORY OF PONTEFRACT, THE SIEGE OF PONTEFRACT CASTLE, 1644–1648, Richard Holmes, ed. (Printed by the liberality of Thomas William Tew, esq., 1887).

Hughes, Ann. THE CAUSES OF THE ENGLISH CIVIL WARS, Second Edition. London: Macmillan, 1998.

Hyde, Edward, Lord Clarendon. THE HISTORY OF THE REBELLION and Civil Wars in England, a new edition. Oxford: Oxford University Press, 1843.

Lambert, John A. "A Declaration of the Northerne Army with Instructions concluded at a Councill of Warre, concerning the Northerne Forces also a Letter concerning the Countries resolution in relation to the Scots." York: printed by Thomas Broad, 1648. Thomason Tracts, E421(31).

Ohlmeyer, Jane. "The War of the Three Kingdoms," *History Today*, November, 1998.

"Parliamentary Army Council of War Minutes, 1647–1648." York and Pontefract: Document C469, West Yorkshire Archives, Wakefield.

THE RIDER OF THE WHITE HORSE And His Army, Their late good successe in Yorkshiere. London: Thomas Underhill, 1643. Thomason Tracts, E88(23).

Rogers, Colonel H.C.B. BATTLES AND GENERALS OF THE CIVIL WARS, 1642–1651. London: Seeley Service & Co., 1968.

PAPERS RELATING TO THE DELINQUENCY OF LORD SAVILE, 1642–1646. James J Cartwright, ed. Westminster: *The Camden Miscellany*, 1883 Vol. Eighth.

Snowden, Keith. THE CIVIL WAR IN YORKSHIRE AND ACCOUNT OF THE BATTLES AND SIEGES AND YORKSHIRE'S INVOLVEMENT. Pickering: Castledon Publications, 1998.

Solt, Leo F. *SAINTS IN ARMS, Puritanism and Democracy in Cromwell's Army.* London: Oxford University Press, 1959.

"A True Account of the Great Expressions of Love from the Kingdom of Scotland unto Lieutenant General Cromwell and Officers and Soldiers Under His Command." London: 1648. Thomason Tracts E 468(26).

Tyas, George. THE BATTLES OF WAKEFIELD. London: A. Hall & Co., 1854.

Young, Peter. *MARSTON MOOR, 1644, The Campaign and the Battle.* Moreton-in-Marsh, Gloucestershire: Windrush Press, 1997.

Wedgwood, C.V. *A COFFIN FOR KING CHARLES, The Trial and Execution of Charles I.* New York: Time, 1964.

———. *THE KING'S PEACE, 1637–1641.* New York: Macmillan, 1956.

Wilson, John. *FAIRFAX, A Life of Thomas, Lord Fairfax, Captain-General of all the Parliament's forces in the English Civil war, Creator & Commander of the New Model Army.* New York: Franklin Watts, 1985.

PURITANS AND INDEPEDENTS

"The Abolishing of the Booke of Common Prayer by Reason of above fifty grosse Corruptions in it," etc. "Being the Substance of a Booke which the Ministers of Lincoln Diocesse delivered to King James the first of December, 1605. Well worthy of the serious consideration of the High Court of Parliament." London: Samuel Satterthwaite, 1643. Thomason Tracts, E178(2).

"an abridgement of that book which the ministers of Lincoln diocese delivered to his Majestie, being the first part of an Apologye for themselves and their brethren that refuse the subscription and conformitie which is required." Diocese of Lincoln, 1605, Reprinted 1617, 1638. British Library Doc. STC 15646.

Babbage, Stuart Barton. *PURITANISM AND RICHARD BANCROFT.* London: S.P.C.K., 1962.

Brandon, John C. "The English Origins of Hatevil Nutter of Dover, N.H.," *The American Genealogist*, July/October, 1997, Vol. 72, Numbers 3–4.

Collinson, Patrick. *THE ELIZABETHAN PURITAN MOVEMENT.* Berkeley and Los Angeles: University of California Press, 1967.

Hutchinson, Lucy. *MEMOIRS OF THE LIFE OF COLONEL HUTCHINSON, Charles I's Puritan Nemesis.* N.H. Keeble, ed. London: Phoenix Press, 2000.

Marchant, Ronald A. *THE PURITANS AND THE CHURCH COURTS IN THE DIOCESE OF YORK 1560–1642.* London: Longman's, 1960.

Nuttall, Geoffry F. *VISIBLE SAINTS, The Congregational Way, 1640–1660.* Oxford: Blackwell, 1957.

Pearson, A.F. Scott. *THOMAS CARTWRIGHT AND ELIZABETHAN PURITANISM 1535–1603.* Cambridge: Cambridge University Press, 1925.

Rose, Elliot. *CASES OF CONSCIENCE: alternatives open to recusants and Puritans under Elizabeth I and James I.* London and New York: Cambridge University Press, 1975.

THE AUTOBIOGRAPHY OF JOSEPH LISTER OF BRADFORD IN YORKSHIRE, to which is added a contemporary account of the defense of Bradford and capture of Leeds by the Parliamentarians in 1642. Thos. Wright, ed. London: J.R. Smith, 1842.

EARLY FRIENDS

Barbour, Hugh. *THE QUAKERS IN PURITAN ENGLAND.* New Haven: Yale University Press, 1964 and Richmond, Indiana: Friends United Press, 1985.

Besse, Joseph. *SUFFERINGS OF EARLY QUAKERS IN YORKSHIRE, 1652 TO 1690.* Facsimile of part of the 1753 edition. York: Sessions Book Trust, 1998.

Braithwaite, William C. *THE BEGINNINGS OF QUAKERISM*, Second Edition. York: Sessions, 1981.

EARLY QUAKER WRITINGS 1650–1700. Hugh Barbour and Arthur O. Roberts, ed. Wallingford, Pennsylvania: Pendle Hill Publications, reprinted 2004.

Feola, Maryann S. *GEORGE BISHOP, SEVENTEENTH-CENTURY SOLDIER TURNED QUAKER.* York: William Sessions Limited, The Ebor Press, 1996.

Fox, George. *JOURNAL OF GEORGE FOX, A Revised Edition,* John J. Nickalls, ed. London, Religious Society of Friends, 1975.

Gough, James. *A HISTORY OF THE PEOPLE CALLED QUAKERS, From their First Rise to the Present Time,* 4 Volumes. Dublin: Jackson, 1789.

Gwyn, Douglas. *THE COVENANT CRUCIFIED, Quakers and the Rise of Capitalism.* Wallingford, Pennsylvania: Pendle Hill Publications, 1995.

HIDDEN IN PLAIN SIGHT, Quaker Women's Writings 1650–1700. Mary Garman, Judith Applegate, Margaret Benefiel and Dortha Meredith, eds. Wallingford, Pennsylvania, Pendle Hill Publications, 1996.

Hoare, Richard J. "The Balby Seekers and Richard Farnsworth," Quaker Studies, Vol. 8, Issue 2, March 2004.

Ingle, H. Larry. *FIRST AMONG FRIENDS, George Fox and the Creation of Quakerism.* New York, Oxford: Oxford University Press, 1994.

LETTERS OF EARLY FRIENDS, A.R. Barclay, ed. London: Harvey and Darton, 1841.

Moore, Rosemary. *THE LIGHT IN THEIR CONSCIENCES, Early Quaker in Britain, 1646–1666.* University Park, Pennsylvania: Pennsylvania State University Press, 2000

Nuttal, Geoffrey. *STUDIES IN CHRISTIAN ENTHUSIASM.* Pendle Hill Pamphlet Number 41. Wallingford, Pennsylvania, Pendle Hill, 1948.

Penney, Norman. *THE FIRST PUBLISHERS OF TRUTH, Being early records (now first printed) of the introduction of Quakerism into the counties of England and Wales.* London: Headley brothers; New York: D.S. Taber; 1907.

Peters, Kate. *PRINT CULTURE AND THE EARLY QUAKERS.* Cambridge: Cambridge University Press, 2005).

Reay, Barry. *THE QUAKERS AND THE ENGLISH REVOLUTION.* New York: St. Martin's, 1985.

Rooksby, Donald R. *THE QUAKERS IN NORTH-WEST ENGLAND, PART 3, AND SOMETIME UPON THE HILLS, a guidebook to places of Quaker interest in Cumbria, North Lancashire, the Yorkshire Dales, and the Pennines.* Colwyn Bay, North Wales, 1998.

Ross, Isabel. *MARGARET FELL, Mother of Quakerism.* London: Longman's Green & Co., 1949.

Trevett, Christine. *WOMEN AND QUAKERISM IN THE 17TH CENTURY.* York: Sessions Book Trust, The Ebor Press, 1991, 1995.

UNDAUNTED ZEAL, The Letters of Margaret Fell, Elsa F. Glines, ed. and Introduction, Foreword by Rosemary Moore. Richmond, Indiana, Friends United Meeting, 2003.

JAMES NAYLER

Bittle, William G. *JAMES NAYLER, 1618–1660, The Quaker Indicted by Parliament.* York: William Sessions and Richmond, Indiana: Friends United Press, 1986.

Brailsford, Mabel Richmond. *A QUAKER FROM CROMWELL'S ARMY: JAMES NAYLER.* New York: Macmillan, 1927.

Burton, Thomas. *DIARY OF THOMAS BURTON, ESQ. MEMBER IN THE PARLIAMENT OF OLIVER AND RICHARD CROMWELL FROM 1656–59,* 4 vols. John Towill Rutt, ed. London: Henry Colburn, 1828.

Carroll, Kenneth L. "Martha Simmonds, a Quaker Enigma," *Journal of the Friends Historical Society* 53, 1972–1975.

SIR WILLIAM CLARKE MANUSCRIPTS, 1640–1664, Vol. 4/2, G.E. Aylmer, ed., Oxford: Harvester Press Microfilms, 1977.

COBBETT'S COMPLETE COLLECTION OF STATE TRIALS, Vol. 5. London: Bagshaw, 1810.

Bibliography

Damrosch, Leo. *THE SORROWS OF THE QUAKER JESUS, James Nayler and the Puritan Crackdown on the Free Spirit.* Cambridge, Massachusetts and London: Harvard University Press, 1996.

Deacon, John. *THE GRAND IMPOSTER EXAMINED, or, The life, tryal and examination of James Nayler : the seduced and seducing Quaker : with the manner of his riding into Bristol.* London: Henry Brome, 1656, and Ann Arbor: University Microfilms International, 1982.

———. *AN EXACT HISTORY OF THE LIFE OF JAMES NAYLOR, with his parents, birth, education, profession, actions, and blasphemies, also How he came first to be a Quaker, etc.* London: 1656.

Fogelklou, Emilia. *JAMES NAYLER, The Rebel Saint, 1618–1660.* London Ernest Benn Limited, 1931.

Levy, Leonard W. *BLASPHEMY.* New York: Alfred A. Knopf. 1993.

Matthews, A.G. *CALAMY REVISED, Being a Revision of Edward Calamy's Account of the Ministers and Others Ejected and Silenced, 1660–1662.* Oxford: Clarendon Press, 1934, 1988.

Nayler, James. *A COLLECTION OF SUNDRY BOOKS, EPISTLES, AND PAPERS, written by James Nayler, Some of whih were never before Printed, with an Impartial Relation of the Most Remarkable Transactions relating to His Life,* George Whitehead, ed. London: J. Sowle, 1716.

Nayler, James. *THE EXAMINATION OF JAMES NAYLER UPON AN Indictment OF BLASPHEMY AT THE SESSIONS AT APPLEBY, JANUARY, 1652,* contained in *SAUL'S ERRAND TO DAMASCUS, With his Packet of Letters from the High Priests, against the disciples of the Lord.* London: Giles Calvert, 1653.

Nayler, James. *THE WORKS OF JAMES NAYLER (1618–1660),* 4 vols. Glenside, Pennsylvania and Farmington, Maine: Quaker Heritage Press, 2003–2008.

Neelon, David. "James Nayler In The English Civil Wars," *Quaker Studies,* Volume 6, Issue 1, September, 2001.

Nimmo, Dorothy. *A TESTIMONY TO THE GRACE OF GOD AS SHOWN IN THE LIFE OF JAMES NAYLER, 1618–1660.* York: Sessions, 1993.

"Proceedings in the House of Commons against James Nayler, for Blasphemy, and other Misdemeanors: 8 Charles II, A.D. 1656 Commons Journals.," *THE HARLEIAN MISCELLANY: or, a collection of scarce, curious, and entertaining pamphlets and tracts, as well in manuscript as in print. Selected from the library of Edward Harley, second earl of Oxford.* London: Printed for J. White and J. Murray, 1808–1813, vol. 6.

Whittier, John Greenleaf. *OLD PORTRAITS AND MODERN SKETCHES.* New York: Hurst & Co., 185.

Index

A
Abbott, Archbishop, 32
Abraham, 67
Act for the Punishment of Rogues, Vagabonds, and Sturdy Beggars, xxxii, 105, 111
ACTS, 145
Adultery, 29, 76–77, 139, 142, 160
　Spiritual, 157, 160–161
Adversary, The (see Satan)
Advowson, 70
Adwalton Moor, xxv, 51
Affection, 157, 160–161, 171
Aldham, Thomas, xxviii, 29, 90, 123–124
Aldworth, Robert, 147
AND IN THE DAY WHEN MY GOD LIFTED MY FEET . . . , 159
Anger, 142, 172–173
Anglican church, 14, 19, 20, 23, 25, 30, 71
ANSWER TO A FANATIC HISTORY, 157, 162, 176
Antichrist, xviii, 20, 40, 45, 89, 137, 167
Apocalypse, xviii, 45, 117, 133, 136, 162
Apology, xxxvi, 163–164, 166, 169
Apostles, 85, 90, 93, 114, 120
Appleby, xxvii, xxix, 58, 71, 73, 90
　Assizes, xxx, 73–74, 86, 87, 103
　Castle, 73–74, 82–83
　Jail, 75, 81–84, 94, 105, 130, 155
　Moot Hall, 73–74, 119, 155
　Trial, 28, 63, 67, 73, 76–79, 84, 87, 99, 149
Archbishop, xxiii, 19, 23, 27, 70–71
　of Canterbury, xix, xxii, xxiv, xxvi, 14, 15, 18, 24–25, 32, 35, 37, 39, 40, 55, 92, 109
　of York, xix, 14, 22, 24–25, 27
Ardsley
　East, 1, 4, 5, 6, 32, 49
　West, xxi, xxviii, 1, 3, 4–9, 30, 31, 35, 38, 50, 69–70, 73, 75, 163, 179n
Ardislaw, 1

Army of the North (see Northern Army)
Arminianism, 24–25, 28, 54
Articles of Religion, 15, 19
Assizes courts, xxix, xxx, 73–75, 83, 86, 91, 102
　Justices, xxiii, xxviii, 152
Audland, John, xxxii, xxxv, 104, 118, 124–125, 139
Authority, xviii, xxii, xxxii, 14–15, 21–23, 34, 60, 70, 78, 85, 101, 108, 111, 114, 132, 137, 140, 150, 154

Backsliding, xxxiii, 161–162
Balby, 69, 75, 119
Baptism, 7, 16, 18, 20–21, 23, 33, 84
Baptists, xv, xxxii, xxxiii, 20, 23, 29, 76–77, 86, 116, 120–121, 127–129, 182n
Barley, xxviii, 65–67
Batley, 7, 8, 25, 30
Baynes, Captain, 62–63, 152
Benson, Justice Gervase, 86–87, 90, 95
Bible, xviii, xix, xxii, xxiii, 97, 134
　Authorized (King James), xix, xxi, 17, 47, 67, 168
　Geneva, xix, 45, 47–48, 67, 137, 168
Billingsley, John, xxxi, 119, 122
Bishop, George, 117, 124, 128, 139, 146–148, 153, 166
Bishop of Lincoln, 17–18
Bishops, xv, 13, 14, 19, 21, 25, 36, 55, 109–110
　courts, xxiii, 15, 17, 23–24
　Wars, xxiii, 11, 38, 41, 50
Bishopric(k), 177
Bittle, William, 84, 198n
Black Canons (Augustinians), 7–9
Blasphemy, xv–xxvii, xxix–xxx, 57, 69, 74, 78–79, 86–87, 89–92, 124, 128, 135, 145–152, 155, 157, 173
Blasphemy, Horrid, xv, xxxiv, 87, 149, 157, 167
Boteler, General, 152

Bradford, xxix, xxv, xxxi, 2, 31, 35–36, 38, 40, 43, 45, 48, 50–52, 106–111, 114–117, 119
Brailsford, Mabel Richmond, 65
Braithwaite, William, 163, 178
Bridewell Prison (Hospital), xxxv, 12, 150, 155–157, 161, 163–164, 166, 169, 171–173, 176
Briggs, Justice Colonel, 76–78
Bright, Colonel, 62
Bristol, xiii, xv, xvi, xxxii, xxxiv–xxxv, 57, 77, 114, 117–118, 125, 139, 145–156, 157, 159, 163, 166
Brownist, 14, 30
Bull and Mouth (see London)
Bull baiting, xxxi, 119–120, 122
Burford, xxvii, 64, 78, 153
Burial, Quaker, 178
Burrough, Edward, xxxi–xxxiii, xxxvii, 124–126, 130, 132, 135, 137, 153, 176
Burton, Justice, 72
Burton, Thomas, 28
Buttery, Isabel and companion, xxxi, 123–124

Calvert, Giles, xxxii, 123–124, 136, 153
Cambridge, 14, 70, 77, 177
Camm, John, xxxii, 118, 124–125, 139
Carlisle, xxx, xxxiii, 59, 73, 91, 102–103
Cartwright, Thomas, 14–17, 19, 23
Cater, Samuel, 145
Catholics, xix, xxi, xxiv, xxxii, 13–14, 19–20, 23, 24, 27, 28, 39–40, 81
Cavalry, 11, 46, 50, 61, 65
Celebrations, xxii, 35–36
Censorship, 85, 164
Chancery Court, xxii, 24–25, 31
Chaplain, xxi, xxv, 10, 22, 24–25, 36, 47, 55, 78
Charles I, King, xix, xxii–xxiii, xxv–xxvi, 10–11, 13, 93, 128
  Church of England, xix, xxii, 24–25, 33
  Civil War, xix, xxiv–xxvi, 42, 45, 55–58, 165, 168
  Criminal trial, xxvii, 60–62
  Execution, xv, xxvii, 63, 110
  Personal Rule, xv, xxii, 24, 35–43
Charles II, King, xxxviii, 82, 89
  Civil War, xxviii, 64–65
  Nayler, xv, 176–177
  Restoration, xv, xxxvii, 63, 116–117, 165–166
Chesterfield, xxxi, 118–120, 122

Children of the Light, 77, 113, 115, 161, 179n
Christ, xiv, xviii, xix, 79, 81, 85, 90, 92–93, 97–98, 108, 113, 115, 120, 131–135, 137–138, 145, 147, 151–152, 157–161, 163, 167–174
Christianity, 94, 157
  primitive, 19, 69
Church of England, xv, xix, xxi, xxii, 7, 14–17, 21, 24, 27, 32, 42, 58, 71, 119
Church wardens, 17, 24, 30
Civil War (see War)
Clarendon, Lord, 128
Clifford, Lady Anne, 73–74, 83
Clothing Towns, 1
  blockade, 43, 45
  economy, 2
  occupation and relief, 45
Coal, 2–3
Colchester, 136–137
COLOSSIANS, 173
Commons, House of, xxii, 51, 57, 61–62, 155
Common Prayer, Book of, xix, xxi–xxiii, xxvi, xxxi, 14–15, 17–21, 23–25, 28, 31, 33, 37–38, 55
Commonwealth, xxxii–xxxiii, 65, 93, 106, 108–109, 111, 117, 128
Community, xvii, 27, 33, 75, 100, 115, 117, 134–137
Compassion, xxxvi, 84, 86
Congregationalists (Independents), xv, 14, 32, 174
Convincement, xxx, xxxvii, 128–129
Copley, Colonel Christopher, xxv–xxvi, 49–53, 55, 59, 61, 77
Cornwall, xxxiii, 131
Correspondence amongst Friends, 130, 132, 135, 141, 147, 177
Cotton, John, 77, 174
Council of State ("Major Generals"), xxix, xxxii, 93, 110, 116, 148
Council of War (Officers), xxvii, 55, 57–58, 60–63
Covenant, 38, 94, 133
Covenant, Solemn League and (see Scotland)
Crab, Robert, 145
Cromwell, Oliver, xiii, xxxiv, xxxvii, 56, 128, 140, 169, 177
  birth, xxi
  death, xxxvi, 165–166, 169
  Fox, xxxii, 89, 102, 124–125
  Independent, xix, xxvi–xxvii, 61–62, 117

Index

Ireland, 64
Nayler, xxx, xxxv–xxxvi, 45, 49, 65, 78, 93, 102, 110, 116, 146, 151, 169, 176–177
 Protectorate, xvi, xxviii–xxx, xxxiii, 65, 93, 111, 115–117, 124–125, 128, 146, 148, 151–152
 war, xiii, xxvi–xxviii, 45, 49, 52–55, 58–61, 64–65, 71, 73–74, 77, 93, 110, 153
Cromwell, Richard, xxxvi–xxxvii, 165
Cross, 95–97, 131, 133, 158
 Sign of, 16, 20, 23
Crown, xviii, 45, 64, 98, 116, 168, 176, 178
Crouch, William, 123
Crucifixion, xvii, 94–95, 105, 131, 158–159, 162, 167–168, 172

Damrosch, Leo, 84, 163
DANIEL, 90
Darcy, Lady, xxxiii, 127–129
Day of Judgment (of the Lord), xiii, 92, 110, 113, 132, 136, 138, 157, 172
Deacon, John, 4, 29, 76, 182n
Debate, 63, 72, 119, 121, 129
Deceit, 109, 132–133, 138, 167–168, 172–173
Dedham Conferences, 14
Derby, xxvii, xxviii, 89
Desborough, Major, 140
Devil (see Satan)
Dewsbury, William, Mary, xix, xxvii–xxviii, xxxv, xxxvii, 29, 91, 106, 135, 137, 166
Directory of Worship, 55
Discernment, xv–xvii, 90, 102, 133–134, 138, 159
Discipline, xvi–xvii, xx, xxii, 14–16, 18, 21, 28, 30–32, 37, 55, 58, 77, 81, 99, 101, 135–136, 142, 165
A DISCOVERY OF THE FIRST WISDOM . . . , xxix, 94–95, 111, 131
Dissent(ers), xiii, xvi, xix, 13, 16, 20, 23, 27, 33, 56, 62–63, 74, 77, 93
Divine Right of King (see Monarchy)
Drayton, Fenny (-in-the-Clay), xxi, xxxi, 13, 16–18, 21–23
Dring brothers, 123
Dunbar, Battle of, xxviii, 49, 55, 64–65, 78
Durham, xxix, xxx, 103, 105, 116, 177

East Ardsley (see Ardsley)
Economy, 2–3, 8, 45
Edward VI, King, 155
Election, 127, 167, 175

Elizabeth I, Queen, xix, 13, 14, 17, 19, 23, 70, 82
Ellwood, Thomas, xxxvii, 176
Episcopacy, xvi, xix, xxiii–xxiv, xxvi, 10, 21, 55, 58, 128
Epistle
 To Friends at Lincoln, xxxiii, 132
 to All Friends in London, xxxiii, 132, 138
 To Friends about Scalehouse, xxxi, 113
 To Friends about Wakefield, xxix, 95, 97
 to Several Friends about Yorkshire, xxix, 96
 to Them of the Independent Society, xxxi, 78, 115
 to the Rulers of This Nation, 116
Epitaph, 178
Erbury, Dorcas, 145, 148–149, 160, 172
Excommunication, xxii, xxviii, 24–25, 28–29, 31, 76, 78–79, 154
Exeter jail, xxxiv, 81, 140–141, 145–146, 153, 159–160, 171
Exhaustion, 113, 132, 152,

Fairfax, Ferdinando, xxiii–xxiv, 43, 46, 49, 50, 53
 Thomas, xxiii–xxv, xxvii, 27, 42–46, 49–51, 53–54, 61–65, 168
Faith, xiii, xvi, xix, xxxvi, 20, 23, 27, 75, 79, 84, 91, 97, 99, 101, 130–131, 135–138, 158, 161, 164–165, 170–172, 174–175
Farnsworth, Richard, xxviii, xxix, xxxviii, 68–69, 87, 124
Fasting, xxix, xxxiv, 20, 81, 84, 139–140
Fell, Judge Thomas, xxi, xxiii, xxviii, xxix, xxxii, xxxvi, 69, 105, 127
Fell, Margaret (Askew), xix, xxi, xxviii, xxix, xxxiii–xxxviii, 68–69, 95–96, 118, 125–127, 130, 132, 135, 139, 147, 153, 164, 166
Fenny Drayton (see Drayton)
Fifth Monarchy, xv, xxxvii, 89, 110, 116–117, 124, 127, 133, 166, 168
First Publishers of Truth, 72
Fisher, Mary, 91
Fogelklou, Emelia, 6, 75
Fothergill, George, 71–72
Fox, George, xiii–xv, xviii, xix, xxii, xxv–xxvi, xxxviii, 13, 18, 21, 88, 96, 103, 113, 116, 149, 164
 Cromwell, xiii, 116, 124–125
 Derby, xxvii–xxviii, 89
 Imprisonment, xxvii–xxviii, xxx, xxxiii, xxxviii, 91, 93, 102, 105, 166

Fox, George *(Cont.)*
  Journal, xxx, 29, 78, 103, 119–120, 129, 140–142
  Launceston, xxxiii–xxxiv, 131, 139, 141–142, 146
  Leadership of Friends, xiii, xvi–xvii, 73, 77, 89, 102, 105, 114, 116, 124–125, 132, 137–138, 140, 153–154
  Letter to Parliament, xxxv
  London, xxxii, 114, 123–126
  Ministry in the North, xxx, 29, 68–69, 73, 77, 103, 113–114, 116, 119, 127
  Nayler, xiii–xv, xxviii–xxxv, xxxvii, 29, 65–66, 68–69, 71–72, 76–78, 83–90, 92, 96, 99–104, 118, 121, 128–130, 139, 141–143, 147, 151, 153–154, 160, 166, 171, 177
  Simmonds, Stranger, xxxiv, 136, 138, 140, 153
Freedom, 97, 101, 130, 165, 170
  of conscience, 27–33, 55, 93, 106, 111, 116–117, 128
  religious, 91, 154, 177
Friends, xiv, 81, 88, 113, 140, 179n
  principles, xiv–xv, xvii–xviii, xxxii, 85, 89, 94, 177
  Society of, xvii, 179n
  of Truth, 113, 179n
Friends House Library, 3, 28, 95

Games, xxii, 35–36, 50
GENESIS, 67, 97, 129
Gentry, xxii, 3–4, 23, 37, 42, 46, 127
Gilbert, Thomas, 25, 31
Glastonbury, xxxiv, 146
Godly nation (society), xiii, xix, 27, 91, 93, 110–111, 136, 176–177
Goodeaire (Goodyear), Thomas, 68, 90, 104
Goring, General, 50–51, 53
Grains (barley, oats), viii, 3, 8, 65–67
Grammar schools, 10, 36
Gunpowder Plot (see Plots)
Gwyn, Douglas, 185n, 188n
Gypsy horse traders, 9, 50, 73

HABBAKUK, 90
Hacker, Colonel, 125
Haigh Hall, 1, 26, 31, 33
Halifax, xxiv, xxv, 2, 36, 40, 106
Hampton Court Conferences, xxi, 17
HEBREWS, 174–175
Henrietta Maria, Queen, xxii, 40–41
Henry VIII, King, 9, 15, 31, 70, 155

Hepworth Moor, 41
Higginson, Francis, 71–72, 77–79, 83, 86, 107, 121
High Commission, 16, 24, 30
Hill, Christopher, 75
HIS CONFESSIONS AND ANSWERS . . ., 158
Hobbes, Thomas. *Leviathan*, xxviii
Holidays, 20, 35–36
Holland, 89, 128
Homilies, 19, 21, 70
Hooten, Elizabeth, 91, 93
Horbury, 29, 37
Horses, 9, 50, 155
Hotham, 11
House(s) of Correction, xxiii, xxxii, 10, 38, 82–83
Howgill, Francis, xxix, xxxi–xxxiii, 72–75, 79–80, 82, 84, 86–87, 93, 95, 98, 103–105, 124–126, 130, 132, 135–137, 140, 142, 153
Howley Hall, xxi, xxv, 8–10, 12, 22, 37–38, 46, 50
Hubberthorne, Richard, xxxiii–xxxv, 125, 132, 135–138, 141–143, 153, 177
Hull, xxiv, 11–12, 41, 43, 52
Humiliation, xv, xvii, 23, 107, 133–135, 143, 150, 157, 175
Huntingdon, xxi, xxxvii, 177
Husbandman, 1, 4, 78

Idolatry, xiii, xvi, 23, 145, 150, 152, 157, 161, 171–173
Imagination, 115, 127–128, 135, 159
Independents (Congregationalists), xix, xxiii, xxv–xxviii, xxxi–xxxii, 1, 9, 14, 23, 25–26, 27–33, 56, 61–62, 71, 76–79, 115, 117, 121, 169
Ingle, H. Larry, 60, 66
Inner light (see Light of Christ)
Ireland, xxiv, xxvii, xxxii, 39–41, 64, 130, 132
Ireton, Henry, 56, 60, 62
ISAIAH, 90, 97, 138, 146, 174, 176

JAMES, 100
James I, King, xix, xxi, xxii, 13, 17–21, 23, 37, 56
JEREMIAH, 97
Jerusalem, xiii, xxxiv, 86, 123, 137, 145–146, 158, 161, 170
Jesus(Saviour), xiii, 84, 115, 120, 145, 147–149, 159, 161, 168, 170, 172, 179n

Index

JOB, 90
JOHN, 45, 113, 145, 149
Jones, Rice (Rhys), xxxi, 120–122, 127, 158
Jordans, xxxvii
Judicial powers, xvi, 15, 149–150
Jury trial, 16, 78–79, 91

Kendal, 69–70, 73–75, 84
King's Ripton, 177–178
Kirkby Stephen, 58, 71–73, 77
Knollys, Hanserd, 182n

Lamb, xxxiii, 109–110, 132, 159, 167–169, 173
LAMB'S WAR . . . , xxxvi, 156, 167–169, 173
Lambert, General John, xxvi–xxviii, 49, 52–53, 56, 58, 60, 62–65, 71, 152, 165–166
A LAMENTATION . . . , xxx, 81, 91, 93, 116
Lancaster (Lancashire), xxix–xxx, xxxviii, 52, 57, 69–71, 78, 84, 86
Langdale, General, 58–59
Laud, Archbishop William, xix, xxii, 25, 35, 37–40, 93, 110
   imprisonment and execution, xxiv, xxvi, 55, 58
   reforms, xix, xxii, 24, 28, 32–33, 77
Launceston (see Fox, Launceston)
Law, xvi, 14, 16, 25, 87, 89, 94, 102, 105, 107–111, 149–151
Lawrence, Lord, 152
Lawson, Joseph, 84
Leading, spiritual(guidance), xiv–xvii, 64, 67, 78, 81, 95–97, 99–103, 106, 110, 113, 115, 118, 120–122, 126, 142, 152–154, 161, 172, 176–177
Lee Fair, 8–9, 50, 73
Leeds, xxiv, xxv, 2, 7, 43, 45–48, 50, 52, 75, 77
Levellers, xxv–xxvii, 56, 59, 63–64, 78, 89, 123–125, 128, 153–154
Leviathan (see, Hobbes)
LEVITICUS, 149, 154
Light of Christ (Light within), xiv, xix, xxxiv, 90, 94–97, 101, 110, 112, 115, 121, 126, 132, 157, 163, 167, 169–171, 174–175, 177
Lilburne, Henry, 54, 63–64
   John, xxv, 54, 63, 123
   Robert, xxv, xxvii, 53, 57, 61–63
   Thomas, 188n
Lister, Joseph, 35–36, 38–41
Literacy, 36–37

Liturgy, 20, 25
Locke, John, 152
London, xvi, xxxvii–xxxviii, 10–12, 15, 17, 28–29, 39–42, 46, 54, 60–64, 70, 73, 75–77, 80–81, 87, 89, 91, 93, 102, 106, 114, 117, 119–122, 123–130, 131–133, 146, 148, 154–157, 165, 176
   Bull and Mouth, xxxii, 126–127
   George Fox, xvi, xxxii, 114, 124–126, 154
   Meetings, xvi, 124–127, 130, 135, 161
   Population, 114
   Quaker ministry begins, xxxi–xxxiii, 123–127, 160
   Schism, xvi, xxxiii–xxxiv, 134–141, 151, 154, 159
   to All Friends in London, xxxiii, 132, 138
Lords, House of, xxvii
Love, xviii, 83–85, 90, 93, 95–97, 100–101, 113, 115, 133, 148, 158, 161, 163, 167, 169, 173, 178
Love to the Lost and a Hand Held Forth to the Helpless . . . , xxxiii
LUKE, 97, 114, 118, 145
Lust, 157, 160, 169, 172, 175

Magistrates, 88–91, 94, 100, 107, 146–149, 152
Mallerstang, xxix, 72–73
Man of Sin, xxxi, 138, 167, 175
Margetts, Thomas, 58, 63
MARK, 145
Marshall, Christopher, xxv, xxviii, xxxi, 29, 76–78
Marston Moor, xxv, 52–53, 55–56
MATTHEW, 145
Messiah, xiii–xiv, 133–134, 150, 157
MILK FOR BABES . . . , xxxvii, 156, 173–176
Millenary Petition, xxi, 17, 19, 22
Ministry, xix, xxi, xxiii, 13, 15–32, 36, 39, 42, 70–72, 78, 80, 84, 86–88, 90, 107–109, 129
   interruption of, xvi, xxxiii, 126, 135–137, 142, 162
   itinerant, 67, 69, 72–73, 99–104, 111, 113, 118–122, 127, 146
   paid, xxx, 29–30, 88, 118, 130, 136
   prophetic, 114, 125, 131, 136
Monarchy, xv, xxii, 9, 15–16, 19, 21, 28, 33, 35, 40, 42, 62, 116
   divine right, xv, 27, 60
   overthrow, xv, xix, xxvi, 37, 41, 55, 57–58, 61, 62, 93, 121
   Restoration, xv, 63, 89, 116, 165–166, 177

Monastic period, 8, 9, 70
Monck, General, xxxvii, 116, 165–166
Money, xxii–xxiii, 4, 12, 25, 33, 37, 38,
    49–51, 53, 57, 64, 77, 83, 88, 90, 111,
    118, 155
Monopoly, publishing, xix, xxii–xxiii, xix,
    85, 121
Morality, 113–122
Morley, 4, 7, 29, 30, 31
Muggleton, Ludovic, 154
  Muggletonians, xv
Mutiny, xxvii, 57
Mystery of iniquity, 133, 138

Nantwich, Battle of, xxv, 52, 165
Nayler, Ann, xxix, xxxv, 5–6, 12, 67, 75–77,
    95, 111–112, 155–156, 166
Nayler (Naylor), James
  Adulation and idolatry, xiii, xvi, 131,
    134–135, 145, 150, 152, 157, 159,
    160, 171–173
  Adultery, 29, 76–77, 139, 142, 159–161
    spiritual, 157, 160
  Affection, 100, 157, 160–161, 171, 173
  Appeals to Fox, 99–104, 129
  Appleby, xxvii, xxix–xxx, 73–75, 79, 119,
    155
    jail, xxix, 75, 79, 81–84, 90–91, 94–95,
      99, 104–105, 130, 140
    trial, xxix, 6, 28–29, 63–64, 67, 73–79,
      81, 84, 86–87, 89, 91, 99, 103, 105,
      111, 149
  Army service, xiii, xxv–xxviii, 4, 10, 37,
    43, 45, 47, 49–66, 71, 75, 79,
    123–124, 152
  Arrests, xxix, 67, 72, 99, 140
  Baptism, 7, 23, 84
  Baptists, xxxiii, 29, 76–77, 121, 127, 129
  Battle of Dunbar, 65
  Battle of Leeds, xxv, 47
  Battle of Marston Moor, xxv, 52–53
  Battle of Wakefield, xxv, 49–50
  Birth, xix, xxi, 22
  Blasphemy, xiii, xv, xxix–xxx, 57, 69, 76,
    78–79, 86–87, 90–92, 124, 128,
    145–152, 160
    horrid, xv, xxxiv, 87, 149–150, 157, 167
  Bradford, xxxi, 107–112, 117–120, 122
  Bristol, xiii, xv, xxxiii–xxxiv, 124, 139,
    145–152, 157, 159–162, 166, 171
  Burial, 178
  Charles I, xv, xix, xxiii, xxv, xxvii, 10, 33,
    55, 60–61, 93, 110

  Charles II, xv, xxxvii, 65, 89, 176–177
  Children, xxiii, xxviii, 4, 36, 38, 41, 75, 95,
    112, 156
  Cromwell, xiii, xxviii, xxx, xxxv, xxxvi, 45,
    49, 65, 93, 102, 110, 116, 146, 151,
    165
  Council of War (Officers), xxvii, 55,
    57–58, 60–63
  Crucifixion, xvii, 94–95, 131, 157–158,
    167–168, 172,
  Death, xiii, xv, xvii, xxxvii, 6, 73, 141–142,
    149, 155, 158, 163, 169, 177–178
  Education, 4, 10, 36–37
  Epiphany, xiii, xxviii, 65–67, 78, 85, 91,
    121
  Epistles (see)
  Exeter jail, xxxiv, 81, 140, 160, 171
  Family home, farm, xxi, 1, 3–6, 65, 67,
    156
  Family members, xxiii, xxviii, 4, 41, 60
  Fasting, 81, 84, 140
  Fatigue, xxx, 104, 132, 152
  and Margaret Fell, xxxiii, xxxv–xxxvi,
    69, 99, 103–104, 123, 127–129, 166,
    169
  and Fox, xiii–xv, xxxv, xxxvii, 65–66, 78,
    85, 87, 89, 91–92, 99–102, 121,
    129–130, 132, 134, 141–143, 147,
    166, 171, 177
  Health and illness, xxxv–xxxvi, 65, 67,
    139–141, 152, 156, 163, 166, 169,
    172–173, 176–177
  Humiliation, xv, xvii, xxxv, 131, 150, 154,
    157
  Husbandman, 1, 4, 78
  Imprisonments, xv, xxxiv–xxxv, xxxvii,
    73, 75, 79, 81, 91, 145, 150, 155–156,
    161, 163–169, 172–173
  Independent Minister, xix, 29
  Intimacy, 95, 130
  Lambert, xxvi–xxviii, 49, 52–54, 56–58,
    60–65, 71, 123, 152, 166
  Last words, xvii, xxxvii, 178
  Leadership qualities, 99, 105, 110, 116,
    127, 130, 139–140
  Letters, xxix, xxxiii, xxxvi, 69, 83, 95,
    99–104, 123, 127, 166, 176–177
  Letters, incriminating, 147, 153, 159
  Levellers, 63–64, 78, 124–125
  London ministry, xvi, xxxii–xxxiv, xxxvii,
    120–122, 123–131, 154, 160, 163,
    171, 176
  Property, xxi, 1, 5–6, 12, 65–67, 75, 156

Prophet, xiii–xv, xvi–xvii, xxx, 29, 81, 85, 91–92, 99, 110, 116, 131, 157, 164, 175, 177
Quartermaster, xxv–xxvi, 51–52, 54, 57–58, 71
and Ranters, 89, 114, 127, 140, 153–154, 159, 162
and Mrs. Roper, xxviii, 29, 65, 76–77, 91, 139
Self–abnegation, xvii, 157, 172, 174–175, 178
and Martha Simmonds, xxxii–xxxvi, 124, 135–142, 145–146, 148–149, 151, 153, 161, 163, 172
Traveling ministry, xv, xxix–xxx, 67–104, 107–110, 113–114, 118–119, 127
Trial at Bristol, 147, 152
Trial before Parliament, xv, xvi, xxxiv–xxxv, 28–29, 56–57, 76, 128, 147–152, 154, 162
Will, 4, 6, 187n
Writing in prison, xiii, xxxv, 82, 84, 86, 94–95, 156, 164, 167–176
Writings, xiii, xv, xxxvi, xxxviii, 73, 79, 81, 85–86, 89, 93, 94, 121, 111, 124, 136, 158, 165–176, 178
Nayler, John, 4, 60, 187n
  Joseph, 60
  Robert, 60
  William, Jr, 49, 60
Naylier, John, 64
Neile, Archbishop, 24–25
New England, xxv, xxxvi, 27, 31, 32, 39, 77, 128
New Model Army, xxvi–xxvii, 54–56, 60, 117
Newcastle, Lord, 43, 51
Nimmo, Dorothy, 75
Nonconformity, xvi, xix, xxi, xxxii, 13, 17–18, 22–25, 28, 30–31, 42, 86, 121
Northern Army, xxvi, 45, 52, 54, 57, 60–63, 152
Northumberland, xxix–xxx, 104
Nostell Priory, 8–9
Nottingham, xxiv, 118–121
Nutter, Anthony, xix, xxi–xxiii, 13–26, 36–37
  Excommunication, xxii, 25
  Fenny Drayton, xix, xxi, xxxi, 16–18, 21–22
  Imprisonment, 16–17, 181n
  Puritan nonconformity, xix, xxi–xxiii, 13–28
  Star Chamber, 16, 30

Woodkirk, xix, xxi, 13, 21–26, 27, 30–31, 36, 46, 78
Nutter, Hatevil, 32

Oath(s), xxxii, xxxviii, 16, 32, 79
Obedience, 159, 162, 170–171, 173, 175, 177
Old Hall, 4
Orton, 69–73, 75, 84, 89, 94, 164
Overton, Robert, 124
Oxford, 56, 70, 152

Painted Chamber, 155
Pamphlet Wars, xxxi, 86, 119, 121
Papists, xxiv, 12, 25, 28, 36, 39–41, 45, 53, 55
Parker, Alexander, xxxii, 125–126
Parliament, xv, xvi, xxi–xxiv, xxvi–xxvii, xxix–xxx, xxxiv, 10–12, 15, 19, 24, 28, 37–42, 53, 55, 57–64, 70, 87–91, 93, 102, 105, 116–117, 128, 147–158, 160, 163, 165–166, 169–170, 176
  Army, xxiv, xxvi–xxviii, xxxvii, 10–12, 37, 41–43, 45–66, 70–71, 74, 86–87, 89, 91, 93, 117, 123, 147, 150, 165
  Barebone's, xxix
  Protectorate, xv, xvi, xxx, xxxiv–xxxv, xxxvii, 116, 128, 147–158, 160, 163, 165–166, 169–170, 177
  Rump, xxvii, xxix, 116
Parnell, James, 137
  Thomas, 178
Patience, 83, 96, 99, 159
Patronage, 22, 70, 128
Paul, xxxiii, 85, 113, 133–135, 173–175
Payroll records, xxv–xxvi, 49, 54, 56–57
Peace Testimony, xxxii, 89, 94, 125
Pearson, Justice Anthony, xxx, 86–87, 103, 105, 114, 124, 127, 152
Penington, Isaac, xxxvii
Pentacostal church, 193n
Perfectibility, xiv, 126
Persecution, xv, xxi, 81, 85–86, 88, 90, 93–94, 107, 125, 151, 153, 157, 164, 168, 174–175, 177
1 PETER, 174
Plots, xxi, 39, 63, 78, 82, 107–109, 116, 124
Pollard, Joan, 156
Pontefract, xxiv, xxxi, 10, 43, 48, 57–58, 64, 75, 78
  Deanery, 25, 119
  Sieges, xxv, xxvi, xxvii, 53, 55–56, 59
Population, 36, 46, 57–58, 70, 83, 114, 117, 127, 131, 146
Poyntz, General, 54, 57–58, 63

Prayer Book, Common (see Common Prayer, Book of)
Scottish (see Scotland, Prayer Book)
Prayerbook Rebellion, xxiii, 38–39, 41
Preaching without license, 16, 31–32
Presbyterian, xix, xxv, 14, 25, 28, 30, 37–38, 52, 55–56, 58, 115
  Book of Discipline, 15–16
  classis meetings and preaching, 14, 16–17, 30, 36
  in Parliament, xxvi–xxvii, 61, 63
Press, 112, 121, 136
Pride's Purge, xxvii, 61–62
Priests, xviii, xxv, xxix, xxxi, xxxiii, 15, 19, 20, 24, 33, 78, 84, 88, 99, 102, 105–110, 113, 120, 127, 135, 176
Prophecy, xiv, xvii–xviii, xx, 85–86, 91, 96–97, 103, 112–113, 136, 155, 157, 171, 178
Prophet, xiii–xiv, xvii, xx, xxx, 29, 44, 81, 85, 90–92, 96–97, 110, 113–114, 116, 120, 138, 146, 155, 162, 168, 175–176
Prophetic ministry, xiii–xvii, xx, 86, 99, 126, 128, 131, 136–137, 145, 164, 171, 177
Protector, xvi, xix, xxx, xxxvi, 93, 116, 125, 146, 148, 150–152, 154, 169, 177
Protectorate, xvi, xxviii, xxxi–xxxii, xxxiv, 65, 111, 117, 124, 128, 148, 165–166
Protest, xxi, 91, 93, 177
PSALMS, 47–48
Publication, xiii, xv, xix, xxi–xxiii, xxviii–xxxiii, xxxv–xxxviii, 7, 33, 35, 45, 47, 58, 64, 72–73, 76–77, 80–81, 84–88, 91, 93–94, 107, 117, 119, 121, 123–124, 136, 153, 156, 158–159, 163–164, 167, 169, 176, 178
Purefey, 22
Puritan(ism), xv, xviii, xxvi, xxxii, xxxvii, 9, 13–26, 27, 35–36, 39, 42, 55, 71, 81, 91, 119, 127–128, 152, 174
  Revolution, xiii, xv, xix, xxi–xxii, xxv, xxxvii, 9–10, 13–26, 28, 32, 69, 77, 111
Putney, xxvi, 63
Pym, John, xxiv, 39, 40–41

Quaker (see also Friend), xiii, xiv–xix, xxvii–xxix, xxxi–xxxii, xxxv–xxxviii, 10, 29, 32, 49, 63, 65–66, 69–79, 81, 84, 86–87, 91, 103, 107–112, 116, 119, 121, 123–143, 146–156, 165–168, 176, 179n
  Christ within, xiv, xix, 81, 85, 94–95, 113, 120, 126, 136
  continuing revelation, xiv, xviii, 81, 85, 92, 95, 130
  peace testimony (see)
  principles, xiv, xviii, xxxii, 84, 89–90, 94, 100–101, 124, 130, 142, 152, 154, 157, 177–178
  quaking and trembling, xxviii, 90, 113
  unity, 131–135, 151
Quaker Act, xxxviii

Rainsborough, Colonel, 59
Ranters, xxvii, 89, 114, 124, 127, 140, 153–154, 162
Reading, xxxvii, 57, 142
Reading ministers, 16, 70
Recantation, 158–159, 163
Reeve, John, 155
Remonstrance, xxiv, 60–63
Repentance, xiii, xviii, xxxv, 81, 92, 95, 146, 161–162
Republic, xvi, 62, 116, 128
Restoration, xv, xxxvii, 61–62, 89, 117, 165, 177
REVELATION, xviii, 45, 91, 110, 117, 134, 137–138, 155, 168
Revelation, continuing (see Quaker)
Revolution, xiii, xv, xvi, xix, 7, 9, 13, 27, 35, 46–47, 54, 62–63, 77, 85, 90, 92, 111, 116, 128, 165, 168–169
Reyner, John, 32, 42
Rich, Robert, xxxvi, 143, 169
Rider of the White Horse, 45, 54, 168
Ridgely, James, John, 25, 31, 42
Ripon, Treaty of, xxiii, 38
Ripton Regis (Kings Ripton), xxxvii, 177
Ritual, 14, 20, 23, 27–28, 35, 39, 81
Roads, 75
Roper, Lt., Mrs., xxviii, 29, 76–77, 91, 139
Royalists, xxiv–xxviii, xxxii, 10, 12, 43, 45–66, 70–71, 73–74, 86, 89, 107, 109, 111, 116–118, 124, 128, 165–166, 168
Rupert, Prince, 52

Sackcloth and ashes, 136–137
St. Elizabeth's School, Wakefield, 10, 36–37
Salvation, xiii–xiv, xvii–xviii, 91, 97, 107, 117, 132, 135, 151, 157, 159, 167–168, 173, 175–177

Index

Satan, xviii, xxxiii, 36, 40, 89, 103, 106, 109, 113–115, 126, 130–134, 137, 140, 142, 153, 161–162, 164, 167, 172–173
Saul of Tarsus (Paul), 85
SAUL'S ERRAND TO DAMASCUS . . . , xxix, 28, 68, 71–72, 76, 79, 84–88, 91, 93, 94, 123
Savile, 3, 5–6, 9, 10, 25, 39, 70
   John, 3–4, 8–11, 22, 36–37
   George, 10, 36
   Thomas, 3, 10–11, 36–38, 42, 50
   William, 10, 46
Scapegoat, 154
Scatcherd, 4, 7, 29
Schools, 3, 10, 22, 36, 37
Scotland, 8, 69, 165–166
   Bishops' Wars, xxiii, 11, 38, 40–42, 50
   Church, xxiii, 37–38, 58
   Civil War, xxv, xxvii–xxviii, 52, 55–59, 61, 63–65, 69, 71, 75, 78, 108–109, 128, 165
   King Charles I, 37–38, 56, 58, 60, 63
   Prayer book, xxiii, 38, 41
   Presbyterianism, xxv, 58
   Rebellion, xxiii, xxvii, xxxii
   Solemn League and Covenant, 52, 128
Scripture, xiv, xvii–xx, 15, 19–20, 23, 28, 33, 35, 84–85, 88, 90–92, 94–95, 97, 101, 108–109, 111, 113, 115, 130, 138, 146, 149–150, 170–171, 174
Second Coming, xxxv, xxxvii, 89, 116–117, 133
Seed, xiv, xxxiii, xxxvi, 88, 94–95, 119, 126, 131, 151, 159, 161, 171
Seekers, xxxii, 69, 74, 81, 101
SEVERAL PETITIONS ANSWERED, xxix, 87, 123
Sexual
   abuse, 107, 111
   misconduct, accusations and denials, 29, 76–77, 139, 160
Silence, xxx, 99, 101–102, 111, 139, 142, 154
Simmonds, Martha, xxii, xxxi–xxxv, 124, 135–138, 140, 142, 145–146, 148–149, 151, 161, 163, 172
Simmonds, Thomas, xxxv, 124, 136, 153, 167, 169
Sign(s), 20, 134, 172
   at Bristol, xv, xxxiv, 146, 148, 153, 157, 159–162
   enactment of, 136, 145, 146
   to the nation and world, 161–162

Sin, xxxi, xxxvi, 51, 92, 97, 109, 112, 126, 133, 136, 138, 146, 152, 154, 156–157, 160, 162, 165, 167, 170, 172, 174–175
SIN KEPT OUT OF THE KINGDOM, 82
Sixty, Valiant (see Valiant Sixty)
Skippon, Major General Philip, 149, 152–153
Sowgelder, 4
Spirit of Christ within (see Quaker, Christ within)
Spiritual adultery (see Adultery, spiritual)
Spiritual leading (see Leading)
Sports, King's Book of, xxii, 35, 36
Stanley, 65, 76–77, 91
Star Chamber, 10, 15–17, 21
Stoddard, Amor, 123
Strafford, Lord (Thomas Wentworth), 11, 39–40
Stranger, Hannah, xxxv, 135–138, 140, 142, 145, 148–149, 172
   John, 145, 147–149, 159, 163, 172
Strickland (Great), xxix–xxx, 103, 163–164
Suffering, 85, 91, 97, 141, 158–159, 166–167, 174–176, 178
Sunbiggen, 73
Surplice, xxii, 17–18, 20, 24–25, 31, 33
Swannington, 124–125
Swarthmore (Swarthmoor) Hall, xxix–xxx, xxxviii, 68–69, 77, 81, 96, 101–103, 105–106
Sydenham, William, 128

Tabitha (Dorcas), 145
Taxation, xv, xxiii, 37, 39, 42, 75
Temptation, xxx, xxxiii, 20, 102, 105–106, 114, 129–132, 159, 162, 171, 175, 178
Temptor (see Satan)
Tenderness, 76, 83–84, 90, 161, 165, 168
Testimony, 16–17, 22, 30, 69
   Appleby, 1, 4, 27–28, 67, 79, 86, 88, 94, 99
   Friends', xx, 90, 94, 103, 121, 126, 167
   last, xvii, 178
   Parliament, 145, 147–149, 152, 157–158, 163
   peace, xxxii, 89, 94, 125
A TESTIMONY TO CHRIST JESUS . . . , 157
2THESSALONIANS, xxxiii, 133–134, 138
Thirty Years War, xxvii, 46
Thomason Tracts, 121
Three Kingdoms, War of the, 41, 55, 58, 117
Tithes, xxx, 25, 70, 88–90, 102, 116

TO ALL WHO WOULD KNOW THE WAY TO THE KINGDOM, 123
TO THE LIFE OF GOD IN ALL, 160
TO THE RULERS OF THIS NATION, 116
Tomlinson, William, 136
Topcliffe, 8, 29, 31
Torture, xv, 16, 85, 149, 154, 166, 168
Tower of London, xxiv, 11–12, 40, 55, 63, 124, 165
Trained Bands, xxiii, 41
Trapnel, Anna, 127, 155
Travers, Rebecca, xxxiii, xxxvi, xxxvii, 129, 154, 164, 176
　William, xxxvii, 164, 176
Treason, xxiv, xxvi–xxvii, 11–12, 21, 40–41, 55, 60, 82, 89,

Ulverston, xxi, 68
Unity, xvi–xvii, 14, 16–17, 28, 94, 115, 131, 134–135, 142, 151
University education, xxii, 22, 36–37,

Vagrancy, xxix, xxxii, xxxiv, 72, 79, 82, 87, 105, 111, 131, 146
Valiant Sixty, xiv, xxxviii, 164
Vane, Henry, the younger, xxvi, xxxiii, 127–128
　the elder, 127–128
Vanity, xxxi, 10, 92, 101, 157, 160, 162
Visitations, Bishops', 17, 24–25, 28, 30–31, 33

Wakefield, xxiii–xxv, xxviii–xxix, xxxi, xxxiii, 1–2, 6, 8, 10, 22, 29–31, 33, 36, 38, 43, 45–50, 53–54, 60, 65, 67, 69, 75, 77, 95, 97, 119, 132, 163
Walney Island, xxix, 69
War, xv, xviii, xix, xxii, xxvii, 36–37, 42, 85, 90–91, 116, 119, 155, 168–169
　Bishops', xix, xxiii, 11, 38–40
　Civil, xv–xvi, xviii, xxiii–xxvi, xxxi, 6, 9–13, 27, 31, 33, 35, 41, 45–66, 70, 73–77, 82, 85–86, 88–92, 106–109, 117, 119, 128, 132, 149, 152, 165, 169
　Lamb's, xxxvi, 91, 109–110, 156, 167–169, 173
　seeds of, 119
　Three Kingdoms, 38, 41, 55, 58, 117
Warwickshire Synod, 16
Wedlock, Timothy, 145
Wells, xxxiv, 146

West Ardsley (see Ardsley)
West Riding, xxiii, 1, 10, 38, 40, 49, 54, 106
Westby, Captain, 62
Westerton, 1, 3–4, 6, 8–9, 31
Westmoreland, xxvii, xxix, 58, 69, 71–75, 79, 82–83, 86, 90–91, 94, 100–101, 103–104, 106–107, 155, 163
WHAT THE POSSESSION OF THE LIVING FAITH IS . . . , xxix, xxxvi, 156, 165, 169–173
Whitehall, 61, 93, 127, 148
Whitehead, George, xxxviii, 73, 107, 158, 162–164, 166–167, 173, 176, 178
Whitelocke, Bulstrode, 150
Whitgift, John, 14–15, 18
Whiting, John, 129
Whitsunday, xxv, 20, 35, 49–50
Whittier, John Greenleaf, 78
Wildman, John, 124
Will of God, xiv, xxxiv, 104, 120
Winstanley, Gerrard, 123
Women, 39, 107, 129, 145–146, 152–153, 160
　Abuse of, 107–108, 111–112
　Ministry, xxxi, 123, 136–137
　turbulent, 129, 140, 164
Woodkirk, xxiii, xxv, 1, 4, 42, 60, 67, 70, 76–77, 106, 155, 171, 177
　church, xxviii, 2, 6–7, 23
　history of, 6–10, 119
　Independent congregation, xix, xxiii, xxxi, 26, 27–33, 76, 78, 115
　Anthony Nutter, xix, xxi, xxiii, 13, 21–26
Wool, 2
Worcester, xxviii, 65–66, 89
Word(s) of God, xiv, xviii, xxviii, 15, 20–21, 33, 79, 88
World turned upside down, 90

Yeoman, , 4, 36
York, Archbishop of, xix, xxi, xxiii, 14, 22–25, 27
York, , xxxiii, 22–25, 31, 46, 90–91, 93, 177
　in Civil War, xxiv, xxvi, 41–43, 48–49, 52–54, 56–58
Yorkshire, xxi–xxv, xxviii–xxix, xxxi, xxxiii, 1, 2, 4, 6, 8, 10–11, 13, 21–23, 27–28, 30, 32, 36, 38–43, 45–46, 49, 52, 54, 57–58, 60–61, 69, 87, 90–91, 96, 106, 114, 119, 123, 132, 134, 139, 155, 168, 177

England and Wales
1649–1910.

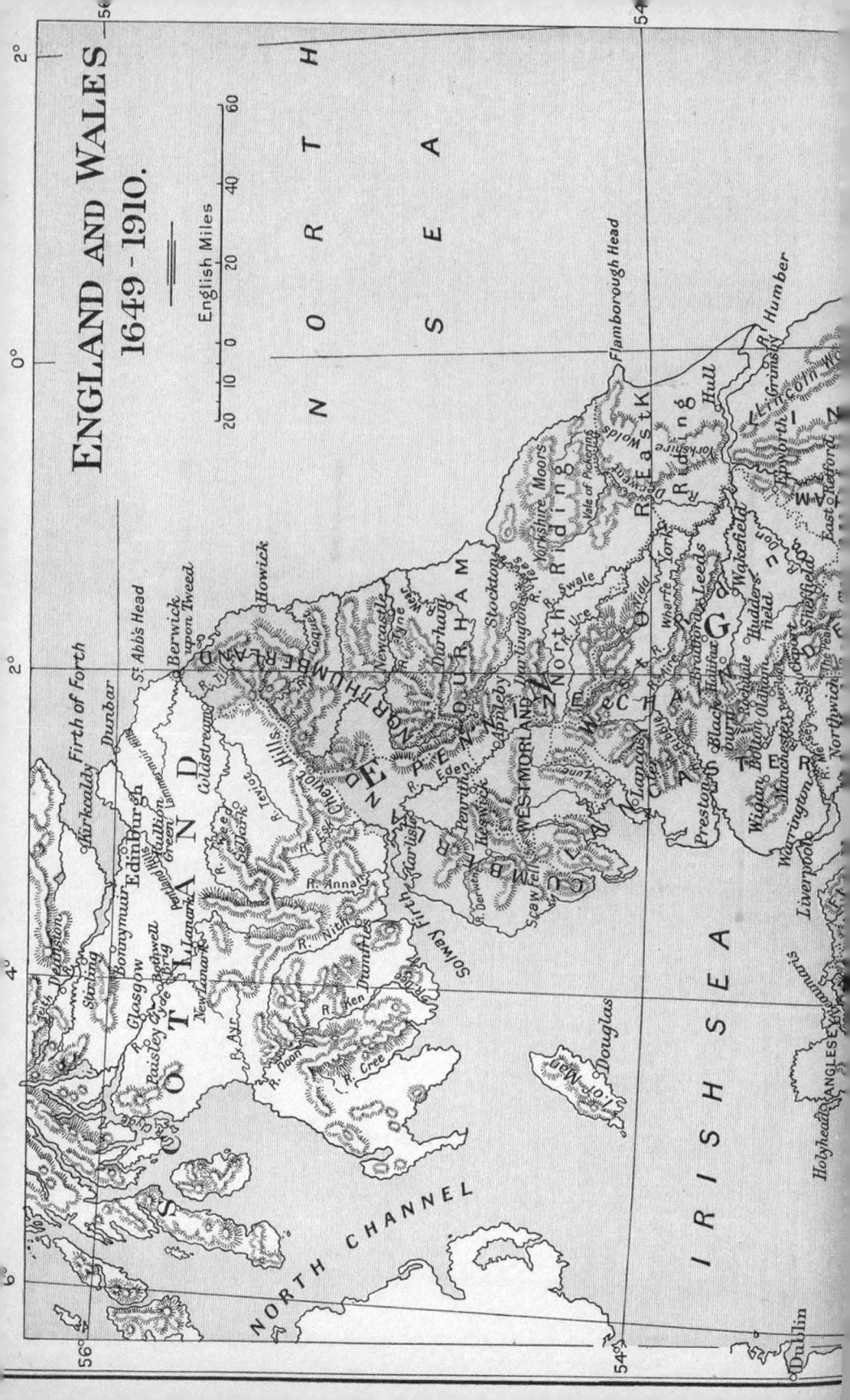